W9-CTM-606

GENIUS CAME EARLY

CREATIVITY IN THE TWENTIETH CENTURY

For Morley —

GENIUS CAME
EARLY

CREATIVITY IN THE
TWENTIETH CENTURY

Lee Cullum

In celebration of creative life — with warmest friendship,

Lee Cullum

WINDSOR HOUSE
PUBLISHING GROUP INC.

Windsor House Publishing Group
Austin, Texas

April 28, 2000

GENIUS CAME EARLY
CREATIVITY IN THE TWENTIETH CENTURY

PRINTING HISTORY
First Edition November 1999

ISBN: 1-881636-90-9
Library of Congress Card Number: 99-72792

For information address:
Windsor House Publishing Group, Inc.
802 N. Milam, Fredericksburg, Texas 78624

The Windsor House logo is a trademark belonging to
The Windsor House Publishing Group, Inc.

PRINTED IN THE UNITED STATES OF AMERICA
10 9 8 7 6 5 4 3 2

Acknowledgments

With gratitude to the following for permission to reprint previously published material:

Reprinted by permission of Alfred A. Knopf, Inc., a Division of Random House, Inc., all of the following: Excerpts from *A Distant Mirror: The Calamitous 14th Century* by Barbara W. Tuchman. Copyright © by Barbara W. Tuchman. Excerpts from *The American Political Tradition* by Richard Hofstadter. Copyright 1948 by Alfred A. Knopf, Inc. Excerpts from *Fin-de-Siècle Vienna* by Carl E. Schorske. Copyright © 1961, 1967, 1973, 1979 by Carl E. Schorske. Excerpts from *Stephen Sondheim: A Life* by Meryle Secrest. Copyright © 1998 by Meryle Secrest Beveridge. Excerpts from *Howard's End* by E.M. Forster. Copyright 1921 by E.M. Forster. Reprinted also by permission of The Provost and Scholars of Kings College, Cambridge, and The Society of Authors as the literary representative of the E.M. Forster Estate. Excerpts from *Memoirs* by Andrei D. Sakharov. Copyright © 1990 by Alfred A. Knopf, Inc.

Reprinted by permission of Bantam Books: Excerpts from *A Brief History of Time* by Stephen Hawking. Copyright © 1988 by Stephen W. Hawking.

Reprinted by permission of Barnes & Noble, Inc.: Excerpt from *History of the English-Speaking Peoples* by Winston Churchill. Copyright © 1955, 1957, 1958 by The Right Honorable Sir Winston Leonard Spencer Churchill K.G. O.M. C.H. M.P.

Reprinted by permission of The Provost and Scholars of Kings College, Cambridge: Excerpts from *Virginia Woolf: The Rede Lecture, 1941* by E.M. Forster. Copyrighted © in the United States of America by Harcourt Brace & Co. Reprinted also by permission of The Society of Authors as the literary representatives of the E.M. Forster Estate.

Reprinted by permission of Charlotte Sheedy Literary Agency. Excerpt from *A Very Close Conspiracy* by Jane Dunn, Little, Brown and Company. Copyright © 1990 by Jane Dunn.

Reprinted by permission of Doubleday, a Division of Random House, Inc.: Excerpts from *Soul: God, Self, and the New Cosmology* by Angela Tilby. Copyright © 1992 by Angela Tilby. Excerpt from "My

Dedication

For Mac and Charlie
and
for Nita and Cullum

Table of Contents

Author's Note

First of all, special thanks to Sally Allen Smith and Marie Basalone for their high competence and their exhaustive (also exhausting) work getting this project ready for publication. It would have been impossible without them. Thank you too to Eileen Gregory for her expert advice on the handling of endnotes as well as her elegant, seamless editing. I'm grateful too to C. C. Marsh and Alexandra Kise for their contribution to this enterprise, which, at times resembled a cottage industry. (It's amazing how work that is so solitary can suddenly demand the attention of so many crucial people.) And Matthew Ervin's effort on literature, musical theatre, and Leni Riefenstahl was a great help. So was Emily Kelley's energetic, informed attack on tracking down photographs.

Genius Came Early began as a speech on creativity in the twentieth century. Erin-Jo Jurow heard it and remarked, "That could be a course." I thought: well, if it could be a course, maybe it could be a book. Then came conversations with Gail Thomas about St. Michael, Flo Wiedemann about Carl Jung, Schubert Ogden and Cullum Clark about the decline of theology, Marjorie Currey and Thomas Moore about philosophy, Tom Knock and Cullum Clark about Teddy Roosevelt, and Zrinjka Perusko Culek about post-modern media. I talked with Jo Brans and Nancy O'Boyle about writers and Louise Cowan about literature and the century to come. Sue Graze and Barnaby Fitzgerald answered art questions, and Dr. Richard Meyer, Vincent Prothro, and Ron Davis offered excellent counsel on film. To those who consented to be quoted in this book, my thanks.

I am forever indebted to Charles Silver, curator of the Film Study Center at the Museum of Modern Art in New York. He opened MoMA's splendid archive to me and even sent me classic movies of his own, on video, to view at home. Even more, he told me what to see, explained the context for each major motion picture, and literally gave me a film education.

Thanks to Robert Coles, Lady Thatcher, James Watson, and Jane Jacobs for allowing me to draw upon interviews I did with them for the public television stations in Dallas-Fort Worth and Denton. I also appreciate those stations, KERA-TV and KDTN-TV, permitting me to use that material and KERA-FM, the public radio affiliate in North Texas, consenting to the incorporation in this book of thoughts from commentaries I've done there. Thank you as well to the *Dallas Morning News* and American Publishing for rights to include passages from columns written for them, including a piece on Jack Kilby who kindly gave permission for its use. Alexandra Wilhelmsen generously said yes to my request to paraphrase a wonderful letter written to me by her father, Frederick Wilhelmsen, a professor of philosophy and politics, before he died. The same is true of Ada Louise Huxtable when I asked to quote from a speech of hers on the necessity of art. This also was the case with Frederick Turner when I wanted to cite an observation he had made about the importance of the past at the Dallas Institute for Humanities and Culture and also with Lorin Hollander, whose dazzling ideas about the great cathedrals have been an inspiration to me.

I'm grateful to Evan Fogelman for his encouragement at critical moments in the writing of this book, to Susan and Don Sanders for their help in giving it a life, to Chuck Joseph for his flair and discerning eye, to Ann Lang for her meticulous care in the preparation of the book, and to Clara Cole for her kind and efficient courtesies. Of course, I give special thanks to Dwight Wallington of Windsor House for publishing and maintaining constant enthusiasm for *Genius Came Early*.

Chapter
One

The Archangel Michael
*The twentieth century, drenched in
dread not seen since the Middle Ages,
turned finally to the brighter aspects of
Medieval inspiration and found there a
fountain of hope.*

In Spite of the Horror, Genius

You have destroyed it,
The beautiful world;
Build it again,
In your heart rebuild it.

Johann Wolfgang von Goethe

The genius of the twentieth century bloomed early then lapsed into a long afternoon of limbo, utterly spent, except for a few bursts of brilliance, by the exertion required to gather the essence of a troubled epoch. The age was greeted in America by the dawn of Progressivism as Teddy Roosevelt, a master of statecraft, stood in striking contrast to the languid energies of Europe, which soon was consumed in the flames of battle that took at least 100 million lives. Before the century was over, another 100 million were lost elsewhere in the world in purges and atrocities. Civilian casualties in war climbed from five percent at the beginning of the century to 90 percent at the end.[1] Marxism rose. Marxism fell. Colonial empires crumbled only to have some seers call finally for a new, benign trusteeship of the West, especially in Africa. This idea was quickly retracted after Somalia.

Art reached back to elemental, archetypal forms (reconfirming Jacques Barzun's profound insight that the arts do not progress though styles may change) while technology lunged ahead, first terrorizing the world at Hiroshima and Nagasaki, which began a nuclear dance that dominated half the century, then landing a man on the moon and knitting the world together in an amazing web of cultural, political and psychic interchange.

"Only connect," said E. M. Forster, in *Howard's End*. The computer revolution has done just that. Following John Naisbitt's admonition to mate high-tech with high-touch, it culminated in Microsoft, a triumph of cozy circuitry. More powerful than Marx, the new communications toppled governments and created global communities beyond the dreams of futurists.

In the United States, splendid architecture told the story. Americans began in 1900 with the weight of centuries on their shoulders and built monuments to their European past. Then they beheld the new engineering and, sensing their agonizing opportunity, they invented the skyscraper and climbed to a stature all their own, at first decorated and exuberant, then skin-tight, the better to display their discipline and awesome achievement. Finally they took their towers and tried to invest them with ornamental history, hoping for some ancestral rescue from the times.

Think of what these 100 years have brought: Picasso, Einstein, Freud. Cubism, relativity, the unconscious. Hitler, Tojo, Stalin, Mao, Pol Pot. Technology and atonal music. Gershwin, Charlie Chaplin, Virginia Woolf. All shaped the twentieth century. The era erupted from reckless expressionism and punishing rationality, Dionysus and Apollo run amok. The result was barbarism, dissonance, dynamism and, sometimes, astonishing beauty.

The twentieth century established itself as an age of relentless logic. This was a perverted legacy of the Enlightenment, and it led Secretary of Defense Robert McNamara, an idolater of reason as quantification, to assess the war in Vietnam not by territory gained but by bodies counted.

Not too many years after that, the era turned to magic to compensate for the rigors of science. Even Unitarians, America's most rational branch of Christianity, were holding healing services with a laying on of hands.[2]

Finally, by the 1990s, reenchantment of art, of philosophy and religion, even of science itself preoccupied the new mystics.[3] Even those of more prosaic persuasion were caught up in the fever: An Episcopal bishop in Dallas took part in an exorcism to banish evil spirits from his diocesan headquarters and still the rash of resident autumn illnesses.[4]

But it was more than the flu that needed to be exorcized at century's end. Magic was invoked no doubt to shape the horrors of the age into a configuration of memory that could be borne. It was a daunting enterprise, even for magic. After all, there hardly has been a more catastrophic century in the history of the West, unless it was the fourteenth. That's what Barbara Tuchman believed and she wrote a book about it called *A Distant Mirror*.

"No epoch was more naturally mad," she said of the fourteenth century, quoting a French historian. With its systematic and brutal suppression of European Jews, it foretold the central madness of the twentieth century— the Holocaust. The ugly seeds were sown early. In the thirteenth century,

Jewish communities were isolated by church decree from Christian society. The star of David that Hitler forced Jews to wear in Nazi Germany was a grim reflection of 1215, when Innocent III (oddly named) ordered "the wearing of a . . . circular patch of yellow felt, said to represent a piece of money."[5]

Jews held major administrative posts in fourteenth century Spain. But that was not enough to shield them from barbaric pogroms that afflicted the country in 1391, forcing many to convert to Christianity. Even so, conversos were burned in the Inquisition that began some ninety years later.[6]

Another eerie echo from the fourteenth century was the Black Death, a scourge even more awful than AIDS. Spread by bacteria from rats, it surfaced again in India in 1994.[7] The medieval Black Death wiped out half the population of Europe.

Religious extremists held forth in the fourteenth century, too, in the form of the flagellants who marched two-hundred strong or more from city to city, "stripped to the waist, scouring themselves with leather whips tipped with iron spikes until they bled." Later charged with "orgies in which whipping combined with sex," they could be said to resemble the grotesquerie that gathered around Jim Jones and David Koresh in the last decades of the twentieth century.

So arrogant did the flagellants become that they thought nothing of affronting the established church. Their masters, observed Tuchman, "assumed the right to hear confessions and grant absolution or impose penance, which not only denied the priests their fee for these services but challenged ecclesiastical authority at its core." Those priests who fought back were stoned not only by flagellants but also by willing parishioners. They were not the only dissenters from the central church. Tuchman noted stories of some "seeking God through mystical sects," not unlike today's New Age. Their doubts intensified by the horror of the Plague, these apostates were "ultimately to break apart the empire of Catholic unity." The Age of Faith began to give way to more worldly wisdom. What followed in time was a turning from theology to the study of natural science. The disillusionment began with the Black Death which, Tuchman perceived, "may have been the unrecognized beginning of modern man." She likened this period to the First World War in its residue of pessimism, "self-doubt and self-disgust." The Plague also led, Tuchman believed, to a cult of death in medieval art.[8] This was to survive in twentieth century Mexico and not necessarily in a way that was harmful.

Indeed, it has been noted that Mexico, tied in spirit to the Middle Ages, has a far healthier, earthier, more realistic sense of death than exists in the United States.

Even so, the medieval imagination has hardly been lost to Americans. Angels reappeared in the 1990s to compensate for the ebbing energies of the age. They presided in books, at conferences, in jewelry and art, and, spectacularly, in Tony Kushner's Tony-Award-winning plays, *Angels in America, Parts I and II*. A heavenly being even made it to the cover of *Time* magazine in 1993.

The celestial return was foretold in a 1978 Gallup poll which found that over half the Americans questioned professed a belief in spiritual beings.[9] *Christianity Today* cited later Gallup surveys showing faith in angels among teenagers had risen from 64 percent in 1978 (itself a substantial figure) to 76 percent by 1992. *Time's* cover story a year later put the figure at 69 percent for all Americans. In 1995, the *Economist* wrote that 72 percent of Americans believe in angels and four out of five in miracles.

Karen Armstrong uncovered a partial explanation for this phenomenon in the work of Father Wilhelm Schmidt. Writing in 1912, he suggested that when the High God becomes too remote, too inaccessible, people turn to lesser spirits and saints. And certainly God had become highly abstract. Some sought Him in modern physics. Others called Him the "ground of being," echoing not only Paul Tillich and Julian of Norwich but also the Vedic *Upanishads*. What has resulted is a sense of God as pervasive, but no longer personal.[10] Hence the need for a guardian angel.

Carl Jung, a giant of the century, foresaw it all when he deplored "the spiritual catastrophe of the Reformation."[11] Jung divined what the loss of mystery would mean to people once they woke up to their impoverishment. It would bring forth in them a yearning for medieval life. Dr. Louise Cowan, a professor of literature, was one of the first to understand this. She prophesied in 1980 that the decades ahead would be like the Middle Ages, though different and not dark.

She was more prescient than she knew. Before the eighties were out, the chants of Hildegard of Bingen, the twelfth century Benedictine abbess, were pealing forth, pure and pristine, from college dormitories. To recordings would be added campus seminars on her ecstatic revelations.

In the fall of 1993 fashion joined the movement with Donna Karan's medieval look. Only a few months later, Gregorian chants hit the top ten compact-disc chart in Spain. Then began the rush to visit Ireland, land of mystery and miracles, where passion reigns. And there's Valerie Van Winkle of Maine, a woman said to be unusually fond of cats and black clothes, who was tried by her church for declaring herself a witch.[12] Also in France, authorities reported that close to fifty-thousand taxpayers "had declared income from their work as star-gazers, healers, mediums and [from] similar occupations" including that of a "self-styled druid" who offered clients "a mix of ancient Celtic rituals he says were handed down through his family in Brittany."[13]

Even scientists, pledged to reason, caught the spirit, however obliquely. Stuart Kauffman, a distinguished biochemist who's been called "perhaps the most ambitious and radical modern challenger of Darwin,"[14] has been making credible scientific claims for a generating mechanism that brings natural organization to chaos, creating a system that grows along ordered lines. Given certain circumstances, he explained, certain species could be *expected* to emerge. This is not the stuff of Gabriel or the spiritualists, but it goes well beyond random selection in its implications. Indeed, Mitchell Waldrop reported that Dr. Kauffman, once a student of philosophy, has acknowledged feeling that Divine Intention has revealed its secrets to him.

"'I knew that God had revealed to me a part of how his universe works,' [Waldrop quoted Kauffman]. It was not a personal God, certainly; Kauffman had never been able to believe in such a being. 'But I had a holy sense of a knowing universe, a universe unfolding, a universe of which we are privileged to be a part. In fact it was quite the opposite of a vainglorious feeling. I felt that God would reveal how the world works to anyone who cared to listen. It was a lovely moment,' he said, 'the closest I've ever come to a religious experience.'"[15]

Michael J. Behe, born a Catholic and now an associate professor of chemistry at Lehigh University, has argued for "intelligent design" of the universe. He stressed that Darwin's theory does not explain the development of the cell in its irreducible complexity.[16]

John Eccles, a British neuroscientist and Nobel Prize winner, candidly admitted that he's a religious person. He voiced the belief that "the very nature of the mind is the same as the nature of life. It's a divine creation."[17]

While some searched for spiritual consolation at century's end, others were caught up in a declaration of endings. Announcements flowed predicting the end of history and the death of science because all the key matters have been accomplished. All that is left, some said, was to work out the triumph of liberal democracy and discover the unified field, which would yield the final answer to everything and fill in the blanks left by Darwinism, Mendelian genetics and DNA.[18]

The end of philosophy was proclaimed as well, not because the great questions have been resolved, but because they never will be. What is truth? Do we have free will? All lie still, as always, beyond our cognitive ability. What will follow from all these endings, if indeed they really occur? Some foresee—inevitably—a renewed interest in religion.[19]

In 1933, when the twentieth century was well underway, G.K. Chesterton, a British writer with a lively mind, wrote that "each generation is converted by the saint that contradicts it most." St. Francis, he noted, "had a curious and almost uncanny attraction for the Victorians."[20] Proud of their commerce and their common sense and obsessed with moral progress through a thousand self-restraints, the Victorians, Angela Tilby confirmed, were alienated from nature. They "knew they were powerful," she wrote, "but also sensed their distance from some of the most important sources of joy." Instead of pleasure, she said, they strove for eternal rest, which to them meant perfection.[21]

But the Victorians sensed their predicament. Searching for their own balm in Gilead, Chesterton pointed out, they found "something in the story of St. Francis that pierced through all those English qualities which are most famous and fatuous, to all those English qualities which are most hidden and human: the secret softness of heart; the poetical vagueness of mind, the love of landscape and of animals."

For the twentieth century, Chesterton believed, the redeeming saint is Thomas Aquinas. His rational theology, reconciling Aristotle to Christ and religion to intellect, seemed a necessary antidote for the utter lack of reason that has characterized the age. "In a world that has grown a great deal too wild," said Chesterton, "Christianity has returned in the form of a teacher of logic."

As for the scholasticism of Aquinas, "it was in every sense a movement of enlargement, always moving towards greater light and even greater liberty." It was Thomas, he said, who expanded Christianity "towards experimental science, who insisted that the senses were the windows of the soul and that the reason had a divine right to feed upon facts, and that it was the business of the faith to digest the strong meat of the toughest and most practical of pagan philosophies."

It is understandable that Chesterton, having just lived through the

1920s, would see this century as "wild," as "the age of uncommon non-sense," bereft of "really solid ground." True enough. But as the thirties took shape, something appalling overtook the times. Relentless horror stalked Europe and spilled over into Stalin's Russia, spreading as far as Tojo's Japan and seeping into Mao's China, where it would lay dormant, waiting for an opportunity which was not long in coming. Pol Pot's Cambodia would follow. Wild spirits were extinguished by an icy, grue-some logic. It was worse than the Hundred Years War, which bled Britain and France but didn't blight the fourteenth century in the same way that Hitler and the others marked the twentieth.

The death camps of Central Europe made the rise of Israel a moral imperative. And so the effects of German atrocities reverberated for another fifty years in the Middle East, yielding at last to the remarkable handshake of Arafat and Rabin in the glow of pragmatic enlightenment, wondrous no matter how difficult and tragic the days that lay ahead. But for most of the century the bewildered West seemed hardly prepared to receive the gently reasoned argument of Thomas Aquinas. His light was too bright, his freedom too sweet for the ravages of an age turned macabre beyond comprehension. Reason had been perverted into abject evil.

It may be that the saint most antithetical to the twentieth century in its final unfolding is Michael, armed with his sword and the scales of jus-tice. While reason continued to reign in the last half of the century through the triumph of technology, it was not sufficient to establish a moral order. The epoch, in fact, despite the discipline of science and engineering, was marked at its deepest level by disintegration of the human personality including its capacity for orderly thought. Genius had to contend with an atmosphere of spiritual and intellectual anarchy. What grander contradiction could there be than Michael and his scales of justice?

Jung would call the trouble an inability to reconcile opposites—male and female, light and dark, Apollonian control and Dionysian abandon. Hence the extreme experience of this century.

St. Michael was called upon to slay the dragon and then to drink his blood, thus uniting with the enemy and putting an end to immature projection. Aspects thought to be alien had to be reckoned with on the inside, where it counts. Michael stood not only for justice, but for integration of opposing forces.

The inability of the twentieth century to grapple with these issues has led to a decline of theology. This must be traced in turn to a similar deterioration in philosophy, which has not ended but may as well have. Where Paul Tillich, Reinhold Niebuhr, Karl Barth, and Martin Buber presided with elegance and profound genius over the serious thought of the first half of the era, the last decades have seen the rule of technique over insight, especially in the United States.

Schubert Ogden, formerly at Southern Methodist University's Perkins School of Theology, agreed.[22] "The public role of the theologian that we became accustomed to . . . in the form of Tillich and Niebuhr has not been occupied in the last twenty-five years," he confirmed. "Theology has no claim on public attention. The growth of popular culture after the war created a market for intellectuals, for theologians who talked about fundamental questions . . . . Americans had won victory over evil after World War II and there was a lack of clarity about where we were going." Hence the urgent turning to theologians.

Philosophy, Ogden explained, "has become technical, analytic," as its practitioners have grown obsessed with "proving they're technically competent thinkers."

"Philosophers have a public role in Europe," he added, "but not in America." (He's right. Czech President Václav Havel comes immediately to mind.)

The "lust for results, answers, solutions" is undermining theology and philosophy, Ogden continued. Both disciplines have forgotten that their purpose is "to question our solutions, not to find them."

"If our public life had more vitality," he concluded, "philosophy and theology would have more of a role to play." (Again Havel's example shines through.)

Students of theology apparently have done little to protest the tepid gruel they're receiving. An observer of one seminary reported that the average age of students there in the early 1990s was thirty-eight. Embarked on second if not third careers, they were concerned with practical things—pastoral care, budget management—and had little interest in deep matters of the mind and soul. Intuitive genius was overwhelmed by the looming details of administration.

Unable to bear the liberating work of Aquinas, the twentieth century turned not only to functionalism but also to fundamentalism, with too many of the planet's peoples in full retreat from any freedom of the intellect or the individual. Rigid, primitive, dour, they eschewed subtlety and regarded salvation as a weapon to be wielded on behalf of the faithful against everybody else. It was not so unlike the fourteenth century.

As for that early age, for all its bestiality, it was not devoid of inspiration. Chaucer produced his poetry, religious reformer John Wyclif the first translation of the Bible into English,[23] and artists in a burst of glory their illuminated Books of Hours. So even a century as dreadful as the fourteenth was animated by creative wonder. Our own time has brought forth startling genius too, but that genius came early and vanished too soon.

Chapter
Two

Sigmund Freud
   Sigmund Freud took the human personality apart and put it back together again, drastically altering art, literature, politics, and all personal relations.

Animator of the Era

*For me the real miracle is life, not
art. And you can only have art if
you see, really see, what life is.*
                    Oskar Kokoschka

There have been five shaping artists of the twentieth century. So said
Agnes de Mille,[1] the choreographer. They are Igor Stravinsky, Béla
Bartók, Frank Lloyd Wright, Pablo Picasso, and Martha Graham,
whom she viewed as greater even than George Balanchine, which is
saying a lot.

"No artist," said Martha Graham, "is ahead of his time. He is his
time." For that reason we turn to the arts to comprehend an era. As Ada
Louise Huxtable observed, "Art never lies. It tells us exactly what we
are."[2]

A look at Martha Graham's work reveals heroines who "emerged
from crisis through the sheer force of self-understanding."[3] Graham's
dances mirrored the psychoanalytic insight that came to suffuse the twentieth century. She was one of the signposts pointing to the animating
genius of the age—Sigmund Freud.

The work of Picasso and the Cubists would have been impossible
without Freud. He took the human personality apart and put it back
together again, just as the Cubists did with the human body, informing
every aspect of modern art that followed. And twentieth century literature
is marked more by Freud than by any other thinker. Indeed, Harold
Bloom has called Freud "possibly the best mind of our century." Freud,
said Bloom, was "the mind of our age, just as Montaigne was the mind of
Shakespeare's."[4]

Freud has been called a "nineteenth century physician," but his seminal
work, *Interpretation of Dreams*, stood on the cusp between that epoch
and our own. Indeed, it was published in 1899, but the date on the title
page said 1900.

This was the book that presented Freud to the world. It embodied the achievements of his early research and pointed to much that would follow. This work, said biographer Peter Gay, summed up "all that he had learned—indeed all that he was . . . ."

But the monumentality of this work—with its critical insight: "at the bottom of every dream there is a wish"—was little comfort to Freud at the turn of the century. He felt isolated from the great capitals of science and shunned in Vienna. His "dream book," he lamented, was mostly shunned by reviewers.

Nonetheless, buoyed by a band of adherents, his movement began to grow. The publication of *Three Essays on the Theory of Sexuality* in 1905 provided his second cardinal text. From its pages flowed those ideas for which Freud is best known. *The Ego and the Id*—"a triumph of lucid mental energy"—was added in 1923. So were other notable efforts. But the principles of psychoanalysis were laid down in the space of only six years, when Freud was in his forties.

As for the "dream book," Gay calls it the "product of a mind shaped in the nineteenth century, yet it has become the property—cherished, reviled, inescapable—of the twentieth." So has Freud himself become the special property of the age. No one has so deeply influenced the way human beings view themselves. It's evident in our art, literature, politics and language. His insights have become so absorbed into the common wisdom that we can't imagine our world without them.

Freud alone did not discover the unconscious. Indeed it appeared earlier in the thinking of Goethe and Schiller, Coleridge and Henry James, Schopenhauer, and Nietzsche. But Freud gave the unconscious shape and definition. "His particular contribution," said Gay, "was to take a shadowy, as it were poetic, notion, lend it precision, and make it into the foundation of a psychology by specifying the origins and contents of the unconscious and its imperious ways of pressing toward expression."

From a nebulous concept the unconscious burst to the forefront of thought in much of the developed world. Is there any educated person any longer who does not automatically assume an unconscious life? Is there any work of twentieth century literature that does not acknowledge the unconscious and its potential for treachery?

It's hard now to realize that before Freud societies thought exclusively in terms of the *political* person whose social contract with other political persons created a nation. His work brought forth *psychological* man and woman. This was a transformation of profound significance.[5] It affected everything from personal relations to jurisprudence. No longer was the human being merely an atom of the state. He, and even she, had complex, subterranean lives that could not be ignored.

By fate and psychological necessity Freud did his work in Vienna, a good place to study evil. Vienna is such a sublime exaggeration it is in danger always of becoming too much. The Baroque buildings of the Ringstrasse are elegant but overwhelming in their lush concentration. The Viennese pastry is seductive, but alarming in its ability to satiate. The paintings of women by Gustav Klimt are the most sensual in all of art history, foretelling sure disruption of the social order. The Vienna Opera is so perfect the very soul of the music shines through in all its clarity laced with complications.

Art in the service of inspiration can be magnificent, but there is a hidden threat when art is itself the heart of human experience. This Carl Schorske saw in Freud's Vienna. Beware, he warned, when the life of art becomes a substitute for the life of action. Indeed, as civic action grew increasingly futile in Vienna, art assumed the dimensions of religion.

What happened in Vienna in the late nineteenth century was a false feminization of masculine culture, which disempowered both principles. Nowhere was this illustrated more chillingly than in Prince Rudolf's double suicide with Mary Vetsera. Denied any responsibility by his father, Emperor Franz Joseph, Rudolf retreated into fantasy, offering the hapless Mary no fine masculine fiber against which to hone her own nature. Both died tragic, ineffectual people.[6]

Schorske traced the trouble in Vienna to the economic crash of 1873, when, he wrote, "the wholly unexpected failure of free enterprise evoked both guilt and nostalgia in the new ruling class." The debacle could be traced to the liberals, who had come to power twenty-five years before endowed with brilliance but not an aptitude for governing. The liberals were strong enough to end the old political order, but they could not master the social forces this dissolution unleashed.[7] It was the perfect milieu for the birthplace of psychoanalysis.

Listen to the music of the day: From Brahms (that towering German master, beloved by the Viennese) to the lyrical Schubert who died too young; from Mahler, away much of the time, conducting in Budapest or Prague, to Bruckner, unluckily idolized by the Nazis after his death[8]; from Zemlinsky, who taught his brother-in-law Schoenberg as well as Mahler's wife, to Schoenberg himself. Listen to their music, its rapturous melodic line giving way finally to jarring dissonance, and you can hear the rupture at the core of the culture, wrecking psychic and civic life.

It was not that the devastation was caused by atonal music. But an attentive listener could hear the catastrophe coming.

It all led to Hitler, born in upper Austria in 1889. He arrived on a wave of anti-Semitism, openly proclaimed eight years later by the demagogue Karl Lueger in his winning campaign for mayor of Vienna. Schorske believed the well of city politics was poisoned by the emotions of simple people who had no outlets in the elegant, rational order of liberal Vienna.[9] (The United States has seen some of the same effect in the religious right, railing still against the long-spent liberal hegemony of the 1960s.)

Freud both loved and hated Vienna. He never was completely at home in the city. In fact, he felt truncated there. Nonetheless he refused to leave even when Nazi attacks on Jews escalated in Germany and threatened to spread over the whole of Europe.

He continued to live, as he had always lived, in Vienna, against the grain (often conducive to creativity), contriving not to see the side of the city that was frivolous, vain, not serious. "Freud had little interest in this excited, overstimulated Viennese world," wrote Gay. He "kept aloof from the modern poets and painters and café philosophers, and pursued his research in the austere isolation of his consulting room." The "Vienna that Freud gradually constructed for himself was not the Vienna of the court, the café, the salon or the operetta. Those Viennas did very little to advance Freud's work. It is not for nothing that his bride should have been from Hamburg, his favorite adherents from Zurich, Budapest, Berlin, London and even more far-flung places, his psychological theories formed in an intellectual universe large enough to embrace all of Western culture."

"Freud vehemently demurred when the French psychologist Pierre Janet suggested that psychoanalysis could have sprung only from the sensual atmosphere of Vienna," Gay reported. "In truth, Freud could have developed his ideas in any city endowed with a first-rate medical school and an educated public large and affluent enough to furnish him with patients." Perhaps. But the rich, complex compost of Vienna had to contribute in a significant way. The tension between the man and the city surely did much to fertilize his genius.

Freud left Vienna finally for London in 1938, feeling relief, of course, but regret too over the rich world of emotion he had left behind.

He lived at first in a rented house near Regent's Park, then moved to Hampstead where his antiquities and Persian rugs were arranged just as they had been in his study at Bergstrasse 79. He still needed his Vienna world around him.

Ill with cancer, Freud lived only one more year. Perhaps in those final months he pondered the riddle of Vienna. Possibly it occurred to him that one should beware of too much good. It can bring forth evil.

At the time he died, few would have believed that the work of Freud would live into the twenty-first century, while that of Karl Marx would not. Though Marx, creator of "the other grand unified theory"[10] that shaped and rattled the twentieth century, cast a longer shadow in 1939, in time he faded, to the astonishment of both those who followed and those who feared him. Freud, however, grew so pervasive that human beings came to understand themselves primarily by the light of his genius. Whatever the adaptation, his thinking prepared the ground in which all psychology, the great informer of humanistic disciplines, would germinate.

Freud has had his bitter detractors. Though some have compared him to Copernicus, Galileo, Darwin and Einstein, others have labeled him the corrupter of Western culture. Then there are those who charge that Freud has destroyed our values by urging people to "blame somebody else."

In 1995, in a storm of controversy, the Library of Congress postponed (then later held) a major exhibition of its holdings from the Freud archive. James Billington, the Librarian of Congress, pleaded financial problems, but he also conceded that he had been utterly unaware of the intense antagonism to Freud among some scholars.[11] In a petition, various critics including Freud's granddaughter, Sophie Freud, a retired professor of social work at Boston's Simmons College, protested that the effort, as it was planned, would not present adequately the case against psychoanalysis. Gloria Steinem added that Freud did not understand female sexuality. Undoubtedly she was right. Freud knew as little about feminine responses as any Victorian. But women have benefitted nonetheless from the therapy that he invented, and his deepest insights belong to all humankind.

Even so, opposition continues, and at a high level: Sir Peter Medawar, a Nobel Prize winner for medicine, called Freud's theories "one of the saddest and strangest of all landmarks in the history of twentieth century thought."[12]

But it was Freud's patients who were sometimes strange and sad. Freud himself was a very moral man, as Dr. Robert Coles, child psychiatrist at Harvard, has insisted.[13] Much drawn to Michelangelo's *Moses*, Freud saw a connection between himself and the lawgiver of Israel. Curiously, he argued that Moses was an Egyptian nobleman—not a popular position in the Jewish community. Perhaps Freud saw himself in the idea of an authoritative voice from an alien place. Also, he wanted for his work the same absolute acceptance Moses had received when he descended from Mt. Sinai. Freud fought to assure that his science, begun largely by Jews, would indeed become a light unto the Gentiles and the world.

For all his disavowal of religion, "Jewish mysticism was never far below the level of his conscious thoughts," wrote biographer Ronald Clark, "and at times he felt that the shadow of the biblical Joseph, whose interpretation of dreams had brought him prominence in Pharaoh's kingdom, was walking by his side."[14] And there was a moment, Gay noted, when Freud "thought of himself as a 'fisher of men,' and did his best to live up to that biblical self-designation."

Freud, according to Gay, grew up in a house that honored "Judaism without religion. Jacob Freud [his father] had emancipated himself from the Hasidic practices of his ancestors . . . . He continued to read the Bible at home, in Hebrew, for his edification . . . . Thus, Jacob Freud established an atmosphere in which the young Freud acquired an enduring fascination with 'biblical history,' that is to say, the Old Testament, when he had barely acquired the art of reading."

Until he was two and a half, Freud had a nursemaid who was a devout Catholic. She "fed her charge pious stories and dragged him to church. 'Then' Freud's mother told him, 'when you got home, you would preach and tell us what God Almighty does.'" None of this endeared Catholicism to Freud. "He viewed the Church of Rome and its Austrian minions as the principal obstacles in the way of full Jewish integration into Austrian society," according to Gay.

Freud at various times called religion "an illusion," religious feeling "a purely subjective fact," and religious need an infantile longing for the father to ameliorate helplessness and fear of "the superior power of Fate." Nonetheless, for all his militant atheism, Freud could not set aside entirely the spiritual realm. "Once again," he wrote, "only religion can answer the question of the purpose of life. One can hardly be wrong in concluding that the idea of life having a purpose stands and falls with the religious system."[15]

Still, he returned more than once to the notion of religion as a "delusional remolding of reality." Ernest Becker, in his study of the work of Otto Rank, a follower of Freud, took this idea to paradoxical depths when he spoke of the need human beings have "for an illusion that does not lie."[16] Thomas Moore, once a Catholic seminarian, now a therapist and writer, went a step further when he said we have to stop worrying about such things and open ourselves instead to the supraintuitive world beyond truth.[17]

Ironically, Freud was charged persistently with having started a secular religion. When his Wednesday Psychological Society met, Gay reports, "there was an atmosphere of the foundation of a religion in that room." Indeed, years later, playwright Arthur Miller would point to friends and acquaintances who had been through analysis and accuse them of smugness, "the smugness of the saved."[18]

It was Carl Jung who brought the Freudian inspiration to the realm of religion. Jung took the basic insight of Freud—the repression of feelings and experience which can wreak havoc unless brought to the light of consciousness—and grounded it in spiritual longing. When deprived of religious roots, Jung said, people lose their moorings. "The need for a meaning of their lives remains unanswered," he observed, "because the rational, biological goals are unable to express the irrational wholeness of human life."[19]

Never a slave to science (as his critics are eager to point out), Freud admitted that Shakespeare, Goethe, and Dostoevski "had come closer to the fundamental truths of psychoanalysis than had the physicians."[20] They indeed foreshadowed Freud. But his thinking was brought to fullest flower by Jung.

Alfred Adler traced neurosis to "an urge to power arising from a sense of inferiority."[21] This certainly was a notion that infused Freud's sexual theory with greater complexity. Then came Jung to argue that "however far-fetched it may sound, experience shows that many neuroses are caused by the fact that people blind themselves to their own religious promptings because of a childish passion for rational enlightenment."[22]

Jung could not rest quietly with this apostasy. In time he challenged Freud directly: "To the psyche," he wrote, "the spirit is no less the spirit even though it be called sexuality."[23] An emerging genius had suddenly confronted the master.

The truth is Jung simply could not accept Freud's definition of libido. According to Gay he "steadily attempted to widen the meaning of Freud's term, to make it stand not just for sexual drives, but for a general mental energy." Moreover, he threw over "most of the psychoanalytic baggage—childhood sexuality, the sexual etiology of neurosis, the Oedipus complex . . . ."

There also was conflict over the concept of the unconscious: "Freud had elaborated a theory of the personal unconscious; Jung extended it into a collective unconscious that contains archetypal images and figures that exist in all cultures, all people."[24]

Freud was heartbroken. Jung was his chosen heir, the extension of his life's work into the future. Freud, Gay points out, had "compared Jung to Joshua who would take possession of the promised land of psychiatry while he, Freud, the Moses, was destined to glimpse it only from afar."

But like Adler before him, Jung had to break away. The Oedipal son had to struggle free from the father figure. What Jung gained from his years with Freud, Gay notes "was more than a private quarrel and a broken friendship; he generated a psychological doctrine that was recognizably his own." Jung's analytical psychology was based on "the archetypes, the collective unconscious, the ubiquity of the uncanny, the sympathy with religious experience, the fascination with myth and alchemy . . . . Jung developed a psychology that naturally shows marked affinities with Freudian psychoanalysis. But the differences are fundamental."

Jung went beyond Freud in many respects, not least when he included the feminine as an essential aspect of psychology as well as religion. He believed the Catholic inclusion of Mary at the center of worship made the godhead complete.

Their two points of view, Freud's and Jung's, are mirrored in twentieth-century painting: If Picasso, inventor of Cubism who took things apart and put them back together again in a new way, can be called Freudian, bound by a masculine response to life, it was Matisse who celebrated woman in the spirit of Jung. Indeed, Matisse seemed to be painting from the female side of his personality, not merely observing women but creating as a woman would.

It is this successful Jungian integration of the feminine that made Matisse so appealing through the whole of his productive life. While Picasso continued always as a great virtuoso, in later years his original inspiration too often turned into "geriatric rage," as one critic has pointed out. His view of women echoed the uncomprehending attitude of Freud. However, the wellsprings of his genius were always there to be drawn upon. A simple peasant boy in a straw hat at the Picasso Museum in Paris, done not long before he died, reveals Picasso once again in all his poignant power. There Freud has been reunited with Jung.

Freud never won the Nobel Prize. One persistent problem was where to place him. Though he yearned to be known as a scientist, his association with medicine was ambiguous, and there were those who insisted, and still insist, that his achievement was in literature, not science. In 1928 and again in 1930 a young German psychoanalyst orchestrated a campaign for him with signatures from Bertrand Russell, Lytton Strachey, Julian Huxley, and Thomas Mann. Mann, however, not agreeing with the critics and wanting, perhaps, to keep Freud off his own turf, stipulated that the prize be awarded in medicine. Albert Einstein (often linked with Freud as the two dominant figures of modern thought) refused to sign, explaining that a psychologist hardly seemed eligible for the Nobel Prize in medicine.

The only category open to Freud, then, was literature, the area that Mann (and apparently others) wanted to protect. "So Freud," Gay remarks, "joined a long list of stylists, from Proust to Joyce, Franz Kafka to Virginia Woolf, who never went to Stockholm."

But literature could not contain him any more than medicine could. His work was too immense, his thinking too seminal. Prozac and other mind-altering drugs may diminish the practice of psychoanalysis. Literary critics may repudiate Freud's theories while acknowledging his talents. But Freud stands nonetheless at the juncture of twentieth century thought. His work transcended art and science. He is indeed the animating genius of the age.

Chapter Three

Franklin Delano Roosevelt
    Franklin Delano Roosevelt not only created American government as public benefactor, he also saved his country and the world from domination by Germany and Japan.

Minds That Made Statecraft

*Leadership, in short, is power governed by
principle, directed toward raising people to
their highest levels of personal motive and
social morality, and tested by the achieving
of results, measured by original purpose.
Power is different. Power manipulates
people as they are; leadership as they could
be. Power manages; leadership mobilizes.
Power impacts; leadership engages. Power
tends to corrupt, leadership to create.*

James MacGregor Burns

Certainly the twentieth century was born in a political vacuum.
Franz Joseph was lingering over the House of Hapsburg, refusing
to vest any authority in his son, Prince Rudolf, who committed a
strange double suicide with his friend Mary Vetsera. It was a case of
failed succession. Franz Joseph would not plan for the future or confer
any responsibility on his son. So he lost both.

Like the Austrian emperor, Britain's Queen Victoria kept Prince
Edward waiting much too long with nothing to do but dally. Fecklessness
was eating away at the royal house of Russia, while Nicholas II foolishly
dreamed of hegemony over Asia.[1] He did make an unexpected gesture
toward world peace, calling in 1899 for an international conference on
disarmament. But his gesture was dismissed as an act of "immature dilet-
tantism," not really serious.[2]

Only the genius of Theodore Roosevelt offered the world any energy
or any hope. He reached the White House in 1901—the year Victoria
died—following the assassination of President William McKinley. It was
six weeks before TR's forty-third birthday, and he remains the youngest
president in American history with John F. Kennedy close behind.

A look at the written works of Roosevelt reveals much about his scope and his magic. It's an amazing collection: twenty-four volumes on the American West, African game, Brazilian wilderness, the Naval War of 1812, essays on literature and foreign policy—and that's only a fraction of the opus.

Known as the "reading president," Teddy Roosevelt has been called "the most eminent intellectual to sit in the White House since John Quincy Adams." He was widely read in American and European literature and he celebrated the work of contemporary authors. Though academicians have disparaged his critical capacity (a biographer said he lacked the "introspective turn of mind to assess 'Hamlet' and 'Macbeth' in depth"), nonetheless TR's "patronage of writers (also of sculptors and architects) influence[d] the national mood," much as happened during the era of Jack and Jackie Kennedy.

No wonder Teddy Roosevelt is so often invoked by those now nearing the end of the century. In the space of two weeks, Margaret Thatcher, Ross Perot, and Bill Clinton all quoted TR, and it was to Roosevelt that Richard Nixon turned on the painful morning of his resignation from the presidency.

Theodore Roosevelt had a bold imagination. Though he never had to face the challenge of a major military conflict while in the White House, he was the first American president to envision a global role for the United States. Roosevelt mediated the end of the Russo-Japanese War and helped resolve a dispute in Morocco. For these efforts he was awarded the Nobel Peace Prize in 1906.

Roosevelt's intuitive powers must have been stimulated by his work to settle the Russo-Japanese War because something inspired him to foretell the rise of East Asia. "The Mediterranean era died with the discovery of America," he said. "The Atlantic era has reached the height of its development. The Pacific era, destined to be the greatest, is just at dawn."[3] Long before World War I, he saw trouble down the road with Japan.

In domestic affairs, Roosevelt grasped fully the implications of the industrial revolution. Where some, such as Supreme Court Justice Louis Brandeis, wanted to bust the trusts, restore competition and return to a Jeffersonian republic of country squires, TR saw the inevitability of big business and he fought to regulate, not destroy it. Like Brandeis, he worried about the effect huge concentrations of capital would have on the spirit of citizenship, but he chose a more realistic way of containing the problem.[4] His approach, according to Michael Sandel, was designed "to regulate big business by increasing the capacity of the national

government . . . . Like Brandeis, Roosevelt feared the political consequences of concentrated economic power. Where Roosevelt disagreed
with the decentralizers was over how to reassert democratic authority. He
considered big business an inevitable product of industrial development
and saw little point in trying to recover the decentralized political economy
of the nineteenth century. Since most big corporations operated in interstate or foreign commerce, beyond the reach of individual states, only the
federal government was suited to the task of controlling them. The power
of the national government had to grow to match the scale of corporate
power."

Roosevelt, observed historian Richard Hofstadter, "identified himself
with the authority of the State." Contemptuous of the "vulgar tyranny of
mere wealth" (TR's words), he felt "the trusts must never be allowed to
grow stronger than the State; they must yield to its superior moral force."[5]
He filed a case against railroad monopolists James J. Hill and J.P.
Morgan, and he brought rates under the control of the Interstate
Commerce Commission. He supported workers' compensation, child
labor laws, and an inheritance tax. Though friendly to business people he
didn't shrink from provoking them. Indeed Henry Clay Frick once complained, "We bought the son of a bitch and then he did not stay bought."[6]

Roosevelt had a rudimentary instinct for civil rights and "infuriated
Southerners by inviting Booker T. Washington to dine at the White
House."[7] He opposed prayer in public schools and government funds for
religious schools. And he was way out in front on the environment,
promoting forest management, water power and national parks, often in
the face of implacable opposition from commercial interests and their
lackeys in Congress.

From his political birthing in the New York Assembly (first elected
when he was only twenty-three) to his years as civil service commissioner
in Washington and police commissioner in New York as well as governor,
Roosevelt was an inveterate reformer. And he never rested. William
Henry Harbaugh suggests that his "most dramatic contribution to
American life . . . was the arousal of the public conscience to the need for
even further reform."

TR has often been accused of "seeking war for its own sake."
Adamant that the country prepare to battle Spain in 1898, he resigned as
assistant secretary of the Navy to join the fight in Cuba himself. Forming
the First Volunteer Cavalry Regiment, he charged up San Juan Hill in
what he called his "crowded hour."

Known ever after as the Rough Rider, Roosevelt as president allowed the construction of the Panama Canal to become a bitter controversy in Colombia. Nonetheless, he did build the canal. He also was heavy-handed in China. But that can't obscure the important things he accomplished for the American military. Harbaugh has written that TR "was perhaps more responsible than any other individual . . . for the shaping of the Navy into an effective instrument of war and diplomacy."

True, Hofstadter dismisses Roosevelt as a man with "the intellectual fiber of a muscular and combative Polonius." Ridiculing TR's strenuous efforts to overcome boyhood frailty (he had terrible asthma as a youth), he notes that Roosevelt "was still boxing in the White House at forty-three."[8] But was this so different from John Kennedy—also sickly as a youth—and his emphasis on "vigah"?

Actually the two had much in common: Not only were they compensating for boyhood physical deficiencies, both were children of privilege and Harvard men. Both achieved the White House in their early forties, read books, and consorted with writers. Both stood on a platform of social justice while working quietly to placate business interests. But TR, the visionary, stood at the beginning of the Progressive Era while Kennedy stood at the end, a bridge to Lyndon Johnson, who with Medicare and Medicaid wrote the last chapter of TR's Square Deal and Franklin Roosevelt's New Deal. (The Clintons tried to add their own health-care epilogue thirty years later, a brave if quixotic initiative since Ronald Reagan had long since tolled the bell for liberalism.)

Roosevelt clearly fascinated his writer friends. Edith Wharton shaped a character after him in *The Age of Innocence*. So did Henry James, occasionally a guest at TR's White House, in *The Bostonians*. Henry Adams dismissed TR as "pure act," but Robert Frost remembered him as "the only president who ever took that much interest in poetry." Van Wyck Brooks said, "If ever there was obviously a man of genius, it was Theodore Roosevelt."[9]

Roosevelt operated on a grand scale. He took a young nation at the dawn of the century and prepared its people for great things. He lived in his imagination. And he imagined for America much that lay ahead.

If Teddy Roosevelt set the tone for twentieth century America, it was his fifth cousin, Franklin Delano Roosevelt, who saved the nation at its moments of gravest peril since the Civil War. Even a Republican businessman from Texas, no fan of FDR, admitted, "We wouldn't have had a country without him."

This Roosevelt won the presidency in 1932, having followed TR's path as assistant secretary of the Navy (under Wilson) and as governor of New York. Crippled by polio, he moved into the White House just as the Depression was nearing its nadir. Unemployment was at 25 percent, where it would stay until 1938, then easing only to 20 percent. General Motors' stock price had dropped from 73 at the time of the 1929 crash to 8, and the Goldman Sachs Trading Co. from 104 to 1 3/4. "The singular feature of the great crash of 1929," wrote John Kenneth Galbraith, "was that the worst continued to worsen. What looked one day like the end proved the next day to have been only the beginning."[10]

That fateful year, 1929, was marked by the Florida real estate boom, made vivid by such disreputables as Charles Ponzi. That was a time when non-bank banks were joyously lending money for speculation in securities; holding companies were scooping up operations and moving, Galbraith observed wickedly, to eliminate "the incompetence, somnambulance, naivete or even the unwarranted integrity of local managements"; and investors were possessed by the craze to buy equities on margin.[11]

When everything fell apart, massive denial was the reaction all around. President Hoover assured Americans the economy was sound. The esteemed Harvard Economic Society announced that a "severe depression like that of 1920-21 is outside the range of possibility. We are not facing protracted liquidation." "This view the Society reiterated," said Galbraith, "until it was liquidated." Nor does Galbraith spare Yale. He wrote that its Professor Irving Fisher insisted that "the market had not yet reflected the beneficent effects of Prohibition, which had made the American worker 'more productive and dependable.'" There were a few who saw the truth: Roger Babson, "educator, philosopher, theologian, statistician, forecaster, economist, and friend of the law of gravity," warned of more trouble ahead. He was roundly rebuked by *Barron's* and other sages of Wall Street.[12]

But the market kept right on disintegrating. By the time FDR reached the White House, it could hardly have been more desperate. He responded with a fever of action, announcing that "the country needs, and, unless I mistake its temper, the country demands bold, persistent experimentation. It is common sense to take a method and try it. If it fails, admit it frankly and try another. But above all, try something."[13]

Try something he did. Try everything in fact. What resulted was the New Deal, the most dramatic domestic innovation in American history.

As Doris Kearns Goodwin said, the New Deal "profoundly altered the relationship between the government and the people, giving the state the final responsibility for the well-being of its citizens."

The scope of the experiment was breathtaking: The stock market was regulated. Control was established over the nation's money supply. Savings were protected by the Federal Deposit Insurance Corporation. Labor won a guaranteed right to collective bargaining. Workers gained a minimum wage. It was the end of Social Darwinism in the American economy. It was the beginning of the safety net that saved millions from ruin.

"At the heart of the New Deal," Richard Hofstadter observed, "there was not a philosophy but a temperament." Indeed it has been noted that FDR had a second-rate mind but a first-class temperament. "The essence of this temperament was Roosevelt's confidence that even when he was operating in unfamiliar territory he could do no wrong, commit no serious mistakes."[14]

Franklin Roosevelt, like TR, was by temperament an "artisan," according to a study of presidential personalities by David Keirsey and Ray Choiniere.[15] Both were drawn to artful action, to change, as long as it was appropriate change. They liked the concrete and the practical and had little use for abstraction. FDR "was not a long-term strategist . . . but he was a prodigal tactician, a very clever maneuverer of people and immediate events with the extraordinary timing so often seen in the Artisans."[16]

Roosevelt had only the flimsiest grasp of economic policy. He vamped during his transition meeting with the deeply knowledgeable Herbert Hoover. His ignorance of economics disappointed John Maynard Keynes when he came to call. And Roosevelt astonished and frustrated staff members with instructions to "weave together" directly contradictory policy options. "And yet," Hofstadter admitted, "there was a kind of intuitive wisdom under the harum-scarum surface of his methods."[17]

That intuitive wisdom was linked by Isaiah Berlin to "an exceptionally sensitive awareness" of people. This, he believed, was the source of Roosevelt's genius. It was as if "the inner currents [and] tremors" of human society registered themselves within him "with a kind of seismographical accuracy."[18]

Out of his wild improvisations, FDR created some programs that blessedly went to an early grave, struck down by the Supreme Court. Of those Hofstadter especially scorned the National Recovery Act—the

NRA—as an effort to seek recovery "through systematic monopolization, high prices and low production" and the Agricultural Adjustment Act as "recovery through scarcity."[19]

Actually, recovery was long in coming. By 1940, noted Goodwin, "almost 10 million Americans, 17 percent of the work force, were still without jobs; about two and a half million found their only source of income in government programs. Of those who worked, one half of the men and two-thirds of the women earned less than $1,000 a year. Only 48,000 taxpayers in a population of 132 million earned more than $2,500 a year."[20]

Nonetheless, FDR salvaged the American spirit during the Depression, and he invented a great new engine for national domestic life. It was fueled by federal pump-priming and lubricated by the most far-reaching of FDR innovations, Social Security. All told, it was an enormous achievement even if war was the thing finally that restored the economy to health.

FDR met the threat of World War II with unflinching boldness and courage. He had, wrote Isaiah Berlin, "apparently complete freedom from fear of the future . . . . What he could not abide was, before all, passivity, stillness, melancholy, fear of life or preoccupation with eternity or death . . . . [F]ree from the obsessions of an inner life, [he had] an unparalleled capacity for creating confidence in the power of his insight . . . ."[21]

After Hitler marched into the Low Countries and France in May, 1940, FDR addressed Congress, asking for huge appropriations to prepare the country to fight. In a staggering show of bravado, the president called for the manufacture of fifty thousand planes a year, a production goal "way beyond the best hopes of his army and navy combined . . . more than ten times the current capacity." It's unclear where Roosevelt got that number, but army historian Irving Holley concludes, the President's big round number was a psychological target to lift sights and accustom planners in military and industrial circles alike to thinking big."[22]

And big thinking was crucial. Not only were U.S. weapons antiquated, war games in Louisiana also made evident the abysmal condition of American forces. Some of the commanders were facing resolutely backwards in their notions of warfare. So were arms experts who continued to insist that the horse cavalry was far superior to tanks. This group included even Gen. George Patton and his junior at that time, Dwight Eisenhower.[23]

Roosevelt confronted not only the need to recapture American might but also the dangerous decision to send scarce equipment to the European front. Advisors such as Gen. George Marshall and Ambassador Joseph P. Kennedy argued against it, pressing the President to husband all available resources for American troops. "With France on the verge of defeat," wrote Doris Kearns Goodwin, "United States military leaders were unanimous in urging Roosevelt to stop supplying the Allies and to focus instead on rearming at home." With great daring, FDR continued to send materiel to Europe. "The only answer, he believed . . . was to bet on the prospects that, if the U.S. did everything in its power to help, the Allies [essentially Britain] would somehow survive until such time as America could get itself into shape to enter the war."

If Roosevelt had been wrong, if Britain had fallen along with France, the Germans would have taken possession of all that precious American equipment and U.S. forces would have been even weaker. But Britain did not fall, and Roosevelt intensified his efforts to keep Churchill's troops alive. He sent destroyers without the approval of Congress, bypassing a balky Republican minority. Then he persuaded lawmakers to approve his lend-lease program for supplying the British. When Hitler invaded Russia in June, 1941, he extended lend-lease to Moscow as well.

FDR refused to respond to German atrocities against Jews. Eleanor tried to persuade him to help after a small dinner with two members of the European underground made her aware of the refugees and the desperate odds they faced. But Roosevelt was worried about Nazi infiltration. He had heard that before invading Norway and the Netherlands Germans had sneaked into both countries disguised as tourists, newspeople and intellectuals. He was determined that would not happen to the United States.

Undeterred, Eleanor sent lists of names to the State Department and pressed her friend Sumner Welles to take action. He accommodated her to a limited extent. Some visitor visas were issued after a board had been set up to ensure security, but it was not nearly enough.[24]

Roosevelt, like Churchill, was convinced that the only way he could help the Jews was to win the war as quickly as possible. "There were no military options to liberate the prisoners of the extermination camps other than the direct assault and conquest by Allied armies," wrote William J. vanden Heuvel, president of the Franklin and Eleanor Roosevelt Institute. "The possibility of bombing the camps was never seriously suggested, and Jewish leaders like Ben-Gurion opposed the very idea of the Allies participating in bombing attacks that would kill large numbers of Jews and leave the survivors to the unrelenting brutality of Nazi violence. Postwar studies showed the bombing of railroad tracks had no appreciable impact because of the Nazi capacity to repair such facilities almost immediately."[25]

The Jews, of course, were subject to Nazi brutality in any case. Even so, bombardment of the camps once the war was underway might indeed have accomplished little except more carnage, wiping out Jews who perhaps could and did survive. The question of refugees, however, still lingers.

There were other blights on Roosevelt's wartime record. The detention of Japanese-Americans was not pretty (Eleanor was appalled), and the losses that stemmed from Yalta haunt Europe still. Here FDR's famous temperament was not suited to the demands of the situation. The problem, Hofstadter believed, was one of misconceived role: "His position between Churchill and Stalin was that of a mediator, in the spirit of 'weave the two together'. . . ."[26]

But the kind of forward-looking perception needed to protect Central Europe from Soviet imperialism simply wasn't in him. "His lack of foresight and his strategic failure should not be a great surprise," said Choiniere and Keirsey. His temperament had "the ability to pinpoint advantageous immediate gains, but little interest or flair for long-range goals. Roosevelt was . . . an optimist. He had a war to fight, and Stalin and the Russians were important allies. Winning the war was what he wanted now; the final fate of Europe could wait and one way or another he would handle it."[27]

There is another view that might also be close to the truth: By the time of Yalta, the Red Army already occupied all of Eastern Europe except the former Czechoslovakia. The war with Japan still raged and Roosevelt hoped Stalin would open that front once Germany had surrendered. The U.S. and Britain were in no position to oppose Soviet troops with force. And force is what it would have taken. The words formulated at Yalta to protect Poland from a Moscow-run regime and ensure free elections "as soon as possible" turned out to be useless.[28]

Two months after Yalta, Roosevelt was dead. Europe was slashed by a cruel chasm, with one side able to rebuild and prosper while the other, Eastern side was put in the deep freeze for forty-four years. Harry Truman was obliged to take over the running of the war and its aftermath, having been given no information whatsoever by his predecessor.

FDR saved the country not once but twice. He saved the world from domination by Germany and Japan. But he could not save Central Europe or millions in Russia from the ravages of Stalin. Even so, he created the social order that endured to the end of the century in the United States, and he made America a preeminent world power. He was a genius at survival, until he could survive no longer.

The Roosevelts were worldly people, connected to the bounty of the seasons and the pleasures of the earth. They came to high office in a country on the verge of fulfilling its capacity for power. Continents away, also in the early years of the century, another kind of leader germinated in the shadow of the British raj. There, in India. Mohandas Gandhi grew from lawyer to political agitator to mystical saint to liberator of his people. Churchill, famously wrong, dismissed him as "a half-naked, seditious fakir." But another British official (E.S. Montagu) saw Gandhi more clearly: "He dresses like a coolie, forswears all personal advancement, lives practically on the air, and is a pure visionary."

Gandhi was born in 1869 to a comfortable, middle-cast family whose men were senior officials at various princely courts. In keeping with Hindu custom, he married when barely a teenager. Much schooling still awaited him after the wedding. He advanced steadily through his classes but without distinction. After some setbacks in college, Gandhi embarked for England to study law at the Inns of the Court, having promised his mother to "abstain from wine, women and meat." So horrified were his relatives, who did not believe in ventures abroad, they outcast him. How, they asked, could he possibly keep ritual purity in London?

Ritual purity was not on Gandhi's mind at first. Instead he embraced Western life, from clothes to dancing. Determined to become an English gentleman, he spent time before the mirror, perfecting his appearance. But he could not suppress his own radical simplicity. He joined the Vegetarian Society and began to see diet in terms of religion as well as health. By the time he returned to India he was not the Gandhi who would move a nation and rock an empire, but he had tested the temptations of the material world and found that he belonged elsewhere. He was ready for the alchemical fires of South Africa, where he moved to practice law.

Gandhi never knew discrimination in England. So he was unprepared for South Africa's obsession with race. It drove him into public life. But not before he had pursued his profession, fathered children (one of whom he delivered himself) and grown ever more ascetic and austere. This included a vow of celibacy when he was thirty-seven, a necessary prerequisite, he felt, for true service.[29]

But before the years of service came reading and a search for God, whom he called Truth. Through friends who were Christian and Muslim, Gandhi explored these religions and found much to admire. But he came upon his own ground in his own tradition, Hinduism. Though he abhorred the caste system and the cruel treatment of untouchables, he discovered in the faith of his father what sustained him. The revelation came to him gradually through intense introspection. "At last," he wrote, "I looked into my heart and found Him there, only there and nowhere else."

Even so, he maintained a high rapport with Christians and Muslims: "I regard both the religions as equally true with my own," he said. "But my own gives me full satisfaction. It contains all that I need for my growth. It teaches me to pray not that others may believe as I believe but that they may grow to their full height in their own religion."

Gandhi took a transcendent view of faith: "Let me explain," he wrote, "what I mean by religion. It is not the Hindu religion, which I certainly prize above all other religions, but the religion which transcends Hinduism, which changes one's very nature, which binds one indissolubly to the truth within and which ever purifies. It is the permanent element in human nature which counts no cost too great in order to find full expression and which leaves the soul utterly restless until it has found itself . . . ."[30]

Gandhi was deeply influenced by reading, and nothing meant more to him than John Ruskin's *Unto This Last*. Here, according to Judith M. Brown, he imbibed the conviction that "the individual's good lies in the good of all, that all work is of equal value, and that the supremely desirable life is one of labour, whether as a farmer or a craftsman."

It led to the founding of Phoenix, a communal settlement on one hundred acres of fruit trees near Durban. There people worked to be self-supporting and Gandhi strove to shape them into a new kind of Indian, productive and free. His principles for this enterprise he elucidated regularly in his own newspaper, *Indian Opinion*. It grew to be a major voice for Gandhi's politics, which to him were inseparable from daily life and faith.

It was Tolstoy who gave Gandhi the fundamental concept of his work—non-violence. In *The Kingdom of God Is Within You* Tolstoy condemned the state as aggressive and unnecessary and urged that people not participate in it but rather that they seek the true kingdom in their own hearts. From this Gandhi began to understand how dependent the British were on the cooperation of Indians and what it would mean if that cooperation were withheld in a peaceable way.

Gandhi's reverence for the Russian writer issued forth in Tolstoy Farm, which he established near Johannesburg with the help of a European supporter. Much larger than Phoenix, with one thousand acres, it accommodated Hindus, Muslims, Christians, and Parsis, who, like their compatriots at the first commune, sought self-reliance. Brown relates that they "built their own houses, and lived on as simple a diet as possible, grinding their own flour, making their own bread, butter and marmalade, and growing their own oranges. Generally they walked into Johannesburg rather than travel even third class on the train, though the round trip was twenty-one miles . . . ." Gandhi paid "detailed attention to sanitation," a lifelong obsession, and he "supervised the health of the members according to his faith in natural medicine."

In the midst of communal life, between the start of Phoenix and of Tolstoy, began the budding of Gandhi as a political force. He believed still, and wholeheartedly, in the British Empire. He just wanted Indians to have their rightful place in the realm. When colonial rulers in South Africa ordered former indentured Indian workers to pay an exorbitant annual tax, Brown relates, Gandhi fought "in the press, in the courts and through petitions." When Indians were denied the vote and limited in their right to immigrate and get a license to do business, he fought some more.

His political work in South Africa took a decisive turn when the Black Act was passed saying that all Indians had to register. To them this was an intolerable encroachment on their rights as free citizens of the empire. It was then that passive resistance, the movement that made Gandhi renowned, was born, only he called it "soul force." He led Indians in mounting a big iron cauldron in Johannesburg where thousands of registration certificates were set ablaze. He launched a long march of over two thousand men, women and children across the Transvaal border without permits. All were thrown in jail.

As Nelson Mandela would do sixty years later, Gandhi maintained an active schedule behind bars, negotiating conditions for Indian prisoners. He also used the time to read, mainly the Bible, the Koran, the *Gita* and other Hindu devotional writings as well as works by Bacon, Carlyle,

Emerson, Huxley, Plato and of course Ruskin and Tolstoy.

Finally Gandhi and J.C. Smuts, the Minister of the Interior, reached an agreement under which the Black Act was repealed. Peace did not last long. There were other issues and other battles before Gandhi left South Africa to return to India in 1915, in the midst of world war. By then he was regarded not only as a political leader but as a saint and a Mahatma. Even so, Smuts was glad to see him go.

Throughout his twenty years in South Africa Gandhi remained loyal to the British Empire. He offered to help colonial officers during the Boer War and the Zulu Rebellion despite his sympathies for the Boers and the Zulus. He believed that as long as he was demanding rights of the British he owed them loyalty. This view he carried into World War I, and he set aside his vow of non-violence to urge Indians to participate. It was, he felt, an opportunity for his countrymen to gain courage and the ability to defend themselves. Foretelling Zhou Enlai in China, he wanted to create "a new society from the roots upwards."

Not only did Gandhi feel an obligation to the British, there was much that he admired about them. He saw in the British strength of character and "love of justice, fair dealing, equality and liberty." But in time he turned against modern civilization to embrace the ancient ways of India. He envisioned a battle between the "Kingdom of Satan" who is the "God of War" and the "Kingdom of God" who is of Love. He warned his countrymen against using "modern methods of violence to drive out the English." In fact, he dreamed of, according to Brown, "a total reversal of all the patterns of Westernization the British presence had set in motion in India, including education, medical practice and industrial development, as well as the practice of government."

Such was the idealism of Mahatma Gandhi. He would be criticized for his "prejudice . . . against modernity," but that would deter him not at all.

Once home in India, Gandhi, by now forty-six, followed the same pattern he had developed in South Africa: He founded an ashram for communal living where he encouraged vows of truth and non-violence along with chastity, even for married couples. He involved himself in issues, and for the first time he had a public fast, to force mill owners to deal decently with weavers who worked for them. From that point on, fasting would be a major weapon in his arsenal against cruelty.

Sometimes, in spite of all his admonitions, his followers in civil disobedience erupted in violence. Frequently Gandhi was sent to prison.

Always he emerged more determined than ever to shame the British into concessions.

In time, spinning was added to his schedule, for half an hour a day. This he saw as holy work which bound him to the poor. It became the symbol of his teaching as he urged Indians to give up British goods and make their own cloth through hand-weaving. In addition, he kept each Monday as a day of silence, when he pursued quiet activities and gave his mind a chance to recuperate. Then his pace would resume again, with constant travel and speaking, living by conviction on five items of food a day.

Meanwhile the tension with London was ever building, ever building. It was a subtle combat as both sides struggled for moral authority. If Gandhi's people lost control and burst forth in mayhem, Whitehall won. If they remained calm, and worthy objects of world sympathy, Gandhi and his Congress Party won. It was also a high-stakes game within India as the Congress group strove to establish itself as *the* legitimate entity to negotiate with the British on behalf of the entire subcontinent.

The tooing and froing was as delicate as it was difficult. The British proposed Dominion Status for India, the position enjoyed by white members of the empire-commonwealth. It meant complete autonomy, but it was not complete independence, and that's what Gandhi fought for, partly at the insistence of his young protege, Jawaharlal Nehru. Determined not to divide Congress and weaken the party's negotiating position in London, Gandhi called for more civil disobedience.

The issue of confrontation was chosen—salt. Brown regards this decision as an act of political genius. She points out that Gandhi seized the high moral ground without touching any vital interests in India or denying the government significant revenue. Yet it was an emotional matter—"a tax by an alien regime on a basic necessity of life" about which gathered "a long tradition of Indian political opposition to the raj." Also, it touched everybody, both Hindu and Muslim, and it could be readily understood by ordinary people.

So in 1930, Gandhi and close to eighty men—Christians, Muslims, Hindus, and untouchables, chosen from his ashram and from groups he could trust—set forth to march 240 miles to the sea. It took nearly a month to reach the Bombay coastline, and once there they made salt on the shore, in direct violation of the British monopoly. It had members of the government utterly paralyzed as they wondered what Gandhi would do next and when to arrest him.

Gandhi, in faltering health, invested his full life force in this march. "I must put forth all my effort or retire altogether and for all time from public life," he said. "I feel that now is the time or it will be never."

His time it certainly was, as the Viceroy admitted. Gandhi, he observed, was "regrettably hale and hearty."

Arrests were ordered, finally, and Gandhi returned to prison. There he stayed almost a year.

Then began the talks between Gandhi and Lord Irwin, the Viceroy, known to be a sensitive, devout Anglican. "This afternoon," a moderate Indian leader reported to his brother, "the two uncrucified Christs met. [We] have prepared each for the other! . . . If they hit it off, then serious negotiations will begin."

Serious negotiations did begin indeed. What emerged was the Gandhi-Irwin Pact on civil disobedience. It cleared the way for Congress to join constitutional talks in London. Nehru greeted the agreement with fearful tears, Churchill with tirades in Parliament.

The London conference in the fall of 1931 did not work. Muslims and untouchables insisted on speaking for themselves when Gandhi badly wanted to represent the whole of India. Hemmed in by the Congress mandate, he had no room for maneuver. He had nothing to offer. He had nothing to withhold. So he set about instead to influence British public opinion. This would stand him in good stead down the road, when colonial officials in India had to answer for their treatment of him.

More time in jail awaited Gandhi upon his return to India, then fasting, which caused the British, apprehensive about what would happen if he should die, to release him. He distanced himself from Congress to devote his time to the development of village life, especially small industry. London pressed ahead with constitutional reform in 1935 and two years later the party joined in cooperative governance of India, especially in the provinces. Its members discovered that actually being responsible for what happened was an unexpected pressure.

With the outbreak of World War II, Congress withdrew from government and in 1942—with odd judgment—launched an all-out "Quit India" campaign against the British. Party leaders spent much of the next few years in jail, including Gandhi, who was thrust to the forefront once again. During the war his powers of perception utterly failed him. He opposed the fighting in the name of non-violence as if non-violence could stop the Nazis. Indeed, he wrote the Fuhrer to advance his idea (the

British refused to mail the letters) and asked to meet with Hitler for the
same purpose. (The Viceroy said no.) Hitler, he was convinced, would
back down if met with massive passive resistance.

Gandhi had no notion of real evil in the world. Hinduism recognized
no such duality, and besides, he was used to Westminster, which did care
about public opinion, especially in the United States. Moreover, he was
convinced that if the British left India, Japan would have no reason to
invade. If he were wrong, and the raj departed, followed by the arrival of
the Japanese, he put his faith in passive resistance to defend India. He
could not fathom that non-violence and fasting would be of little interest
to Tojo.

London offered India independence in 1942 (Churchill wanted to
demonstrate to his American allies British good will) and again after the
war, but Gandhi's Congress Party took issue with the terms. Finally, on
August 15, 1947, freedom did come, hurriedly, abruptly, with devastating
results. Pakistan was created as a Muslim state, and bloody carnage
ensued as Hindus and Muslims scrambled to get on their side of the new
divide. As many as one million people died. Two million fled their
homes. To stem the rampage, Gandhi held a fast in Calcutta, and, miracu-
lously, the killing was quelled for awhile. Lord Mountbatten, the last
Viceroy, even wrote to congratulate him. Another fast for peace followed,
in Delhi. This time it was the politicians who relented and agreed to press
for a resumption of normal life in the city.

But there could be no normal life for Gandhi. He was in constant
danger, and he knew it. He insisted that God would protect him as long
as his work was needed on earth. That work was ended January 30, 1948,
when three shots, fired point-blank by an angry young Hindu, bitter
about Gandhi's evenhanded treatment of Muslims, sent the Mahatma
slumping to the ground as he walked to a prayer meeting. It brought to a
close one of the most strangely successful lives of the twentieth century.

Though a pure idealist and almost certainly a saint, Gandhi also was
recognized by those who dealt with him as a superior politician. He
understood the arts of negotiation and the importance of symbols to an
illiterate people. Through simple, white robes and a spinning wheel he
managed to convey to a vast continent a concern for the poor. He awoke
in Indians the spirit of their own culture and an aspiration to be their own
people.

Gandhi tried hard for a simple life, but simplicity eluded him at the
deepest levels. Judith Brown wrote that he "wrestled with guilt, anger,

depression and lust" during much of his life. But he prevailed over all of them. He achieved sufficient self-mastery to break the moral authority of the British and bring his people to freedom. No doubt nationalism would have won out finally in India in any case, but without the elegance that Gandhi brought to his historic moment. And without the spiritual power that would reach across the years to inspire another liberator, Martin Luther King, Jr., in the United States

Across the northern border of India lay China. It too emerged from World War II with revolutionary aspirations. The seeds had long since been planted, and no one was more central to their final fruition than Zhou Enlai. Mao Dzedong may be the vivid anti-hero of the era, but it was the single-minded persistence of Zhou Enlai that brought China into the modern world after a century of humiliating exploitation.

Zhou Enlai was "the greatest statesman of his day," wrote Harrison Salisbury.[31] Henry Kissinger ranked him with de Gaulle.[32] Han Suyin, his biographer, called him "an enlightened Confucian." Another observer likened the magic of his presence to that of the Dalai Lama.

But there was a dark side: A former State Department official told Richard Nixon that Zhou Enlai, "charming as he was, had killed people with his own hands and then departed, calmly smoking a cigarette." Nixon also related this view from another diplomat: "There was not a grain of truth in him . . . . It's all acting. He is the greatest actor I have ever met. He'd laugh one moment and cry the next and make his audience laugh and cry with him. But it is all acting."[33]

Acting or not, Zhou gave his life to China. It was China that he loved. Communism was merely the vehicle for saving the country from years of degradation at the hands of the West. "He was, for me, for so many," writes Han Suyin, "both the old China that we had known and the striving toward that unknown China to come."

Zhou Enlai was born into a Confucian culture in 1898. So steeped in this tradition was his family that a dying childless uncle was permitted to adopt Zhou at the age of two. This assured that the uncle would be remembered as part of the family genealogy and his widow would not be spurned. As a result, young Enlai had three doting mothers: his own, his aunt and his nurse. From them, Han Suyin proposed, he learned an easy respect for women that was not at all Confucian.

Both Zhou's mothers died young, leaving his father struggling apart from the family in a clerk's job. This time another uncle stepped in and invited the boy, by now ten years old, to live with him in Manchuria. There Enlai went to a school sponsored by American missionaries and studied Western science, history and thought. John Hersey's mother was one of his teachers.[34]

Zhou read newspapers, magazines, Darwin, Rousseau and John Stuart Mill, but his most important lesson came from the harsh Manchurian winters. If he could survive those, he reasoned, he could withstand anything. With endurance came also frugality, according to Han Suyin, both essential to serious revolutionaries. And, unlike many of his comrades, he cultivated the gift of friendship, which for him would mean more than mere sentimentality—feeling without the obligation of action. Zhou would be a loyal friend, often in circumstances stripped of all humanity. Perhaps his code permitted him to kill, as Nixon's source suggested, but it also required him to save the lives of people within his orbit, whenever he could.

Zhou Enlai wrote poetry. Sixteen different pseudonyms accompanied his work through the years, and in his writing could be discerned a Buddhist search for truth. But though he believed in the power of a heart transformed, his primary impulses flowed always from Confucius. He sought salvation in guiding principles that would change not just him but the whole of China. He was an intellectual who tried to perfect the spirit through action, much like that anti-intellectual, Gandhi. And like Gandhi, he considered this a national, not simply a personal, quest.

When revolution struck Russia in 1917, Zhou was in Japan, depressed and failing as a university student. He shortly returned to a campus in China where he registered in literature but seldom graced the classroom. Instead he became, according to Han Suyin, "a professional agitator, organizing protest marches, meetings, picketing pro-Japanese shops," for he both loved and resented Japan. This was the moment that Marxism entered his life, but he took a while to commit himself to the new philosophy. Finally, convinced that China required an overarching ideology, he embraced Communism as the saving truth for his country.

By then Zhou was in France on a program for Chinese students to study and work in local factories. But most of his time he gave to recruiting and organizing for the Socialist Youth League, not only in France, but in Belgium and Germany as well. One of his compatriots was Deng Xiaoping who later would lead China into an age of astonishing prosperity. Zhou also met Vietnam's Ho Chi Minh who would be an ally in years to come.

Zhou discovered his true forte when Sun Yatsen's Guomindang

(Nationalist Party) and the Communists formed a united front in China and asked him to put the two groups together in Paris. This was a difficult assignment, demanding extraordinary finesse. It foretold all that lay ahead for Zhou Enlai. He had, Han Suyin points out, "a genius for reconciling the unreconcilable." He was "many-faced, but consistent unto himself, like a rainbow which displays a many-colored arc by refracting colorless light."

The united front did not last. Sun Yatsen died, and with him went all hope of holding China together. Chiang Kaishek, commander-in-chief of the Guomindang armies, turned adversarial. So then did the Communists. The inevitable blow-up came when Zhou, by now a military man, led an uprising of workers in Shanghai in 1927. He won. Soon Chiang arrived and demanded that the workers lay down their arms. Zhou said no. Then came the massacre: Chiang's people swept through the city and machine-gunned as many as five thousand workers. Zhou was arrested but not held long. The killing spread all over the country.

Zhou led a fledgling people's army against Chiang's forces in Nanchang, then withdrew to Shantou, a port that lay south. He captured Shantou only to retreat again in the face of rampaging warlords. He head-ed to Hong Kong to recover from malaria which had decimated his troops. Next came Shanghai, bastion of capitalism but ever the refuge for budding Communists, where, after a trip to Moscow, Germany and France, he set about rebuilding the party which had dwindled from fifty-eight thousand members in January, 1927, to ten thousand by December.

This was the moment when the hard side of Zhou Enlai came to the fore. He created the Te Ke, which Han Suyin refers to as "a tightly-knit organization." "The Te Ke kept Party files on each party member, collected information, punished betrayals, operated radio stations, and instituted protection teams and justice squads . . . ." When a high-ranking, deeply informed operative defected to Chiang Kaishek, having sent a letter home about his plans, Zhou ordered his entire family killed, all seventeen of them. Only a twelve-year-old boy was spared.

All the while Mao Dzedong was in a mountain stronghold, develop-ing his strategy of rural bases while Zhou held out for occupying cities. It was years before Zhou understood that Mao was right: The power to move China lay in the countryside. Zhou had been taking the Moscow line, the admonition of Lenin who said "All power to the center." That meant Shanghai. In time, Zhou stopped being a rival to Mao and the two joined forces, a fateful union.[35]

The painful bond between Zhou Enlai and Mao Dzedong has been called "an indissoluble linkage, until their deaths," both in 1976. "The two men," wrote Han Suyin, "exercised upon each other a mutual fascination, because they were so utterly different, in character, mentality, physical build." Suyin further observes, "Zhou had discovered Mao Dzedong. Discovered genius, an amplitude, a breadth of vision, in which his own passion for China could recognize itself. The tragedy of this bond would come later, much later. When Mao, betrayed by the power lust of all around him, feared and envied Zhou Enlai, the only man who had never betrayed him . . . ."

A Chinese scholar, Han Suyin points out, took another view: "Zhou Enlai knew Mao was a tiger. He, Zhou, thought he could ride that tiger." An American observer agreed: Zhou, he said, realized Mao was going to be in charge. So he set about to get along with him. Thus Zhou joined his genius for organization to Mao's creative force.

By the time the Long March, an arduous westward retreat, began in October, 1934, Mao, Han Suyin relates, had "got into the habit of letting Zhou do all the convincing. He would sketch out his vision, his plans, maps spread before him. And Zhou would discuss, refine, sometimes add an item of importance. In the end he always knew exactly how things should be done." Mao became the mastermind. Zhou the master of logistics.

The leaders of the Long March, Harrison Salisbury relates, "worked by night, slept by day. They stayed up until dawn receiving messages from far-flung units and sending out battle plans for the day. Exhausted they fell into their litters and were carried on these swaying beds during the Long March. Without sleeping pills they could not manage. To a man they became sleeping pill addicts. Those pills were morphine, codeine or plain opium capsules. Nothing else was available." This *modus operandi* continued long after the revolution had been won. Both Zhou and Mao spent their lives working through the night after only two or three hours of sleep. Both became addicted to sleeping pills. This had no discernible effect on Zhou's behavior, but Mao "fell into a pattern of lengthy disengagement from the world, lolling for days, weeks and months on his pyramid of pillows, whether in Beijing, Hangzhou, or some other resort. These periods were broken by frenzied activity, meetings, conferences, new grandiose schemes, 'inspection trips' through the countryside."[36] It's impossible not to wonder if these strong drugs impaired Mao's personality, accentuating the streak of evil for which he has come to be remembered.

After the Long March there was more than civil war to rivet Zhou and his compatriots. The Japanese had occupied Manchuria in September, 1931 and attacked Shanghai a few months later. But Chiang Kaishek refused to fight the Japanese. He insisted instead on quelling the Communists first. Finally, working throughout 1936 and 1937, Zhou helped persuade Chiang to join forces with the Red Army against Japan.

Once World War II was over, the Communists drove Chiang out of China to Taiwan. Then it fell to Zhou, as soon-to-be premier, to form a government that would preside over the building of the new China. Careful to reach beyond the party, he installed a cabinet by November, 1949 in which forty-seven of the ministers and vice-ministers were non-Communists. So were half the members of official commissions. Zhou also placed high importance on bringing intellectuals to the fore, as he had once before, to oppose Chaing Kaichek. They were resented as bourgeois, but Zhou defended them as "part of the working class" by virtue of their "mental labor."

Zhou understood perfectly what eluded many of his comrades: that unless China could engage the brainpower of its scientists and experts, the dream of advanced development would be dead. Finally he convinced Mao to launch the movement called "Let a hundred flowers bloom / A hundred schools of thought contend." The tragedy was that Mao's conception differed drastically from Zhou's. Where Zhou wanted "A hundred flowers" to liberate the mind of China so its intellectuals could soar into new elevations of creativity and technology, Mao, according to Han Suyin, saw it merely as a means of remotivation and quite possibly as a way of shaking up the party which he feared was growing beyond his grasp. Its command now was vested in committees, leaving him powerless to control events and people. So began another purge of intellectuals.

Mao's destruction of his own work happened over and over, beginning with the "rectification" of 1942, when Zhou was attacked and everything he had ever said or done subjected to intense review. "Each decade," observed Henry Kissinger, "an assault was launched against the huge, bloated bureaucracies—the government, the Party, the economy, the military. For several years all universities were closed. At one point China had only a single ambassador abroad . . . . And so each decade the fading Chairman would smash what he had created, forgoing modernization, shaking up the bureaucracy, purging its leadership, resisting progress in order to maintain undefiled values that could be implemented, if at all, by a simple peasant society . . . ."[37] A society, need it be added, dominated by Mao Dzedong.

Zhou had many friends who were artists and intellectuals. Protecting them from the havoc of "Hundred Flowers" took all his gifts of duplicity and guile. No sooner had some begun to speak out than they were set upon as "rightists" and denounced by restive Communists ready always for a bloodletting. Responsibility for the devastation belonged to Zhou, who had proposed the project in the first place, hoping for new ideas, not vituperation and chaos. It cost him mightily, especially in his relationship with Mao who didn't take well to a loss of face.

Zhou clashed with Mao yet again, Han Suyin notes, when the chairman proclaimed his Great Leap Forward in 1957. The premier denounced it as "haste . . . adventurism . . . quite incompatible with the running of modern industrial plants." The plan was to decentralize the economy, and it worked well for a year, which emboldened Mao to castigate Zhou unmercifully, plunging him into a deep depression.

But the Great Leap turned decidedly sour, not least because Mao insisted that schools, hospitals, everything, become foundries for steel. People were told to bring bed springs, cooking woks and utensils as well as iron railings from city pavements and toss them into vats and makeshift brick furnaces to make steel. According to Jung Chang, "Mountains were stripped bare of trees for fuel" so firewood could be fed to the vats night and day. It was Mao's "half-baked dream of turning China into a first-class modern power . . . . This absurd situation reflected not only Mao's ignorance of how an economy worked, but also an almost metaphysical disregard for reality, which might have been interesting in a poet [as Mao sometimes was], but in a political leader with absolute power was quite another matter."[38]

Famine ensued, caused entirely by Mao's maniacal scheme, which he insisted would boost China's production so dramatically it would surpass Britain's in fifteen years. This he later, incomprehensibly, shortened to two years. But what happened was a total collapse of Chinese agriculture. As a result, an astounding 30 million people died between 1959 and 1961.[39]

Party leaders railed against Mao. However, when the chairman didn't fall but instead regained his footing, they meekly embraced the old order. Mao apologized to Zhou Enlai, who picked up the pieces of the economy, established austerity and "became the man around whom hope crystallized . . . . Once again honored, respected, listened to . . . ." Han Suyin, clearly an admirer of Zhou, calls him "a consummate artist in double-dealing." To that, along with his indispensable skill as an administrator, he probably owed his survival during the Cultural Revolution, one of the oddest occurrences in the twentieth century. It was another, and by far the most drastic, effort of Mao Dzedong to destroy the Communist Party he had created. (He figured he controlled only a third of it, therefore he would smash the whole thing and rebuild from the ground up.) More specifically, the aim of Mao's operation was to rid himself of a rival, Liu Shaoqi, China's president, and also Deng Xiaoping, who worked with Liu.[40]

In 1955 Mao had turned over routine party affairs to Liu, whose position was further strengthened after the Leap went awry and central party control returned. Zhou respected Liu's competence and discipline, but he never violated his loyalty to Mao. Instead, according to Jung Chang, he functioned "as the peacekeeper in the power struggle . . . [while he tried] to head off Mao's witch hunt."[41]

In 1966 Mao "declared that all dissident scholars and their ideas must be 'eliminated.'" He emphasized that these offending intellectuals and other "class enemies" had been protected by Communist officials following the capitalist road. Thus was born the dreaded epithet, "capitalist-roader."[42]

Students all over the country were inducted into the Red Guards and unleashed upon Beijing by the millions via free rail transportation. It fell to Zhou to see that they were housed and fed. When they rioted against teachers and other intellectuals, Zhou saved as many as he could. Some, according to Han Suyin, he sent to "the safety of Hospital No. 301, reserved for high cadres. The medical staff there fully understood the situation, and in collusion with Zhou discovered in their patients diseases which would not permit their leaving the hospital grounds." Others Zhou and his wife sheltered in their own home.

Zhou, according to Han Suyin, developed the tactic of excoriating a suspect in public in order to get himself named to the judicial panel. Then he would find "extenuating circumstances" that got the person released or at least a jail sentence instead of death. When the Red Guards demolished books, antiques and other treasures, thinking they were following the dictum to destroy the "four olds"—old ideas, behavior, customs and attitudes—Zhou closed museums to protect their contents and sent the army to guard the Forbidden City.

Hundreds called Zhou for help. He did his best for them while coping with the business of government almost single-handedly, since his departments were badly depleted, their ministers and staff having been hauled off by Red Guards to be "struggled against," contended with, attacked and possibly killed. When Deng Xiaoping was ousted, Zhou had to take over the party Secretariat as well.

Liu Shaoqi made a slow, excruciating exit. In 1967 he was called for a cozy chat with Mao Dzedong, who apparently liked to end things this way.[43] Liu offered to resign and take his family back to the countryside where they would farm. Mao urged him instead to do some reading, perhaps a little Hegel or Diderot, and to take care of his health. But this would not be possible since within two days Mao unleashed savages to storm Liu's house and office, attacking the president and his wife, a great beauty, and cutting all their telephone lines.

Then followed more torture and beatings which went on for months. Liu's sleeping pills were confiscated. So was his medication for diabetes. He grew desperately ill, and finally, after being expelled from the party, he was wrapped in an old cotton blanket and flown to Henan province, where his doctors left him alone to die, lying on a cement floor in the basement of an old prison.[44]

Zhou Enlai was no friend of Liu Shaoqi. Back in the early 1940s, when Mao was determined to establish indigenous Chinese Communism, free from Soviet direction, his chief supporter, Liu, had harshly assailed Zhou, not yet ready to renounce Russia. Years later, as president, Liu had tried to bypass the premier in the handling of foreign affairs. Yet Zhou defended Liu in speeches during the first convulsion of the Cultural Revolution, and he stayed in touch with Liu and his wife when their torment began, sending two special nurses to care for the broken president near the end.

Still, Zhou acquiesced in Mao's cruelty even while he tried to alleviate it. "Why did he not stand up to Mao?" some ask. "The party would have followed Zhou." "No, the party would not have followed Zhou," Han Suyin retorted. "Zhou was an intellectual, immensely liked, popular, but he was not a peasant, not a worker. Mao's charisma was enormous with the rank and file, who came from the peasantry. Liu Shaoqi and Deng Xiaoping might have controlled a strong bureaucratic machine . . . . But they could not win against Mao. Zhou had no chance to win, except by doing what he did, biding his time, and getting rid of the demons, one by one . . . ."

"Zhou's score was not bad, but he was not a white knight," wrote Harrison Salisbury. "He was one of the most skilled courtiers the world has seen, always carefully husbanding himself against the day when China entered total chaos and only he, perhaps, could save it."[45]

The moment for which Zhou had saved himself arrived, finally, in 1971, when Henry Kissinger landed in Beijing, having flown in total secrecy from Pakistan, armed with instructions from President Richard Nixon to achieve an opening to China. For Zhou it was the fulfillment of a dream. In the heady days of the revolution he had hoped that after World War II was over the United States would help his country industrialize. But there was no response from Washington. So he and Mao had turned to the Soviets. Now relations with the USSR had soured, with high-level talks ending in 1965, not to be resumed for twenty-four years when Gorbachev would come to Beijing during the debacle at Tiananmen Square.

So Nixon's signal was auspicious in its timing. And for Zhou personally, Kissinger was a Godsend. Kissinger offered a wealth of good talk flowing from a mind both elegant and sophisticated, something Zhou had yearned for during long years of isolation, when he geared down to half a cylinder, his intelligence in heavy camouflage. It was an urgent necessity in an atmosphere dominated by the maniacs of the Cultural Revolution.

According to Han Suyin, "[t]he two implicitly recognized that they would be natural partners in a strategy which, for the Pacific region, would define the twenty-first century." Theirs was a high moment in the history of diplomacy. They were shaping an epoch with no military action, no territory gained, lost or transferred, just a broad opening of what had been closed, a dramatic change of heart.

Nixon went to China on February 21, 1972. It was the ultimate moment of Zhou Enlai's career.

That summer Zhou found he had cancer. He lived until early 1976, hounded in his last days by Jiang Qing, Mao's power-crazed, estranged wife, and her Gang of Four. At the end, Mao himself never visited Zhou nor made any contact with him. Nor did he attend the premier's funeral. He too died, later that year.

Kissinger was convinced that only illness and death saved Zhou from annihilation by the Gang of Four, "tolerated if not backed by Mao." During the last year of Zhou's life, said Kissinger, "he was rarely mentioned in the Chinese press or by other Chinese leaders to me."[46]

Zhou and Mao, in their time together, built a new China, but at an appalling cost. As many as 830,000 "enemies of the people" were killed from 1934 to 1954 by Zhou's reckoning. Mao put the figure at between two million and three million. Harrison Salisbury said this is probably an underestimate.[47] And of course there were the 30 million peasants who died of starvation during the Great Leap Forward. So Zhou was contaminated by an ugly era. But within the confines of a barbaric regime he tried for a moral life, though those are not words he ever would have used. He went along with much that was unforgivable, but when he could, he saved lives.

Zhou understood better than anyone, Han Suyin asserts, that China had "to accomplish two revolutions at once: first the industrial revolution, which had taken place in Europe three centuries ago; then the technological revolution, which had started at the end of World War II." To that he added a third revolution: opening China to the West. Then, far-sighted still, even while dying, he brought Deng Xiaoping back to Beijing from the exile into which he had been driven by the Cultural Revolution. Zhou brought Deng Xiaoping back to Beijing to create a Chinese economy that would challenge the world.

Ronald Reagan went to Washington in 1981 to confront the Communists. It was not the Communists of China he had in mind. It was those of the "evil empire," the Soviet Union. Four years later he would have an extraordinary adversary on the other side of the table—Mikhail Gorbachev. As it turned out, the American president would hold more cards than he knew. The Soviet economy was *in extremis*, but it took a leader with the courage of Gorbachev to admit it and to call off the arms race and bring an end to the Cold War. That his reforms stirred up a whirlwind even he could not survive does not for an instant diminish his importance to history.

Gorbachev may have been outpaced by his own program. Certainly he did lag behind after the coup of August, 1991, clinging to the Communist Party when it was clearly a corpse. His long loyalty to Communism is curious given that both his grandfathers were persecuted by the regime—one exiled for two years, the other tortured—and his wife's grandfather was executed.[48] One can only assume that as an activist he remained engaged in the only reality he knew, and, when given a chance, he worked to transform it from within. He was the Erasmus, not the Martin Luther, of his day. He sought a gradual turning to market socialism and social democracy, not the dismemberment of the system itself.[49] But it was Gorbachev, nonetheless, who set in motion the forces that brought about the final dissolution. Boris Yeltsin may have been the winner of the new day in Russia, but without Gorbachev that dawn never would have occurred.

For years, perhaps with an inkling of destiny, Gorbachev, son of a tractor driver, prepared himself for his high moment. As a young man he embraced the literature of the West, steeping himself in Rousseau, Thomas Aquinas, Hobbes, Machiavelli, and Mill. A dreamer of achievable dreams, he was fond of quoting Hegel's maxim, "Truth is always concrete."[50] This did not, however, turn out to be the case for Gorbachev. Truth, he would learn later, has a metaphysics that cannot always be divined in the concrete and the observable.

Eager to grasp the modern world beyond Moscow, Gorbachev developed a taste for the plays of Arthur Miller. He read English novels, including *Corridors of Power* by C.P. Snow. It was a telling choice. Snow's main character was a politician who was destroyed because he would not mount a tactical retreat from a passionately held position. (Later, beset by fate, Gorbachev would make tactical retreats one after another, not realizing it was too late to tame the centrifugal forces set in motion by his own inspiration.)

Anatoly Dobrynin, longtime Soviet ambassador to the United States, condemned Gorbachev as a man in too much of a hurry. His "fundamental failing was that he did not really understand economic problems and the policies to deal with them."[51] Certainly that was the case.

But there were other things that Gorbachev did not understand, things of the spirit that might have made him a leader of greater resonance. Though secretly baptized as a child, he was not religious. While he did restore freedom of worship in 1988, the millennium of Christianity in Russia, this was not enough to connect him to the soul of the nation.

Biographers Dusko Doder and Louise Branson have pointed out that in trying to modernize the Soviet economy and build a managerial class, Gorbachev collided with "the very Slavophile core of the country, the eternal mother Russia, whose history and traditions had left her burdened with a collective incapacity to respond to changes without a theoretical (or religious) basis . . ."

"Unlike the commercial West," they wrote, "Russia is a country that fervently needs an ideology, a set of beliefs, a religion—and Gorbachev was offering his people a set of laws, accounting procedures and efficiency standards . . ." The necessary truth was not entirely, or even primarily, concrete.

"There is no such thing as a happy reformer." Gorbachev quoted this saying to an interviewer long after leaving office. "Remember the French revolution," he also said. "Robespierre, two days before his execution, marched before the crowd as an idol, and then his head was cut off. So this is the fate of the politician who assumes the burden of reforms . . . ."[52]

Reduced to making commercials for Apple Computer and Pizza Hut, Gorbachev's sense of persecution grew even stronger as he tried for a comeback in the 1996 elections. (He won less than one percent of the vote.) By then it wasn't Robespierre he saw in himself, it was the Lord of Christendom. "I will fight to the bitter end even if you crucify me," he cried to hecklers during the campaign. "I am reminded of Jesus Christ on the way to Golgotha. How he walked through the streets and people spat at him."[53]

Gorbachev, Doder and Branson relate, said he wanted "to be remembered as a man of vision, not illusion, a man capable of transforming Soviet society." He told some Indian journalists that nuclear disarmament was "the only possible way that mankind can regain immortality." Certainly Gorbachev attained a kind of immortality by calling a halt to the nuclear arms race and, however reluctantly, freeing the Soviet republics and Eastern Europe, thus undoing the ugly aftermath of Yalta. And it cannot be forgotten that it was Gorbachev who agreed to the reunification of Germany under the aegis of NATO. Much credit must go to German Chancellor Helmut Kohl for this great historical moment, but without Gorbachev it never would have happened.

In the end, however, the times turned cruelly against him and there were colleagues who resolved to remember him only as the one who destroyed the Soviet empire.[54] Doder and Branson explained it like this: Gorbachev forced his people "to make a choice of civilizations, a choice between Europe and Asia, between West and East, between Westernizers and latter-day Slavophiles."[55] Russians are still struggling with this dilemma, but not Gorbachev. He did indeed make a choice. Even as he fought to hold the middle ground, Gorbachev, in spite of his own conservatism, chose in favor of a new nation, freed from the agony of the past. And for all his machinations he made that choice stick.

Gorbachev's genius was in his daring. Risking everything, he set in motion the great intellectual reversal of the twentieth century, the fall of Marxism.[56]

The Soviet capitulation helped confirm this as the American century, as Henry Luce once proclaimed. Even so, Britain, star of the 1800s, supplanted by the U.S., went down with great gallantry only to rise again, inexplicably, on the strength of a single leader.

The British giant of the twentieth century, of course, was Winston Churchill. He towered over his times. Protesting the last gasp of empire with an eloquence surpassed only by Shakespeare, he kept the torch of British genius burning.

"In the summer of 1940 Churchill's vision and the ghost of Britain's faded grandeur met for one last moment of glory," wrote biographer John Charmley; "after that the twilight fell."

Charmley, a determined revisionist, embraced the odd idea that Churchill himself ushered in the twilight. Incomprehensibly, he argued that it was Neville Chamberlain who "offered the only way of preserving what was left of British power." The victory of 1945 was not for Britain, Charmley insisted; "it was, as Chamberlain had foreseen, for the Soviets and the Americans."

But there are those who believe that Hitler's government would never have survived, much less waged war, if Chamberlain had not given him a decisive boost at Munich.[57] Moreover, appeasement had no chance of preserving what remained of British power. Nothing would remain of it, no matter what happened. After all, in 1940, when Churchill went to Buckingham Palace to receive the King's charge to form a government, the U. K. was broke.[58]

The trouble could be traced to the last years of the nineteenth century when British education began to be eroded along with industrial supremacy. Instead of reinvesting their profits, successful entrepreneurs began buying country houses, and British steel allowed itself to be overtaken by competitors in Germany and the United States. In addition, London's far-flung colonies became more of a drain than an advantage. In her memoirs Margaret Thatcher acknowledged "the deceptive might of an empire which continued to expand until 1919 but which cost more to defend than it contributed to national wealth."[59]

This was not an insight visited upon Churchill. Defying the inevitable decline of colonialism and refusing to recognize the price of empire, he railed against freedom for India, declaring to the House of Commons in 1931, the high moment of Gandhi, that "the loss of India would be final and fatal to us. It could not fail to be part of a process that would reduce us to the scale of a minor power."[60]

Certainly Churchill understood the diminution that lay ahead. What he could not see was there was nothing he or anybody else could do to hold off the wave of nationalism that would sweep the globe during the twentieth century. But accepting the verdict of history in matters colonial was not the same thing as acquiescing to Hitler's domination of Europe. There Churchill was everlastingly right. After all, were not the British in real danger of German conquest? After Chamberlain's capitulation, of course they were.

Churchill is a hero of the twentieth century, but his roots are deep in the Victorian era, nurtured by the Parliamentary politics of his father. Hampered by a learning disability and thus denied a classical education at Oxford or Cambridge, Churchill went to Sandhurst for military training. But he didn't give up on books. Later, while posted in Cuba, India and elsewhere, he pursued history, political economy and philosophy on his own, reading Schopenhauer, Kant, Hegel, Gibbon, Macaulay and Darwin. He also memorized all his father's speeches and practiced them constantly to master oratory.

Darwin's theory of evolution was especially important to Churchill and he drew from it evidence of "motive force" in the universe. This he applied to his own romantic view of statecraft. "We cannot say that a good man will always overcome a knave," said Churchill, "but the evolutionist will not hesitate to affirm that the nation with the highest ideals will succeed."[61]

Charmley called Churchill a "Whig-imperialist," and probably this was true. Certainly his aristocratic nature, unaccommodated to the modern world, showed itself in his chapters on the American Civil War in *History of the English-Speaking Peoples*. He closed the account grandly, pronouncing that war "the noblest and least avoidable of all the great mass-conflicts of which till then there was record."[62]

Churchill showed considerable understanding of the United States in his study of the Civil War. When aroused, he said, the Americans will fight. It was an insight that eluded Hitler.

Churchill once wrote that "a man's life must be nailed to a cross either of Thought or Action." Like both Roosevelts, Churchill chose action, even though one colleague credited him with the "brain of a genius."[63] Some did not agree. "He can only think in phrases," said one detractor, "and close argument is lost on him."

But his phrases had within them the seeds of greatness. Churchill's writing won the Nobel Prize for Literature in 1953. Long before that Arthur Balfour had praised his prodigious output: "Five volumes of immortal history is a wonderful addition to this great period of administrative activity," he said. In fact, there were years when Churchill paid his bills through journalism and other literary work, producing pieces for the

Daily Mail in London, *Colliers Magazine* in the U.S. and even a screen treatment for a film on George V, not to mention his monumental *History of the English-Speaking Peoples*, followed in time by his work on the Second World War.

The truth is the genius of Churchill lay in his words. Those words were drawn from another era, said Isaiah Berlin, and carefully crafted to "convey his particular vision." Elaborating on "the formal mode" of Gibbon, Dr. Johnson and Macaulay, "always public, Ciceronian, addressed to the world, remote from the hesitancies and stresses of introspection and private life," he fashioned a style that was "too bright, too big, too vivid, too unstable" for the 1920s, but that carried the whole of the British people through the desperate days that followed.[64]

"There are those," wrote Berlin, "who, inhibited by the furniture of the ordinary world, come to life only when they feel themselves actors upon a stage . . . . There are those who can function freely only in uniform or armour or court dress . . . act fearlessly only in situations which in some way are formalised for them . . . . So it happens . . . that people of a shrinking disposition perform miracles of courage when life has been dramatised for them, when they are on the battlefield . . . ."[65] This Churchill did for the British. He dramatized the war for them. He set a scene in which they found their own courage.

". . . [T]he single, central, organizing principle of his moral and intellectual universe," Berlin continued, "[was] a historical imagination so strong, so comprehensive, as to encase the whole of the present and the whole of the future in a framework of a rich and multicoloured past." And while he spoke as a public man, what he said was based always on pervasive private thought. Where Franklin Roosevelt fled from introspection, Churchill, said Berlin, built "his own massive, simple, impregnably fortified inner world . . . . His nature [possessed] a dimension of depth—and a corresponding sense of tragic possibilities—which Roosevelt's light-hearted genius instinctively passed by . . . . [W]hereas Roosevelt, like all great innovators, had a half-conscious premonitory awareness of the coming shape of society, not wholly unlike that of an artist, Churchill, for all his extrovert air, [looked] within, and his strongest sense [was] the sense of the past."[66]

It was from his soul that Churchill fortified the British people. "The spirit which they found within them," said Berlin, "he had created within himself from his inner resources, and poured it into his nation . . . . He created a heroic mood and turned the fortunes of the Battle of Britain not by catching the mood of his surroundings . . . but by being stubbornly impervious to it . . . . [His genius sprang] from a capacity for sustained introspective brooding, great depth and constancy of feeling . . . ." But, Berlin pointed out, Churchill's "Periclean reign" in a state of extreme emergency never subverted the democratic institutions of Britain: ". . . [I]t was Churchill's unique and unforgettable achievement that he created this necessary illusion within the framework of a free system without destroying or even twisting it; that he called forth spirits that did not stay to oppress and enslave the population after the hour of need had passed."[67]

Churchill was not always far-sighted. At the admiralty during World War I he championed an operation in the Dardanelles that turned out disastrously. And during the 1920s, when he was Chancellor of the Exchequer, he underestimated the Japanese threat, announcing he did "not believe there is the slightest chance" of war against Japan "in our lifetime." (Charmley attributes this misperception to Churchill's habitual absorption in his assignment of the moment. At the Treasury he was obsessed with saving money, not spending it on the military.) However, from the beginning, long before his Iron Curtain speech, Churchill understood the threat of Communist Russia. In 1917 he urged Lloyd George to take some stand against it. But the Prime Minister refused. By 1943, Churchill saw clearly what the Soviet threat would mean to the West: "Stalin is an unnatural man," he said. "There will be grave troubles."

Even so, Stalin was a necessary ally during World War II, and Churchill did not shrink from turning over parts of Poland to him. "The Poles," he exclaimed, "must be very silly if they imagine we are going to begin a new war with Russia for the sake of the Polish eastern border." Though Britain initially declared war on Germany because of the invasion of Poland, it was not possible in the end to defend those frontiers from Soviet armies. Foresight Churchill certainly had in this case, but endless military reserves he did not. And Roosevelt was equally determined to have an end to the fighting in Europe as soon as German forces were defeated.

Certainly Churchill grasped the implications of Hitler when many of his compatriots in the Conservative government did not. Held at arm's length, out of the cabinet during the accumulating crises of the 1930s,[68] he rallied Franklin Roosevelt to the defense of Britain at the crucial moment and he kept his country alive through the strength of his oratory. In that effort and the imperturbable will behind it lies his vast importance. That he was up against staggering odds which could not in the aftermath of war be overcome makes his achievement as poignant as it is compelling.

Churchill fought the war with a problematic heart that worried his doctor and with a steady consumption of alcohol, Charmley relates, that would have stupefied most people: "beer, three ports, and three brandies" at lunch and "two or three glasses of 'iced whiskey and soda' before dinner, at which he 'always had champagne, followed by several doses of brandy . . . .'" There would be more whiskey and sodas "as the night wore on."

Churchill's strength was not in his strategy, though betting everything on Franklin Roosevelt was instinctively wise. Nor was it in his political acumen. (The Tory Party was often on the verge of mutiny and would have dismissed Churchill if there had been any alternative.) The prime minister's great gift aside from language was in the boldness of his will. Even as some members of Parliament were pressing for a peace agreement with Germany, he was declaring that his country would never, never surrender.

Charmley wrote that "Churchill's leadership was inspiring, but at the end it was barren, it led nowhere, and there were no heirs to his tradition." Charmley was wrong.

Churchill implanted the possibility of resilience, giving birth to a hope that quietly endured through the dry, dismal years of shrinkage. Churchill kept alive the idea of Britain.

When Churchill died, he was called the last great Englishman. But that didn't turn out to be true. Another leader of remarkable force, heir after all to the Churchill tradition, arose in the 1980s to restore British prestige and prosperity. She could not return power to the island-nation, long past its prime, but she did leverage her own strength and a special relationship with America's Ronald Reagan into a position of singular influence and respect.

Margaret Thatcher, the longest-serving British prime minister of the twentieth century, put her mark not only on her country but on the world. She fought a brief war in the Falklands and prevailed, but it was economic not military leadership that made her memorable. Her highest achievement was the market economy that transformed Britain and swept the globe. Indeed that movement will forever be known by her name, Thatcherism, not Reaganomics as it was called in the U.S.

"In my case you just had to have a star to steer by," Thatcher said in a television interview three months after she resigned as prime minister, "and mine was to stop Britain being satisfied with decline and to bring it out into a new confidence, a new enterprise, a new success, and we did just that."[69] Indeed she did.

Her successes are beyond dispute, even though they were bought at the price of great upheaval and later were diluted by recession. Here is her miracle, itemized in the bloodless language of business:

• Rover: cut loose from government subsidies, streamlined, partnered with Honda, profitable in 1993 in spite of a sales slump, acquired in 1994 by BMW.

• British Airways: a money maker in the face of falling profits for most of its competitors, "one of the world's few truly global carriers through investments in airlines like USAir and Qantas."

• British Telecommunications: "long a stodgy, high-cost phone company" that slashed prices and improved its poor service, then took a "20 percent stake in MCI of the United States, a move that should allow it to expand worldwide."

• BAA: "the company that owns and operates Heathrow, Gatwick and other international airports in Britain . . . more than doubled its profits since 1987 . . . expanding its management services into the United States and Asia."

• NFC: formerly National Freight Consortium, privatized through an employee-led buyout in 1982, stock price has soared, bought Allied Van Lines in the U.S.

• Cable and Wireless: "slashed the work force at its headquarters, pushed authority and responsibility out to its operating units around the world," profits up from about $100 million a year to an estimated $1.5 billion in 1993.

It wasn't just privatization that generated these successes. It was "a wide range of government policies that had the intention of deregulating industry, creating more competition and removing barriers to foreign trade and investments."[70] It all sounds automatic in this press account. But those were treacherous days, bitter and always on the brink of catastrophe. That she waged her revolution, day after day, crisis after crisis, working often in a storm of controversy, is evidence of her formidable power as a person.

Thatcherism, it has been pointed out, was not presented to the nation whole. It grew in response to immediate problems. It was "never a coherent set of economic and political ideas (though it often had pretensions to be)," the *Economist* insisted. "Rather, it was a list of instinctively selected friends and enemies. At a rough approximation, the friends were the property-owning (and would-be property-owning) middle, lower-middle and aspiring working classes. The enemies were trade unions, public-sector workers, the intelligentsia and (as she saw them) spongers of every kind who were content to live off the state."[71]

The *Economist*, however, was too close to Thatcher to see her true qualities. There is no question that she cared far more than most politicians about developing a coherent economic plan with firm philosophical underpinnings. When she took over at the Conservative helm in 1975 she arrived with anti-Keynesian convictions firmly in place.[72] That's because she had joined in starting a think tank before ever becoming party leader, and those colleagues had helped her shape a working ideology for her party and later her government. It amounted to far more than just a list of friends and enemies. Thatcher in fact—along with Reagan—made ideology respectable again. Together they battled the weary pragmatism that had overtaken politics on both sides of the Atlantic.

Some charge that Britain's resurgence under Thatcher was short lived, and certainly the U.K. did plummet into recession in the late 1980s. But that was a world-wide phenomenon, spreading finally as far as Japan. Not even the Iron Lady could have shielded her country from such an epidemic. But the British economy rebounded, and by the time Labor swept out the Tories in 1997, many of Thatcher's issues had been settled in her favor: Britain has had none of the paralyzing strikes that before her time brought the nation to a halt. Her battle with the coal miners changed all that and changed it for good.

Also, Thatcher has been vindicated somewhat in her dogged opposition to the European Union. The British got safely out of the exchange rate mechanism and gained unified trade on their own terms. Closer ties no doubt will come, but Thatcher held them off as long as possible so the British economy could compose itself.

In foreign affairs, Thatcher did much to make Gorbachev respectable in the West when she pronounced him someone with whom she could do business. It was in fact Thatcher who discovered Gorbachev when, casting about for the next generation of Soviet leaders, she invited him to London in 1984, shortly before he ascended to the leadership of the former U.S.S.R. "I spotted him because I was searching for someone like him," she wrote in her memoirs. "His line was no different from what I would have expected," she said. But "his style was." "He smiled, laughed, used his hands for emphasis, modulated his voice, followed an argument through and was a sharp debater," she recounted. "He was self-confident and . . . he did not seem in the least uneasy about entering into controversial areas of high politics."[73] Gorbachev was just the sort of adversary Thatcher could respect and enjoy.

The Prime Minister made the most of her association with Gorbachev and also of her truly special relationship with Reagan. She would fly to Washington to set the president straight, usually on defense matters. "During the Reagan administration," noted Kissinger, "she achieved an influence over American decisions, especially with respect to NATO and arms control policy, not seen since Churchill's day."[74]

But it was in economic policy that Thatcher made her reputation. So pervasive did Thatcherism become that even left-of-center parties started moving to the middle during the 1980s. This could be seen in France, Spain, Portugal, Greece, Norway, Sweden, Australia and New Zealand.[75] Mexico embraced the market. And even Britain's Labor Party got so tired of losing to Thatcher it disavowed nationalization in favor of a mixed economy. When Labor's Tony Blair became Prime Minister in 1997, he took office in full obeisance to the Thatcher revolution. While a majority of European governments had leftist regimes by century's end, few were ready to abandon the market, though some fretted about its punishing discipline, a discipline Thatcher understood better than most.

Through the strength of her own mind and spirit, buttressed by a coherence of upbringing, education, thought, and policy not seen since Churchill, Margaret Thatcher put herself at the center of action. When it looked as if the century was running out of steam, Thatcher proved once again the power and importance of a single, inspired leader.

From the earliest days of her prominence, Thatcher wore a bracelet from South Africa brought to her by her husband, Denis. She had strong feelings about South Africa and blunt advice for Nelson Mandela when he came to call at Number Ten Downing Street in July, 1990, after his release from twenty-seven years in prison: "Mr. Mandela," she said, "before we discuss any issues, I must warn you that your schedule is too heavy. You must cut it in half. Even a man half your age would have trouble meeting the demands that are being made on you. If you keep this up, you will not come out of America alive. That is my advice to you."

Mandela did not take her advice, and when he landed on her doorstep again, after the American tour, he had pneumonia. She chided him "like a schoolmarm . . . ." And though Mandela called her "always a forthright and solicitous lady," he could not budge her from her view that all sanctions against Pretoria should be lifted at once. He wanted to wait, and keep as much pressure on F.W. de Klerk's regime as possible.

As for Thatcher, she found Mandela that day to be a man with "nobility of bearing" but "outdated in his attitudes, stuck in a kind of socialist timewarp in which nothing had moved on, not least in economic thinking, since the 1940s." Nonetheless, she felt South Africa was lucky to have someone "of Mr. Mandela's stature."[76] (Thatcher had not always been so generous. In earlier years she had called Mandela a "terrorist" and declared the possibility that he might one day govern South Africa to be a notion out of "cloud-cuckoo land."[77]) Whatever her early misjudgments, in her assessment of Mandela's stature she was surely right. For it was not his approach to policy that made Nelson Mandela a man of the century, it was his spirit.

Mandela walked a long, treacherous road from the moment of his birth in 1918, the son of a royal Thembu who had four wives. Like his father, Mandela was groomed not to rule, but to counsel the kings of his people. Perhaps that training—to observe, listen and assess as well as to speak; to be wise, not willful—prepared Mandela for his unique role as the guardian of the African National Congress and later of South Africa itself. No ruler by right of inheritance would have cultivated the intuition, the patience necessary for such a role.

Mandela's father died when he was nine, so the boy went to live with the Thembu regent in his elaborate house. Mandela learned much from this patriarch who would have long, all-day meetings with the chiefs. Each would speak, sometimes in vehement criticism of the regent, who always sat in utmost quiet and attentiveness. At sundown, he would sum up all that had been said. If there was no consensus, they would agree to leave things suspended until a more propitious time.

The ability to listen closely, to absorb criticism and to tolerate the tension of unresolved issues must have been imbibed by Mandela, because they are just the qualities that saw him through the dark years on Robben Island and two other prisons after that, where he kept his fellow inmates from the ANC alive and functioning as active, political beings.

Mandela described himself as introverted in those early days, and serious. "I did well in school not so much through cleverness," he wrote, "as through doggedness . . . . I had to drill myself." Mandela, in fact, failed his L.L.B. exam in law several times and pursued it later, while in prison, through a correspondence course at the University of London. There, behind bars, his love of solitude paid off. He had realized its benefits for him years before, living underground in Johannesburg: "Although I am a gregarious person," he said, "I love solitude even more. I welcomed the opportunity to be by myself, to plan, to think, to plot."

The law was a vehicle for Mandela, an outlet for his moral energies, and he used it to great advantage. With a colleague he started the only African firm in Johannesburg, then devoted the bulk of his time to defending blacks caught in the web of apartheid. ". . . [I]t was a crime to walk through a Whites Only door, a crime to ride a Whites Only bus, a crime to use a Whites Only drinking fountain, a crime to walk on a Whites Only beach, a crime to be on the streets past eleven, a crime not to have a pass book, and a crime to have the wrong signature in that book, a crime to be unemployed and a crime to be employed in the wrong place, a crime to live in certain places and a crime to have no place to live." Thus did Mandela describe the system he gave his life to abolish.

Apartheid. It began after World War II when the Afrikaners took what had been *de facto* and made it *de jure*. Apartheid had two corner-stones: the Population and Registration Act and the Group Areas Act.

The first, as Mandela put it, "authorized the government officially to classify all South Africans according to race . . . . The arbitrary and meaningless tests to decide black from Coloured and Coloured from white often resulted in tragic cases where members of the same family were classified differently all depending on whether one child had a lighter or darker complexion." On such distinctions rode where one could work and live. The other measure provided that "each racial group could own land, occupy premises, and trade only in its own separate area . . . . If whites wanted the land or houses of other groups, they could simply declare the land a white area and take them."

Along with the Suppression of Communism Act, always handy when an indictment was wanted, these two laws created a vise that contained and controlled an entire nation save for a tiny minority of uneasy but prosperous settlers, descended from the British and the Dutch. They were determined to assure their fortune through a twentieth century form of barbarism. A black leader in Natal was asked what would have happened to South Africa if the Europeans never had come. "Well," he answered, thinking carefully, "then it never would have developed." It was a strikingly candid answer, filled, no doubt, with irony as well as pain.

The Europeans did come, of course, and they did develop the nation. But at an appalling price. No sooner had Parliament passed these onerous acts in 1950 than a year later Nelson Mandela, native of the Transkei countryside, by now established in his own world in Johannesburg, became president of the Youth League of the African National Congress. And so was born a career that would bring down the ugly Afrikaner dispensation and at the same time accomplish the apotheosis of a young freedom fighter who surely was not always as sweet of spirit as he became in a prison cell. But those 330 or so months in a contained setting gave him time to think, and to simplify himself.

Mandela was no Gandhi, though at one time he had pictures of Gandhi on his wall along with some of Roosevelt, Churchill, Stalin and the storming of the winter palace in St. Petersburg in 1917. In the early years Mandela saw nonviolence not as an "inviolable principle" but as a "practical necessity," to be deployed only as long as it was effective. This did nothing to ally him with Manilal Gandhi, the Mahatma's son who was also an editor and member of the South African Indian Congress. The young Gandhi believed strongly in his father's precepts. The young Mandela, however, did not.

The young Mandela, in fact, was put in charge of building an army for the ANC. It was called Umkhonto we Sizwe—the Spear of the Nation. He set about this job armed with books, reading works by and about Che Guevara, Fidel Castro, Mao Dzedong and Menachem Begin. He examined Clausewitz and he studied the Communist Party of Cuba during its illegal years under the Battista regime as well as the guerrilla tactics of the Boers in South Africa during their war with the British. He sought out information about the struggle of the Ethiopians against Mussolini and the guerrilla armies of Kenya, Algeria and the Camaroons.

His idea was to fight apartheid in ways that were "least violent to individuals but most violent to the state." This approach was arrived at only after a milder program of defiance had failed. According to that plan, the first stage involved "a small number of well trained volunteers [who] would break selected laws in a handful of urban areas. They would enter proscribed areas without permits, use Whites Only facilities such as toilets, Whites Only railway compartments, waiting rooms and post office entrances. They would deliberately remain in town after curfew. Each batch of defiers would have a leader who would inform the police in advance of the act of disobedience so that arrests could take place with a minimum of disturbance. The second stage was envisioned as mass defiance, accompanied by strikes and industrial actions across the country."

By then Mandela had acquired the "reputation of being a firebrand." His life was full and hectic as he moved from nighttime meetings to days in his law office to the prisoner's dock in court where increasingly he appeared, on trial under the Suppression of Communism Act or some other legal restriction. Mandela has sworn he was never a Communist but certainly he believed the ANC should cooperate with "anyone who was against racial oppression."

Even so, he hesitated at first to work with whites or Indians. And his spiritual composure took years to germinate. Oliver Tambo, an ANC leader, remembered Mandela as "passionate, emotional, sensitive, quickly stung to bitterness and retaliation." Walter Sisulu, another associate in the party, said Mandela "can become very stubborn, very arrogant. His anger becomes extreme." Yet this is the man who was so generous to whites at his first news conference after leaving prison that three hundred journalists "broke all rules of professional distance and burst into applause."[78]

Nonviolence never worked in South Africa as it did in India, wrote Mandela, because "Gandhi had been dealing with a foreign power that ultimately was more realistic and farsighted. That was not the case with the Afrikaners . . . . Nonviolent passive resistance is effective as long as your opposition adheres to the same rules as you do. But if peaceful protest is met with violence, its efficacy is at an end."

Time ran out on Mandela. After a deferred sentence in the Communism trial and an acquittal in the treason trial that followed, he went underground, trying to ward off the incarceration that he knew could not be avoided forever. Striving to be inconspicuous, Mandela dressed in overalls and a chauffeur's cap, surely not easy for a tall, attractive man who admired British style and manners and one day, many years later, showed up at a lunch in Johannesburg with American journalists wearing a Harvard sweatshirt. Predictably, Mandela could not achieve obscurity. He continued to fascinate, and became known during this incognito period as the "Black Pimpernel."

Holed up in a farmhouse in Rivonia, a suburb near Johannesburg, Mandela, along with his cohorts, continued to shape the armed struggle. Sometimes using the name David Motsamayi, he traveled to London and throughout Africa drumming up support for the ANC. But he was too vital, too active to last for long underground. After a raid on the farmhouse, where police confiscated plans for sabotage and guerrilla war, Mandela and the others were tried and sentenced to life in prison.

Then began the years at Robben Island. Allowed only one visitor and one letter (heavily censored) every six months, forbidden to attend his mother's funeral or the service for his son who was killed in an automobile accident, Mandela coped with a situation that actually suited his temperament. With confinement came peace and with hardship the strength of Stoics.

Mandela and his fellow inmates organized a university, each teaching courses, using the Socratic method. Mandela also spent volumes of time preparing judicial appeals for other prisoners. In addition, he registered constant reminders with prison officials that he and his colleagues were political prisoners, not criminals, and they were owed under the law certain respect. They demanded long pants, not short, and they refused to appear in photographs, because it was demeaning to be pictured as a prisoner. And through various ruses Mandela stayed in touch with the movement on the outside.

Years went by. Then more years. No mention of Nelson Mandela was permitted in the South African media. But the Black Pimpernel could not be forgotten. Just as pressure was easing in prison—Mandela, close to sixty, finally was allowed to garden and to play tennis—pressure was building in the country for his release.

It took a long, long time. And the way was never smooth. Mandela's study privileges were suspended when he was found to have been writing a memoir and to have buried the original draft in the courtyard. This turned him to reading novels—Nadine Gordimer (the ones not banned), Tolstoy's *War and Peace* (most books with "war" in the title were forbidden) and *The Grapes of Wrath* by John Steinbeck. Literature must have been a refining influence after the rigors of preparation for armed struggle.

The opening to freedom began with a call from a cabinet member who offered to let Mandela out of prison if he would move to Transkei, now a "quasi-independent homeland." Mandela said no. He intended to live in Johannesburg, not a make-believe jurisdiction, and besides, he said, "It was an offer only a turncoat would accept." At least six other feelers followed, but none would work. In one instance, Mandela and the ANC were unwilling to renounce terror without receiving in return full political rights.

In 1985, after prostate surgery, Mandela was put in isolation quarters, apart from the comrades with whom he had been moved to Pollsmoor Prison near Cape Town a few years before. His three rooms, designated for sleeping, studying and exercise, were more than adequate, and he had his own bathroom. But, in addition, he had something even more valuable—solitude. Mandela put it to use by starting a serious communication with the government. This he did without prior approval from the ANC, unusual for him, but he realized it would give the organization a way out if things went badly.

The communication commenced, but two more years went by before the government offered Mandela a formal meeting. He accepted. Dressed in a suit provided him for the occasion, he gathered secretly with various officials in May, 1988, at an officers' club at Pollsmoor. These sessions had to be suspended briefly in December when Mandela came down with the early stages of tuberculosis, caused probably by his damp cell. Upon leaving the recovery clinic (a luxurious facility that had never had a black patient before), he was taken, not back to Pollsmoor, but to a cottage on the grounds of a prison in the wine-growing country, also near Cape Town.

The authorities felt that Mandela should have a proper place in which to hold private discussions. And proper it was. He had a swimming pool and his own chef who prepared three meals a day and cooked for guests. In this auspicious setting, Mandela heard the news that P.W. Botha had resigned as president of South Africa in August, 1989. His replacement was a man whose name will always be linked with Nelson Mandela's— F.W. de Klerk.

The two of them met for the first time in de Klerk's office in Cape Town. Mandela immediately pronounced the new president "a man we can do business with," echoing Margaret Thatcher's assessment of Gorbachev. Ironically, Thatcher herself would note the deep similarity between the fate of the South African and the Soviet leader when she had de Klerk and his wife for lunch at her country house.[79]

On February 2, 1990, in his first opening speech to Parliament, de Klerk startled the world by freeing Mandela and other political prisoners, lifting the ban on the ANC and declaring that "the time for negotiation has arrived." After ten thousand days in prison, Mandela was released as a hero at the age of seventy-one. It was a triumph of discipline and realism.[80]

The negotiations that followed were arduous and threatened always by violence. Mandela soon discovered that de Klerk did indeed resemble Gorbachev in that he wanted to reform the system not dismantle it altogether. "Despite his seemingly progressive action," wrote Mandela, "Mr. de Klerk was by no means the great emancipator. He was a gradualist, a careful pragmatist. He did not make any of his reforms with the intention of putting himself out of power. He made them for precisely the opposite reason: to ensure power for the Afrikaner in a new dispensation. He was not yet prepared to negotiate the end of white rule."

De Klerk's goal, said Mandela, "was to create a system of power-sharing based on group rights, which would preserve a modified form of minority power in South Africa. He was decidedly opposed to majority rule, or 'simple majoritarianism' as he sometimes called it, because that would end white domination in a single stroke. We knew early on that the government was fiercely opposed to a winner-take-all Westminster parliamentary system, and advocated instead a system of proportional representation with built-in structural guarantees for the white minority. Although he was prepared to allow the black majority to vote and create legislation, he wanted to retain a minority veto. From the start I would have no truck with the plan. I described it to Mr. de Klerk as apartheid in disguise, a 'loser-take-all.'"

Mandela won. A new constitution was written, elections were held and he was sworn in as president on May 10, 1994. De Klerk accepted the post of second deputy president. Together they were awarded the Nobel Peace Prize. Though not friends, they accomplished an astonishing national reconciliation and shared a redeeming moment in twentieth century history.

From firebrand to peacemaker, from violence to order, from tension to serenity, from the law to the prophets, Mandela traveled the tortuous road to mature leadership. Through years of cruel testing, he developed the mind of a statesman and the heart of a wise man. He became the kind of integrating personality Havel talks about, able to contain within himself—tall, straight, slender, youthful, and frail—the horror and the hope of his nation, and of the world.

The twentieth century ended in limbo, its best energies spent, with Mandela the last great leader to exit the stage of statecraft. The peoples of the globe, obliged to practice patience until they were over the hurdle into the new century, the new millennium, could recall for comfort that 1901, after all, had brought forth Theodore Roosevelt.

From Teddy Roosevelt came the beginning of a progressive social order and a new sense of America's place in the world. Franklin D. Roosevelt advanced both those dreams. He invented a solid system of public responsibility for private well-being and established the United States as a global power. It was he who ushered in the American century.

Gandhi created an independent, secular, democratic India and administered the coup de grace to the British Empire. Modern China owes its being to Zhou Enlai, who sustained the nation through countless catastrophes and opened it up to the West. Without Zhou, Deng Xiaoping's economic revolution never would have happened. Gorbachev pushed Russia into the modern world even at the price of his own power and the Communist Party, which he revered and hoped to save.

Churchill strengthened the British to stand alone for a year against Hitler and made possible the rise of a united Western Europe, sure to extend in time to the states of the former Warsaw Pact. Ironically his heir, Margaret Thatcher, iron lady of the great British revival, could barely tolerate the idea of the E.U.

Mandela finished the century with amazing moral force, freeing South Africa to take its place in the civilized world.

All shaped new eras for their nations and left the world vastly changed by their creative statecraft.

Chapter
Four

James Watson
    James Watson (along with Francis Crick) discovered the structure of DNA—the double helix—and created the most famous moment in biology since Darwin or Mendel. From this work flow enormous advances in genetics.

The Supremacy of Science

*In the twentieth century we shall live in the midst
of strange faces, new images, and unheard-of
sounds. Many of those who do not have the spark
within themselves will feel cold and they will
escape into the ruin of their memories.*
                                        Franz Marc

More than any epoch in history, ours has been an Age of Science.
Cut loose from the constraints of religion, twentieth-century
scientists have located humankind in a new, vastly expanded
universe. Leading the way was a man of faith, Albert Einstein, who was
hailed by George Bernard Shaw at a London dinner as the greatest of his
contemporaries.

Einstein, said Shaw that October evening in 1930, stood in the company
of a handful of makers of universes stretching back over twenty-five hundred years. Shaw could, in fact, count them on two hands: Pythagoras,
founder of the ancient movement that celebrated numbers and shaped
geometry; Aristotle, conceiver of all matter as earth, air, fire, and water
acted upon by forces such as gravity; Ptolemy, elaborator of a cosmos
with earth at the center (Aristotle's view also); Copernicus,
perceiver of the sun at the center instead; Galileo, confirmer of the
Copernican breakthrough (to the hostile dismay of the Catholic church);
Kepler, proclaimer of the planets in elliptical motion; Newton, formulator
of the universal law of gravitation; and Einstein, discoverer of the general
and special theories of relativity.[1]

As Shaw put it, Newton's universe lasted three hundred years. But
along came Einstein to prove that Newton did not really know what happened to the apple. Einstein's theory of relativity disputed Newton's
argument that an apple fell to the earth because the apple and the earth—
like all masses—attract each other.

According to Einstein, there is no such attraction. Objects are naturally in motion, and they follow the contour of space as they move. Or as science writer Tom Siegfried explained, "An apple hits the earth because the earth gets in the way of the apple's motion."[2]

Siegfried also noted that Einstein wreaked havoc with the long-standing idea that the universe was eternal and infinite. It always had been and always would be, world without end, amen. But Einstein's equations showed that the universe ought to be expanding—or collapsing. It could not be static. Horrified, Einstein refused to accept the direction of his own work. Instead he proposed a cosmological constant that acted as a counterforce to gravity, preserving the stable universe he had inherited from Newton. But Einstein could not escape the implications of his own genius. By 1929 his original idea had been proved correct by Edwin Hubble and his famous telescope. Space indeed was expanding, causing the galaxies to be spread farther and farther apart, much like raisins in a rising loaf of bread.[3]

It was not the only time Einstein would be proved right (or possibly right) in spite of his own reservations. His notion of a cosmological constant, which he dismissed as "the greatest blunder of my life," returned to serious consideration in 1994 when physicists were trying desperately to cope with an odd suspicion that some stars are perhaps older than the universe itself. If this were true, it would mean that the big-bang theory of universal creation, generally favored in scientific circles by the end of the century, would require drastic shoring up, perhaps by the discovery of another force.[4]

Two years later, however, Dr. Allan Sandage of Carnegie Observatories, concluded that the stars in question are 13 billion years old while the universe itself dates back 15 billion years. Then came data from the European Space Agency satellite Hipparcos to indicate that "the oldest stars are about 11 billion years old, while the universe is believed to be 10 to 13 billion years old." Still later research pointed to an age of 15 billion years for the universe. But yet another estimate has circled back to the old worry that the universe may indeed be younger than some of its stars.[5]

So the big-bang debate has not ended because no one knows for sure how rapidly the universe is expanding, though some have come to believe the expansion will go on forever. Einstein supplied the beginning but not the end of the argument.[6]

It didn't take long for the world to realize what it had in Albert Einstein, as his biographer, Abraham Pais, relates. In 1919, when he was forty, the *London Times* trumpeted, "Revolution in science/New theory of the universe/Newtonian ideas overthrown," and the *New York Times* echoed, "Lights all askew in the heavens/Einstein theory triumphs." Two years later he won the Nobel Prize.

The work that was honored in Stockholm dated back to 1905, when, at the age of twenty-six, the young German Einstein, then living in Switzerland, published six papers, including one that explained why ultra-violet light could knock electrons out of a metal plate. The answer: Light in that instance behaved not as a wave, as most people believed, but as a stream of particles, producing the "photoelectric effect." So there was duality at the heart of light.[7]

Einstein is most often celebrated for his theories of relativity, special and general. So pervasive have they become that even those who have no idea of their meaning refer to relativity, not always with approval, as a way of defining the era. Indeed, the loss of absolutes implicit in this thinking became a special torment for some unsuited to their century. The truth is they might well look again. Einstein's theory of special relativity has in it great hope.

What Einstein realized is that energy could be converted into mass. Later he came to see that the reverse is also true. Mass is locked-up energy. The result was his famous equation $E=mc^2$. It says that mass and energy are interchangeable. Or as one biographer put it, "Every clod of earth, every feather, every speck of earth becomes a prodigious reservoir of entrapped energy."[8] This means that nothing is lost. Nothing.

Einstein showed that as an object moves faster it contracts with every bit of velocity gained. But as it approaches the speed of light, suddenly it reverses itself and gets heavier. "The energy that impels an object to move faster gets somehow added to its mass. This is the beginning of the breakdown of the idea that things are solid objects, separate from the forces that move them. Energy can turn into mass."[9]

Einstein's genius revealed itself at an early age. He was only sixteen when "questions that lie at the root of the special theory of relativity dawned on him." It took ten years for those intuitions to blossom into understanding, but once they did he wrote quickly, finishing his first paper only five weeks after the insight had settled. And no sooner had the 1905 reports been written than he began to gestate with the general theory. Finally, after years of trial and error, he brought forth this work in 1915 in a fever of activity, completing the major formulation in about two months.

It wasn't long before Einstein had to confront the master, Newton. There was no way Einstein could avoid dealing with gravity and the apple. What he concluded, according to Angela Tilby, is that "gravity is not simply a fundamental force of nature acting instantaneously and at any distance between bodies, as Newton had believed. It is rather to be understood as a field, like a magnetic field . . . To describe what this field was, Einstein introduced the concept of spacetime. Spacetime is everything."[10]

Spacetime was indeed, as Shaw observed, a whole new universe. Einstein made assumptions rarely considered by the human mind and proved them true. He discovered in his work on special relativity that there is no such thing as absolute rest for material things, as Aristotle had supposed, and no such thing as absolute motion either. The absolutes, in fact, took a beating as Einstein completed his extraordinary *tour de force*.

He also concluded that there is no universal time. Tilby explains: "Every object has its own time which is affected by its movement through space . . . . The faster something moves the slower time flows for it . . . . Even clocks will go at different speeds. So a space traveller coming back to earth would find he had aged less quickly than his family or friends." Expanding that insight, Einstein showed in the general theory that gravity also affects the flow of time which "runs faster in outer space, where there is no gravity, than it does on the earth's surface."[11]

Einstein was not always the iconoclast. Frequently, inevitably, his work built on past discoveries. But at other moments he was startlingly fresh. "Special relativity brought clarity to old physics and created new physics," wrote Abraham Pais. In this effort Einstein was inspired by the previous work of H.A. Lorentz. But in general relativity he was truly original. There he started "the long road alone." Where it led was to the fantastic studies of mass, energy, motion and light. Einstein recognized that as energy is emitted and absorbed by matter (causing an object to grow smaller then larger as it moves faster) light is "created or annihilated in similar discrete parcels of energy." This Pais declared to be "Einstein's one revolutionary contribution to physics. It upset all existing ideas about the interaction between light and matter."

None of this was accomplished in a mood of calm detachment. "The emotional state which enables such achievements," Pais observed, is like that of "the religious person or the person in love; the daily pursuit does not originate from a design or program but from a direct need." So out of Einstein's need came his towering victory—the general theory of relativity, still "the cosmological framework for most of twentieth-century physics."[12]

Out of Einstein too, as noted earlier, came the notion of the big bang. The idea can also be traced to Hubble, who first estimated the universe to be about two billion years old. His figure had to be revised upwards in 1963 after a new telescope at Mt. Palomar, California, four times stronger than Hubble's, spotted quasars (quasistellar radio sources) whose light must have started its journey toward earth ten, if not fifteen, billion years ago. "It was also discovered," said Tilby, "that the farther away the quasars were, the more dense they were. Their mass was compacted into smaller and smaller areas. Scientists interpreted this as evidence that they belonged to an ancient era of the universe [which had] changed over time." Thus was born the view that the universe had not existed always but in fact had begun in a big bang that brought about "the creation not only of all matter, but of space and time as well."[13] It's a measure of the ignorance of physics that creationists don't spend more time attacking Einstein and Hubble and less Charles Darwin.

They might also give some thought to Stephen Hawking, who developed the concept of "the nature and behavior of black holes, those voracious gravitational sinkholes in space predicted by relativity but never really accepted by Einstein . . . . As he [Hawking] saw it, the expansion of the universe must be like the time reverse of the collapse of matter creating a black hole; running the process backwards should lead to a beginning. In that case, if Einstein's math is correct, the primeval atom out of which the universe supposedly emerged in the Big Bang must have been the mother of all singularities." (A singularity occurs when stellar matter collapses into a black hole and keeps on collapsing until it reaches a tiny point of infinite density, where "all the basic laws of physics would have broken down.")[14]

The most ambitious effort to test the big-bang theory was to have been the superconducting super collider in Waxahachie, Texas. This was a fifty-four-mile-long tunnel in which particles were to have been smashed at high speeds to emulate the birth of the universe in which was embedded the origin of life. The effect then would have been studied by computers. It was partially completed when Congress pulled the plug on the $11 billion funding—a fatally short-sighted decision.

Since then, serious observers such as science writer Dick Teresi have predicted the death of physics. Members of Congress, Teresi charged, seem to have no understanding that theoretical physicists merely make predictions about the universe based on incomplete data that can only be confirmed through real experiments, such as the vital collision planned at the SSC. Scientists produce elegant mathematical models that are little more than the stuff of "Star Trek." It is particle accelerators that permit physicists to "go back in time by creating very hot conditions similar to those present in the very early universe. The bigger the accelerator, the farther back one can travel." Nobody's traveling anywhere now, however, at least not in the United States. (A number of the scientists and engineers who left the SSC are working now on the Large Hadron Collider at CERN, near Geneva.) Instead, Teresi snorted, American lawmakers seem entranced by the idea of "small, cheap physics." Foolishly, naively, they suppose that "a frizzy-haired scientist with a foreign accent makes an accelerator out of an eight-track stereo, some toaster wire and a used Cuisinart. Particle physics doesn't work that way."[15]

No, it doesn't. As Teresi rightly warned, "When, millenniums hence, archaeologists dig up the U.S., they will find two odd features: a well-maintained Disney World in the Florida swamps and the enormous, half-finished tunnel for the supercollider in the Texas prairie. They will do some quick extrapolations and jump to some harsh conclusions about our culture."[16] Genius, they will realize, need not apply. It's a sad end to a century that began with blazing hopes.

Einstein pointed the way with general relativity, though it took a while for him to accept the implications of his discovery—that the universe might have changed over time. He was no more happy with quantum mechanics, which can be traced in part to his experiments with light waves and particles (where he affirmed that light comes in bullet-like jumps called quanta).

Quantum mechanics, the forerunner to modern electronics as well as the nuclear bomb, has been called "a far greater break with the past" than the relativities. Einstein disliked that break. He was far more comfortable with transitions than with revolutions. "He could be radical," Pais observed, "but never was a rebel." He preferred to play "the role of the instrument of the Lord, Who he deeply believed, was subtle but not malicious."

While he admired the achievements of younger physicists who pushed ahead in quantum mechanics, Einstein, a naturalized American by 1940, continued his solitary search for a principle that would maintain cause and effect in an orderly way. His scientific genius had spent itself. The time had come for his greatness of spirit.

Einstein read philosophy most of his life. On several occasions he gathered a small group, including Bertrand Russell, at his house in Princeton to discuss the philosophy of science. Pais believed this interest harmed Einstein as a scientist though it "stretched his personality." The biographer argued that Einstein's philosophical nature froze him into an attitude that could not generate creative work during the last thirty years of his life. And yet, was it not philosophy that sustained him after the inevitable end of scientific creativity, that honed his character, that made him, in Pais' own words, "the freest man I have known"? Of course by freedom Pais meant the "freedom to ask scientific questions, the genius to so often ask the right ones. He had no choice but to accept the answer." So in his view liberation of the intellect involves certain limitations imposed by logic. But perhaps there is a freedom beyond logic.

Einstein's freedom could be construed as something that grew from a grounding not only in philosophy but also in music (he played the violin, and his favorite composers were Mozart, Bach, Vivaldi, Corelli, and Scarlatti—early masters of order) as well as art, where his affection lay with Giotto, Fra Angelico, Piero della Francesca, Rembrandt—venerable masters once again, which shows that no one can live on the cutting edge all the time. It may in fact require the deep roots of the old world to bring forth the new.

Like Freud, who as a young man also had a liking for philosophy, Einstein was a Germanic Jew who suffered at the hands of the Nazis. (Einstein's cousin, Lina, died at Auschwitz and another at Theresienstadt. Freud lost four sisters in a German concentration camp.) Both left their countries, Einstein as a young man, Freud not until the end of his life. The two of them exchanged letters on the frightful prospect of war.

In 1939 Einstein feared that Germany would get the bomb. He wrote to Franklin Roosevelt, Pais reports, about "the military implications of nuclear fission." Roosevelt came to understand well those implications and later put Einstein to work as a consultant to the Research and Development Division of the U.S. Navy.

According to one report he was never actually attached to the Manhattan Project because the War Department denied him security clearance. This was due to an F.B.I. dossier that suggested he was involved with Moscow. Bureau director J. Edgar Hoover stepped up his obsession with Einstein in 1950 and began running down rumors that the great physicist had tried to involve Soviet agent Klaus Fuchs in the development of the atom bomb—absurd since Einstein was kept at a distance from it—or that after the death of his second wife he had been in love with Margarita Konenkova, another suspected spy for the Kremlin, when she lived in Princeton. Her husband, a noted sculptor, created the bronze bust of Einstein at the university's Institute for Advanced Studies. Though Hoover kept Einstein on his enemies list, along with Eleanor Roosevelt, Charles Chaplin, and later, Martin Luther King, Jr., there is no evidence that his relationship with Konenkova was anything but an amorous passion. She did succeed in introducing him to the Soviet vice consul in New York. His letters to her mention the occasion, but nothing else of political note.[17]

Einstein was not of a political temperament, though he readily admitted that his life was "divided between politics and equations." He became a strong advocate of Zionism and was even offered the post as Israel's first president, though not with total enthusiasm. Indeed, Ben-Gurion asked his personal secretary, "What are we going to do if he accepts?" Einstein did not accept. He pleaded he was too naive in politics. But there may have been another reason that went directly to his core: "Equations," he acknowledged, "are more important to me, because politics is for the present, but an equation is something for eternity."[18]

Einstein saw nothing eternal in quantum mechanics, but it turned out to be one of the most enduring intellectual breakthroughs of the century. Defined as "an attempt to understand the movement and behavior of things which cannot be described by classical Newtonian physics . . . . very small things like atoms or molecules," it is a mystifying adventure. It all goes back to Einstein's ambiguity about light, which he described as both waves and particles. The same thing turned out to be true of sub-atomic objects that bubble up from the quantum realm. Governed by the uncertainty principle, by probability, "things pop into existence and dance out again, without rhyme or reason."[19]

"To get a grip on reality at the quantum level," wrote Tilby, one must realize that it works "not in certainties, but in probabilities." The scientist's role is "no longer to read the answers off the book of nature, but to lay out the betting odds." The quantum arena is there "as potential rather than as actuality." It exists as a theoretical realm, not as anything ever empirically observed. What you see is not what you get. "Go deeper and deeper into the concrete world of tables and chairs," Tilby continued, "go beyond individual molecules to the bonded atoms that make them up; go inside the . . . atom and the solidity disappears. Instead of ending up with a world of tiny discrete building-blocks, you come to a seething turbulence of possibility."

The basic theory suggests that nature itself is indeterminate. It "fatally undermines" the causal order that both science and theology once imposed upon the universe. Niels Bohr called quantum mechanics shocking and Werner Heisenberg (father of the uncertainty principle) said it was absurd. Both physicists pursued quantum mechanics after Einstein had abandoned it, proclaiming, "God does not play dice."[20]

For all its quirkiness, Stephen Hawking has pronounced quantum mechanics, along with the general theory of relativity, "the great intellectual achievements of the first half of this century." The general theory, he explained, "describes the force of gravity and the large scale structure of the universe" while quantum mechanics "deals with phenomena on extremely small scales . . . ." The problem is, he said, that "these two theories are known to be inconsistent with each other—they cannot both be correct." Hence the search today "for a new theory that will incorporate them both—a quantum theory of gravity."[21]

For the past fifty years, a unified theory has been the Holy Grail of physicists. Indeed Einstein gave the last years of his life to the search. What is longed for is "to see the universe as an overall unity composed of its ninety-odd elements and four forces." At first those four forces were one, but that didn't last. Gravity, it's likely, "split off from the unified force in the first fragment of time." The electromagnetic field spun off the weak nuclear force, which along with the strong nuclear force, governs the inner world of atoms.[22]

"The main difficulty in finding a theory that unifies gravity with the other forces," observed Hawking, "is that general relativity is a 'classical' theory; that is, it does not incorporate the uncertainty principle of quantum mechanics . . . . A necessary first step, therefore, is to combine general relativity with the uncertainty principle."[23]

So the great dream now is this: Combine relativity with uncertainty to make a unified field, a unity of the four forces, a whole that will indeed be holy and satisfy the human craving for universal order, though it would be a paradoxical order born of probability.

Quantum mechanics led the way to modern electronics. This suggests a direct line from the world of Einstein in Bern, Berlin and Princeton to that of Jack Kilby at Texas Instruments in Dallas. In 1958, three years after the death of Einstein, Kilby, a genius of engineering, invented the integrated circuit, called the monolithic integrated circuit because it was formed from a single crystal. Also known as the semiconductor microchip, this is the magical miniature element that made computers manageable for ordinary people, putting them on desks and airline tray-tables at ever descending cost. Kilby remade the world, not in his own image (in spite of his commanding stature which totally fills a doorframe, he is a modest man), but in the image of connection.

Connecting is what Kilby helped the world accomplish in a manner wholly new and immediate. This he did along with Robert Noyce, who pursued a parallel path in California.

"The development of the integrated circuit was the single most important event that helped usher in the Information Age," said Robert M. White when he was president of the American Academy of Engineering. "Like the invention of the telephone, the light bulb, or the automobile, the creation and widespread application of the integrated circuit has fundamentally changed our lives."[24]

What would such a man think about the world he helped to create? An interview produced some answers, but not many. This genius, who answers his own phone with "Kilby," is not fond of talking.

Like others he deplored the decision of Congress to disband the superconducting super collider. Only with data obtained from the SSC or something like it, he said, can the existence of the unified field be established. He too believes in the Grail.

Congress kept the space station which Kilby pronounced "not important to science." Its only value is in public relations and prestige and, of course, jobs. It would have been better, he said, to save the SSC and let the space station go.

Kilby expressed intense concern about the decline of basic research in the U.S. and the accompanying disdain for adventurers who have no idea what they might find but whose discoveries can define an age. Bell Labs "has turned off its work in this area," he lamented, and General Electric and DuPont have reduced their efforts. So if government and business are turning their backs on basic research in favor of more limited, applied projects, who in the United States is going to accomplish the great work? It will have to be done in the universities, he explained. But where will the money come from? Possibly abroad.[25]

Asked who the foremost scientists of the twentieth century have been, here was the answer from this master engineer: Einstein, of course, and James Watson and Francis Crick.[26]

James Watson in the 1950s was a wild-haired, Chicago-born American. Francis Crick was urbane, British and twelve years older. Together, at Cambridge, they discovered the structure of DNA—the double helix. This has been called the most important moment in science since Mendel, the nineteenth-century father of genetics,[27] and the most famous event in biology since Darwin published his theory of evolution in 1859.[28] Along with Maurice Wilkins, also working in England at the time, Watson and Crick won the Nobel Prize.

How did they come to see, when most scientists did not, that DNA was at the heart of everything? Surely it was a momentous leap of intuition grounded in the belief that innocents so often hold in the simplicity of things. "Worrying about complications before ruling out the possibility that the answer is simple would be foolishness," Watson said years later, adding that he had always believed that "the truth, once found, would be simple as well as pretty." Crick also wrote of the "intrinsic beauty of the DNA double helix. It is the molecule," he declared, "that has style, quite as much as the scientists."[29]

But the scientists had style too. What's more, they refused to be inhibited by the decorum of their professional community. While traditionalists might look askance at eminent biologists jousting in the public print, they went about it with relish. First Watson wrote a memoir of the DNA discovery in which he confided, "I have never seen Francis Crick in a modest mood . . . Although some of his closest colleagues realized the value of his quick, penetrating mind and frequently sought his advice, he was often not appreciated and most people thought he talked too much."[30]

Crick rejoined that Watson was "regarded in most circles as too bright to be really sound."[31]

But for all that, their collaboration changed the world. Their great discovery was this: "That the master DNA molecule is a gently twisted spiral ladder, a double helix, that carries the genes, the messengers of heredity, and that is capable of endlessly copying itself."[32] From this came the tantalizing possibility of genetic engineering.

It led to fears in the early 1970s that genetic tinkering might produce a monster—perhaps a ghastly form of cancer—that would escape from the lab and wreak destruction. That worry subsided by the end of the decade as DNA technology began to fuel hot new venture capital companies, turning scientists into business successes.[33]

But James Watson and Francis Crick never crossed over into the world of commerce. Both remained men of pure science. Crick now is studying consciousness at the Salk Institute for Biological Research near San Diego, and Watson took on the leadership of Cold Spring Harbor Laboratory on Long Island and restored its sagging fortunes to make it the top independent lab in the country. Later he ran the Human Genome Project in Washington—an amazing effort by the National Institutes of Health to identify the 100,000 or so genes that encode human life. Already they've found or soon will discover the genes responsible for Huntington's disease, colon cancer, breast cancer, heart disease, diabetes, and mental retardation.

Watson explained in an interview that eventually doctors will be able to spot these defective genes in the fetus. Will that lead to a wave of abortions? Watson admitted that it will, and he refused to condemn those who make that choice. "Some people say you shouldn't interfere with natural conditions," he observed, "but I find that remark rather cruel."[34]

So extensive and exotic has genetic research become that Dr. Luigi Cavalli-Sforza, a geneticist at Stanford, has examined the chemical sequencing of genes (by reading the sometimes thousands of "letters" in a gene one by one) to map the movement of peoples around the globe— out of Africa one to two million years ago, spreading across the world 100,000 years ago, reaching every continent 40,000 years later.[35]

DNA was a watchword, of course, at the criminal murder trial of O.J. Simpson. Like psychoanalysis, relativity, quantum leaps and other high moments of science, DNA is being absorbed into the culture without much understanding of what it means. Now it will seep its way into unconsciousness, gathering interpretations as it goes along, carrying the projection of the times. Little will be known of the vibrant pair from Britain and the American Midwest who found their destiny together in Cambridge. But their work will live in the laboratories of the next century with vast consequences for human health.

Watson has called himself a total Darwinian who believes human beings are completely a function of evolution.[36] One who's beginning to question Darwin is Dr. Stuart Kauffman, a biochemist formerly at the Santa Fe Institute. Whether his work will carry the day is not yet known, but he's raising questions certain to influence our understanding of the origin of the species. In challenging natural selection, random and unpredictable, he's opening the way to a new conception of natural order.

"Most biologists have believed for over a century that selection is the sole source of order in biology, that selection alone is the 'tinkerer' that crafts the forms," wrote Kauffman. "But if the forms selection chooses among were generated by laws of complexity, then selection has always had a handmaiden. It is not, after all, the sole source of order, and organisms are not just tinkered-together contraptions, but expressions of deeper natural laws. If all this is true, what a revision of the Darwinian worldview will lie before us! Not we the accidental, but we the expected."[37]

Arguing from complexity theory, Kauffman, blessed both with brilliance and incandescent intuition, insists that natural selection is not the only key to evolution. The principle of self-organization also is involved, whereby the seemingly chaotic amorphous soup of creation put forth its own implicit order.

Mitchell Waldrop described the context in which Kauffman is working:

> According to the standard theory in the biology textbooks . . . DNA, RNA, protein, polysacharides and all the other molecules of life must have arisen billions of years ago in some warm little pond, where simple building blocks like amino acids and such had accumulated from the primordial atmosphere . . . . So over time, went the argument, these simple compounds would have collected in ponds and lakes, undergoing further chemical reactions and growing more and more complex. Eventually there would have arisen a collection of molecules that included the DNA double helix and/or its single-strand cousin, RNA—both of which have the power to reproduce themselves. And once there was self-reproduction, all the rest would then follow from natural selection. Or so went the standard theory.

> But Kauffman didn't buy it.

> For one thing most biological molecules are enormous objects. To make a single protein molecule, for example, you might have to chain together several hundred amino-acid building blocks in a precise order. That's hard enough to do in a modern laboratory, where you have access to all the latest tools of biotechnology. So how could such a thing form all by itself in a pond? Lots of people had tried to calculate the odds of that happening, and their answer came out pretty much the same: if the formation were truly random, you would have to wait for longer than the lifetime

of the universe to produce even one useful protein molecule, much less all the myriads of proteins and sugars and lipids and nucleic acids that you need to make a fully functioning cell. Even if you assumed that all the trillions of stars in all the millions of galaxies in the observable universe had planets like Earth, with warm oceans and an atmosphere, the probability that any of them would bring forth life would still be—infinitesimal. If the origin of life had really been a random event, then it had really been a miracle.[38]

Describing Kauffman's thinking, Waldrop further speculated that the "amino acids and sugars and such banging around" might have had "at least some random reactions with one another," producing "a fair number of smallish molecules." Then some of these smallish molecules might have acted as catalysts—"submicroscopic matchmakers"—grabbing "two other molecules as they go tumbling by" and bringing them together "so that they interact and fuse very quickly."[39]

"If the conditions in your primordial soup were right," he continued, "then you wouldn't have to wait for random reactions at all. The compounds in the soup could have formed a coherent, self-reinforcing web of reactions . . . . If it were true, it meant the origin of life didn't have to wait for some ridiculously improbable event to produce a set of enormously complicated molecules; it meant that life could indeed have bootstrapped its way into existence from very simple molecules, and it meant that life had not been just a random accident, but was part of nature's incessant compulsion for self-organization."[40]

Physicist Fred Hoyle has come to a similar conclusion, as Tilby explains. "His explorations of the nuclear processes in stars suggest that the laws of nuclear physics have been designed with consequences favorable to life in mind. Otherwise . . . we are left explaining a monstrous chain of coincidences and accidents."[41]

So Kauffman is not the only voice of Darwinian revision. But he is probably the most passionate and articulate. For one thing, he knows how to dramatize an idea. That's because he set out at first to be a playwright, but abandoned that ambition to study philosophy, at Dartmouth and Oxford. In time he grew impatient with philosophy—"you couldn't find out if you were right," he lamented—and went to medical school instead. "If I had to choose," he told Mitchell Waldrop, "I'd rather be Einstein than Wittgenstein."[42]

There is comfort in the courage of his speculation. It means a lot not to be living the life of a fluke in a universe born of chance. In the midst of all this fresh investigation, it has became possible to see the universe as a whole even though the unified field—our new ground of being—remains elusive.

"The challenge was to discover how the complexity had emerged from simplicity through time," wrote Tilby.[43] This quest has given birth to chaos and complexity theory, the most sophisticated of today's sciences. Of course, that's where Stuart Kauffman, who has the most sophisticated of minds, would have to be working. Kauffman may never know if he is right. But his path has deep emotional appeal. Intuitive truth is on his side. So is the philosophical tenor of the times.

As for the study of complexity, this is a way of reconnecting the will-o'-the-wisps of quantum mechanics and modern biotechnology. It cuts across disciplines from physics and biology to economics and computer science. And it does not shrink from large subjects. One of its disciples, Ilya Prigogine, the Nobel-winning Russian chemist, has insisted, for example, that time has a real role to play in the universe. It is not reversible, capable of being played backwards. Nor is it on its way to extinction. To those who can't imagine the natural order without time, this is a relief. Much has been gained from the genius of Prigogine.

Ilya Prigogine was born in Moscow in 1917, nine months before the revolution. By 1921 his father, a chemical engineer, had moved the family to Lithuania, then Berlin and finally Brussels in an effort to make a new life, apart from the Bolsheviks. His mother was a musician, and from her Prigogine learned to love notes before he could even read words. He dreamed of becoming a classical pianist, but his parents urged him in the direction of law.

To prepare for the legal profession, it seemed to him a good idea to study the workings of the criminal mind. This led him to read about brain chemistry, and the course of his life was altered. It was chemistry, not law, or even music (also a love of Einstein's) that held Prigogine for the rest of his days.

Also like Einstein and so many other thinkers in science, Prigogine's work was informed by philosophy. For him it wasn't just another interest, like archaeology was an interest. He saw philosophical implications in his theories, and he stressed that the "relentless movement of the universe toward a state of maximum entropy" (disorder) predicted by the second law of thermodynamics need not be a cause for social pessimism. His discovery of "self-organizing systems," he is convinced, lends itself to a more hopeful view.[44]

But order and equilibrium are not the same thing. One arises in the absence of the other. Equilibrium means that either "a body has no forces acting on it or it has forces acting on it in such a way that they balance and there is no change of energy between the body and its environment." What Prigogine showed is this: When they are "far from equilibrium, systems have an astonishing capacity to produce a high degree of order."[45] That is reason for optimism. If we are patient, the chaos that's been roiling the last years of the century will yield finally to a new, more complex level of order.

He further has insisted that "the universe we live in has been organized by a progressive breaking of symmetries . . . . Creation is achieved through the *loss* of perfect symmetry." In fact, "the further you go from equilibrium, from the perfect, symmetrical world, the more the universe seems to be able to organize itself into higher and higher degrees of complexity." Perfection, then, is the enemy of creativity. So is balance. "Creativity and chaos belong together," Tilby observed. "Equilibrium is sterility and death."[46]

For those who see science as metaphor, this insight is strikingly important. In giving it to the world, Prigogine, the philosophical man of music, gave us a great deal more than chemistry. He gave dignity to turmoil and turned chaos into hope.

Einstein may have preferred equations to politics, but for Andrei Sakharov it was the reverse, not by choice or even temperament, but because politics—and greatness—were thrust upon him. Indeed, Glasnost can be attributed as much to Sakharov as to Gorbachev.[47]

Sakharov was the son of a physics teacher who earned most of his income and a measure of prestige from his scientific writing. But for all his family background and later achievement in physics, Sakharov in his memoirs recalls a persistent sense of insecurity about his "unsystematic education."

He tried to make up for it with intensive preparation for classes he taught as a graduate student, then regretted that there hadn't been time to do more. "I often think how wonderful it would have been if I'd had the time to go through all the disciplines of theoretical physics that way," he wrote. "If in the 1950s and 1960s I'd taught courses in quantum mechanics and quantum field theory, elementary particles including the theory of symmetry and courses in statistical physics (with those new methods borrowed from field theory), gas dynamics, hydrodynamics, and astrophysics, the gaping holes in my education that for decades hindered my work might not have existed. But my life shaped up differently."

It took time for that different destiny to reveal itself. Sakharov looked at first and for quite a while like a typical, gifted, loyal Russian scientist. In college in Turkmenistan—a month's ride from Moscow by train— Sakharov looked so promising to Soviet authorities that they sent him to a munitions factory after graduation to help with World War II.

Later he began a twenty-year career developing thermonuclear weapons in a "secret, closed town" called the Installation. It had a taut atmosphere in which "all notes had to be made in special tablets with numbered pages. At the end of the working day, they were placed in suitcases, sealed and handed in for safekeeping."

The restrictions extended to science itself. During the 1930s there was great hostility toward Einstein's "anti-materialist" theory of relativity. Some who espoused it were arrested and sent to prison. Also, "belief in Mendelian genetics was regarded as an indication of disloyalty." When Sakharov had the temerity to say once at a meeting that genetic theory "seemed scientifically correct," it was not well received. Nonetheless, his prestige kept trouble at bay. As he noted in his memoirs, officials "exchanged glances but said nothing. Evidently my position and reputation at the Installation disposed them to overlook my sins."

Indeed his reputation was soaring. He relates in his memoirs that one colleague referred to him as "our gold reserve," and another was fond of saying, "Let's apply the Sakharov principle—let's use our brains." After a major hydrogen bomb test in 1953, Georgy Malenkov, Soviet leader after Stalin's death, asked the head of the project "to congratulate and embrace Sakharov in particular for his exceptional contribution to the cause of peace." That same year Sakharov was named a Hero of Socialist Labor, won a Stalin prize and was awarded an expensive dacha in a Moscow suburb. And all this just as he was receiving his doctorate.

Sakharov was so prized, in fact, that he was not allowed to fly lest the Soviets risk losing him in a crash. Moreover he had body guards called "secretaries." But privilege and adulation did not prevent the KGB from tapping his phone or reading his mail. No doubt this surveillance was intensified after Sakharov refused to join the Communist Party.

Nonetheless he believed in what he was doing. He was convinced, he wrote, "that our enterprise was absolutely vital for our national security and the preservation of peace."

This changed forever as Sakharov grew increasingly concerned about the effects of nuclear testing. His quiet life quaked as he began to dissent publicly. By the 1960s he was confronting the Kremlin, calling for an end to tests, opposing honors for politically connected "pseudo-scientists" and signing a letter denouncing Stalin's rehabilitation.

He paid a price for his activism. Officials at the Installation kicked him out as a department head and cut his salary almost in half. But they were up against more than they knew.

Whence came this transformation? "What," asked Yevgeny Yevtushenko, the poet, "had changed the young successful atomic scientist, winner of three gold Hero of Socialist Labor stars, and who according to law should have had a monument erected to him in his lifetime? What had turned him, a man so removed from politics by nature, into one of the era's central political figures?" It was, said Yevtushenko, "the pangs of conscience, traditional to the Russian intelligentsia." Sakharov was not a religious man, but he had in his own way set his face toward Jerusalem. No harassment, no punishment deterred him. He could not be worn down by the "cult of impersonality" that ground away the resolve of so many others. With infinite courtesy, "sadly but firmly" as Yevtushenko liked to say, he continued his quiet crusade.[48]

"By the beginning of 1968," wrote Sakharov, "I felt a growing compulsion to speak out on the fundamental issues of our age . . . . I shared the hopes of Einstein, Bohr, Russell, Szilard, and other Western intellectuals that these notions which had gained currency after World War II might ease the tragic crisis of our age. In 1968 I took my decisive step by publishing *Reflections on Progress, Peaceful Coexistence and Intellectual Freedom.*"

The title may sound tame, but the work electrified the West. It occupied three pages in the *New York Times*. According to Edward Kline this long essay "urged an end to the Cold War, stimulated Western interest in disarmament and scientific exchanges and set forth a constructive blueprint for remaking the Soviet Union and the World." As Sakharov described it, "*Reflections* rejected all extremes, the intransigence shared by revolutionaries and reactionaries alike. It called for compromise and for progress moderated by enlightened conservatism and caution."

Yevtushenko called the work amateurish yet prophetic. Much that Sakharov urged, all unthinkable at the time, has come to pass. What are

today's joint ventures in the former communist world if not the conver-
gence between socialist and capitalist countries espoused by this brave
physicist more than twenty-five years ago?[49]

But the soundness of Sakharov's thinking counted for nothing.
Trouble erupted almost immediately as the paper was widely and illegally
circulated in Moscow. Before long his clearance was revoked and he was
expelled from the Installation. Then began his fullblown dissident years
that led to the Nobel Peace Prize in 1975 and exile from Moscow in 1980
after he had come out against the Soviet invasion of Afghanistan.

"Sakharov," wrote Yevtushenko, "found himself in [the novelist
Boris] Pasternak's position, not a politician but in the epicenter of
politics, because in a conscienceless administrative system, an unkilled
conscience is a political phenomenon. But Sakharov went further than
Pasternak and heroically sacrificed his science, consciously becoming a
political fighter. As a political fighter, Sakharov was unique—history has
not known such a gentle, shy fighter, such a polite and awkward hero."[50]

Sakharov and his wife, Elena Bonner, were sent to Gorky, where they
lived in a four-room apartment with no telephone and heavy
oversight. A "landlady" hired by the KGB spent two hours a day simply
sitting in one of the rooms, keeping an eye on everything.

Sakharov continued to write papers and speeches which Bonner
would smuggle to Moscow by train and slip to foreign correspondents or
send to her children in Boston for publication. Some of his articles
appeared in the *New York Times Magazine*, others in *Foreign Affairs*.

The KGB kept a constant lookout for his work and stole critical man-
uscripts more than once. Whenever he went out Sakharov always stuffed
his important papers into a bag and took it with him since the apartment
was certain to be searched while he was out. Three times he had to
rewrite parts of his memoirs because material had been taken. This
included nine hundred pages purloined from Bonner on the train to
Moscow.

Sakharov was no sentimentalist of foreign relations. He applied great
realism to his view of the interminable arms talks between the Soviets
and Washington: "It seemed clear to me," he said, "that the West could
expect no real progress in disarmament negotiations unless it had some
bargaining chip; therefore it had to be prepared to go ahead with the MX
missile as a potential trade-off for the USSR's powerful silo-based
missiles (effectively first-strike weapons since being MIRVed) and to
install Pershing and cruise missiles in Europe."

This sensible (and correct) assessment was twisted by the KGB to say that Sakharov wanted the U.S. to increase its military forces and thus threaten the Soviets all the more. Sakharov's admirers were mystified. Even his neighbors were upset and angry with him. Always there were dark intimations that Bonner was behind the trouble.

Elena Bonner—he called her Luisa and depended on her totally— married Sakharov after his first wife died. She resisted a match with so controversial a figure. As it turned out, her fears were justified. Immediately after the marriage reprisals began. A pediatrician by training, she suddenly found assignments harder to come by at the medical school where she was on staff. Before long she resigned.

Sakharov believed there was a strategy at work. "The brunt of the authorities' pressure tactics—slander, threats and various attempts to intimidate—shifted first to her," he wrote, "and soon to the children and grandchildren who were forced to emigrate." The KGB apparently planned to reclaim Sakharov at Bonner's expense.

"There is some evidence," Sakharov continued, "that suggests that the KGB intended to portray my public activities as a delusion produced by the influence of Luisa, who would be presented as a corrupt, self-serving, loose-living, egotistical, depraved, and immoral Jew prostitute, an agent of international Zionism. I would be transformed back into a distinguished Soviet (*Russian* of course) scientist who had made invaluable contributions to the Motherland and world science, whose name could be exploited for ideological warfare. This process was to be accomplished either posthumously or while I was alive, by means of forgery, false evidence or breaking me in some fashion, for example in a special psychiatric hospital . . . or by using my children . . . ."

In 1984 Bonner was put on trial and convicted of "slandering the Soviet system" and sentenced to five years' internal exile. Her trips to Moscow were over. But she didn't stay much longer in Gorky. Sakharov launched a hunger strike to force the Kremlin to permit his wife to go abroad to get medical treatment for her bad heart. Finally he succeeded.

Bonner went to Boston for by-pass surgery. Travelling afterwards in the U.S. and Europe she urged people to work for Sakharov's return to Moscow, the center of Soviet action. Why did she not call for his release from the country? Because he would never accept.

Return to Moscow he did. Two years later Mikhail Gorbachev reached Sakharov in Gorky and invited him back to the capital, Sakharov reflects, to become "in effect, the regime's loyal opposition." KGB agents had showed up the day before to install a telephone and tell the famous dissident to expect an important call.

Sakharov was elected to the Congress of People's Deputies, and only a few days before he died, suddenly and unexpectedly, he finished a new constitution for the "Union of Soviet Republics of Europe and Asia." That was December, 1989, at the very hour the Eastern European states were liberating themselves. The Soviet republics would not be far behind. There would be no union to speak of. But the Russia that survived would owe much to Andrei Sakharov.

Václav Havel, president of the Czech Republic, said in an interview that if Sakharov had lived, he might have become president of Russia and in that role he would have been an "integrating personality" (like Mandela in South Africa), uniting the man of thought with the man of action, the old Russia with the new.

Yevtushenko wrote this about Sakharov: "He did not appear out of the blue. He was born out of all the best of the great Russian intelligentsia. From Tolstoy he took and put into practice the thesis of nonviolent resistance [just as Gandhi did]. From Dostoevsky, the thesis that all the best ideals of mankind are not worth the tears of an innocent child. From Chekhov, that there are no little people or little sufferings. Sakharov won. Sadly, but firmly."[51]

It was Sakharov the philosopher who won, more than Sakharov the scientist. He did not think of himself as having an inner life, but that was where he bloomed the most decisively. "Today, deep in my heart," he wrote, "I do not know where I stand on religion. I don't believe in any dogma and I dislike official churches, especially those closely tied to the state, those of a predominantly ceremonial character or those tainted by fanaticism and intolerance. And yet I am unable to imagine the universe and human life without some guiding principle, without a source of spiritual 'warmth' that is nonmaterial and not bound by physical laws. Probably this sense of things could be called 'religious'."

And about the human adventure he said this: "The meaning of life is life itself: that daily routine which demands its own form of unobtrusive heroism."

"It turned out," Yevtushenko observed, "that political amateurism with a pure conscience is much more effective than professional politicking with a dirty conscience. When just yesterday, the live Sakharov, deputy badge on his lapel, walked along the Kremlin cobblestones, slick with spilled blood, his figure seemed tiny and defenseless before the gigantic shadows of Ivan the Terrible and Stalin. But after Sakharov's death, his shadow, imprinted on the Kremlin walls forever, will keep growing bigger as the shadows of the tyrants will diminish."[52] Thus far there has been no one in Russia to assume the mantle of moral authority that adorned Sakharov. His heir apparent, biologist Sergei Kovalyov, resigned as human rights commissioner when he could not persuade Boris Yeltsin to call off the war in Chechnya.[53]

Yet in Israel, Natan Sharansky, who emigrated there from the former Soviet Union, kept in his office as Minister of Trade and Industry a portrait of Andrei Sakharov, his "higher authority." Of Sakharov Sharansky said this: "His expression was like a saint's—straight, pure, clear moral thought."[54]

Sakharov triumphed in the end, and so did science. Some say, in fact, that science has been so transcendent in the twentieth century that there is nothing left to be discovered. "There will be no great revelations in the future comparable to those bestowed upon us by Darwin or Einstein or Watson and Crick," said John Horgan, who wrote a book called *The End of Science*.[55]

As Gunther Stent of the University of California at Berkeley put it, only three critical issues remain in biology: "how life began, how a single fertilized cell develops into a multicellular organism, and how the central nervous system processes information. When those goals are achieved," Stent said, "the basic task of biology, pure biology, will be completed."[56]

In physics, the last great achievement would be a final theory that explains everything. But some are wistful at the prospect of finding it. "There will be a sense of sadness," admitted Steven Weinberg, who has relished the pursuit of ultimate truth.[57]

The overarching effort of scientists for hundreds of years has been to establish the fundamental laws of the universe. Once they have been discovered, said one physicist plaintively, "you can't do that again." And merely applying the implications of fundamental laws is "in a way less interesting" and "less deep," he said, than forcing the laws to reveal themselves.[58]

Another physicist, Richard Feynman, predicted "a degeneration of ideas" once the universal laws are well understood. Then the philosophers will move in, he lamented.[59]

One of those philosophers, Colin McGinn of Rutgers University, expects a general retreat from science. "It wouldn't surprise me," he said, "if sometime during the next century people started veering away from studying science as much, except just to learn what they need to know about things, and started to go back into the humanities. [This last scientific epoch has been] a phase, a brilliant phase. People do forget that just one thousand years ago there was just religious doctrine, that was it. [After the fading of science] religion may start to appeal to people again."[60]

Sheldon Glashow, a physician at Harvard, agreed, not happily, that we may be going back to the Middle Ages: "Contemplation of super-strings," he wrote with a colleague, "may evolve into an activity as remote from conventional particle physics as particle physics is from chemistry, to be conducted at schools of divinity by future equivalents of medieval theologians . . . . For the first time since the Dark Ages, we can see how our noble search may end, with faith replacing science once again."[61]

It was all foretold by Oswald Spengler as early as 1918 when he wrote that scientists, if they became too estranged from other beliefs, would drive people into the arms of religion. He predicted this would happen by the end of the millennium. How right he has turned out to be.

But the renewed interest in faith need not mean the end of science. They simply need to recognize each other as two different, and powerful, ways of knowing. Nor is there any reason to suppose that great scientific discoveries do not lie ahead, things as yet unimagined, in spite of the current funding problems which won't last forever.

Einstein himself said that his theory of relativity "will have to yield to another one, for reasons which at present we do not yet surmise. I believe that the process of deepening the theory has no limits."[62] Or as David Bohm, the physicist-philosopher, said, "I think there are no limits to this . . . . We're not ever going to get a final essence which isn't also the appearance of something." Then he added, "This division of art and science is temporary. It didn't exist in the past, and there's no reason it should go on in the future . . . . The ability to perceive or think differently is more important than the knowledge gained."[63] (Some may disdain the arrival of the philosophers but it should be apparent from this insight how crucial they are to keeping the world whole.)

So science may be in limbo now, caught up in invention, which is not the same thing as creativity. But still, much creative work is left to be done. John Maddox has pointed out that a whole new physics may await a deeper understanding of matter and empty space, new conceptions of genetics and DNA sequencing will follow more complex rendering of the human genome, and new wisdom lures us to an accelerated study of brain, mind, memory, and imagination.[64] There's no reason to doubt the fresh perception and riper knowledge that surely lie ahead. Science anticipated its own demise at the end of the nineteenth century. It didn't happen then. It won't happen now, either.

Chapter
Five

Pablo Picasso
  *Pablo Picasso followed the lead of
Freud: He too took human beings apart
and put them back together again—as
cubes, cylinders, and spheres. His
geometry of the spirit reflected the deep
disintegration of the twentieth century.*

Shattered Images of Art

*And there was only one way out—the
artist had to fling himself into the
abyss in the belief that when he
reached bottom he would not be dead,
but would be newly born.*
El Lissitzky

The twentieth century inherited the glories of Impressionism, which replaced the formality of the past with shimmering scenes of everyday life. Bathed in light, these boating parties, ballet dancers, fields of flowers, and luscious women promised a world of happy grace. Then came a hundred years of horror and retrenchment. They led to the shattered images of art.

No one was more responsible for the new vision, searing and sorrowful, than Pablo Picasso, the giant of the age. Picasso surveyed Impressionism, spreading beauty all about, and rejected it. He rejected beauty (which he was supremely capable of creating) for something else, something deeply psychological. Jung described Picasso's work as a descent into the Hades of his own unconscious. There he sought out "the ugly, the morbid, the grotesque, the incomprehensible" in order to tell his own truth.

Though Picasso shattered the art that went before, he nonetheless brought to his work a psyche steeped in centuries of Spanish culture. Malaga, the sunny, southern city where he was born in 1891, was, biographer Patrick O'Brian noted, "much nearer to the middle ages than to the twentieth century." The Catholic household in which he grew up echoed that earlier inspiration.

Picasso's mother was Doña María Picasso y Lopez. His father, a painter, teacher, and local curator, was Don José Ruiz y Blasco. For some reason Picasso decided to drop his father's name in favor of his mother's—most unusual in Spain and all but unprecedented except for Velásquez. Picasso had a warm relationship with his mother, who adored him, but that affection didn't prevent his regarding women as "sex-objects or as domestic animals," there to be "exploited." It was the prevailing attitude of Spanish men, and Picasso never overcame it. His "feeling for women oscillated between extreme tenderness and appreciation on the one hand," wrote O'Brian, "and violent hatred on the other, the mid-point being nearer dislike if not contempt."

His father was "a good teacher, with a considerable share of technical knowledge," but the moment came when he was outstripped by his son and he knew it. Don José "ceremonially handed his brushes over to the boy and never painted again." He gave Picasso a studio of his own at the age of fifteen and the money to go to Paris when he was nineteen. Yet when his father died, Picasso did not go to the funeral, even though he was only a hundred miles away.

The family lived in "secret, hidden, bourgeois poverty." However, this did not preclude servants.

It was a devoutly Catholic culture, and Picasso was christened only sixteen days after he was born. Nonetheless, O'Brian noted, he "rebelled against the church, as he rebelled against everything else, but he retained a deep religious sense: deep, but also obscure, Manichaean, and in many ways far from anything that could possibly be called Christian." Still, he got Françoise Gilot, whom he never married, to pledge him "eternal love in a church," with holy water.

He had a "sympathy with such mystics as El Greco and St. John of the Cross" and spoke of "the spiritual essence of African carvings." Moreover, he said that a good painting was "something holy, that's what it is . . . because it has been touched by God." However, O'Brian points out, Picasso nonetheless denied the existence of God.

Religion rarely surfaced in Picasso's work though there were some crucifixion drawings as well as bullfight engravings with Christ-figures. Also, he did a Calvary painting, according to O'Brian, that was "a passionate, savage outcry of an essentially religious nature and a statement about death, agony, and sacrifice." This was an important picture to Picasso, and "he never parted with it."

Picasso drew constantly, from his earliest years, even before he could talk. He was an uninspired student who often arrived late. Reading, writing and math held no interest for him. Neither did languages. O'Brian concludes that he had "a brilliant and original mind, but it did not do its . . . work in words; it was not primarily a verbal mind." Nor in later years could he tolerate art criticism. Picasso's philosophy was "to be seen on the wall."

After the museum closed in Malaga, Don José was forced to move his family to a small town on the Atlantic coast. After a few years, they moved again, to Barcelona, where Picasso first acquired the accouterments of a personal style. This was a rough, hard-working city whose urban poor gave rise to anarchists and bomb-throwers. They had great impact on Picasso, who wanted to accomplish some disruption of his own. "The Barcelona that Picasso explored in 1895 presented some analogies with Joyce's Dublin," wrote O'Brian. "There was the same nationalist revival, the same passionate resentment of a foreign government, the same memory of a glorious past now overshadowed, the same tradition of deep opposition to central authority, the same conviction of a higher culture oppressed by a lower."

Picasso was an outsider. He spoke Andalan Spanish, not Catalan. He was considered akin to the Gypsies and thus indolent. But at thirteen he was admitted to advanced art classes when the minimum age was twenty. It accentuated the feeling in Picasso that he was different, set apart. Already his genius was affecting him, cutting him off, making it hard "to find any equals." In time he came to see, according to O'Brian, that except on the most superficial level, the only way he could communicate was "in a language that [would] not be generally understood for years."

Nonetheless, he did find friends, and they remained important to his life. After a stint studying art in Madrid—mainly copying El Greco, Velásquez and Goya at the Prado—he returned to Barcelona and began frequenting the Quatre Gats, a café where gathered a group of painters, writers and poets who shared an enthusiasm for anarchist ideas as well as the Modernismo movement (as the swirls and shapes of Art Nouveau were known in Spain). They immersed themselves in "an atmosphere of Ibsen, Tolstoy, Wagner . . . Schopenhauer, the Symbolists, Nietzsche . . . ." Picasso was "no great reader," O'Brian notes, but he did develop a "second-hand" grasp of this thinking.

Though never a man of letters, he did fall in love with poetry. Its concise, intense concentration enthralled him, just as a painting did. He also loved poets, and Max Jacobs, Guillaume Apollinaire, Paul Eluard, Jean Cocteau, and André Breton were among the closest friends of the Paris years to come.

But at Quatre Gats, destruction reigned, especially destruction as a creative passion, a view Picasso entirely appropriated. Years later, he would say, "In my case a picture is a sum of destruction."

It has been noted that Picasso in many ways resembled Goethe: Both

had great staying power and physical stamina. "[B]ut whereas Goethe
was an insider," observed O'Brian, "solidly based in his social and
national contexts, endowed with an elaborate education and with money,
and supported on all sides by the culture of his time, Picasso was socially
peripheral, his sense of national identity was at least troubled, his schooling had scarcely passed the elementary stage, and the culture of his time,
such as it was, oppressed him on every hand. His eventual aim was to
revolutionize a great part of this culture, and apart from his native genius
all he had to help him in his intellectual formation . . . were his contacts
in Barcelona and his early years in Paris: the Quatre Gats and
Montparnasse were to be his Leipzig and Strassburg, his Greek, Latin,
and philosophy."

If Barcelona supplied Picasso with a world view, his grounding in art
as a discipline, derived from centuries of effort, awaited him in Paris.
There he went at nineteen to work in a studio loaned by a friend in
Montmartre, near Sacre Coeur.

Toulouse-Lautrec was the inspiration of the hour. But it wasn't long
before Picasso had digested this muse of the night and plunged himself
into a world of blue. "Blue," said he, "so full of grace." It was his favorite
color, and with it he created some of the most entrancing pictures of the
twentieth century. Poignant, heartbreakingly beautiful, with none of the
grotesquerie that would follow, they sang a plaintive song of solitude and
deprivation. Some said they had "too much soul," as if that were possible.

Solitude evoked conflicting feelings in Picasso. He insisted upon it
for his work, then, when work was over, sometimes well into the
evening, he seemed "afraid of being alone." He was gregarious (though
easily bored), and his creativity came at a cost not suffered by more
introverted natures.

Inevitably he would seek a woman to fill his need for company in the
midst of a carefully protected daily routine. Fernande Olivier, wife of a
troubled sculptor, appeared when Picasso was twenty-two. She has been
described as "remarkably idle," never helping Picasso when times were
lean except by persuading the coal dealer to deliver on credit. Nor did she
take much interest in his work. Even so, Fernande, whose lassitude combined with a canny intelligence, lived with Picasso for twelve years.

It was in those early days together that the Blue Period, with its deep
pools of melancholy, gave way to the Rose, often realized in grand, radiant, classical figures, full of comfort and repose. Picasso and Fernande
went often to the circus with friends, and there he discovered still another

strain of his work, according to O'Brian—the "saltimbanque" pictures of "dusty vagrants, wandering through bare, indeterminate landscapes in the clothes they [wore] for their performance." They also met Gertrude Stein and her brother Leo. These American collectors became mainstays for Picasso, inviting him and Fernande to dinner and buying his pictures to hang alongside their Matisses, Gauguins, and Cézannes.

Of Cézanne Picasso said repeatedly, "He was my one and only master." O'Brian notes that his was "almost the only influence, apart from Van Gogh, that Picasso ever directly acknowledged." It was Cézanne who pointed the way to cubism—the first artistic breakthrough of the twentieth century—with his admonition to "deal with nature by the cylinder, the sphere and the cone."

Cézanne died in 1906, one year before his legacy burst upon the world in the first great cubist work—Picasso's *Demoiselles d'Avignon*. These five whores with their "mask-like faces" and their humanity "abstracted, left behind," comprise the pivotal painting of the century. With its brutal distortion and obliteration of feeling, *Demoiselles* has been called "one of the most dynamic, liberating pictures of our age." But liberated from whom and for what? The era was even younger than the artist. Both would learn in time what had been unleashed. The dragons of the unconscious were about to clamp themselves upon the thinking mind and make it believe that atrocity could be the child of reason.

Demoiselles was denounced all around. Vollard, the art dealer, called it "the work of a madman." Braque, who soon would become Picasso's soulmate in the cubist experiment, likened it to drinking paraffin. Leo Stein dismissed cubism as "Godalmighty rubbish" and observed that the painter of *Demoiselles* had "been trying to paint the fourth dimension" in some monstrous Einsteinian joke. The laugh that followed, O'Brian related, let Picasso know that his patron was not amused.

Neither was Fernande Olivier. She seemed oblivious, in fact, to what Picasso had accomplished. Not one mention of the d'*Avignon* earthquake occurred in her memoirs and the importance of cubism always eluded her.

Though Picasso's success allowed them to move from their accustomed squalor to a nicer flat, that brought them contentment only for a few years more. In 1912 they parted, and Picasso took off for Avignon, his mythical city of triumph, with Marcelle Humbert, the mistress of an artist friend. He called her Eva, and they were happy for a time. But Eva died of tuberculosis, during World War I, just as Picasso was about to move into a whole new, dramatic phase—the ballet.

Diaghilev summoned Picasso to Italy to design scenery and costumes for a Ballets Russes production with Jean Cocteau the poet and composer Erik Satie. The show was called *Parade*, and when it opened in Paris, its cubist figures, moving to the sounds of typewriters, were greeted with shocked hostility, though Proust and his friends were enthralled. Picasso's friend Apollinaire, who did the program notes, was there fresh from the battlefield, in uniform and bandages. Also, there was another who was making her way into Picasso's life: Olga Koklova, a Russian dancer. Before long, they were married in an Orthodox cathedral in Paris, just three months after Apollinaire took to wife his war-time nurse.

But well before that, through Gertrude and Leo Stein, Picasso had met the artist who always would be linked with him—Henri Matisse. Together they would be called the titans of the twentieth century.[1] At that point (probably about 1905), Matisse, twelve years older, was known as the controversial leader of the Fauves, or "wild beasts," who expressed themselves in raging, savage color, arousing the predictable howl of protest.

Yet Matisse was cultivated, educated, bourgeois; and he had a gift for domestic life. His wife and daughter Marguerite (two more children would follow) were crucial to him. Picasso noticed this and envied Matisse his serenity. He also felt that the gentle painter with the penchant for bold color was a rival for the friendship of the Steins. In fact, Matisse introduced Picasso to other new friends who were also collectors, cloth-merchant Sergei Shchukine and sugar operator Ivan Morosov. Both bought numerous pictures to take home to Russia.

Picasso felt jealous of Matisse, and once, when hearing that the colorist was doing the curtain, sets and costumes for a show by Stravinsky, cried out, "Matisse! What is a Matisse? A balcony with a big red flowerpot falling all over it." Yet, as O'Brian pointed out, "Matisse was the only painter to whose achievements Picasso reacted all his life long, the one standard by which he judged his own . . . . It was Matisse who really worried him, then and for the rest of his life, Matisse at whom he looked with a mixture of uneasiness, respect and emulation." Indeed, the moment came, when Picasso pronounced Matisse "our greatest painter."

Matisse not only saw to it that Picasso got to know people who could help, O'Brian notes, he also introduced the younger painter to a revelation that changed his eye and filled his heart—African masks and carvings. To Picasso these pieces were more than art; they were magic.

Their creators were "intercessors . . . against unknown, threatening spirits." He came to see himself as a kind of "witchdoctor," defending people from their demons. "If you give spirits a shape," he said, "you break free from them. [It's very Freudian though Picasso hated Freud.] Spirits and the subconscious . . . and emotion—they're all the same thing. I grasped why I was a painter . . . . The *Demoiselles* must have come that day: not at all because of their forms, no; but because it was my first exorcising picture . . . ."[2]

So Picasso felt himself "surrounded by an inimical world: a true outsider." According to O'Brian, this sense of evil (and good) embodied all about "constituted his largely but not wholly pagan religion." Matisse did not share this view at all. Neither did George Braque, Picasso's friend and compatriot in cubism. And it separated the two, Picasso from Braque. Braque "never felt what I've called Everything, or life, or what shall I say—the World? Everything around us," Picasso explained to Malraux, "everything that is not us, he never thought it hostile . . . . He was always at home."[3]

Picasso was never at home, so his men friends meant a great deal to him. They connected him to life and to his own mind and emotions in a way that women simply could not do. During the cubist years, he would talk with Braque for hours. But World War I intervened, and once Braque returned from the front they had trouble reviving the old rapport. Braque remained loyal to cubism. Picasso moved on, and was heard to remark to Gertrude Stein, "Yes, Braque and James Joyce, they were the incomprehensibles whom anyone can understand." But eventually Picasso and Braque found each other again, not on the same basis as before, but with some consanguinity of spirit.

As for women, they came and went like the tide, though seldom did they disappear forever. Olga bore a son, Paulo, and, as Picasso grew more successful, she took to wearing clothes by Chanel. Together they embraced a world of late nights and fashion. When the manic mood had spent itself, Olga landed in a lonely place, wealthy but with nothing to do, detached from her husband and his work. Picasso responded with rage, which, O'Brian notes, he poured into paintings of "toothed, predatory women."

But in time these female monsters yielded to paintings that overflowed with sensuality and joy. Had Olga been paying attention she surely would have noticed that she was nowhere to be seen in the glorious nudes of this period. The body instead belonged to Marie-

Thérèse Walter, whose carnal generosity Picasso had imagined on canvas long before they met. Swiss and very beautiful, she was close to twenty years old; he was fifty. Unlike Fernande and Olga, and later Françoise Gilot, Marie-Thérèse never wrote about Picasso. She was discreet. And while she had no interest in painting or sculpture, she showed more affection for Picasso than ever did his chic Russian dancer.

Picasso tried living a double life, but by the time Marie Thérèse had a daughter—Maria Concepcion, whom he called Maya and adored—he was in divorce proceedings with Olga. It was painful and expensive. To reach a settlement that allowed him to keep his pictures, Picasso had to give his wife a generous allowance; Boisgeloup, a chateau forty miles from Paris, which he had bought as a working retreat especially for sculpture (Olga despised it); and custody of Paulo.

Picasso gave up his dinner jackets and went back to Gypsy clothes. The divorce was so draining it sabotaged his work for several months, Gertrude Stein said for two years. He survived by writing poetry—verse which the Surrealists were happy to claim as their own. He also removed himself from Paris, heading south to Juan-les-Pins, site of many holidays with Olga, where he lived under the name Pablo Ruiz, resurrecting his father at last.

Whether Marie-Thérèse was with Picasso in the south is not clear. Certainly it wasn't long before he returned to Paris, repaired to the Deux Magots, and there encountered a remarkable woman, who, O'Brian reports, took off her "elegant embroidered gloves, [laid] her hand on the table with its fingers spread, and [stabbed] between them with a pointed knife: her aim was imperfect and every miss was marked with blood." This was Dora Maar.

Dora Maar has been called "far and away the most intelligent woman Picasso had ever met: the only intellectual with whom he ever shared part of his life." The daughter of a Yugoslav architect and a Frenchwoman, she had spent some time in Argentina before becoming a Surrealist photographer in Paris. She was devoted to painting and had tried it herself but stopped, because her work did not "come up to her own exacting standards." Later Picasso persuaded her to take it up again.

Dora took a flat near Picasso, who continued to see Marie-Thérèse and Maya as well. Though Maar became the model for many of Picasso's most important pictures, including the "weeping women," their relationship did not go well for her. Within nine years, Picasso's drive to dominate drove her to a nervous breakdown. According to Françoise Gilot, no indifferent observer, Dora told Picasso, "As an artist you may be extraordinary, but morally speaking, you're worthless." Even so, she preserved a sizable collection of Picasso's works that brought $30 million at auction in Paris.[4]

Picasso's moral sensibilities were aroused by the Spanish Civil War. When it broke out in 1936, he immediately pledged himself to the Republic. To show its appreciation, the government named Picasso director of the Prado. There was not a lot for him to do. The museum's treasures were stored in Valencia to protect them from Franco's bombs.

But another treasure emerged from the war: It was Picasso's great *Guernica*. He painted it in a fever of concentration after German planes under Franco attacked the little town by that name and obliterated it. For Picasso, O'Brian observes, art was "a means of waging offensive and defensive war against the enemy." This he did with ferocious effort, producing all the drawings and preliminary studies in little more than a month—unheard of since Picasso usually let an experience germinate for months, if not years, before he expressed it on canvas. Then his ideas poured forth in a flood (not unlike Einstein's science). In *Guernica*, large, anguished and overwhelming, Picasso gave the world one of its most passionate protests of war. Then followed the weeping women, portraits of agony, drawn from Dora Maar, who felt keenly the devastation at hand and to come.

Hitler and Stalin dismembered Poland in 1939. Then, in 1940, Germany invaded Denmark and Norway. Finally France fell. Picasso rushed to Royan, but soon returned to Paris. Matisse got a visa for Brazil, but couldn't bring himself to board the boat. "If everything of any worth runs away," he asked, "what will remain of France?"

Picasso had reason to be nervous. His work was hated by Hitler as degenerate. To keep him on edge, the Gestapo would come to Picasso's apartment, asking him if he were Jewish. Then, later, other German emissaries would arrive, with promises of special consideration in a land of war and rations. Picasso offered them nothing, O'Brian relates, except post cards of *Guernica*.

It was near the end of the war that Picasso, influenced by Dora Maar, finally declared himself a Communist. Though hardly a man of politics, he was drawn to the heroism of Communists during the French resistance. And their cause had been his in Spain. While he never read Marx or anything else on the subject, he had a visceral sense of belonging to the Communist Party, of no longer being an exile with no country of his own.

The war also brought Françoise Gilot, whom Picasso met in a café. Françoise was twenty-one, a student at the Sorbonne and the daughter of a wealthy businessman. Picasso was forty years older. She agreed to live with him and stayed seven years, bearing two children, Claude and Paloma.

None of it was easy, of course. When they went off to the South of France, Olga and her son Paulo, now twenty-six, hovered on the beach. Olga herself came to call from time to time, and there would occur slaps, scratches and pinches from the aggrieved wife. Marie-Thérèse and Maya spent their holidays close by. And, early on, Dora Maar had her nervous breakdown and had to be cared for. Françoise dealt with all of it in a book, *Life with Picasso*, in which, it has been said, she presented Picasso as a "small man, ill-tempered, unkind, self-indulgent, and essentially weak." But this, O'Brian insisted, was not the Picasso people knew, either personally or through his work.

There was another young woman from the war years: Geneviève Laporte. She was a student who came to interview Picasso for her school newspaper. He was taken with her and invited her back often, in the after-noons, for quiet talk. He helped her go to Swarthmore College in the U.S., and when she returned, grown up into a poet, he took a small house with her as a respite from Françoise. Those were lovely times, and she wrote of them, "I believe I was Picasso's only deep love and in all likelihood his last."

But not his last woman. After the departure of Françoise (Picasso begged her to stay), there appeared Jacqueline Hutin, twenty-seven, with a daughter. Employed as a saleswoman at the Ramié workshop that made Picasso's ceramics, she arrived in time for the final act. Jacqueline worshiped Picasso, threw herself at him, and finally married him, in a secret ceremony. By then she was thirty-five. He was eighty.

Whatever tranquillity they were able to establish was ruptured by the publication of Françoise Gilot's book. Picasso went to court to try to stop it or get it changed, but his efforts were futile. He turned against Françoise and her children and never saw Claude and Paloma again except for one awkward encounter. Jacqueline kept all Picasso's children and grandchildren at a distance, and when he died, in 1973, the inevitable battle began over his estate. He had made provision for very little except *Guernica*.

The total legacy was immense, the sheer volume of it staggering.

Through years of persistent effort, Picasso is thought to have created "over fifteen thousand paintings to say nothing of his sculpture, engravings, and countless drawings." Among those works were masterpieces that marked the twentieth century as the age of Picasso.

Clive Bell, the critic, said "Two people I have known from whom there emanated simply and unmistakably a sense of genius: one is Picasso." The other was Virginia Woolf. "Virginia and Picasso," he explained, "belonged to another order of beings; They were of a species distinct from the common; their mental processes were different from ours; they arrived at conclusions by ways to us unknown."[5]

Picasso saw the century for what it was. He foretold the horror, prophesied the deep disintegration, wailed for lost worlds as they were swept away. He never flinched in the face of atrocity. He expressed the times and made of them immortal art.

Picasso and Matisse: Together they are called the two pre-eminent painters of the twentieth century.

Their differences were many: Where Matisse glorified the female body, Picasso often painted women as witches. Where Picasso was personally flamboyant, Matisse was reticent. Where Picasso came from straitened circumstances, Matisse's background was solidly bourgeois. Picasso had little education. Matisse was well versed in the classics. Matisse "exalted colour." Picasso "smashed form into pieces."[6] Picasso carried within himself the turmoil of the era. Matisse, for all his depressive tendencies, was committed to joy.

Henri Matisse was born on New Year's Eve, 1869, in the northern French town of Picardy. His mother was from a well established family of tanners and glove-makers, dating back to the sixteenth century. Before her marriage she worked as a milliner in Paris, and, as time went on, she developed skills in painting china. She also sold house paints in her husband's store and developed a reputation for her taste in recommending colors. Matisse's father ran retail businesses, first in hardware, then grain.

Matisse was close to his mother, and identified himself with her "sensitive and artistic nature." From her he gained his love of textiles and elegant hats which turned up later in his pictures. While his father may have contributed to this interest in lovely cloth—the elder Matisse was working in a fabric shop in Paris when he first met his wife—it was business-like habits and a strong will that he mainly bequeathed his son.

After graduation, Matisse's father arranged for him a clerk's job in a lawyer's office. Next came law school in Paris, but it wasn't long, his biographer, Hayden Herrera, points out, before Matisse was overcome by "boredom and restlessness" (traits that also drove Picasso). Even so, he returned to Picardy and the life of a clerk.

Matisse was saved from listless obscurity at twenty when appendicitis forced him to bed and his mother bought him a paint box and some brushes. For the first time, perhaps ever, Matisse was truly engaged. ". . . [T]he moment I had this box of colors in my hands," he said, "I had the feeling that my life was there . . . . I was completely free, alone, tranquil, whereas I had always been anxious and bored by the various things I had been made to do."

From a popular handbook on painting Matisse learned how to create an academic picture. But this new knowledge did not prevent his return to the law office after he recovered. His father expected it, as Matisse well knew.

Without telling anyone, Matisse enrolled in a school for textile and tapestry designers. Each morning he would draw for an hour before going to his office, then paint for an another hour at lunch time. He snatched moments from copying documents to draw some more on legal paper. Then, on summer evenings, in his room, he would get in a little more art work before dark.

Finally Matisse worked up the courage to quit his job and go to art school. His father was furious, fearing that Matisse would starve. His mother, however, felt differently. She persuaded her husband to let their son study painting in Paris.

Matisse enrolled in a private program to prepare for the prestigious Ecole des Beaux-Arts. He failed his entrance exam, twice, confirming his father's skepticism. But this did not stop the allowance arriving each month from Picardy. Finally, on the third try, Matisse was admitted to the Ecole des Beaux-Arts.

As the struggle intensified, Matisse found comfort with Caroline Jobland. Eventually they had a daughter, named Marguerite. Matisse was devoted to the little girl, and when the liaison with Caroline ended he legally recognized Marguerite but apparently had little contact ever again with her mother.

It wasn't long before he met Amélie Parayre at a friend's wedding. Described as "tall, slender . . . charming, vivacious, intelligent, and totally devoted to Matisse and to his art," Amélie was the granddaughter of a Spanish pirate. When they married, she took on a large assignment. Not only was she the primary model for Matisse's painting and an important support for the household, working as a milliner (like his mother), she also calmed her husband during recurrent moments of anxiety. Their life together was not as serene as it appeared to Picasso.

"Matisse the anxious, the madly anxious." That view came from a painter friend, and he was hardly wrong. Matisse was indeed "tortured by insomnia,"[7] and found relief only in work. Though Amélie would awaken and read to her husband late at night, it was only through his painting that he found any repose. Even then, he was "often in agonies of doubt" and he would talk to himself as he painted. Herrera relates, "Frequently he experienced panic: he perspired, trembled, cursed, and wept." Sometimes, when beginning a picture, he would stand in front of the blank canvas for ten minutes, then smoke a cigarette to ease the tension.

Complete silence was necessary for Matisse's work (just like Picasso's), with no distractions. Hence Amélie was expected to keep the children quiet—there were three: Jean, Pierre and Marguerite, whom she adopted—as well as endure her husband's utter self-absorption. "Brutal egotism" was what Gertrude Stein called it. Another friend said the artist's obsession with his own work choked "almost everyone off."[8]

Yet what work it was. Rapturous color and voluptuous expression of the female body rendered Matisse the greatest sensualist of modern art, belying his businessman's dress and reserved demeanor. He sought, he said, to "awaken the ancient sensuality of man." His goal was heightened feeling: "I go toward sentiment, toward ecstasy . . . . And there I find calm."[9]

The calm was not easy to come by. Matisse worked at it, by working at his easel. For him the stakes were enormous. His friend André Derain used to say to him, "For you doing a picture is like risking your life." To which Matisse replied, "We have to live over a volcano." But there he lived, and with phenomenal success. "I have chosen to put torments and anxieties behind me," he declared, "committing myself to the transcription of the beauty of the world and the joy of painting . . . . My art is said to come from the intellect. That is not true; everything I have done I have done through passion."[10]

Like all superior performers, he made his act look effortless. "I have always . . . wanted my work to have the lightness and joyousness of a springtime which never lets anyone suspect the labors it has cost." So said one who suffered mightily for his art and shaped it into a thing of magic.

Matisse was "born to simplify." That's what his teacher, Gustave

Moreau, told him. Simplicity became his watchword, Herrera observed, and when he began a huge commission for Shchukin, the Moscow collector, Matisse ruminated on the project thusly: "I will attain this [complete calm—always calm was the object] by the simplest and most reduced means, those which permit the painter pertinently to express all his interior vision.

If ever a painter got his vision out completely (to paraphrase Virginia Woolf on Shakespeare) it was Matisse, and with such economy of means that he became "the precursor and the accomplice of all the simplifiers of our time, from Malevich to Mondrian."[11]

Matisse did manage to simplify himself, and it saved him. But the road was treacherous, and there were many years of deprivation before the inner effort paid off. One winter he and a colleague took jobs in Paris painting garlands to decorate the Grand Palais. Matisse caught bronchitis from the cold and quit after a week. Frequently, when money ran out, he took Amelia and the children to live with his family or hers. This was especially necessary after Matisse's father cut off his allowance in disgust.

Desperation did not stop Matisse from buying a small painting by Cézanne from the dealer Vollard. Gertrude Stein opined that it was paid for by selling Amélie's large sapphire engagement ring, something the artist denied. The picture—*Three Bathers*—became "a talisman" for Matisse. When friends urged him to sell it to raise money for his family, he refused. Cézanne was for him, as for Picasso, "a sort of god of painting . . . the father of us all . . . ." It was to Cézanne, he said, that he owed the most, and the little painting, he proclaimed years later, "sustained me morally in the critical moments of my venture as an artist; I have drawn from it my faith and my perseverance."[12]

Persevere he did. And finally there were friends to help. Paul Signac, the painter, lent Matisse a house near his own in Saint-Tropez one summer. Signac even bought one of Matisse's paintings—*Luxe, calme et volupté*—thrilled that it almost embraced his divisionist system of little colored dots. But that didn't last long, and Signac turned against a later picture by Matisse (*Le Bonheur de Vivre*), attacking its creator as "having gone to the dogs." Leo Stein, however, after initial reservations, pronounced the piece "the most important painting done in our time." He bought it.

Signac's was not the only bad review Matisse endured in those years. His work was castigated as "a madness," as "the barbaric and naive sport of a child who plays with a box of colors he has just got as a Christmas present," and in Paris wall graffiti, "Matisse makes you crazy, Matisse is more dangerous than absinthe."

This was the furor that greeted Fauvism, the fantastically colorful movement that counted Matisse as its undisputed leader. It was, according to Herrera, the "first avant-garde art style of the twentieth century," and it all began in 1905, when Matisse, Derain, Vlaminck, and Rouault, among others, had their work hung at the Salon d'Automne. Right away, a critic dubbed them Fauves—or wild beasts.

One of the most remarked upon pictures in the show was Matisse's *Woman with a Hat*. The president of the salon thought it too far out and he advised against hanging it, but the work was purchased by Leo and Gertrude Stein, along with their brother Michel and his wife. It was the beginning of Matisse's friendship with the Steins.

Picasso also spent time with these collectors from America. At their house he and Matisse papered over their rivalry with good will. Leo Stein was quick to note the difference between them: "Matisse," he wrote, "bearded, but with propriety; spectacled neatly; intelligent; freely spoken, but a little shy—in an immaculate room, a place, both within his head and without. Picasso—with nothing to say except an occasional sparkle, his work developing with no plan, but with immediate outpourings of an intuition which kept on to exhaustion, after which there was nothing till another came."[13]

Fernande Olivier, Picasso's lady at that time, observed this: Matisse "was very much master of himself. Unlike Picasso, who was usually rather sullen and inhibited at occasions like the Steins' Saturday gatherings, Matisse shone and impressed people."

Indeed, Matisse did impress people. So did his work. As he moved from Fauvism to a more decorative approach, his art began to sell. Matisse made enough to take Amélie to Algeria for two weeks. There he bought textiles and ceramics that would appear later in his paintings, making them rich with pattern and texture. He acquired a country house near a Paris suburb with a pond, garden and greenhouse. He dressed splendidly, like Picasso, and sent his wife and daughter to a fine dressmaker in Paris.

But it was not all happiness for Amélie. Her husband opened a school, and found there Olga Merson, a young Russian Jewish woman. He painted her, sculpted her, made love to her. Next came Lorette, an Italian model who appeared in some fifty of Matisse's pictures. In time,

Amélie sank into psychosomatic illness, often in bed with a bad back. By the time Matisse painted his last portrait of her, this once confident, vibrant woman had shrunk to a sad, ghost-like visage.

Matisse's father never did acknowledge his son's success. Nonetheless, despite the strain between them, Matisse was devastated when his father died. He went to Spain a month later, and there he fought depression and a near nervous breakdown with three hot baths a day.

His distress was made worse by Shchukin's refusal to hang two huge commissioned panels—*Dance II* and *Music*. Protesting that he had two young nieces living with him, Shchukin said he could not have nudes in the house. Finally, he accepted the work, though he covered the genitals of the flutist in *Music* with red paint.

This was not the first time Matisse had been shaken professionally, Herrera noted. Three years earlier, cubism had shattered his repose, displacing the Fauvist style and disturbing his sense of self-confidence. He "clashed" with Picasso "over the birth of cubism," Fernande Olivier recalled. Matisse "lost his temper and talked of getting even with Picasso, of making him beg for mercy."

Finally Matisse fled the cubist craze. He went to Tangier with Amélie and a painter friend. There he produced some his most scintillating canvases, many of which were purchased by Morosov and Shchukin in Moscow. Matisse returned to Paris confirmed in his own "deeply sensory nature." Cubism be damned.

World War I was also a time of terrible tension. Though forty-four, Matisse volunteered for the military but was rejected. Then he and his family went south, where constantly he played the violin—the instrument of his youth—to fend off anxiety.

Before the war was over, Matisse decided he belonged in Nice. "One can't live in a house too well kept, a house kept by country aunts," he had said in another context, but surely these sentiments could be applied as well to his life with the fading Amélie. He stayed in various hotels and "rose at seven [to play] the violin for two hours in some remote bathroom so as not to disturb the other . . . guests." Then to work.

In time he took up rowing and kept two small boats at the Club Nautique where he even won a gold medal. He also met Renoir, who lived near Nice. Though old and arthritic, Renoir was a radiant spirit and a great inspiration to Matisse. In fact, he came to think of Renoir in the same league as Cézanne.

Solitude and boredom, Herrera reported, were what drove Matisse to paint. (His work was also an antidote to depression.) Certainly he had plenty of solitude in Nice, although his children did come to visit and Amélie showed up occasionally, even living there for awhile.

But she could not penetrate Matisse's absorption in his work or rapport with his models. Many of them came from a nearby movie-extra agency, and one, Henriette Darricarrère, worked with Matisse for seven years, posing for some of his most erotic odalisques.

By 1930 Amélie had gone completely to bed, surrendering herself to the life of an invalid. It was the natural moment for the entrance of Lydia Delectorskaya, another Russian beauty. Lydia became Amélie's nurse, and before long she also was Matisse's model as well as his "secretary, studio assistant, household manager, hostess, and, until the end of his life, beloved companion."

It was too much for Amélie. She cried. She grew hysterical. She shrieked, "You may be a great artist, but you're a filthy bastard." (It sounds like Dora Maar to Picasso.) She demanded that her husband choose between Lydia and his wife. When he could not, she got up out of bed and left. So energized was Amélie by the parting, Herrera relates, that she joined the French resistance during World War II, along with Marguerite. Both women were arrested by the Gestapo. Amélie was seventy-three but hardly an invalid any longer.[14]

Amélie was sentenced to prison for six months for typing secret newsletters. For Marguerite it was even more terrifying. Discovered in Brittany working to prepare for the Allied landing, she was tortured by the Gestapo, then sent by train to Ravensbruck concentration camp in Germany. Luckily the train was stopped en route by an Allied air attack. Marguerite escaped into the woods and made her way finally to Paris.

Matisse, as his wife came late in life to know, was one of those artists who was not meant for marriage. "Watch out for the influence of wives," he told an interviewer. "The priest and the doctor should never marry, so as not to risk letting temporal considerations come before their profession; the same goes for the artist." Love, he said, "is not compatible with hard work."

And work hard Matisse did. When, in 1930, he was asked by Dr. Albert Barnes, wealthy developer of the antiseptic Argyrol, to do another version of *The Dance* for his house near Philadelphia, Matisse "drew directly on the canvas with a piece of charcoal fastened to a long bamboo pole."[15] It was the most imposing work he would ever paint. "I set about drawing the whole thing in one stroke," he explained. "It was inside me, like a rhythm that carried me along." (Virginia Woolf believed that good writing was entirely a matter of rhythm.)

World War II was hard on Matisse. Not only did he worry about Amélie and Marguerite and endure the Nazis denouncing his work as degenerate, he had surgery for intestinal cancer followed by two pulmonary embolisms and another operation. His health wrecked, he nonetheless kept on working. It was, he said, "as if I had all my life ahead of me, or rather a whole other life . . . . Everything that I did before this illness, before this operation, gives the feeling of too much effort; before this, I always lived with my belt buckled. Only what I created after the illness constitutes my real self: free, liberated . . ."

The liberated Matisse was at his core a man of great spiritual dimension. He had a "religion of happiness," "a religious awe toward life."[16] When he traveled in Moscow he was drawn to the Russian icons, and he felt, according to Herrera, an "almost mystical urge to find an essential order underlying change." In his later years, *Imitation of Christ* by Thomas à Kempis was his favorite bedtime reading. And when he drew, Matisse often sensed the presence of a higher power. "I am guided," he said, "I do not lead."

He began, Herrera said, to see art as "a living world which is in itself an infallible sign of the Divinity, a reflection of Divinity." The paper cutouts he did in the 1950s show signs of ethereal spirituality. He was, he said, drawing "closer to the absolute, with greater abstraction I pursue the essential wherever it leads." In his text for *Jazz*, he answered the question, "Do I believe in God?" with "Yes, when I work. When I am submissive and modest, I sense myself helped immensely by someone who makes me do things by which I surpass myself." And to his students, Matisse said, "Retain only what cannot be seen."

For all that, Matisse had still a practical nature: "It took sheer nerve to paint in this manner," he observed, "and it took sheer nerve to buy."

In the last years of his life, Matisse was too infirm to go out, so he made his own house a garden of delight. To the walls he attached cutouts of fruits and flowers, and the ceiling he adorned with heads of women and his grandchildren, drawing them himself with a charcoal attached to a fishing pole, just as he had done when creating the *Dancers* for Barnes. During the war, Herrera notes, he began to worry that he "would not be able to finish my life's work for lack of time." "[A] painter's life is never long enough," he said, "you leave your work in the middle."

In 1954, Matisse "died of a heart attack in Marguerite's arms." He left the world some of the most luminous art of the century.

Picasso, a volcanic force, shattered the images of art. Matisse, the sensualist, reassembled them in a quest for beauty. And Mondrian, philosopher of painting and of life, strove to make of his work the deepest possible expression of universal truth. His pristine white canvases, carefully balanced with sacred squares of red, blue, or yellow, the spaces defined by black lines as decisive as any in history, were meant to convey cosmic order, which, if properly internalized, could change lives and civilize societies.

Ever a hedgehog, Piet Mondrian took years to fulfill himself. He journeyed through naturalism, neo-impressionism, fauvism and cubism on his intense, deliberate road to purity. Nor was he kind to his previous work. Each picture, according to Yve-Alain Bois, he expected to outdo and even destroy its predecessor—quite different from Picasso or Matisse, both of whom felt strongly that each work stood on its own, with no reference to the past or progression to the future.

Pieter Mondriaan, as he was first known, was born in 1872, three years after Matisse and nine before Picasso, in the Netherlands. His father was steeped in the world of Dutch Reformed activism. Over the years he ran two Protestant elementary schools, and threw himself into politics, working with Abraham Kuyper, head of the anti-revolutionary party.

When Mondrian graduated at fourteen, his father urged him to get a diploma that would allow him to teach drawing. By then his uncle Frits, who had taken over the family barber, perfume and wigmaking shop in The Hague, had turned seriously to painting himself. He came as often as he could to help young Pieter learn art.

In time Mondrian moved to Amsterdam to study at the Rijksacademie. He lived with old friends above their Dutch Reformed bookstore and joined Kuyper's congregation even though by then his father had left Kuyper over dissension in the church. Mondrian helped pay the bills by copying pictures at the museum, "giving private lessons, making bacteriological drawings, painting decorative tiles, designing bookplates, producing portraits on commission, and occasionally selling a landscape painting."

Where Picasso astonished everyone with his virtuosity at art school in Barcelona, Mondrian, like Matisse, was not much of a student. In fact, he failed his first entrance exam for the Dutch Prix de Rome competition with a male nude drawing that was thought disappointing. Three years later he passed, but even then a male nude painting came in for harsh criticism. The human body, supreme province of Picasso and glory of Matisse, simply was not the forte of Mondrian. Two pictures with biblical themes fared badly too. Mondrian was a religious man, but his inspiration was not scriptural.

What moved him was theosophy. Founded by an esoteric thinker named Helena Blavatsky, theosophy held that "'art' and 'nature' are both manifestations of the universal." They are linked by a "common principle" to the "Great Whole," Bois explained.

Joined they may be, but for Mondrian, nature was the downfall of art. If art tried to imitate the beauty of nature, he believed, it would only encourage a false sense of unity with the Absolute, where the true One could only be perceived through pure abstraction—pure white; pure red, yellow and blue, rendered as essence and intensity.

For Mondrian, theosophy was the galvanizing revelation. Had he not come in contact with it, said Yve-Alain Bois, he might have remained a "minor-league landscape painter." Mondrian himself realized that the difference between his work and that of his peers was his "assertive relationship with philosophy." He was lackluster at painting male nudes, but his zeal to become the conduit for ultimate reality, indeed to create a kind of transubstantial reality himself, drove him to genius.

Mondrian waited until he was forty to move to Paris. By then he had resisted the temptation to marry a woman in Holland. "Fortunately," he wrote, "I realized in time that it was only an illusion, all that prettiness." Actually his work was a priestly calling that precluded close relationships. He and Theo van Doesburg, the Dutch artist and critic, were friends, but they stayed in touch mainly through correspondence and there was a period when they fell out with each other over issues of art.

Still, Mondrian was highly regarded, and there was always someone providing him an allowance or organizing a fund to cover part of his studio rent or a lottery to purchase one of his pictures as the prize. Women were always offering to represent his work. And when World War II broke out and he needed to escape from France, Ben Nicholson was there to help him get to London and find a house in Hampstead, where Freud too soon would flee. Harry Holtzman, another supporter, took care of Mondrian later, in New York.

So while Mondrian's life was ascetic (even though punctuated by learning the Charleston with the painter Georges Vantongerloo and his wife), and always financially strained, his work was celebrated and sought after. In fact, when Katherine Dreier, the American collector, put together a show for the Brooklyn Museum in 1926, the three Dutch masters she named in the accompanying book were Rembrandt, van Gogh, and Mondrian.

Mondrian took a long time to unfold. He was "the fabled tortoise (van Doesburg, the hare)." Through years of cubist experiments Mondrian labored before arriving, when he was nearly fifty, at the abstractions, with their vertical and horizontal declarations, that would make him renowned. And never was he satisfied. According to Bois, each time he came to a point where he felt that "a perfect equilibrium [had] been reached in his art, he [concluded] that he [had] rushed too much, attained an untimely perfection, and that he must change course."

Thus it was that in wartime New York, during his happiest years, Mondrian worked feverishly to destroy "every morning what he had made the night before"—like Penelope. The picture was *Victory Boogie Woogie*. Relentlessly he struggled to complicate it, to overlay the grid with small, vibrant squares of color.

It grew out of his taste for music, which Mondrian enjoyed at home, on a gramophone. "Although he loves jazz," wrote the *New Yorker*, Mondrian "has been hardly anywhere. He has a collection of boogie-woogie records which he plays, often dancing around the room to their accompaniment all by himself."[17]

Perhaps Mondrian stayed away from night spots, but he did go out socially in the art world of New York, at least when he wasn't working, which often he was, late into the night, seeking always to advance humankind to a new and richer unity with the One.

Mondrian, like Churchill and Teddy Roosevelt, believed in Darwinian progress. When he began to foresee new weapons, for example, he wrote that though they might be horrible, they would be too grotesque to use, so they would of themselves make war impossible. Hence evolution would carry the world to a higher plane.

Such were his thoughts when Mondrian died unexpectedly of pneumonia in February, 1944, leaving *Victory Boogie Woogie* unfinished.[18]

Art News called Mondrian "the purest, the most austere abstractionist of our day." But actually, at the end, his austerity was turning exuberant, as if in some new, wondrous wisdom. And his radical simplicity was growing more complex, foretelling the physics to come.

Where Picasso erupted and Matisse gently bloomed, Mondrian

evolved into a prophet of the Whole.

The early decades of the twentieth century were suffused with meta-physical longing. Mondrian was not the only painter whose quest for the universal consumed his life. In Russia another voice arose to proclaim the spiritual in art. Steeped in the high moment of Tolstoy, Dostoevsky, Pushkin, and Gogol, Wassily Kandinsky produced pictures that danced to the mystery of quantum mechanics and dreamed of the unified field, long before these notions brought physics to a new world of uncertainty.

Kandinsky was never uncertain. Though abstraction came late to him, and he lost time early on in law and economics, he moved with resolution through life, thinking deeply at every turn and pursuing each new venture as if it had been there all along in his imagination.

Kandinsky was born in Moscow in 1866, a time of great social progress—for serfs, for schools and for exiles, many of whom were per-mitted to come back from Siberia. Among those returning were Kandinsky's parents who had been living on the border of Mongolia in a community devoted to the tea trade. That part of the world remained with Kandinsky though he never lived there. It was in his blood, through his great-grandmother, a Mongolian princess. The family remained upper-class, and after the move to Moscow Kandinsky's father managed a Russian tea firm until ill health forced him to leave for Odessa.

Kandinsky endured the new setting, far inferior to Moscow he felt. He also lived patiently through his parents' divorce. Finally he returned to the city that he considered the "source of his artistic aspirations" to study at the university. But it was law and economics, not art, that he pursued in Moscow. Though Kandinsky had bought himself some oil paints a few years earlier and loved working with them, so impractical a profession never occurred to him, his biographer Will Grohmann noted. Unlike Matisse, Kandinsky saw practicing law as a natural thing to do. Something useful did accrue to Kandinsky from those years: a "capacity for abstract thinking."

Progress gave way to repression in Russia as agitators forced the czar to defend his regime with the zeal of the autocrat. Among those who resisted was Kandinsky, who threw himself into politics—but not very far. He was not prevented from passing his law examination and taking a job as instructor. He also got married—to a cousin named Ania Chimiakin.

But none of it worked. Art kept intruding. Kandinsky visited the

Hermitage and encountered Rembrandt. He saw an Impressionist show and experienced Monet. In time he also discovered himself and his own calling. When a university professorship was offered in 1896, Kandinsky said no. Instead he went to Munich to become a painter.

At the age of thirty Kandinsky embarked on his life's work. He enrolled in art school and pursued drawing from nude models. But the nude didn't suit him any more than it did Mondrian. And like Matisse, Kandinsky failed the entrance exam for the Munich Academy. After a year on his own, he finally got into the painting class.

His progress was sure and steady, though it took more than a decade to break through to abstraction. Even so, those early works—mainly woodcuts along with paintings in oil and tempera, often drawn, in a melancholy key, from Russian folk tales and religious icons—came to be shown, and Kandinsky traveled about to view the exhibitions and, often, to stay for awhile. He went to Venice, Odessa, Moscow, Tunis, Dresden, then lived for a year near Paris. There he was awarded medals and elected to the jury of the prestigious Salon D'Automne whose Grand Prix he won in 1906.

Still, his work was far from avant-garde. Gertrude Stein came to his studio and left in disappointment. She was too Western for Kandinsky, who was torn still between Russia and Europe. Ever a foreigner wherever he went, he remained immersed in the Orthodox Church and delighted in the music, literature and language of his country. His incessant travel, biographer Will Grohmann believed, relieved the pressure of place and helped him become a citizen of the world. Then he might belong somewhere.

But those were painful days. Kandinsky came close to a nervous breakdown in Paris, and only a rest cure in Munich brought him back to full life.

Kandinsky was not alone during the peripatetic years. With him through all of it, except in Russia, was Gabriele Münter who had been his student when he was teaching in Munich. Having long since left Ania behind, he took an apartment with Münter and also a summer house in Bavaria. He stopped his restless travel, with only an occasional visit home to Russia, and there, in Munich, accomplished the most important work of his life.

Kandinsky broke through to abstraction in 1910. It all began earlier, with some colorful Fauvist landscapes. (Grohmann insisted that these pictures were created alongside Fauvism, not as a part of the movement.

The Fauves were sophisticated, he said, where Kandinsky had a "naive inwardness" that made for a "rural quality.") What followed were paintings bursting with energy, vibrating with a vision as immediate as youth and as distant as the heavens. Surely he had been shown a glimpse of the ground of being.

These *Improvisations* and *Compsitions* pushed Kandinsky beyond the specifically Christian works he had been doing (with themes such as St. George, the Resurrection of the Dead, the Last Judgment and the Feast of All Saints—executed in oil, on glass, in woodcuts) to a mystical manifestation that echoed the Zen of Asia. "I do not consciously choose the form," he said, echoing Matisse, "the form spontaneously chooses itself in me." Grounded in Orthodoxy, drawn to theosophy (like Mondrian), Kandinsky evolved into a seer of the universe.

He also made some friends, especially Franz Marc, and together they started the Blue Rider group. (Blue, with its celestial qualities, was their favorite color, as it was Picasso's. Marc loved horses. Kandinsky loved riders. Thus the name.) Exhibitions followed, and also the *Blue Rider Almanac*, a compendium of "all the really new ideas of our day," as Marc said, including "painting, music, drama." The *Blue Rider Almanac*, he explained, "has become the focus of all our hopes."[19]

Kandinsky wrote almost half the text, and works by Picasso, Matisse and Rousseau were among those featured. The *Blue Rider* effort was a bold experiment in a conservative city, and Germany was slow to respond, except with epithets. "Imbecile" was the word one critic applied to Kandinsky. His friends rallied with a protest signed by such luminaries as Léger, Klee, Arp, and Apollinaire.

The almanac was not Kandinsky's first book. A year before, he had published *On the Spiritual in Art*. It too attracted vitriol: "The muddle-headed may speak of the 'spiritual'" wrote a detractor, "but the spirit does not muddle, it makes things clear . . . . A painting without an object is meaningless. Half object and half soul is simple delusion."

What that opponent could not grasp was Kandinsky's insight that pictures of real things got in the way of the true reality of his work. "The end," he said, "(and hence also the means) of nature and art differ essentially, organically, and by virtue of a universal law." Here he sounds strikingly like Mondrian.

So Kandinsky set forth to paint the transcendent spirit, working from his own "inner necessity." Natural objects he left behind, though circles and triangles surfaced in later work, a geometric ordering of exuberance, foretelling the wisdom of chaos in science.

Poetry gave him an outlet also, and he published some of that work in *Klänge*, along with woodcuts. It was part of an amazing period, hugely productive, when the introverted Kandinsky, prone to depression, came to bloom. The man who once wrote to Gabriele Münter, "I am sadly happy," achieved an ecstatic artistry.

But, Grohmann noted, he hardly looked the part. Like Matisse, who gave the appearance of a professor, Kandinsky had a diplomatic air. He dressed "with meticulous care, spoke quietly and attentively . . . . [and] sought to reduce the tensions around him." (This too was like Matisse, who couldn't bear disruption.) Kandinsky could be self-contained and aloof, preferring to keep himself private, unrevealed. "I hate it that people should see what I really feel," he wrote to Gabriele Münter. Before Munich could know him too well, World War I broke out, sending him home to Russia for refuge.

"The more horrible the world . . . the more abstract art becomes . . ." So said Paul Klee, later to become Kandinsky's great friend. Actually, the world became so horrible that Kandinsky made no art at all, not for a year. Once he started painting again, the Russian Revolution erupted, turning his days into long treks all over Moscow, tracking down consumer products and getting the proper documents to buy them, if he could find them.

But daily life improved when he was assigned to the Commissariat for Public Instruction. This was an administrative as well as a teaching job and it carried certain privileges. He worked not only in schools, but also in museums, the theatre and art publishing. In time he founded the Institute for Art Culture. While his own work suffered in an atmosphere that was deadening, Kandinsky did manage to cope with the new dispensation far better than most people.

Before the revolution, in 1915, at Christmastime, Kandinsky met Gabriele Münter in Stockholm and stayed until March. That was the last time they were together. It wasn't many months after his return to Russia that Kandinsky met Nina de Andreevsky, daughter of a Russian general. Though she was considerably younger than he was (Kandinsky by then was fifty), they found themselves so congenial that they wed almost immediately. It was a good decision, for both of them.

Münter spent the war in Scandinavia, waiting for Kandinsky. She didn't learn that he had finally divorced and remarried until he sent a lawyer to collect some of his paintings that he had left with her. Thus ended a tempestuous relationship between two artists who contributed a great deal to each other's work.

Kandinsky and his new wife stayed in Moscow until 1921, but by then he could bear no more. He had to find a place compatible with his own sensibilities. Berlin seemed a workable choice. Arriving there with few possessions, he and Nina hoped that the extensive work he had left behind with a dealer and others would give him an economic base. It didn't. The gallery had sold all Kandinsky's pictures, but inflation had so eroded the mark that the proceeds had dwindled to nothing. Finally, after years of negotiation, he recovered some of the other works, but by no means all. And it was 1957 before his papers appeared.

Life in Berlin was hard. Money was worthless. Sanitation was terrible. Moreover, when the Soviets realized Kandinsky was not returning to Russia, they revoked his citizenship, leaving him stateless. Relief came when an invitation arrived from Weimar, asking Kandinsky to teach at the Bauhaus. He seized it, and life began again.

The Bauhaus was an experiment in unifying the high and the decorative arts, the studio and the workshop, the aesthetic of elegance with the details of industry and everyday life. Started by Walter Gropius, it offered classes in typography, furniture, weaving and plastics. The faculty was a constellation of talent: Kandinsky, Paul Klee, Lyonel Feininger, Moholy-Nagy, and, later, Josef Albers and Marcel Breuer. Visiting lecturers included Stravinsky and Bartók. At one point, Einstein and Schonberg served on the board.

Agitators were never far away. Attacking Kandinsky as "Communist" and his colleagues as "immoral," they hounded the Bauhaus out of Weimar in 1924, Grohmann related, only to see it spring up again in Dessau a year later.

Kandinsky's life in the new setting was vastly better than it had been in Weimar. From a modest apartment he and Nina moved into a double house on the edge of a lovely wooded park with Klee in the other half. Whereas in Weimar times had been so tough a collector friend had formed a "Kandinsky Society" to help the artist pay his bills (each member received a watercolor), in Dessau the Bauhaus made money from manufacturing furniture, lighting fixtures and wallpaper as well as running a printing plant. So Kandinsky was nicely compensated, especially since by then he was one of the executive directors.

After seven years with no country of their own, the Kandinskys became German citizens. So now they had passports as well as income, which enabled them to travel extensively. In addition, Kandinsky's work had come to be so well received that he had his first show in Paris. At that point his paintings had entered a phase that was geometric, intellectual, classical and cool. They had the same spirit of play and adventure, but an element of order asserted itself.

The first issue of the Bauhaus magazine celebrated Kandinsky's sixtieth birthday. It found him in a wave of reflection. Here is what he wrote to a friend: "We are really forced to stop much, much too early, at the very moment when we have begun to understand something." It sounded like Matisse. Remember his lament: "You leave your work in the middle."

Kandinsky was forced to abandon Germany in 1933 after the Nazis shut down the Bauhaus in Dessau, then blocked an effort to revive it in Berlin. His last years he spent in Paris.

It was not easy. Kandinsky was sixty-seven and once again short of money. He felt alienated from the French art world where he was regarded as "too Russian." Léger, Arp and Delaunay were friendly, and he met Miro, Mondrian, Chagall, Max Ernst, Brancusi, and Pevsner. But he took an apartment for only a year and decorated the dining room exactly like the one he had had in Dessau. The truth is he expected to return to Germany as soon as the trouble ended. Because now Germany was home.

But the trouble grew worse, and he grew attached to France. When Paris fell, he fled to the Pyrénées for a couple of months, but then returned to the capital as Picasso had done. And there he stayed for the rest of his life.

The war brought isolation and illness and finally death, in 1944. Memorial exhibitions immediately were organized, the first by the Guggenheim Foundation in New York. Gradually the world began to grasp what it had in Kandinsky. What it had was an enduring document of universal inspiration.

The early obsession of the century—a spiritual world, standing in Platonic splendor behind this one—found its most electrifying expression in Kazimir Malevich. His Suprematism, Charlotte Douglas wrote, foretold in art all that physics later would reveal. If there is a unified field, surely Malevich (along with Miro and Kandinsky) imagined best how it might be visualized.

Malevich's moment was as brief as it was brilliant. After spending his youth in Symbolist apprenticeship, painting peasants and experimenting with Cubo-Futurism, he burst into his own adventure, spirited and wildly energetic, only to be savaged by the Bolsheviks. Forced to retreat to figurative work, he embraced the idea of Russian icons and produced pictures of strength and mastery, but the magic was gone.

Malevich was born in Kiev in 1878 to Polish-Ukrainian parents who had nine children. His father worked as a manager in sugar refining and was obliged to move his family often from one rural town to another. Malevich graduated from agricultural school, but the sugar business was not for him. Already he had discovered the artistic impulse, first learning to embroider and crochet from his mother (a lasting influence, somewhat like Matisse's mother), then watching the work of artisans who came from St. Petersburg to decorate the country churches.

In time Malevich married a doctor who was also the sister-in-law of one of his brothers. He took a job as a draftsman, showed his work with an art group and had a son and a daughter. It was a normal progression for a young man of the provinces, but this was not a life that could hold him for long. He left by train for Moscow, all on his own, to study in a studio that he hoped would prepare him to pass the entrance exam for the Moscow School of Painting, Sculpture and Architecture. Like Matisse and Kandinsky, Malevich failed the exam. In fact, he failed it three times.

But he was undeterred. Malevich moved his family, including his mother, to Moscow. Before long he and his wife were divorced, and Malevich married a psychiatrist's daughter who wrote children's books. He also made an advantageous connection with the Moscow Artists' Society, which put on two shows a year. There he found his community —painters such as David Burliuk, Natalia Goncharova, and Mikhail Larionov plus a collection of poets. Together they formed the nucleus of the Russian Avant-Garde, one of the most original movements in twentieth century art.

They worked far away from the great cultural world of Paris, but they weren't ignorant of what was happening there. Shchukin made his growing collection available to them. At his house they imbibed Picasso, Matisse, and Gauguin. To this fresh impetus they added their own Slavic ancestry, producing a style that reached its apotheosis in the work of Malevich.

The Russian avant-garde had great panache and humor. Boldly they mounted exhibitions called *Jack of Diamonds*, *Donkey's Tail*, and *Target*. There were books as well, with provocative titles such as *A Trap for Judges* and *A Slap in the Face of Public Taste*. They also put on an opera called *Victory Over the Sun* with costumes and set by Malevich. And they argued passionately about art: was it born for the service of the state or was it sufficient unto itself?[20]

Certainly Malevich believed that the work of the avant-garde should transform "not only painting, poetry, sculpture and music . . . [but also] textiles, architecture, film, and technology." Like the Bauhaus, soon to follow, the Russian avant-garde committed itself to a democratic ideal of art for everyone in everyday life.

Through all of it Malevich maintained a sustained quest for a higher reality. Influenced by Aleksei Kruchenykh, a poet of the avant-garde who drew from theosophy, and other poetic compatriots, Malevich sought to depict in his painting a vision of universal truth. Just as Mondrian and Kandinsky were driven toward the spiritual realm, so was Malevich, only his sense of it was the most dynamic of them all. His was a world in motion, though suffused throughout by divine order. It was called Suprematism, and it soared in space, weightless and free. Echoing Kandinsky once again, Malevich embraced the wisdom of science, and saw in it the path to God. His flights from the earth culminated in the *Black Cross* and the *Black Square*, both, Douglas proposed, "emblematic [of the] absolute."

When Russia erupted in revolution in October, 1917, Malevich was in the army, though by then he strongly opposed World War I. Glad to see the Czar gone, he served the new regime (like Kandinsky) as head of the newly organized art section of the Moscow Soviet of Soldiers' Deputies. He moved on to other assignments in Moscow, protecting cultural treasures and teaching, and landed finally at the art school in Vitebsk, Belarus.

There Malevich had another daughter whom he named Una for Unovis, which meant Advocates for the New Art, the name of the group that gathered in Vitebsk. It was not a happy time. Conditions were so deplorable that faculty and students had to sell whatever they could, including classroom equipment and their own belongings, just to survive. Even worse, the school came under suspicion in Soviet circles. It was far too creative to be politically acceptable.

The situation was dangerous, and Malevich knew it. He decided to move to Petrograd and seek protective coloration there. It worked for awhile. In 1923, he was named director of what became the Petrograd State Institute of Artistic Culture. But he simply could not hunker down and paint the party line. A show mounted by his organization drew harsh criticism from *Pravda*. His artists were attacked as "holy crackpots," beset by "creative impotence" and producing "counterrevolutionary propaganda."

Malevich was fired, the institute was closed and nineteenth century reactionary art became the order of the hour. The only good thing that happened was Malevich was allowed to travel to Poland and Germany, something he had longed to do. He visited the Bauhaus in Dessau and exhibited his work in Warsaw and Berlin. Abruptly recalled to Russia, he left over one hundred paintings, drawings, and charts behind in Germany.

Malevich wanted desperately to return to the West one day, and if that were not possible he still believed the pieces would have a better chance at life there than in the Soviet Union. Indeed they did. Some paintings made their way to New York wrapped in the umbrella of Alfred Barr, director of the Museum of Modern Art, who feared the Nazis wouldn't let the work out of Germany. Drawings Barr stuffed in his suitcase. If anybody asked, he said they were "study materials."[21]

Once home, Malevich found the same dull horror. He was given a spot at the Institute of the History of Art, where he started painting again, this time clinging to the peasants of his early days. Some of these pictures he backdated as stand-ins for the work of his Suprematist years which would only appall the authorities if they knew about it. Before long he turned to Surrealism, with a bow to de Chirico, but that drew vituperation both ugly and ominous. His show in Kiev was closed and Malevich was vilified as a class enemy for painting in the bourgeois style of the West. Workers' committees began turning up at his studio for inspection. His chances for a sane life were over.

Malevich was jailed for two months in 1930 and interrogated about his philosophy of modern art. Once released he returned to his easel and, after a fling with Impressionism, embraced the icon as a matrix for his later years. The Soviets, in their insistent taste for "proletarian" art, had cut him off from the finest fruits of his genius, but they could not extinguish it altogether.

When Malevich grew ill with cancer, he asked permission to travel to the West for treatment. There was no response. He then requested food and medical care in Russia. Nothing was done.

In 1935 Malevich died, leaving a world that would understand only slowly the magnitude of his achievement. By the mid-1970s the Ministry of Culture in Moscow began to realize that the value of his work was rising in the Western market. (Admirers had flocked to those pictures left behind in Germany.) Paintings stored in the Russian Museum in St. Petersburg were resurrected. So was the reputation of Malevich, who blazed for merely five years, if that, but shone brightly enough to mark the art of his century with dazzling insight and innovation.

Henry Moore has been called "the Michelangelo of our times."[22] He worked on a grand scale and he reached deep into the unconscious to recover the symbols of primordial imagination. His muses were the Indian artists of Mexico. From them he divined a direct route to the human psyche. Yet his work was quintessentially public, intended for the forum, not the quiet recesses of private life. He took what had been concealed and made his truth manifest in gathering places all over the world.[23]

Moore was born to a British coal miner and his wife in 1898 in the industrial reaches of Yorkshire. He was the seventh in a brood of eight. To get the children out of the house at least once a week, his parents would send them off to Sunday school at the Congregational chapel. There young Henry first heard of Michelangelo, the "greatest sculptor who ever lived." He knew then, Roger Berthoud noted, that this was what he too wanted to be: not only a sculptor, but a great sculptor, the greatest sculptor of his era.

He was ambitious, but no student. (Few artists are.) Moore failed his first exam to win a scholarship to secondary school, but on the next try he passed it, though the work that followed was undistinguished. When he wanted to move on to art school his father protested, insisting instead that Henry train as a teacher. That was his only hope for security.

Hence Moore became a student teacher at his old elementary school. He called those days the most miserable of his life.

World War I rescued Moore from the classroom only to toss him into a German bomb attack which only a fraction of his regiment survived. Later he showed signs of mustard-gas poisoning. But for all that, his biographer, Roger Berthoud, observed that Moore's letters from France "showed a high degree of self-absorption [like Matisse] and a curious unawareness of the wider tragedy of the war." Yet his stark and poignant *Warrior with Shield*, missing an arm and a leg, done forty-five years later, embodied the residual suffering of combat, surely absorbed by Moore in that early, brutal experience.

After his return to England, a former teacher of Moore's, Alice Gostick, helped him by searching out grants for ex-soldiers. Moore got one and went to Leeds School of Art. It was a breakthrough experience. His world was expanded by the study of Assyrian, Egyptian, Chaldean, and Babylonian sculpture as well as Byzantine, Renaissance, and Gothic architecture, along with Greek and Roman masters of both. And, of course, he pursued his passion for Michelangelo.

At Leeds Moore first met Barbara Hepworth, who would become his only rival in the realm of British sculpture. They had a brief flirtation, then advanced together to the Royal College of Art in London. In time, during the thirties, they both lived in Hampstead and set to bickering over who had influenced whom the most. Hepworth suggested Moore had gotten the idea of piercing a sculpture all the way through from her. (Actually Archipenko was the first to do it, but not in stone.) In truth, as Berthoud has pointed out, they were "at heart very different artists: where Moore was dynamic, disturbing and many-layered, Hepworth was serene and classical in spirit." Yet never was he reconciled to her or her gifts. When Hepworth died in 1975, in a fire at her house in Cornwall, Moore, in a fit of mean-spiritedness, refused to do a tribute to her for the BBC.

The woman in Moore's life was Irina Radetzky, daughter of a wealthy, upper-class Russian who disappeared during the revolution of 1917. Her mother sent Irina to live with her grandmother in the Crimea. However, when the grandmother died of cancer, Irina, then eleven, was thrown on her own in a world of chaos and hunger. A teacher of handicapped children took her in and helped her get to Moscow. There Irina lived, working with her friend's students until her mother, by now in Paris with a British officer, had the child traced through the Polish embassy. Irina was smuggled out of Russia on a Polish passport.

After a few years in Paris, Irina was dispatched to England to live with the British officer's parents. She landed in a lovely Georgian house thirty miles from London. Her step-grandfather, it turned out, was chairman of a family pharmaceutical firm and in a position to give Irina a prosperous and stable life, quite unlike her mother, who was anything but reliable. Nor was the officer, who left for America and never returned.

Irina met Henry Moore when she was a painting student at the Royal College in London. He was by then thirty and working as a teaching assistant in the sculpture department while pursuing his own work. Before meeting Irina, Moore said, sounding like Matisse, "I had argued with all my friends that really serious artists shouldn't get married, they should be married to their art: Michelangelo and Beethoven weren't married, and so on. After meeting Irina I began to say Rembrandt was married. Bach had twenty children . . . ."

Irina was "a nicely rounded beauty" with great shoulders. She had "peaceful charm." And, as the years went on, bringing Henry great success, she proved to be a "steadying influence . . . . his antidote to the calls of wealth and fame, sustaining and restraining."

They wed in 1929 and moved into a studio/flat in Hampstead. Barbara Hepworth, by then herself married to another sculptor, helped them find it.

Moore developed into a remarkably practical and steady man, the sort who kept regular working hours, similar to Matisse, though Moore was spared, to some extent, the depression that hovered over his French counterpart. The only time Moore was ever close to a breakdown was in Italy on an art-student scholarship. In Florence, well before Irina, he met up with friends from the Royal College and fell in love with one of them. The problem was she was already engaged to his closest compatriot back in London and she chose to remain true to him. Moore preserved both friendships and, when the time came for their wedding, he performed as best man. But the emotional cost was high. Also, Berthoud believed Moore suffered from a overdose of culture in Italy with no time to work off strong emotions through his own art.

Moore returned to England riddled with conflict. "The master works" of Europe, he said, had collided with all his "previous ideals." He consoled himself with the "ancient Mexican art in the British Museum" and found his way back to archaic forms, in defiance of the glories of the Renaissance. It was a great help that he got to know Jacob Epstein, a New York sculptor living in London, whose embrace of African motifs was an inspiration to Moore as well, confirming his own response to the ethnic impulse.

What followed was the beginning of the great reclining figures, first in stone and cast concrete, later in elmwood and bronze. To Eric Neumann, the Jungian, these monumental female forms became "more and more clearly the archetype of the earth goddess."[24] Berthoud called one of the early works "a romantic fusion of the eternally feminine and the spirit of the land." Influenced by Picasso and the sculptor, Hans Arp, Moore dug beneath the soil of the century and found there the wisdom of ages. A work of art, he said, was "an expression of the significance of life, a stimulation to a greater effort at living."

By 1930, a year after his marriage, Moore was thought to be one of England's best artists. Of course, he attracted the usual abuse ("the cult of ugliness," and "freak potato" art), but Moore also drew to himself crucial support from Herbert Read, the critic, and Kenneth Clark, youthful director of the National Gallery. Moore was greatly aided as well by the British Council which sent his work on exhibition all over the world. Twice Moore was chosen by the council to represent Britain at the Venice Biennale. In 1947, he won the prize as best sculptor, edging out Henri Laurens of France. Braque beat Rouault as top painter that year, and Chagall captured the award as preeminent engraver. (What a lineup. It makes one weep for the Biennales of the nineties, when Venice was lost in limbo.)

Before that triumph, on the eve of war, Moore lived at the center of an expatriate world, as artists fled Europe for Hampstead. Mondrian was there for a time, before the blitz drove him on to New York. So were Walter Gropius, Marcel Breuer, and László Moholy-Nagy, all refugees from the Bauhaus, shut down by Hitler in 1933. Freud, ill and dying, arrived in 1938, though there is little evidence that he mixed with the artists, though the work of one, Henry Moore, was deeply psychological, and all of them drew upon the Freudian suspicion of conventional surface appearances.

Those years before the Second World War were a time of public action for Moore. He allied himself with Artists International, a group formed to galvanize creative opinion against Fascism, colonialism and aggression toward the Soviet Union. So dedicated was Moore he was asked to join the Communist Party, but declined, saying that "was an active role I didn't want to have."

He did join Jacob Epstein and Herbert Read in a group that sent letters to editors in support of the International Peace Campaign. But when Mussolini invaded Abyssinia, Japan moved against China and Hitler launched his terror in Europe, Moore turned tough-minded and put his name on a missive to the *Yorkshire Post* that asked, "Are we to stand aside while these forces complete the wreck of our civilization?" He raised money to resettle German artists who had fled to Czechoslovakia only to be undone by Munich, and he almost went on a mission to Spain with Epstein, Stephen Spender, Paul Robeson, and others. But the British government refused to allow the trip.

When the war spread to England, Moore took part in an effort chaired by Kenneth Clark to make a record, in drawings, of the national experience. Moore sketched Londoners sleeping in the underground, hiding from the Battle of Britain. This was some of his most moving work. Maynard Keynes, the economist, bought a Moore shelter drawing. So did Kenneth Clark.

By now Henry and Irina had joined the exodus from London. They gave up the studio in Hampstead they had taken over from Barbara Hepworth and Ben Nicholson (to whom she was now married, having parted from her first husband—together they struck out for Cornwall with their triplets, a nursemaid and a cook). The Moores also left the house they had bought in Kent (too vulnerable to German bombs) and found the place where they would spend the rest of their lives—in Much Haddam, northeast of the capital.

The house, a seventeenth century farm structure, was called Hoglands. The Moores lived there in utter simplicity even as their fortunes flourished. The did add a sitting room in the back, and, over the years, nine studios. The garden grew larger. A small park for sculpture was acquired, also a low-key holiday house in Italy. There were some paintings by Cézanne, Seurat, Vuillard, Degas, Millet, and Courbet. But there was also about the Moores a marked restraint in the uses of the considerable wealth that came to them. Before they died, they put millions into the Henry Moore Foundation for the benefit of art and culture.

Henry Moore was, in fact, a man of rural England. "With his shortish, stocky physique, ruddy countryman's complexion, and tweedy taste in clothes," wrote Berthoud, "he might have been a well-to-do Yorkshire farmer." An extrovert, he loved to have visitors at Much Haddam, and he was very good at selling himself. But he also had an addiction to work, similar, once again, to Matisse. Like Matisse, in fact, Moore saw work as an answer to depression. "I get depressed when I'm not working enough," he said." . . . [W]orking is a way of not becoming depressed."

In 1946, at the age of thirty-nine, after several miscarriages, Irina gave birth to the Moores' only child, Mary. Her father doted on her even when, as an adult, she had notorious, noisy fights with him. One of the great hurts of his life was when Mary and her husband left Much Haddam and moved to South Africa with their little boy Gus, Moore's adored grandchild. They returned five years later, with two more offspring, Jane and Henry, but they were careful to settle in Dorset, a three-hour drive from her parents' house.

In a way not typical of many artists, Moore had, according to Berthoud, a "deep respect for the social fabric." He served as a trustee of the Tate Gallery and the National Gallery and on the National Theatre board. In his politics he was a moderate socialist. He deplored the Soviet

Gulag and the invasion of Hungary, and he embraced many causes including an end to capital punishment; help for intellectuals in Hungary, Poland, and Mexico; opposition to treason trials in South Africa; and nuclear disarmament. He said no to a knighthood, believing that if people had to call him Sir Henry it would distance them from him. He did, however, permit himself to be named a Companion of Honor, a high tribute since there are only fifty of these in Britain at one time. In addition, President François Mitterand of France traveled to Much Haddam to present Moore, by then frail and ailing, with the Order of the Commander of the Legion of Honor.

Moore was extraordinarily concerned about his place in history. A dealer recalled that the sculptor would ask him: who's the greatest of them all? He sensed that what was wanted in reply was "Michelangelo, Rodin, and Moore." Then he would disparage contemporaries: Giacometti, he said, was "good but overrated . . . ." Brancusi was too limited in range. And "minimal art," he said, "is for minimal minds."

By this time, Berthoud quoted an admirer, Moore's sculpture "had become so much part of the landscape that a considerable effort was required actually to see it." His imposing bronze figures graced public buildings from Lincoln Center in New York to the city halls of Dallas and Toronto (though not without controversy in the last two). And environmentalists adopted him as their own because of the organic nature of his work.

It's not surprising that younger artists began to snipe. Anthony Caro, the sculptor, once an assistant to Moore, wrote that Henry was isolated at Hoglands and past his moment. He also signed a letter to *The Times* protesting the Labor Government's plan to give matching funds to the Tate for an extension designed to house the sculptures that Moore intended to give the museum. Moore was hurt. Caro was contrite. But the special building never materialized. Moore made the gift anyway, once the Tate acquired more exhibition space.

In 1983, prostate surgery undermined Moore's health and left him in precarious circumstances, ill as often as not. He died three years later, at the age of eighty-eight.

Moore was widely acknowledged as a man of Britain. The *Melbourne Age* called him "the one true sculptor upon a big scale who has matured in England since the Middle Ages." A Belgian artist said that "Henry Moore has accomplished for the prestige of British art what Nelson did for the British navy." At home he was acclaimed as "the greatest living Englishman," and when he died, as "the most honoured abroad since Churchill."

Yet Moore individuated in relation to earthier cultures, especially those of pre-Columbian Mexico. When his work was shown there, a gallery invitation said this: "Moore speaks in a language we believe we know. A man who has never been in Mexico . . . becomes one of the best and most authentic representatives . . . of the spirit of our ancestors . . . . Confronted with his work, we know we are in the presence of an artist of genius, a great creator."

His genius grew within the bounds of a simple life, domestically placid, but informed by deep currents of earlier energy that recalled the lives of people he would never know. Symbols both ethnically exotic and emotionally profound bubbled up in his psyche and animated his work. They made Moore a sculptor of primeval power.

Moore believed in the moral imperative of art. He sought spiritual vitality in his work. Was he the greatest sculptor of the twentieth century, as he so longed to be? Not necessarily. Brancusi had the same transcendence as Moore, though not on as grand a scale. Both were bathed in universal knowledge. They brought deep composure to tormented times.

Where Moore had strength, Brancusi had magic. His carvings are classical, spare, pared-down, primordial. They have about them an aura of inevitability, as if they could not have been other than they are. They resonate with the peace of resolution, free of factors that would complicate.

Constantin Brancusi, however, did not live an uncomplicated life, much as he tried to. He was born in Romania, a richly shadowed part of the world, in a town called Hobitza, in 1876. His biographer, Radu Varia, called this land "a repository of ancient European civilizations, redolent with Celtic mythology . . ."

Brancusi was his parents' sixth son. His father was a farmer, his mother, a spinner descended from a family of priests. Brancusi had a great-grandfather, in fact, who built a wooden church with his own hands and bequeathed to the sculptor, across many years, a mystical spirit that would inform all his work.

The boy grew up deep in the valley of the Carpathian mountains with the Danube River nearby. Summers he spent as a shepherd, until he ran away from home at the age of seven, then again at ten, after his father died, leaving the family in harsh circumstances. The second escape was meant to last. Brancusi went to work as a dyer's apprentice and then moved on, still a child but quite on his own, to Craiova, where he got a job in a liquor store and later with a grocer. A local church gave him a scholarship to the School of Crafts. After graduating he studied in Bucharest, staving off poverty as a dishwasher in a fashionable brasserie.

While in Craiova, Brancusi also sang in a choir, and Varia speculated that he got involved with a fraternity of stone and wood carvers. It was the members of this guild, Varia believed, who supported Brancusi during his exhausting walk to Paris, in his late twenties. By then he had sold his interest in his father's land, and that helped some, but not nearly enough.

En route to Paris, in Lunéville, Brancusi fell dangerously ill with pleural pneumonia. His consolation was a book by Helena Blavatsky, the sage of Mondrian, whose thinking seeped again and again into the culture of the times. While her theosophy was not for Brancusi, he did absorb from her the notion of cycles, stretching back to primal origins which, if ever apprehended, had the power to bestow a destiny.

But what awaited Brancusi in Paris, along with destiny, was the need to support himself. Once more he signed on as a dishwasher. He also applied to the government in Bucharest for a small subsidy and attached himself to the Romanian church where he took an official part in services.

Brancusi showed up at Rodin's studio, and there he did well, at least in his own estimation. "I worked faster and better than the others," he said. But he didn't stay. Three months later, he left, declaring, "Nothing grows in the shade of great trees." (Matisse also found he could not connect with Rodin.) The master understood. "In the long run he's right," observed Rodin of Brancusi. "He's just as stubborn as I am."

His stubbornness paid off. The year 1907 was pivotal for Brancusi, just as it was for Picasso. That was when the Spaniard broke through to Cubism with *Les Demoiselles d'Avignon* and the Romanian created *Wisdom of the Earth*, and *The Prayer*, a haunting figure commissioned for a cemetery in his homeland. Both pieces use the female presence to capture the agonizing dignity of human experience. Brancusi called *The Prayer*, a second spiritual birth for him.

In 1907, Brancusi also did his first *Kiss*, which he called his "road to Damascus." Within a few years *Sleeping Muse* followed, that elegant oval head which was further refined into *The Beginning of the World*. No marble egg was ever so suffused with serene possibility. He also pursued

Birds in Space. ("Like everything else I've ever done, there was a furious struggle to rise heavenward," he explained.) And *Fish.* (Of these he noted that he never tried to give an accurate account of fins and scales. "I want just the flash of its spirit.")

African art never meant as much to Brancusi as it did to Picasso. He did some pieces with African motifs, but then turned away from them. They conflicted, Varia believed, with Brancusi's own sense of magic. African art was concerned with powers in this world. Brancusi dealt only with the realm beyond our own.

Though women were seldom at the center of Brancusi's life, he did find them appealing. According to Varia, he spent the good years, when fame was plentiful, squiring "spectacular young ladies," some from society, to "the most exclusive places."

He did have a "dark, destructive" affair with Marie Bonaparte, wife of Prince George of Greece and later mistress of a French prime minister as well as a follower of Freud. One good thing came out of their relationship—the handsome sculpture *Princesse X*, a highly abstracted portrait of Marie. Invited to exhibit the piece at the Salon des Indépendents, Brancusi carried it to the Grand Palais from Montparnasse in a wheelbarrow only to have the police attack the carving as "phallic and obscene." Before they ordered it removed, Picasso saw the work and exclaimed, "What a great cock!"

Brancusi found true love with Eileen Lane, a dark-haired Irish beauty whom he met through Ezra Pound. He was forty-six. She was thirty. She brought joy and light to his middle years. Indeed she was the only woman he ever took home to Hobitza.

Eileen Lane understood Brancusi's inner urgency and secret strivings. She knew who he was. "He maintained a close link with the mystery of the earth," she wrote, "and at the same time had an inherent enigmatic gift for understanding things that came to him from the invisible, from another world surpassing our understanding."

Lane saw Brancusi for the last time in 1939. "War had just broken out," she said. "I found him infinitely sad, weary in the depths . . . After the war, I often called him from the United States [where she married] and we had long talks. The last time I called it was just before his end. He was too weak to go to the telephone. I understood then that I would never see him again in this life."

Before World War I, Brancusi had substantial support from Romanians, who offered both public commissions and private purchases.

Then, in 1914, an American collector, John Quinn, appeared, and over the next ten years acquired twenty-four sculptures. The French never warmed to Brancusi's work, but museum officials nonetheless pressed him to agree to leave his studio to them after his death. Brancusi became a French citizen to seal the understanding.

Though he lived in Paris as if he were "at home in his native village," looking like a "shepherd from the high hills" and cooking his own food with his sculpture tools, Brancusi was sometimes reclusive but not isolated. James Joyce (whom he also met through Ezra Pound) was a close friend. So were Erik Satie, Marcel Duchamp, Léger, and Modigliani.[25]

When Brancusi reached his later years he left off wearing blue, a shade he loved (blue was Kandinsky's favorite too, also Picasso's) and clothed himself only in white. Blue, he felt, was right for youth, while white was for maturity. It was the color of "great creators and sages." His studio he also made white, like Mondrian's.

Brancusi was not a man of books, though he did admire Giambattista Vico. There was one writing, however, that captured him for the rest of his life. It was by Jetsun Milarepa, an eleventh century Tibetan mystic. So strong was his identification with the ancient master from the Himalayas that Brancusi "believed himself to be the reincarnation of Milarepa."

Like Milarepa, Brancusi practiced solitude. Like Milarepa he was drawn to order. From Milarepa he learned, as Varia put it, that "all is pilgrimage, departure, with everything fatally returning to its point of departure, but equally attaining, with each successive rotation, a higher level than before."

For Brancusi, life was predestined. "All that I had to do, I had to do," he said. And what he had to do, or try to do, was "attain sainthood."

He returned to Romania to accomplish his last great work, *Endless Column*, *Table of Silence* and *Gate of the Kiss at Târgu-Jiu*. It was not just sculpture that he created there, it was an atmosphere, anchored in the earth by a gate of expectation and a table ready to be spread with the bread of life, but soaring, through the tall, tall column, reaching high to heaven.

After that, Brancusi's work was over. The strain of creating sculpture while sustaining saintly aspirations had exhausted him. Better perhaps the profanity of Picasso when it comes to making art than a spirit that strives too hard to transcend itself.

Brancusi lived twenty years more, but a fatal detachment set in. "I no longer belong to the world," he said. "I am far from myself . . . I am already a part of essential things."

No doubt he was, or hoped to be. But still he felt despondent. Solitude overtook him, not the kind of solitude that deepens and refreshes, but the sort that deadens the heart. So did failing health. He didn't fight, wrote Varia. "He simply waited for the end."

The end came, in 1957. Brancusi was eighty-one.

His work remains—pure, solid, evocative, reassuring us that life has inner order and the world has inner truths of which we can only dream.

The most luminous, and troubled, artist of his time was Mark Rothko. His canvases are a glimpse of glory, bathed in the harmony of heaven, but they sprang from a soul that struggled daily with the tyranny of despair.

"I do think there was a great vacuum at the center of his being," said Rothko's friend Stanley Kunitz. Yet he never tried to fill the void with things. Rothko wrestled with his own emptiness the way prophets spar with angels, and from that continual confrontation came paintings of pure enlightenment. His rectangles, numinous, immanent, alive with the shades of the sunset, or darkened like the night sky, are the work of a man whom many called a rabbi of art.

Marcus Rothkowitz was born in 1903 in Dvinsk, a small town in Russia. Drenched in poverty, it was nestled in the Settlement of Pale where most of the country's five million Jews were confined, and often violated by pogroms. They were not allowed to own property, so most of them ran shops, including Rothko's father, Jacob, who had a pharmacy.

The Rothkowitz family loved books and practiced politics. Often Jacob would hold dissident meetings at his house even though they were forbidden by the Russian government. Rothko's father was passionately Marxism but hostile to orthodox Jews who dominated the community. All that changed when pogroms caused him to embrace orthodoxy and even send his son Marcus to a strict religious school while his other two sons were trained to be pharmacists and his daughter a dentist. Rothko rebelled in time, but by then his family was regrouping in Portland, Oregon.

Jacob was the first to emigrate, followed by the two older boys. Finally Marcus, his mother and his sister sailed to America, second class, landing in Brooklyn. What greeted them when they arrived in Oregon was the debilitating anti-Semitism. Portland was only 10 percent Jewish, and the WASPs reigned with callousness, excluding Jews from the debating club in high school (Marcus was a fine debater) and predicting in the yearbook that Rothko would become a "pawnbroker." Even so, had the Rothkowitzes stayed in Dvinsk, it's highly unlikely they would have survived the First World War much less the Nazi purge of World War II.

None of this could help the heart of Marcus Rothkowitz, however. He resented being forced to move to America, and he felt always like an exile there. He grew lonely and melancholy and lived a life apart from the normal flow of things, withdrawn inside himself and given to depression, which only deepened with the death of his father. By then his brothers and sister were married, so Rothko lived with his mother, the redoubtable Kate, whose strength upheld them both.

Rothko won a scholarship to Yale, but he stayed only two years before going to New York to explore either art or theatre. Before long he returned to Portland and got involved in an acting company run by the woman who would become Clark Gable's first wife. Then it was back to New York, where he was refused subsidized admission to the American Laboratory Theatre but admitted to the New School of Design. There he took a class with Arshile Gorky and began the demanding journey to eminence as a painter.

Rothko suffered for his art. The early years he spent hungry, poor, sleeping in subways, or even a bathtub. His education was brief. After eight months in another program he left to teach himself, working occasionally in the garment district to make some money.

In 1932, Rothko married Edith Sachar. Franklin D. Roosevelt had just been elected president, and the worst days of the Depression lay ahead. Both of them taught children part-time at the Brooklyn Jewish Center. He led classes in art, she in crafts. Edith also worked for a dress shop and in FDR's Works Progress Administration. (So did Rothko.) In time she started a business designing and selling silver jewelry. It made her the main earner in the household, which suited Mark perfectly. It meant he could pursue his painting.[26]

Artistic communities opened up for Rothko, first around Milton Avery (a father figure) where Barnett Newman and Adolph Gottlieb also gathered, then at the Ten, a group of Jewish painters including Gottlieb. Their work, according to James Breslin, was marked by "inwardness, its origins in the private self." It was the beginning of Expressionism in America.

Robert Motherwell later said that Rothko pursued a "collective intimacy." He wanted from the group a sense of family and the kind of community he had lost when he broke with orthodox Judaism. All his life he sought "companionship from men, consolation from women, and adulation from both . . . ."

There was not much consolation from Edith. She came to feel her husband was living like a parasite off her efforts and her income. They separated, then reconciled, and Edith persuaded Mark to work as a salesman in her jewelry business. This he detested. Finally they were divorced and Mark collapsed into a breakdown. He liked the regularity of marriage. Being without Edith was desolating to him. Being without her financial support hurt too.

But Marcus Rothkowitz carried on, becoming an American citizen in 1938 and a few years later changing his name to Mark Rothko. It was not long before he married again.

"I was a foreigner and she made an American out of me," said Rothko of Mary Alice (Mell) Beistle. Middle-class and WASP, Mell grew up in Cleveland and went to Skidmore, then landed in New York with a job at a publishing company that put out magazines such as *True Confessions* and *True Story*. Nineteen years younger than Rothko, she brought him warmth and utter adoration. She also earned a living as a commercial artist, freeing her husband to leave his part-time teaching post and devote himself entirely to his own art.

This arrangement shifted when their daughter Kate was born. Then Mell stopped working and Mark became an assistant professor in Brooklyn College's Department of Design.

These were enormously fertile years for Rothko. Cloistered in his studio, with Mozart all around him, he explored mythology and symbols of the archaic. When several Surrealists, including Max Ernst, André Breton and Marcel Duchamp, fled to New York during World War II, he fell under their influence. By 1950 he was on the verge of the signature style that would ever after be synonymous with his name. It was soon clear that no one could animate a room like Rothko. His stacked rectangles exuded transcendence, promising that matter could indeed be made into energy, as Einstein promised, and the spiritual power that resulted could last many lifetimes.

Rothko's community grew in those years to encompass a gathering of giants—Robert Motherwell, Jackson Pollock, Willem de Kooning, Franz Kline, Barnett Newman, and Clyfford Still. These were the

Abstract Expressionists who made New York the center of world art, leaving Paris to ponder its memories of other eras. They grouped themselves into two camps: the downtowners (de Kooning, Kline, and Pollock), who met in Greenwich Village bars, and the uptowners (Rothko, Newman, Motherwell, and Gottlieb), who collected mainly at the home of Herbert Ferber, an artist who made money as a dentist and thus could afford to entertain.

Downtown, the men wore jeans and T-shirts and cavorted with violent abandon. Uptown the dress was suits, the demeanor much more subdued. There was cross-pollination between the two enclaves, but each artist remained solitary and apart from the others. They never collaborated in the manner of Picasso and Braque. Nor did they form a movement like the Surrealists. But they shared a common moment and a common experience, Breslin related, until discord and jealousy made the sharing impossible.

Rothko's ruptures with Newman and Still were especially painful. He yearned for their return, but it never happened. Gottlieb also drifted away, and Rothko refused to see Milton Avery, his one-time father figure, when the older man had a heart attack. Avery's wife said Rothko feared sick people because they might cause him to have the same symptoms.

Rothko had symptoms of his own. Depression struck him again when his mother died. It sapped his spirit but deepened his work.

Dealers had long since recognized the promise of Mark Rothko. Peggy Guggenheim showed his pictures until she moved to Venice. Then Betty Parsons took over. She was wonderful at nurturing artists but not good at selling their paintings. Sidney Janis, a businessman, was. So Rothko, Pollock, Newman, and Still deserted Parsons for Janis. It paid off.

Even the Museum of Modern Art began taking notice of Mark Rothko. Alfred Barr, the director, asked architect Philip Johnson to buy a Rothko and give it to MoMA. That way the trustees, not ready yet for so singular an artist, would be less likely to turn it down.

The trustees came 'round to Rothko, however. In 1961, the museum mounted a one-man show of his work. He was, James Breslin remarked, the "first living member of his generation" to be so honored. Though unable to suppress his resentment that MoMA had not rallied sooner, during the desperate days, Rothko hovered over the exhibition, demanding, as he always did, that the paintings be close together so as to obliterate the wall and dominate the ambience.

Rothko became so established as an important painter that Philip Johnson asked him to do a series of murals for the new Four Seasons Restaurant he was designing for the Seagram Building. Rothko was ambivalent because he despised the expected clientele which he called "the richest bastards in New York." Nonetheless, he set to work producing panels that were dark, somber, mysterious. Some didn't satisfy him, so he sold them and started over again. At the end of two years, he declared, "These are not pictures . . . I have made a place."

Unfortunately, Mark and Mell Rothko had dinner at the Four Seasons before his project was installed. He was horrified. He thought he had "made a place," but it was Philip Johnson who actually had made the place, along with high-powered designers of many callings. Rothko couldn't bear to put the hallowed environment of his imagination into such a commercial setting even if it was elegant. He withdrew his pictures and returned the commission, reassuring himself that he had not been corrupted by good fortune after all. Rothko was still the "embattled outsider."

He got another chance to create a sacred space when John and Dominique de Menil invited him to Houston to bring into being the Rothko Chapel. They also asked Philip Johnson to do the design. Johnson and Rothko were hardly attuned to each other after the Seagram's affair. They quarreled over the details, the de Menils backed Rothko, and the architect resigned. A replacement from Houston completed the building, and Rothko filled it with fourteen paintings, though he did not live to hang them himself.

Rothko had an aneurysm in 1968. From that day forward he lived a restricted life, mired in depression. His habits were no help. He smoked, ate too much and took his first drink of the day at ten a.m., in his studio. Other drinks would follow, every hour. Rothko, steeped in the dark philosophies of Kierkegaard and Nietzsche, was giving in to his own shadow side. But there was no anti-depressant help for him. Ann Douglas called Rothko and his circle the "last unmedicated artists." Psychopharmacology, she said, belongs to post-modernism.[27]

Success did not set well with Rothko. The four-story house on East 95th near Park Ave. brought him only anxiety, and the Cape Cod property was no comfort either. Rothko claimed he hated nature and so he was alienated from a source of solace.

The world of art and money was a torment to him. Though he wanted his pictures to sell, of course, he suffered mightily when his mystical rectangles became a commodity, a brand name, a stamp of prestige for collectors.

Rothko didn't like the business of art, and he did badly at it. Nor was he good at choosing his associates. Foremost among his mistakes was allowing Bernard Reis, a lawyer turned accountant, to represent him. Reis maneuvered himself into the role of cunning father figure, urging Rothko to depend on him for everything, which the artist was only too eager to do. Reis steered Rothko into an association with Marlborough-Gerson Gallery, whose owner, Frank Lloyd was fond of saying, "I don't collect pictures; I collect money." The problem was that Reis also did accounting for Marlborough. While he took no payment for the work he did for Rothko, aside from an occasional gift of a painting (no small consideration), his relationship with both the gallery and the artist was a clear conflict of interest, as a court later would find.

Mell too was strained and relying heavily on alcohol. After the MoMA show, she found herself pressed into a social world where she was seldom recognized, much less valued. The marriage survived through the birth of a son, Christopher, when Rothko was sixty, but it fell apart six years later. Mark separated from Mell and began an affair with the young widow of Ad Reinhardt.

Life was closing in on Mark Rothko, and nothing could make it bearable. Frank Lloyd had long since been selling the artist's pictures in New York, not just Europe, in violation of their contract. Prices were often different from those agreed upon. Still Reis pressed constantly for more sales to Marlborough. Rothko began to wonder whose side his father-adviser was really on. The artist felt devastated, unprotected, betrayed.

In February, 1970, in the gray light of winter, Rothko took a slug of anti-depressant medication, then slashed his forearms below the elbow with a double-edged razor blade.

In a will drawn up by Bernard Reis, Rothko left almost eight hundred pictures to his foundation, a staggering bequest. Reis, and two other executors of the estate, quickly sold the works to Marlborough at deflated prices without telling their fellow directors. The executors then took the proceeds and divided them three ways as fees. Rothko's children sued in what became the most famous case in art history. Reis and the other executors were found guilty of "breach of duty of loyalty."[28]

No one needed loyalty more than Mark Rothko. Uprooted as a child, abandoned by his father who died too young, beset by anti-Semitism, ignored for years by the art world, let down by wives upon whom he depended, he was singularly unable to withstand the machinations of Frank ("I collect money") Lloyd, who later was convicted of keeping false records to hide his sale of Rothko paintings,[29] and smooth, insinuating Bernard Reis. Rothko was too tired to fight, and he had never been equipped for fighting anyway.

Rothko's gift was the gift of spirit. "He had a great deal of dignity, and he had dignity that comes from very serious, long religious background," said Louise Bourgeois. "His demeanor was that of a prophet."[30] Rothko married ancient insights to modern mysticism. The world he intuited was wholly transcendent. He strove for iconic images, Breslin remarked, rendered in radiant color or sometimes in shadow, that would convey cosmic harmony and hope.

Spiritual longing marked the major artists of the twentieth century. Even the earthiest of them, Picasso, sought exorcising magic in African carvings, and the supreme master of sensuality, Matisse, believed he worked in a religious context. Moore pursued archetypal truths through archaic resonance. Mondrian searched for universal absolutes. So did Kandinsky and Malevich in ways that echoed the world of physics. Brancusi brought to his sculpture the simplicity of the seer. And Rothko turned torment into luminous expectation.

Many struggled with depression. Few achieved satisfying marriages. Some were easily bored, others self-absorbed. All of them were strictly disciplined, devoting long and regular hours to their efforts. Taken together, their work documents the deepest examination of ultimate reality since the Middle Ages.

They took the romantic objects of earlier creations and broke them into pieces, sometimes obliterating them altogether, leaving their canvases clear, their sculpture pared down to essential elements. Theirs were the shattered images of art, but those shattered images were a glimpse of eternal truth. Whether perceived in the symbols of science, divined in forms archaic or radically pure, drawn from the earth or expressed in the language of lyricism, this work marked the twentieth century as a time of spiritual questing. It ended with the death of Henry Moore in 1986. Since then, art has been drained of serious intention.

Chapter
Six

Virginia Woolf
*Virginia Woolf brought to her books
an elegance of language and forcefulness
of mind that made her the foremost writer
of our time.*

When Women Writers Came Into Their Own

*It is an extraordinary thing that in all those
arts and all those exercises wherein at any time
women have thought fit to play a part in real
earnest, they have always become most
excellent and famous in no common way.*
Giorgio Vasari

The genius of the twentieth century found its truest literary expression in the novel. While the form goes back at least four hundred years, and certainly flourished in the 1800s, it was in our own time that the novel achieved dominance. ". . . [N]o poet of our century," wrote Harold Bloom, "has matched *In Search of Lost Time*, *Ulysses*, or *Finnegan's Wake* . . . ." Not even Yeats, Rilke and Stevens, he added, spoke with a voice as attuned to the age as Proust and Joyce.[1]

Giants they are, Proust and Joyce, but their achievement cannot obscure the high literary moment of the era—the emergence of women writers. While the masculine sensibility has certainly brought brilliance to twentieth century letters, the age has been distinctly open to the feminine. And it was the ascendancy of the novel that made this apotheosis possible.

The novel is so private, so susceptible to the material of domesticity and the interior life that it seemed born for the special circumstances of women. Drama required productions, theaters, money—the purview of men. So drama was out except in a few cases. Poetry might have worked for women, and indeed in nineteenth century America it did glorify the gifts of Emily Dickinson. But the genre had long since been preempted by men in a way that the novel had not.

The novel was to poetry as painting was to architecture. Women were thought, however unjustly, to be less adept as engineers either of stone or the spirit. Broad brushwork, on page or canvas, seemed somehow to suit them better. This surely will change in the age to come.

Even so, the feminine imagination has been so successful these past hundred years that Harold Bloom was moved to reach back many centuries and declare the author of *Genesis*, *Exodus*, and *Numbers* a woman. And not just a woman, but "a writer of the stature of Homer, Shakespeare, and Tolstoy . . . ." Said to be "of the royal house living at King Solomon's court,"[2] J certainly would have fit Virginia Woolf's dictum that for a woman to write she had to have a little money and a room of one's own. We must suppose that the ruler was wise enough to make these available to her.

A room of one's own Virginia Woolf certainly had. It was a "lodge" built against the garden wall at Monk's House in Rodmell.[3] There she sat, each morning without fail and many afternoons, filling her notebooks with small meticulous script, shaping her fiction (alternated with criticism or what she called her "journalism"), churning out letters, maintaining her diary. As a young woman growing up, she also had the free run of her father's library, compensation perhaps for the Cambridge education only her brothers were allowed.

A little money she had as well (a legacy from a great aunt), but her books never earned much until she was in her forties. Then *Mrs. Dalloway* and *The Common Reader* brought in enough to install two water closets in Monk's House and *Orlando* produced the wherewithal for Woolf to add a new wing for herself with a writing room downstairs and bedroom above. Nonetheless, she thought of her life as limited, writing once of Vita Sackville-West, her intimate friend, "being so much in full sail on the high tides, where I am coasting down backwaters . . . ."[4]

But in those backwaters she brought forth a body of work that suggests she was more insightful than Proust and more lyrical than Joyce. Indeed she did not respond well to Joyce though she conceded he might have been "underrated."[5] *Ulysses* she called a "disaster."[6] "[N]ever did any book so bore me," she confided in a letter to Gerald Brenan,[7] though by the end of her life she saw him somewhat differently. This she wrote of Joyce in her diary:

> Then Joyce is dead, Joyce about a fortnight younger than I am. I remember Miss Weaver, in wool gloves, bringing *Ulysses* in typescript to our teatable at Hogarth House. Roger [Fry] I think sent her. Would we devote our lives to printing it [on the press

she ran with her husband Leonard]? The indecent pages looked so incongruous: she was spinsterly, buttoned up. And the pages reeled with indecency. I put it in a drawer of the inlaid cabinet. One day Katherine Mansfield came, and I had it out. She began to read, ridiculing: then suddenly said, "But there's something in this: a scene that should figure I suppose in the history of literature."[8]

Proust she admired without ambivalence. Proust she acclaimed as "far the greatest modern novelist . . . ."[9] Next to his prose "everything else appeared insipid and worthless."[10]

"There is no subtler ironist than Proust in our century . . . ." So says Harold Bloom who also attributes to Proust great wisdom: "*Search*," he writes (Bloom insists that Proust's towering work be called *In Search of Lost Time*, not *Remembrance of Things Past*), "is wisdom literature." And this wisdom, for Bloom, proceeds directly from the power of art and narrative:

> Aesthetic salvation is the enterprise of his vast novel; Proust challenges Freud as the major mythmaker of the Chaotic Era [Bloom's epithet for the twentieth century]. The story he creates is a visionary romance depicting how the narrator matures from Marcel into the novelist Proust, who in the book's final volume reforms his consciousness and is able to shape his life into a new form of wisdom.[11]

No doubt this is true. Proust quickly confirms the insight of Harold Bloom: "What brings men together is not a community of views but a consanguinity of minds." But for Proust, minds are saturated always by memory: "The memory of a particular image is but regret for a particular moment; and houses, roads, avenues are as fugitive, alas, as the years."

Moments are captured, however, in things, irradiating always our lives with intimations of divinity, however lost it may sometimes seem. Proust's narrator reflects:

> But when a belief vanishes, there survives it—more and more vigorously so as to cloak the absence of the power, now lost to us, of imparting reality to new things—a fetishistic attachment to the old things which it did once animate, as if it was in them and

not in ourselves that the divine spark resided, and as if our present incredulity had a contingent cause—the death of the gods.

Elegant, all of it, and some of it profound, but what's missing is the struggle in the deep recesses of the soul. For that we must turn to Virginia Woolf. Informed by recurring depression, she fought to find light in nihilism and to ameliorate her melancholy with the delights of daily living or to submerge it in work. She writes in her diary:

And so I pitched into my great lake of melancholy. Lord how deep it is! What a born melancholic I am! The only way I keep afloat is by working. A note for the summer—I must take more work than I can possibly get done.—No, I don't know what it comes from. Directly I stop working I feel that I am sinking down, down. And as usual I feel that if I sink further I shall reach the truth. That is the only mitigation; a kind of nobility. Solemnity. I shall make myself face the fact that there is nothing—nothing for any of us. Work, reading, writing are all disguises; and relations with people. Yes, even having children would be useless.

Now is life very solid or very shifting? I am haunted by the two contradictions. This has gone on for ever; will last for ever; goes down to the bottom of the world—this moment I stand on. Also it is transitory, flying, diaphanous. I shall pass like a cloud on the waves. Perhaps it may be that though we change, one flying after another, so quick, so quick, yet we are somehow successive and continuous we human beings, and show the light through. But what is the light? I am impressed by the transitoriness of human life to such an extent that I am often saying a farewell—after dining with Roger for instance; or reckoning how many more times I shall see Nessa.[12]

The narrator of *Orlando* muses:

Here, have lived for more centuries than I can count, the obscure generations of my own obscure family. Not one of these Richards, Johns, Annes, Elizabeths has left a token behind him, yet all, working together with their spades and their needles, their love-making and their child-bearing, have left this.

Never had the house looked more noble and humane.

Why, then, had he wished to raise himself above them? For it seemed vain and arrogant in the extreme to try to better that anonymous work of creation; the labours of those vanished hands. Better was it to go unknown and leave behind you an arch, a potting shed, a wall where peaches ripen, than to burn like a meteor and leave no dust. For after all, he said, kindling as he looked at the great house on the greensward below, the unknown lords and ladies who lived there never forgot to set aside something for those who come after; for the roof that will leak; for the tree that will fall. There was always a warm corner for the old shepherd in the kitchen; always food for the hungry; always their goblets were polished, though they lay sick; and the windows were lit though they were dying. Lords though they were, they were content to go down into obscurity with the mole-catcher and the stonemason. Obscure noblemen, forgotten builders—thus he apostrophised them with a warmth that entirely gainsaid such critics as called him cold, indifferent, slothful (the truth being that a quality often lies just on the other side of the wall from where we seek it) . . . .

Is there not here a richness, an earthiness, an engagement with life somehow missing from Proust, however luscious the prose?

As for Joyce, he and Woolf arrived and departed this world almost simultaneously: Both lived from 1882 to 1941. Both were heavily influenced by the fluency and elegance of Walter Pater. Both were adventurers in their novels, taking huge risks, launching bold experiments with stream of consciousness. But while "Joyce believed he was equal to Shakespeare in his gifts and scope,"[13] Woolf, though well aware of her genius if not burdened by it, was content to be a woman of her time. As a result she was in the end more expressive of the century than Joyce.

Ulysses is "brilliant and dull, intelligible and obscure by turns . . . ." That's what Judge John Woolsey said when he ruled in 1933 that this novel, finally, could be published in the United States after being banned for well over a decade.[14] And brilliant it is, but now that its ability to shock has receded, what is the lasting worth of *Ulysses*?

Some of its joy lies in sheer exuberant impudence:

—We think of Rome, imperial, imperious, imperative.
—What was their civilization? Vast, I allow: but vile. Cloacae:
sewers. The Jews in the wilderness and on the mountaintop said:
It is meet to be here. Let us build *an altar to Jehovah.* The
Roman, like the Englishman who follows in his footsteps,
brought to every new shore on which he set his foot (on our
shore he never set it) only his cloacal obsession. He gazed about
him in his toga and he said: *It is meet to be here. Let us construct
a watercloset.*

And in the dazzling stream of consciousness, when it works:

He looked down at the boots he had blacked and polished. She
had outlived him, lost her husband. More dead for her than for
me. One must outlive the other. Wise men say. There are more
women than men in the world. Condole with her. Your terrible
loss. I hope you'll soon follow him. For Hindu widows only. She
could marry another. Him? No. Yet who knows after?
Widowhood not the thing since the old queen died. Drawn on a
guncarriage. Victoria and Albert. Frogmore memorial mourning.
But in the end she put a few violets in her bonnet. Vain in her
heart of hearts. All for a shadow. Consort not even a king. Her
son was the substance. Something new to hope for not like the
past she wanted back, waiting. It never comes. One must go first:
alone under the ground: and lie no more in her warm bed.

And, of course, in the radiant sensuality of Molly's soliloquy at the
end:

. . . [O]r shall I wear a red yes and how he kissed me under the
Moorish wall and I thought well as well him as another and then
I asked him with my eyes to ask again yes and then he asked me
would I yes to say yes my mountain flower and first I put my
arms around him yes and drew him down to me so he could feel
my breasts all perfumed yes and his heart was going like mad
and yes I said yes I will Yes.

But Woolf too could write of the yearnings of feminine flesh, though
with her they were more complex, less likely to find simple fulfillment,

such as this meditation from *The Waves*:

> There is some check in the flow of my being; a deep stream
> presses on some obstacle; it jerks; it tugs; some knot in the centre
> resists. Oh, this is pain, this is anguish! I faint, I fail. Now my
> body thaws; I am unsealed, I am incandescent. Now the stream
> pours in a deep tide fertilising, opening the shut, forcing the
> tight-folded, flooding free. To whom shall I give all that now
> flows through me, from my warm, my porous body? I will gather
> my flowers and present them—Oh! to whom?"

Joyce possessed the rhythm of language that Woolf herself maintained was all,[15] but would that he had cared as much as she did for the
rendering of the moment:

> I mean to eliminate all waste, deadness, superfluity: to give the
> moment whole; whatever it includes. Say that the moment is a
> combination of thought; sensation; the voice of the sea. Waste,
> deadness, come from the inclusion of things that don't belong to
> the moment.[16]

Woolf in fact had the more powerful mind and this is evident in her
writing. "The better a thing is expressed," she said, "the more completely
it is thought."[17] Thought she gave—to everything: her novels, her criticism, her friendships and the voluminous correspondence that sustained
them. And she had discipline. That she drew from her inexhaustible
attention to beauty. She was convinced "[t]hat beauty teaches, that beauty
is a disciplinarian . . . ."[18] Her response to life was above all aesthetic.
Bloom goes so far as to say that "[h]er religion (no lesser word would be
apt) was Paterian aestheticism: the worship of art . . . . Her aestheticism
is her center . . . ." He also calls Woolf "an Epicurean materialist, like her
precursor Walter Pater."[19]

Yet James Wood has written that Woolf had a religious nature that
reached beyond art, that "looked for 'something more.'" She thought of
herself as "mystical," he said, and she "sought a further metaphysical pattern behind the aesthetic pattern." This unseen wisdom, drenched in mystery, flowed into her work. "[I]t was real, it was revealed, it was given to
her." And, Wood notes, Woolf experienced her greatest fevers of insight
during times of mental instability.[20]

Bloom insisted that Woolf was no 'feminist': "Herself the last of the high aesthetes," he writes, "she has been swallowed up by remorseless Puritans, for whom the beautiful in literature is only another version of the cosmetics industry."[21] Aesthetic of course she was. But look carefully at the writer of *A Room of One's Own*—the only feminist book that need ever be read—not to mention the polemical *Three Guineas*. Here was a personage who "refused to sit on committees or to sign appeals, on the ground that women must not condone this tragic man-made mess, or accept the crumbs of power which men throw them occasionally from their hideous feast."[22] How can it be said that she was not suffused with a sense of women's unjust station in the world? To maintain otherwise is to overlook one of her most important contributions to twentieth century thought. Virginia Woolf foretold the revolution to come.

> All human relations have shifted—those between masters and servants, husbands and wives, parents and children. And when human relations change there is at the same time a change in religion, conduct, politics, and literature . . . . At the present moment we are suffering, not from decay, but from having no code of manners which writers and readers accept as a prelude to the more exciting intercourse of friendship . . . . Signs of this are everywhere apparent. Grammar is violated; syntax disintegrated; . . . Their sincerity is desperate, and their courage tremendous; it is only that they do not know which to use, a fork or their fingers.[23]

Woolf was talking about modern writers, but she brings to mind the absurdity of grown men who cannot fathom what might constitute sexual harassment at work or naval officers whose inexplicable confusion when they try to explain appropriate behavior toward women in the service makes one wonder if they had mothers. It's all so exasperatingly simple: you don't say to a female associate anything you wouldn't say to your mother, or do anything either. Woolf could have predicted all of this.

Even more important, she articulated the deep ambivalence modern women feel about marriage. Her vehicle was Lily Briscoe, the artist in *To the Lighthouse*. Her setting, the most brilliantly rendered dinner party in all of literature, a dinner party planned and assembled by Mrs. Ramsey:

> . . . [A]n exquisite scent of olives and oil and juice rose from the great brown dish as Marthe, with a little flourish, took the cover

off. The cook had spent three days over that dish. And she must take great care, Mrs. Ramsey thought, diving into the soft mass, to choose a specially tender piece for William Bankes. And she peered into the dish, with its shiny walls and its confusion of savoury brown and yellow meats and its bay leaves and its wine, and thought. This will celebrate the occasion—a curious sense rising in her, at once freakish and tender, of celebrating a festival, as if two emotions were called up in her, one profound—for what could be more serious than the love of man for woman, what more commanding, more impressive, bearing in its bosom the seeds of death; at the same time these lovers, these people entering into illusion glittering eyed, must be danced round with mockery, decorated with garlands.

'It is a triumph,' said Mr. Bankes, laying his knife down for a moment. He had eaten attentively. It was rich; it was tender. It was perfectly cooked. How did she manage these things in the depths of the country? he asked her. She was a wonderful woman.
All his love, all his reverence, had returned; and she knew it.

That might be a joy to Mrs. Ramsey, who died of exhaustion before she was fifty, but Lily Briscoe had a different view of love:

He turned on her cheek the heat of love, its horror, its cruelty, its unscrupulosity . . . . She need not marry, thank Heaven: she need not undergo that degradation. She was saved from that dilution. She would move the tree rather more to the middle.

. . . Yet, she said to herself, from the dawn of time odes have been sung to love; wreaths heaped and roses; and if you asked nine people out of ten they would say they wanted nothing but this—love; while the women, judging from her own experience, would all the time be feeling, This is not what we want; there is nothing more tedious, puerile, and inhumane than this; yet it is also beautiful and necessary.

Woolf believed in the sanctity of the self which could not be violated without consequences, as Clarissa reflects in *Mrs. Dalloway*:

And there is a dignity in people; a solitude; even between
husband and wife a gulf; and that one must respect, thought
Clarissa, watching him open the door; for one would not part
with it oneself, or take it, against his will, from one's husband,
without losing one's independence, one's self-respect—
something, after all, priceless.

Virginia's own marriage to Leonard Woolf was deeply successful,
though apparently she was sexually reticent, having been molested by her
two half-brothers while growing up. She suffered a breakdown a year
after the wedding, and while many have attributed this illness to the
pressures of married love, Rosemary Dinnage associates it with the com-
pletion of Woolf's first novel, *The Voyage Out*.[24] (Indeed she did often
experience depression after finishing a work of fiction.) Whatever the
cause of her symptoms, Woolf came to depend upon her husband utterly.
There is no question that his constant care, bringing her breakfast in bed,
looking after everything from the publication of her work to the daily
details of her health, kept Virginia Woolf alive.

Actually Woolf had two guardian angels: Leonard and her sister
Vanessa Bell, the painter. It was to them that Woolf wrote suicide letters
before she walked into the River Ouse at the age of fifty-nine, her jacket
pockets stuffed with stones. That was in 1941. The Battle of Britain had
decimated much of London, including her house and other parts of the
city she had lived in and loved. Bombs were falling still near Monk's
House where the Woolfs had repaired full-time for the duration of the
war. Virginia expected a German invasion at any moment and assumed
that she and Leonard would have to end their lives to avoid capture since
he was Jewish. She was anxious about her almost completed novel
Between the Acts (though it had flowed effortlessly) as she always was
when a book was about to be released to the appraisal of the world.
Indeed, she had written to John Lehmann, who by then was running
Hogarth Press, that it was too silly and trivial and she would revise it for
later publication.[25] Besides, the war had destroyed the audience for her
work, leaving her isolated, cut off from the public affirmation she
required to sustain her life.[26] And she was hearing voices and did not feel
she could fight them again and or that this time she had any hope of
recovery.

Woolf never sought help for her depression from Freud even though
the Hogarth Press which she ran with Leonard published Freud's

Collected Papers and also the *Collected Works*, for which they laid out 800 pounds in 1924.[27] Moreover, some of the most important translations of Freud's writing were done by James Strachey (brother of Woolf's close friend Lytton) and his wife Alix. Both of them studied psychoanalysis under Freud in Vienna. Indeed, Woolf noted in her diary after a visit from the Stracheys, "Freud has certainly brought out the lines in Alix. Even physically, her bones are more prominent. Only her eyes are curiously vague. She has purpose & security; but this may well be marriage."[28]

Woolf was skeptical of Freud and in a letter to Molly MacCarthy trained on him her devastating wit: "I shall be plunged in publishing affairs at once; we are publishing all Dr Freud, and I glance at the proof and read how Mr A.B. threw a bottle of red ink on to the sheets of his marriage bed to excuse his impotence to the housemaid, but threw it in the wrong place, which unhinged his wife's mind,—and to this day she pours claret on the dinner table. We could all go on like that for hours; and yet these Germans think it proves something—besides their own gull-like imbecility."[29]

In 1939 Leonard and Virginia visited Freud for tea at Hampstead, where he spent the last year of his life in refuge from the Nazis, dying of cancer. By then she called him "the great Freud,"[30] surely without irony. She had begun to read him seriously, and announced in her diary, "(I'm gulping up Freud.)" The next day she added, "Freud is upsetting: reducing one to whirlpool; & I daresay truly. If we're all instinct, the unconscious, whats all this about civilisation, the whole man, freedom &c? His savagery against God good. The falseness of loving one's neighbours. The conscience as censor. Hate . . . . But I'm too mixed."[31]

Virginia Woolf seems to have seen Freud as a writer and thinker, not a doctor, though she did draw consolation from him. "I tried to center by reading Freud," she wrote in her dairy in 1940, nine months before her death.[32] Whether he could have helped her or not, it's impossible to say. It may well be that some of the medications that rescued depressives late in the century would have been the only thing that could have dealt successfully with her illness.

Leonard Woolf saw Freud in the same light, as a great man, but not as a physician or an analyst who might have worked with Virginia. After meeting Freud in Hampstead he wrote:

Nearly all famous men are disappointing or bores, or both . . . .
Freud was neither; he had an aura, not of fame, but of greatness .

. . . There was something about him as of a half-extinct volcano, something sombre, suppressed, reserved. He gave me the feeling which only a very few people whom I have met gave me, a feeling of great gentleness, but behind the gentleness, great strength.[33]

Virginia Woolf had expected to have children, but Leonard, fearful for her health, persuaded her against it. This became "a permanent source of grief to her,"[34] and some of her most beautiful writing is devoted to the continuity of generations:

It is, however, true that I cannot deny a sense that life for me is now mysteriously prolonged. Is it that I may have children, may cast a fling of seed wider, beyond this generation, this doom-encircled population, shuffling each other in endless competition along the street? My daughters shall come here, in other summers; my sons shall turn new fields. Hence we are not raindrops, soon dried up by the wind; we make gardens blow and forests roar; we come up differently, for ever and ever. This then serves to explain my confidence, my central stability . . . .

She could also write wickedly about nineteenth century conventions of maternity. This is a comment in *Orlando*:

Were they not all of them weak women? wearing crinolines the better to conceal the fact; the great fact; the only fact; but, nevertheless, the deplorable fact; which every modest woman did her best to deny until denial was impossible; the fact that she was about to bear a child? to bear fifteen or twenty children indeed, so that most of a modest woman's life was spent, after all, in denying what, on one day at least every year, was made obvious.

Woolf looked to Vanessa Bell, not without envy, as the maternal sister. Indeed it has been observed that the two of them divided up the territory of their lives:

Vanessa was the artist, Virginia the writer, but it went much deeper. Vanessa was the practical one, the one who deferred to men, the one who had taken up the mantle of their dead mother.

She was the sensualist, the maternal figure, the inspired creator of homes and circles of friends, the goddess Demeter. Virginia was the quick-witted, verbal one, judged a genius from childhood on, the one who renounced traditional femininity for the life of the mind.[35]

Along with Leonard, Vanessa kept Virginia Woolf alive during all those years, which were astonishingly productive even though she often was in bed with flu, headache or depression. Three years older, Vanessa was central to Virginia's life from the beginning. No doubt there was rivalry between them, and there were awkward moments when Virginia, jealous of her sister's married happiness and missing her attention, struck up a flirtation with Vanessa's husband Clive Bell. But that passed. Clive, though not divorced, moved on to others, and with two sons (a daughter would come later) Vanessa settled into a domestic arrangement with the painter Duncan Grant. Her care for Virginia was unceasing.

But there was a price for all that domestic competence in a complicated situation. (Her daughter Angelica was Duncan's child—though he was mostly homosexual—but Angelica believed until she was eighteen that Clive was her father.) There were galling voids in Vanessa's life. Added to them was the worry about Virginia whom she sought to comfort with daily letters. As a subterranean aggravation she had to cope with the fictional personality that her gifted sister created for her in writing. Apparently Virginia was trying to control her own desperate dependence as well as her jealousy by jockeying Vanessa into "the role of eternal mother, oracle and protector . . . ."[36] Yet in this description of her sister as a child, Virginia, only twenty-five, surely hit the truth:

You see the soft, dreamy and almost melancholy expression of the eyes; and it may not be fanciful to discover some kind of test and rejection in them as though, even then, she considered the thing she saw, and did not always find what she needed in it . . . No hole dug in the gardens however deep, so that it was possible to extract clay of malleable quality from it, gave her all that she needed . . . . She seemed to draw on steadily, as though with her eye on some far object, which attained, she might reveal herself.[37]

In dedicating her second novel, *Night and Day*, to Vanessa, Woolf turned to restraint. By then she was in her thirties, making her way to a new form of fiction and still in awe of her sister: "To Vanessa Bell but, looking for a phrase, I found none to stand beside your name."[38]

And then mature admiration took hold, though even then Virginia seemed to see herself as one of "Nessa's children." Looking back on all they had endured together—the death of their mother when they were young teenagers, of their adored stepsister Stella, then their father and finally their brother Thoby of typhoid fever, all in the space of eleven years, Virginia wrote:

> Nessa's children (I always measure myself against her and find her much the largest, most humane of the two of us), think of her now with an admiration that has no envy in it; with some trace of the old childish feeling that we were in league together against the world; and how proud I am of her triumphant winning of all our battles; as she takes her way so nonchalantly, modestly, almost anonymously, past the goal, with her children round her; and only a little added tenderness (a moving thing in her) which shows me that she too feels wonder, surprise, at having passed so many terrors and sorrows safe . . . .[39]

And finally, the support Virginia was to Vanessa when her son Julian was killed in Spain during the Civil War. Vanessa was so overwhelmed by grief she went to bed for months. Virginia wrote or visited almost daily. Then a letter arrived at the Woolfs' from Vita Sackville-West. It said:

> This is a private postscript. I had a note from Vanessa which ends thus: 'I cannot ever say how Virginia has helped me. Perhaps, some day, not now, you will be able to tell her it's true.'

> Perhaps I ought not to quote this to you, but I don't see why not. In any case, please keep it to yourself.[40]

This was Virginia's reply:

> We have been so ridden with visitors that I never had a moment to write. In fact I was so touched by your letter that I couldnt. Isnt it odd? Nessa's saying that to you, I mean, meant something I cant speak of. And I cant tell anyone—but I think you guess—

how terrible it is to me, watching her: if I could do anything—sometimes I feel hopeless. But that message gives me something to hold to . . . .[41]

If one accepts Martha Graham's maxim that artists are not ahead of their time, they *are* their time, then Virginia Woolf must be seen as representative not only of the first half of the century, when she lived and worked, but also of the sixty years to follow, when her perceptions took on the full force of culture. But the cost to her was high. She never felt undergirded by her own times. And she knew what it would have meant to her to have had that kind of support. It's clear from this passage:

Again, in Mr. [Lytton] Strachey's books, *Eminent Victorians* and *Queen Victoria*, the effort and strain of writing against the grain and current of the times is visible too. It is much less visible, of course, for not only is he dealing with facts, which are stubborn things, but he has fabricated, chiefly from eighteenth-century material, a very discreet code of manners of his own, which allows him to sit at table with the highest in the land and to say a great many things under cover of that exquisite apparel which, had they gone naked, would have been chased by the men-servants from the room. Still, if you compare *Eminent Victorians* with some of Lord Macaulay's essays, though you will feel that Lord Macaulay is always wrong, and Mr. Strachey always right, you will also feel a body, a sweep, a richness in Lord Macaulay's essays which show that his age was behind him; all his strength went straight into his work; none was used for purposes of concealment or of conversion. But Mr. Strachey has had to open our eyes before he made us see; he has had to search out and sew together a very artful manner of speech; and the effort, beautifully though it is concealed, has robbed his work of some of the force that should have gone into it, and limited his scope.[42]

The truth is that Virginia Woolf, for all the lustrous beauty of her writing, did not fashion a fancy dress for camouflage. She presented herself whole in her work, including an examination of mental illness in *Mrs. Dalloway* and her own precarious hold on the material world in *The Waves*. That is very likely the reason that releasing a new novel to the world set off in her severe anxiety and depression, causing her to retreat for a time to literary criticism, where her formidable intellect could protect her fragile emotions. But always she fought her way back to fiction. Today, writes Bloom, "half a century after her death, she has no rivals among women novelists or critics . . . ." Then Bloom went ever farther and admitted, "one could argue that she was the most complete person-of-letters in England in our century."[43] This could be broadened to include the entire world where English is read and appreciated.

Some say that Woolf's masterpiece was *To The Lighthouse*, and they may be right. But others believe, as Leonard and E.M. Forster did, that it was *The Waves*. It is hard to contend against them. *To the Lighthouse* is a brilliant portrait of Virginia's parents, Leslie and Julia Stephen. It sparkles with insights and ideas, with grace of language and economy of feeling. But *The Waves* achieves greater heights and depths. It is pure poetry, elegant and sublime.

Listen to this soliloquy of a young girl, on the cusp of a woman's life:

> . . . I feel myself shining in the dark. Silk is on my knee. My silk legs rub smoothly together. The stones of a necklace lie bold on my throat . . . . I am arrayed, I am prepared . . . .

> This is my calling. This is my world . . . .

> This is what I have dreamt; this is what I have foretold. I am native here . . . . I feel a thousand capacities spring up in me . . . I am rooted, but I flow . . . . My peers may look at me now. I look straight back at you, men and women. I am one of you. This is my world . . . .

> There are girls of my own age, for whom I feel the drawn swords of an honourable antagonism. For these are my peers. I am a native of this world. Here is my risk, here is my adventure.

Woolf wrote superbly about the importance of food, not only to pleasure but to friendship and even to human achievement. Good food, she believed, was terribly important to good talk. Not only did she accomplish the complexities of the dinner party in *To the Lighthouse*, she also laid bare the deprivations of women's colleges and thus of women's lives and possibilities in *A Room of One's Own*:

Prunes and custard followed. And if anyone complains that prunes, even when mitigated by custard, are an uncharitable vegetable (fruit they are not), stringy as a miser's heart and exuding a fluid such as might run in misers' veins who have denied themselves wine and warmth for eighty years and yet not given to the poor, he should reflect that there are people whose charity embraces even the prune.

Biscuits and cheese came next, and here the water-jug was liberally passed round, for it is the nature of biscuits to be dry, and these were biscuits to the core. That was all. The meal was over.[44]

Then there is the lovely satisfaction of bacon and eggs in one's own home after a road trip:

And then the body who had been silent up to now began its song, almost at first as low as the rush of the wheels: 'Eggs and bacon; toast and tea; fire and a bath; fire and a bath; jugged hare,' it went on, and 'red currant jelly; a glass of wine; with coffee to follow—and then to bed; and then to bed.'
'Off with you,' I said to my assembled selves. 'Your work is done. I dismiss you. Good-night.'[45]

It was in *The Waves*, however, that she achieved rapture at the table:

But I eat. I gradually lose all knowledge of particulars as I eat. I am becoming weighed down with food. These delicious mouthfuls of roast duck, fitly piled with vegetables, following each other in exquisite rotation of warmth, weight, sweet and bitter, past my palate, down my gullet, into my stomach, have stabilized my body. I feel quiet, gravity, control. All is solid now. Instinctively my palate now requires and anticipates sweetness and lightness, something sugared and evanescent; and cool wine, fitting glove-like over those finer nerves that seem to tremble from the roof of my mouth . . . .

We have proved, sitting, eating, sitting talking, that we can add to the treasury of moments.

It was also in *The Waves* that she elevated commerce to an art form, laced always with the anxiety that talent might not fulfill itself:

I have signed my name already twenty times. I, and again I, and again I. Clear, firm, unequivocal, there it stands, my name. Clear-cut and unequivocal I am too. Yet a vast inheritance of experience is packed in me. I have lived thousands of years. I am like a worm that has eaten its way through the wood of a very old beam. But now I am compact; now I am gathered together this fine morning . . . .

". . . [A]ll the furled and close-packed leaves of my many-folded life are now summed in my name; incised cleanly and barely on the sheet. Now full grown; now upright in sun or rain, I must drop heavy as a hatchet and cut the oak with my sheer weight, for if I deviate, glancing this way, or that way, I shall fall like snow and be wasted.

I am half in love with the typewriter and the telephone. With letters and cables and brief but courteous commands on the telephone to Paris, Berlin, New York, I have fused my many lives into one; I have helped by my assiduity and decision to score those lines on the map there by which the different parts of the world are laced together . . . .

My shoulder is to the wheel; I roll the dark before me, spreading commerce where there was chaos in the four parts of the world.

Always Woolf returns in *The Waves* to the writer: the writer's need for solitude, for other people, to be praised, and remembered:

Yet it is incredible that I should not be a great poet. What did I write last night if it was not poetry? Am I too fast, too facile? I do not know. I do not know myself sometimes, or how to measure and name and count out the grains that make me what I am . . . .

How curiously one is changed by the addition, even at a distance, of a friend. How useful an office one's friends perform when they recall us. Yet how painful to be recalled, to be mitigated, to have one's self adulterated, mixed up, become part of another.

I need an audience. This is my downfall. That always ruffles the edge of the final statement and prevents it from forming . . . . I need eyes on me to draw out these frills and furbelows. To be myself (I note) I need the illumination of other people's eyes, and therefore cannot be entirely sure what is my self. The authentics, like Louis, like Rhoda, exist most completely in solitude. They resent illumination, reduplication. They toss their pictures, once painted, face downward on the field. On Louis' words the ice is packed thick. His words are issued pressed, condensed, enduring . . . .

Now I am drawn back . . . by the irresistible desire to be myself. I think of people to whom I could say things; Louis; Neville; Susan; Jinny and Rhoda. With them I am many-sided. They retrieve me from darkness . . . . They drum me alive. They brush off these vapours. I begin to be impatient of solitude—to feel its draperies hang sweltering, unwholesome about me. Oh, to toss them off and be active! Anybody will do. I am not fastidious.

As it is, finding sequences everywhere, I cannot bear the pressure of solitude. When I cannot see words curling like rings of smoke round me I am in darkness—I am nothing. When I am alone I fall into lethargy . . . . When Louis is alone he sees with astonishing intensity, and will write some words that may outlast us all. Rhoda loves to be alone. She fears us because we shatter the sense of being which is so extreme in solitude . . . . But I only come into existence when the plumber, or the horse-dealers, or whoever it may be, says something which sets me alight . . . But observe how meretricious the phrase is—made up of what evasions and old lies. Thus my character is in part made up of the stimulus which other people provide, and is not mine, as yours are . . . . I am made and remade continually. Different people draw different words from me.

If I lie open to the pressure of society I often succeed with the dexterity of my tongue in putting something difficult into the currency . . . . But I have sacrificed much. Veined as I am with

iron, with silver and streaks of common mud, I cannot contract
into the firm fist which those clench who do not depend upon
stimulus . . . . I shall never succeed, even in talk, in making a perfect phrase. But I shall have contributed more to the passing
moment than any of you; I shall go into more rooms, more different rooms than any of you. But because there is something
that comes from outside and not from within I shall be forgotten;
when my voice is silent you will not remember me, save as the
echo of a voice that once wreathed the fruits into phrases.

But Woolf meant to be remembered, as she made clear in this passage
from *The Waves* about letter writing. It's self-mocking and bristling with
wit, but she intended it to last:

Yes, all is propitious. I am now in the mood. I can write the letter
straight off which I have begun ever so many times. I am writing
the first thing that comes into my head without troubling to put
the paper straight. It is going to be a brilliant sketch, which, she
must think, was written without a pause, without an erasure.
Look how unformed the letters are—there is a careless blot. All
must be sacrificed to speed and carelessness. I will write a quick,
running, small hand, exaggerating the down stroke of the "y" and
crossing the "t" thus—with a dash. The date shall be only
Tuesday, the 17th, and then a question mark. But also I must give
the impression that though he—for this is not myself—is writing
in such an off-hand, such a slap-dash way, there is some subtle
suggestion of intimacy and respect. I must allude to talks we
have had together—bring back some remembered scene. But I
must seem to her (this is very important) to be passing from
thing to thing with the greatest ease in the world. I shall pass
from the service for the man who was drowned (I have a phrase
for that) to Mrs. Moffat and her sayings (I have a note of them)
and so to some reflections apparently casual but full of profundi-
ty (profound criticism is often written casually) about some book
I have been reading, some out-of-the-way book. I want her to say
as she brushes her hair or puts out the candle, 'where did I read
that? Oh, in Bernard's letter.' It is the speed, the hot, molten
effect, the lava flow of sentence into sentence that I need. Who
am I thinking of? Byron of course. I am, in some ways, like

Byron. Perhaps a sip of Byron will help to put me in the vein.
Let me read a page. No; this is dull; this is scrappy. This is rather
too formal. Now I am getting the hang of it. Now I am getting his
beat into my brain (the rhythm is the main thing in writing).
Now, without pausing I will begin, on the very lilt of the
stroke—Yet it falls flat. It peters out. I cannot get up steam
enough to carry me over the transition.

My true self breaks off from my assumed. And if I begin to
rewrite it, she will feel, "Bernard is posing as a literary man;
Bernard is thinking of his biographer" (which is true). No, I will
write the letter tomorrow directly after breakfast.

But then there's this, the credo, the solemn declaration of her
life's purpose:

I conceive myself called upon to provide, some winter's night, a
meaning for all my observations—a line that runs from one to
another, a summing up that completes.

She did just that—in *The Waves*.

Bloomsbury could boast of two veritable geniuses—Virginia Woolf
and John Maynard Keynes the economist. It also encompassed artists and
critics of voluptuous talent, many of them men, whose achievement was
in no way diminished, of course, by the emergence of women.
Prominently among the writers stood E.M. Forster, three years older than
Woolf and a decade more precocious. Indeed his masterpiece, *Howards
End*, completed when he was only thirty-one, appeared five years before
her first book, The *Voyage Out*, which was notable but not transcendent.
His other great novel, *A Passage to India*, was published in 1924, when
she was on the verge of her breakthrough work, *Mrs Dalloway*.
    "There is something baffling and evasive in the very nature of his
gifts," Woolf wrote of Forster, her friend and occasional colleague. (The
Hogarth Press published some of his work.) Forster, she said, has trouble
"connecting the prose and poetry of life." His theorizing gets in the way.
He can't decide whether to be a preacher and teacher of literature (like
Tolstoy and Dickens) or a pure artist, like Jane Austen or Turgenev.[46]
Woolf felt that Forster interrupted the flow of his fiction to interject a

message. "So, exerting ourselves to find out the meaning," she wrote, "we step from the enchanted world of imagination, where our faculties work freely, to the twilight world of theory, where only our intellect functions dutifully."

Dualism never appealed to Woolf. To her, single-mindedness was everything. ". . . [I]f there is one gift more essential to a novelist than another," she declared, "it is the power of combination—the single vision."[47] Forster understood this about her and noted in a lecture on Woolf right after her death that she worked mightily to assemble all her notes, her sensations, the complexity of her thought into "one thing, one."[48]

Rose Macaulay did see a paradoxical unity in Forster's work where Woolf did not, and that unity she ascribed to the view of life he gained as a Cambridge student. "The thing you may see—with luck—up here [at Cambridge] is Reality," she explained, "and it is this vision of Reality, this passionate antithesis between the real and the unreal, the true and the false, being and not-being, that gives the whole body of E.M. Forster's work, in whatever *genre*, its unity." And on a deeper level, "the importance he attaches to the antithesis has the urgency of a religion. There is a Way, a Truth, a Life . . . ."[49]

Nowhere is the struggle with the opposites more intense than in *Howards End*, where ideas contend with commerce. "Only connect," he wrote on the title page, and he set out to do just that. Furthermore, he makes it a fair fight. "Still two worlds, two ways of thought and life, are at war," said Macaulay, "but now one is not all truth and light, and the other not all sham and darkness: both are bad unless they fuse and cooperate." These two realms, "the outer world of newspapers and golf, empire-building, business and politics" and "the inner world of ideas and of personal relationships"[50] collide in the marriage of Margaret Schlegel to Henry Wilcox. Theirs is the central tension of the book.

For all his commitment to the life of the mind, Forster wrote convincingly of the business ethos and its effect on the intellectual and idealistic Margaret Schlegel:

> She desired to protect them [the Wilcoxes] and often felt that they could protect her, excelling where she was deficient. Once past the rocks of emotion, they knew so well what to do, whom to send for; their hands were on all the ropes, they had grit as well as grittiness, and she valued grit enormously. They led a life

she could not attain to—the outer life of 'telegrams and anger' . .
. . To Margaret this life was to remain a real force . . . . It fostered
such virtues as neatness, decision, and obedience, virtues of the
second rank, no doubt, but they have formed our civilization.
They form character too; Margaret could not doubt it: they keep
the soul from becoming sloppy . . . .
"Don't brood too much," she wrote to [her younger sister] Helen,
"on the superiority of the unseen to the seen. It's true, but to
brood on it is medieval. Our business is not to contrast the two,
but to reconcile them."[51]

And there's no one better to do the work of reconciliation than
Margaret Schlegel. As grounded as she is spiritual, as practical as she is
generous, "Margaret has some of the attributes that please civilized
women in one another," Macaulay pointed out. "Beauty, merely feminine
charm, single-track emotion, biological urge—these qualities, so confusing
and swamping to personality and character, so much the stock-in-trade of
the heroine-maker, in Margaret Schlegel scarcely exist; in consequence we
see her as an individual, with mind, heart, intelligence, sympathies, theories
and ideas. She grows and develops, blunders and advances, she has theories
about life, which she tries to follow herself and somewhat vociferously to
preach to others. She is delightful, adventurous, erratic, at once a
cultured highbrow, a moral enthusiast, a social idealist, a witty talker, and
a nice, sympathetic, sensible woman." Moreover, she knows how to take
domestic life in stride. She would not be diluted in the way Lily Briscoe
feared. "Margaret loves Mr. Wilcox; but love does not engulf her; she
continues to choose to see life whole, even after marriage." As Forster
noted, "It is impossible to see modern life steadily and see it whole, and
she had chosen to see it whole. Mr. Wilcox saw it steadily."[52]

So is Virginia Woolf right? Does Forster interrupt the flow of his
characters with too many insightful asides? Does our experience of
Margaret and Henry suffer from the writer's view of modern life? Of
course not. Their story gets told and told well. But in addition, throughout the novel, we get a wealth of observation that brings us back
to *Howards End* again and again. It is the kind of wisdom that fills
notebooks and guides lives.

Here is what Forster said in *Howards End* about possessions, land
and the world of real estate:

The Age of Property holds bitter moments even for a proprietor
.... The feudal ownership of land did bring dignity, whereas the
modern ownership of movables is reducing us again to a
nomadic horde. We are reverting to the civilization of luggage,
and historians of the future will note how the middle classes
accreted possessions without taking root in the earth, and may
find in this the secret of their imaginative poverty. The Schlegels
were certainly the poorer for the loss of Wickham Place. It had
helped to balance their lives, and almost to counsel them. Nor is
their landlord spiritually the richer. He has built flats on its site,
his motorcars grow swifter, his exposures of Socialism more
trenchant. But he has split the precious distillation of the years,
and no chemistry of his can give it back to society again.

And then there is the brilliant discourse on the meaning of money, as
scintillating in its way as Woolf's dinner party in *To the Lighthouse*:

Money's educational. It's far more educational than the things it
buys ... Well, isn't the most civilized thing going, the man who
has learnt to wear his income properly?
The imagination ought to play upon money and realize it vividly,
for it's the—the second most important thing in the world. It is
so slurred over and hushed up, there is so little clear thinking—
oh, political economy, of course, but so few of us think clearly
about our own private incomes, and admit that independent
thoughts are in nine cases out of ten the result of independent
means.

No one has written with greater wit on the amassing of arms, public
and private, real and metaphorical, than E.M. Forster. This is from
Howards End:

With infinite effort we nerve ourselves for a crisis that never
comes. The most successful career must show a waste of strength
that might have removed mountains, and the most unsuccessful
is not that of the man who is taken unprepared, but of him who
has prepared and is never taken. On a tragedy of that kind our
national morality is duly silent. It assumes that preparation
against danger is in itself a good, and that men, like nations, are

the better for staggering through life fully armed. The tragedy of preparedness has scarcely been handled, save by the Greeks.

In the matter of human relations, Forster expected delicacy and tact. He bestowed some of his best insights on the remarkable Mrs. Wilcox, heir to the house called Howards End and Henry Wilcox's first wife. Here she rescues her son Paul from his older brother Charles and welcomes Mrs. Juley Munt, aunt of the Schlegel sisters, who understandably is confused about an engagement she supposed to have taken place between Paul and her niece Helen:

> "Paul," cried Charles Wilcox, pulling his gloves off . . . "Paul, is there any truth in this? . . . . Yes or no, man; plain question, plain answer. Did or didn't Miss Schlegel—"
> "Charles dear," said a voice from the garden. "Charles, dear Charles, one doesn't ask plain questions. There aren't such things."
> They were all silent. It was Mrs. Wilcox.
> She approached just as Helen's letter had described her, trailing noiselessly over the lawns, and there was actually a wisp of hay in her hands. She seemed to belong not to the young people and their motor, but to the house, and to the tree that overshadowed it. One knew that she worshipped the past, and that the instinctive wisdom that the past alone can bestow had descended upon her . . . . High-born she might not be. But assuredly she cared about her ancestors, and let them help her. When she saw Charles angry, Paul frightened, and Mrs. Munt in tears, she heard her ancestors say: "Separate those human beings who will hurt each other most. The rest can wait." She did not ask questions. Still less did she pretend that nothing had happened, as a competent society hostess would have done. She said: "Miss Schlegel, would you take your aunt up to your room or to my room, whichever you think best. Paul, do find Evie, and tell her lunch for six, but I'm not sure whether we shall all be downstairs for it." And when they had obeyed her, she turned to her elder son, who still stood in the throbbing stinking car, and smiled at him with tenderness, and without a word, turned away from him towards her flowers.
> "Mother," he called, "are you aware that Paul has been playing

the fool again?"

"It's all right, dear. They have broken off the engagement."

"Engagement—!"

"They do not love any longer, if you prefer it put that way," said Mrs. Wilcox, stooping down to smell a rose.

The novel and all its meaning reside in the house. In a quirk of willful intuition, Mrs. Wilcox, at her death leaves Howards End to her new friend Margaret Schlegel, which brings shock and consternation to her husband and family. They suppress the news. Margaret, aware of none of it, marries Mr. Wilcox and thus inherits the house a second time. Her marriage requires her to make peace with the life of commerce. All this Lionel Trilling took as a metaphor for England: "*Howards End* is a novel about England's fate," he wrote. "It is a story of the class war. The war is latent but actual—so actual indeed that a sword is literally drawn and a man is really killed. England herself appears in the novel in palpable form, for the story moves by symbols and not only all its characters but also an elm, a marriage, a symphony, and a scholar's library stand for things beyond themselves. The symbol for England is the house whose name gives the title to the book. Like the plots of so many English novels, the plot of *Howards End* is about the rights of property, about a destroyed will-and-testament and rightful and wrongful heirs. It asks the question, 'Who shall inherit England?'"[53]

Two world wars, the loss of empire, the failure of socialism and Margaret Thatcher settled that question in favor of the business class. But that is only half of *Howards End*. The other side of the ledger, the deeper side, deals, as all his novels do, with the inner self. "His concern is with the private life," observed Virginia Woolf; "his message is addressed to the soul." He was, she said, "the most persistent devotee of the soul."[54] That's why Forster remains so deeply satisfying.

If Forster was devoted to the soul, and Woolf to the aesthetic, Edith Wharton, it's been said, was a novelist of morals. She suffused a certain time and place—*fin-de-siècle* New York—with strong convictions about how the good life is to be lived. She wrote about manners, of course, but her deeper emphasis was on the demanding standards of her world view and her shrewd sense of the tragic as worlds collapse.

"At best there are only three or four American novelists who can be thought of as 'major' and Edith Wharton is one," wrote Gore Vidal.

"Who are the other two or three?" He declined to say except to note that Wharton and Henry James are the "two great American masters of the novel" while "most of our celebrated writers have not been, properly speaking, novelists at all."[55] Wharton and James were close friends, and her biographer, R.W.B. Lewis, has pointed out that "a clear line (perhaps the clearest line of development in the history of the novel in America) connects Mrs. Wharton with Henry James as well as F. Scott Fitzgerald. "All three," he said, "are artistic historians of manners, particularly of the widening breach between manners—the palpable externals of behavior— and a significant morality . . . ." While Wharton adored Henry James (who was two decades older), she fretted about the shadow of his eminence: "The continued cry that I am an echo of Mr. James," she wrote her editor, "makes me feel rather helpless . . ."[56] That letter she dispatched the year before the appearance of her first successful novel, *The House of Mirth*. It was published in 1905 (five years before *Howards End*) when Wharton was forty-three.

Hers was a long road to the committed life of letters. Where Virginia Woolf was born into the household of respected intellectual Leslie Stephen, who nurtured her interest in books even if she was not allowed to enter Cambridge, Edith Wharton had to fight her way out of the Newport-New York circuit of boring chatter and extraneous obligation.

A proper marriage to dull, eligible Teddy Wharton failed to satisfy her. The astonished response of family and friends when she turned to writing surely undermined her inner security. Edith Wharton's doubts and conflicts manifested themselves as recurring illness—"loss of weight, inability to read or write, frequent headaches and constant nausea, profound melancholy." At thirty-two she had "a total nervous collapse that endured, all told, for more than two years."[57]

Finally, Wharton saw a doctor in Philadelphia who put her in the Stenton Hotel and prescribed total rest, daily massage (unheard of at that time in America), large meals and snacks and no visitors, no contact with anybody from home, though she was allowed to receive mail. Teddy and Walter Berry, the literary soulmate she knew from youth and treasured for years but never married, wrote daily. This regimen endured from October through January. After her release, Edith and Teddy took a house in Washington that Berry found for them rather than have her return to the domestic anxieties that had undermined her health in the first place.

But Wharton was seeking a deeper escape and she found it in her writing. She found it also at The Mount, the elegant house she built for herself in Lenox, Massachusetts. And she found it in Paris, where she lived much of the time during her middle and later years. "In Paris," noted Gore Vidal, "a woman could be taken seriously as an intellectual . . . ."[58] In Paris she became completely herself. As a result, illness vanished. There were occasional flareups, such as the asthma that hit her after she finished *The House of Mirth*, but precarious health did not plague her for all her life in the way it did Virginia Woolf.

In *The House of Mirth* Edith Wharton found her own American voice. Like *Howards End*, it deals with the intrusion of commerce into a coherent world of settled principles. But Wharton saw no redemption in business, only social disintegration. Nothing could come from the worship of money but turmoil.

Like Forster, she found her metaphor in the house. Having first discovered the drama of architecture by writing an earlier book on decoration, Wharton used the *House of Mirth* to symbolize the first crack in the old order. Then followed other houses, inhabited by even grosser agents of glitter and greed. But where *Howards End* represents a life of beauty, grace, and continuity of the countryside, protected from the encroachments of the city, the *House of Mirth* has no such salutary connotations. It is the beginning of civic degradation.

While many regard *The House of Mirth* as Wharton's most important novel, it was *The Age of Innocence*, published in 1920, that won the Pulitzer Prize. Indeed Lewis called this novel Wharton's "major accomplishment" in her study of the disconnection between morals and manners, between ethics and actual behavior.[59]

By the time *The Age of Innocence* was written, Edith Wharton had become "the most renowned writer of fiction in America."[60] It was in the decade that followed—the 1920s—that Virginia Woolf, twenty years younger than Wharton, also came into her own. Like Woolf's *To the Lighthouse*, Wharton's *Age of Innocence* features a pivotal dinner party. But while Woolf uses the occasion to convey the complicated relationships and resistance to relationship around the table, Wharton's assemblage is gathered for the express purpose of isolating Madame Olenska from their circle, pronouncing an end to her suspected romance with Newland Archer, a married man, without ever noticing, much less acknowledging the affair, and sending her off grandly to Paris, to live evermore in exile.

There were certain things that had to be done, and if done at all, done handsomely and thoroughly; and one of these, in the old New York code, was the tribal rally around a kinswoman about to be eliminated from the tribe. There was nothing on earth that the Wellands and the Mingotts would not have done to proclaim their unalterable affection for the Countess Olenska now that her passage for Europe was engaged; and Archer, at the head of the table, sat marveling at the silent untiring activity with which her popularity had been retrieved, grievances against her silenced, her past countenanced, and her present irradiated by the family approval . . . .

Archer, who seemed to be assisting at the scene in a state of odd imponderability, as if he floated somewhere between chandelier and ceiling, wondered at nothing so much as his own share in the proceedings. As his glance traveled from one placid well-fed face to another he saw all the harmless looking people engaged upon May's [his wife's] canvasbacks as a band of dumb conspirators, and himself and the pale woman on his right as the center of their conspiracy. And then it came over him, in a vast flash made up of many broken gleams, that to all of them he and Madame Olenska were lovers, lovers in the extreme sense peculiar to 'foreign vocabularies.' He guessed himself to have been, for months, the center of countless silently observing eyes and patiently listening ears, he understood that, by means as yet unknown to him, the separation between himself and the partner of his guilt had been achieved, and that now the whole tribe had rallied about his wife on the tacit assumption that nobody knew anything, and that the occasion of the entertainment was simply May Archer's natural desire to take an affectionate leave of her friend and cousin.

It was the old New York way of taking life "without effusion of blood": the way of people who dreaded scandal more than disease, who placed decency above courage, and who considered that nothing was more ill-bred than 'scenes,' except the behavior of those who gave rise to them.

"Throughout much of the novel," explained Cynthia Griffin Wolff, "Archer longs for a life that moves well beyond the charted realm of the familiar, a life of high emotional intensity and sustained moral and intellectual complexity."[61] This yearning he invests in the elegant Ellen Olenska, his wife's cousin, newly returned to New York from a calamitous marriage in Europe. But their feeling for each other has no hope of resolution, not only because of the violation it would do to the social structure of the day but because of his own internal sense of honor.

Years later, after his wife has died, Newland travels to Paris, where he considers seeing Ellen, living still on her own, but decides against it. She was too remote by then, too removed from his maturity.

"Something he knew he had missed," wrote Wharton,

"the flower of life. But he thought of it now as a thing so unattainable and improbable that to have repined would have been like despairing because one had not drawn first prize at the lottery . . . . That vision, faint and tenuous as it was, had kept him from thinking of other women. He had been what was called a faithful husband; and when May had suddenly died—carried off by the infectious pneumonia through which she had nursed their youngest child—he had honestly mourned her. Their long years together had shown him that it did not so much matter if marriage was a dull duty, as long as it kept the dignity of a duty: lapsing from that it became a mere battle of ugly appetites. Looking about him, he honored his own past, and mourned for it. After all, there was good in the old ways."

In the end, Newland Archer "is not the man he had once dreamed of becoming," Cynthia Wolff observed, "but he is a man . . . who has the satisfaction of having become most truly himself in the ways that were available to him. He has not betrayed his own capacities." He has, in fact, achieved integrity.[62]

Edith Wharton's own marriage did not turn out so well. Though she and Teddy, over ten years older, were of the same world, it was a milieu that to her felt like a "trap, or cage." That Teddy shared none of her literary interests could only have induced her to associate him solely with a cultural setting that nurtured her not at all though it became the stuff of her novels. It could not have been easy for Teddy either. Intimate relations with Edith veered early off the track and never righted themselves. Her gifts were married to a large ambition, and though in every way a great lady she became also a "self-made man," which was for her a "deep necessity."[63] While she pursued a blossoming career, spending more and more of her time in Europe among people who must have seemed to Teddy as if from another planet, he busied himself looking after her investments, which grew ever grander due to her own considerable earnings and a generous inheritance from her father.

For a time Teddy showed himself "to be something of a genius in his handling of Edith's estate, displaying 'immense energy and great astuteness in venturesome transactions in steel.'" But signs of manic-depression became ever more apparent, culminating finally in an odd confession to Edith that the previous summer he had "converted a number of her holdings, including those in steel, into cash, had speculated on his own behalf, and then had purchased an apartment in Boston . . . [where] he had established a young woman . . . as his mistress and lived with her for several months. He also claimed to have let out the spare rooms to several chorus girls as tenants . . . ."[64]

Trying to smooth the way for Teddy's return to his marriage, his doctor wrote Edith that her husband had exaggerated somewhat: there had been a mistress but no chorus girls. However, it was no exaggeration that "Teddy had embezzled—and spent—not less than fifty thousand dollars from Edith's several trusts." To make amends he had to transfer a sizeable share of an inheritance from his mother to Edith's accounts. The shame was devastating. So was the financial loss. Teddy "saw the major portion of his fortune snatched away almost before it came into his hands . . . ."[65]

The situation deteriorated beyond recall when Teddy began cavorting about Europe, registering various women in various hotels as "Mrs. Wharton." The real Mrs. Wharton could take it no longer. She took action, and, painful as it was for her (she was still in many ways a traditionalist), they were divorced.

Through all these difficulties, Edith was not without other resources. Indeed, just as Teddy had been setting up house in Boston, she, living quite apart from him in Paris, was having the great love affair of her life at forty-six. The man was Morton Fullerton, an American journalist. She left no doubt in her own writing that he fulfilled her totally as a woman. Indeed, Fullerton himself "said that Edith Wharton in love displayed the reckless ardor of a George Sand."[66]

Fullerton had many liaisons. As Elizabeth Hardwick wrote, "In his love life, he is something like a telephone, always engaged, and even then with several on hold."[67]

But Wharton was ever the great lady. Though the liaison with

Fullerton waned after about three years (the usual span of his affairs, with either sex), she maintained warm contact with him long after that.

Wharton had many men friends, Bernhard Berenson among them, but the one who meant the most to her was Walter Berry. They first met in their youth at Bar Harbor but nothing came of the obvious attraction they held for each other. Berry "maintained a careful lack of final seriousness in his relations with women," and Wharton then was too naive to give him the encouragement that might have changed everything.[68]

So Berry disappeared from Edith's life for thirteen years only to surface again when she needed him to help her through her breakdown and support her early writing. (In this respect he was to Wharton what Leonard was to Virginia Woolf.) He was there again when Fullerton departed. Having just returned to Paris from a stint in Cairo, Berry moved into the guest suite of the Whartons' apartment in Paris and stayed for six months while he looked for a place of his own. During that time, in "the rhythm of Edith Wharton's personal life, Berry's temporary establishment in her household marked the start of his gradual replacement of Fullerton in her deepest affections." It was not perfect. Berry often showed a preference for "empty-headed pretty women," surely a source of hurt to Edith. But when he died, Wharton wrote in her diary, "The stone closed over all my life."[69]

Wharton's literary taste was not so different from that of Virginia Woolf. She too took a dim view of Joyce's *Ulysses* which she called "a welter of pornography (the rudest school-boy kind), and unformed and unimportant drivel . . . ." "What she resented," noted R.W.B. Lewis, "was not so much the 'pornography,' [indeed she wrote some herself, in the riveting 'Beatrice Palmato' fragment] . . . as its adolescent male tone that she seemed to hear echoing crudely . . . . More than likely," Lewis said, "Edith Wharton had resolved to demonstrate that she could do much better than James Joyce at this kind of writing, and that as against Joyce, Lawrence, and other male observers of female sensuality, she could give a truly accurate portrayal of a woman's sexual response. At the same time she wanted to show that *she* could do it: that she could write elegant pornography as well as her usual fiction of manners, implication, and insinuation. If these were her ambitions, she fulfilled them." By then Wharton was in her sixties. No doubt she feared that, measured against the vibrancy of Joyce, her own work would be regarded as something from the "Dark Ages."[70]

Her fears are understandable in light of a story told by Lionel Trilling of T.S. Eliot, who, while having tea with Virginia Woolf, argued—against her judgment—for the "magnitude" of Joyce's "power by saying that his book [*Ulysses*] 'destroyed the whole of the nineteenth century.' Eliot meant that Joyce by his radical innovation of style had made obsolete the styles of the earlier time . . . [and thus] the concerns and sentiments to which the old styles were appropriate had lost their authority."[71]

And what was it that had lost its authority? It was the novel conceived so as to set the "values of the moral and spiritual life over against the values of the world." This was precisely the central intention of Edith Wharton's work. It's not surprising she worried about being consigned to the Dark Ages. Then too, Wharton must have sensed Trilling's insight that Joyce was very much "a man of the century in which he was born." He shared its "concerns and sentiments," was "deeply rooted" in its "ethos and mythos, its beliefs and its fantasies."[72] So Joyce imbibed the nineteenth century as his own and then he killed it. How Wharton must have hated him for that. How much a violation of her own sacred center this must have been. And, with differing emphasis, of Virginia Woolf's as well.

Edith Wharton and Virginia Woolf had more in common than either was willing to admit. As children, both had been allowed free access to their fathers' libraries. Both were to a considerable extent self-educated. Both rewrote their work endlessly. Both had famous heroines named Lily. Both adhered to certain standards of aesthetic beauty. Yet they were wary of each other.

"Edith was never cordial to the Bloomsbury group as such," noted Lewis, "though she relished her rare meetings with Lytton Strachey. She was on her guard against Virginia Woolf, especially after an article by the latter which seemed to argue that American writers should cultivate their native idiom and not, like Henry James and Edith Wharton, strive after the king's English." "According to Berenson," Lewis continued, "Edith admired none of Virginia Woolf's novels, though recognized that she had 'prodigious gifts in other directions.'"[73]

Woolf struck a similar note when she wrote to her friend Ethel Smyth: "And then I lit the fire and read Mrs. Wharton; Memoirs and she knew Mrs. Hunter [Ethel's sister] and probably you. Please tell me sometime what you thought of her. Theres the shell of a distinguished mind; I like the way she places colour in her sentences, but I vaguely surmise that there's something you hated and loathed in her. Is there?"[74]

Edith evened the score in her remark to Mary Berenson that

Virginia's photographs in the advertisements for Orlando "made me quite ill. I can't believe that where there is exhibitionism of that order there can be any real creative gift."[75]

But creative gifts there were, of a high order, in both these great ladies of literature, and whether they were willing to admit it or not, each knew the other's quality. Moreover, they agreed about one thing—the genius of Marcel Proust.

"Of all the novelists, European or American, whose lives overlapped her own, Marcel Proust was the one that Edith Wharton by background and training was best equipped to appreciate," wrote Lewis. "The analyst of ebbing New York society recognized at once the genius who explored its immensely more complex French counterpart. She sent a copy of *Swann's Way* to Henry James within two months of its publication; James held back a little, but eventually, according to Edith Wharton's memory, he 'devoured it in a passion of curiosity and admiration,' discerning in it 'a new master,' and 'a new vision.'" Wharton wrote that Proust's "endowment as a novelist . . . has probably never been surpassed." She "ranked him with the Tolstoy of *War and Peace* and the Shakespeare of *King Lear*."[76]

Though a friend of Walter Berry's, Proust never met Wharton, not even during sixteen years of proximity in Paris. Ironically, after Proust's death and that of his translator, Scott Moncrieff, Wharton was asked to complete the translation of *Remembrance of Things Past*, but pleaded age and fatigue.

Age and fatigue did indeed cloud her later years, but Edith Wharton was never vanquished by them. "In spite of illness," she wrote, "in spite even of the arch-enemy sorrow, one can remain alive long past the usual date of disintegration if one is unafraid of change, insatiable in intellectual curiosity, interested in big things, and happy in small ways."[77]

Wharton died at the top of her profession and there she has remained for the whole of the century, only now more esteemed than ever. "Henry James has always been placed slightly higher up the slope of Parnassus than Edith Wharton," said Gore Vidal. "But now that the prejudice against the female writer is on the wane, they look to be exactly what they are: giants, equals, the tutelary and benign gods of our American literature."[78] Wharton need not have worried about writing in the shadow of James. She emerged from his spell with a powerful voice of her own, and with a style infinitely more readable than his.

Proust and Woolf remained thoroughly of their own place throughout their lives. As writers and as people Woolf was wedded to England, Proust to France. Forster too was solidly British even when his work was set in India or Italy. Edith Wharton followed her friend Henry James to Europe to live, but where he adopted a Transatlantic view of both worlds, the Old and the New, she never ceased being a novelist of New York. Joyce too has been forever associated with the Ireland he both loathed and loved[79] though he spent years living on the Continent.

Kenya was the land of individuation for Isak Dinesen, who grew up in Denmark, wrote in English, and moved to a coffee plantation near Nairobi after marrying her Swedish cousin Bror Blixen—which made her Baroness Karen Blixen, her real name. Africa thereafter held her heart and her imagination and was the source of her most famous book, *Out of Africa*. But it did not really contain her any more than Denmark did.

Dinesen, born three years later than Virginia Woolf, was an aristocrat who sought extreme experience and endured hardship to find it. Her husband gave her syphilis, then was away most of the time, caught up in other adventures. Inevitably, they were divorced. Denys Finch Hatton, an English adventurer and her great love, died in a plane crash. The coffee farm devoured money and finally failed, sending Baroness Blixen, at age forty-six, back to her mother's house in Denmark. There she felt she was living an "afterlife," but there she wrote brilliant books—not novels, but exotic stories and elegant accounts of her years in Africa. There she became Isak Dinesen.[80]

It was devastating to return to Denmark after years of freedom on the farm in Kenya. "He lives free who has the strength to," she would write.[81] Even before leaving home, Dinesen had recorded that at her family house she had "something of the same feeling, moral and intellectual, that one encounters physically in a crowded apartment or waiting room, where the windows are kept closed: the air has been consumed."[82] But out of that afterlife—where she was sometimes suicidal, often isolated and worried always about money—came *Out of Africa* and the aromatic stories that Dinesen called tales.

Dinesen believed in fate. She once wrote to her mother, apparently quoting someone else, that "in flight from fate there is no happiness. The outward gain brings only inward sadness."[83] Also, later, in *Out of Africa*, came this: "Pride is faith in the idea that God had, when he made us. A proud man is conscious of the idea, and aspires to realize it. He does not strive towards a happiness, or comfort, which may be irrelevant to God's idea of him. His success is in the idea of God, successfully carried through, and he is in love with his destiny. As the good citizen finds his happiness in the fulfilment of his duty to the community, so does the proud man find his happiness in the fulfilment of his fate."

Feeling that fate held nothing more for her, however, she considered ending her life more than once. "I don't belong, I have no place to be anywhere in the world, and yet I must stay in it," she wrote to her brother Thomas when the farm was beginning to fall apart and she had to limit her hopes for Finch Hatton and quell her yearning for a child. But she wanted to live, and she believed she could discover a purpose inside herself, without depending any longer on outside circumstances. "For what I long for is after all life, and what I fear and take flight from is emptiness and annihilation,—and what else can one hope to achieve by dying? I want so terribly much to live, I want so terribly not to die."[84]

Dinesen railed against fate, but not against life which she regarded as a force unto itself. "I believe that life demands of us that we love it," she observed to her brother, "not merely certain sides of it and only one's ideas and ideals, but life itself in all its forms, before it will give us anything in return."[85] Here is what she asked of life: "My life, I will not let you go except you bless me, but then I will let you go."

"By the time Isak Dinesen began to write," said Judith Thurman, "she believed there was an absolute sense, a divine Intention to life. In such a scheme, if you can be faithful to it, the losses will seem inevitable. And it is this confidence that gives her fiction its immense authority to console."[86]

"No-one came into literature more bloody than I," declared Isak Dinesen.[87] She had lived strenuously and suffered grievous losses. Through it all she had learned a style for coping from the young men of Africa, a style she called divine swank or chic. She comments in *Out of Africa*:

> Those young men [the Masai warriors] have, to the utmost extent, that particular form of intelligence which we call chic;— daring, and wildly fantastical as they seem, they are still unswervingly true to their own nature, and to an immanent ideal. Their style is not an assumed manner, nor an imitation of a foreign perfection; it has grown from the inside, and is an expression of the race and its history.

From her father, Dinesen acquired a sense of the great gesture, as explained by Thurman:

> Great gestures recur over and over in Boganis's work [Boganis
> was Wilhelm Dinesen's penname]: something impossible is
> yearned for; it is realized in symbolic form. A task is set, involving
> enormous risk; it is performed as if no effort were involved. A
> great price is demanded. An even greater one is casually paid.
> The essence of all great gestures is to casually mock necessity—
> economic, biological or narrative. The gesture defies the bour-
> geois impulse to appraise an experience in practical terms, in
> terms of its market value. Survival itself, the most basic of neces-
> sities, has the highest price, and therefore the gestures have to do
> with that 'exquisite *savoir mourir*' that Isak Dinesen also
> admired so deeply. One is forced by life to pay the price for
> one's existence, and this is pain, loss, and death. But one is also
> free to laugh at the price and at oneself for caring about it. This
> disdain for the common-sense view of experience . . . was one of
> Wilhelm's most impressive lessons to his daughter. It carried a
> great germ of self-destructiveness.[88]

But it fit Isak Dinesen's fatalistic view of life and her long flirtation
with death, fueled by the profoundest melancholy. She wasn't always
overcome by depression, however, and she had natural sources of joy.
Consider Lulu, the fawn Karen Blixen fed milk from a saucer at her
farmhouse in Kenya. But the moment came when Lulu was grown, or
almost grown, and had about her intimations of freedom. Here is what
Dinesen wrote about Lulu:

> "Oh Lulu," I thought, "I know that you are marvellously strong
> and that you can leap higher than your own height. You are furi-
> ous with us now, you wish that we were all dead, and indeed we
> should be so if you could be bothered to kill us. But the trouble
> is not as you think now, that we have put up obstacles too high
> for you to jump, and how could we possibly do that you great
> leaper? It is that we have put up no obstacles at all. The great
> strength is in you, Lulu, and the obstacles are within you as well,
> and the thing is, that the fullness of time has not yet come."

But the time did come, and Lulu left without warning. Then one day she returned, bringing her husband with her:

> Lulu of the woods was a superior, independent being, a change
> of heart had come upon her, she was in possession . . . . She was
> now the complete Lulu . . . . She was standing quietly on her
> divine rights. She remembered me enough to feel that I was noth-
> ing to be afraid of. For a minute she gazed at me; her purple
> smoky eyes were absolutely without expression and did not
> wink, and I remembered that the Gods or Goddesses never wink,
> and I felt that I was face to face with the ox-eyed Hera . . . .

> The years in which Lulu and her people came round to my house
> were the happiest of my life in Africa. For that reason, I came to
> look upon my acquaintance with the forest antelopes as upon a
> great boon, and a token of friendship from Africa. All the country
> was in it, good omens, old covenants . . . .

But those years could not last. The Ngong farm folded, and Dinesen
had to leave. Thinking back she asked, "Had those hard times really had
all these in them? There was youth in us then, a wild hope . . . . That bad
time blessed us and went away."

Dinesen returned to Denmark, redeemed her losses as literature, and
grew more eccentric with the years. By her seventies, illness and surgery
had so limited her digestive system that she spent her last days living on
oysters, grapes and fruit and vegetable juices and never weighing more
than eighty-five pounds. By then she also was naming her clothes. For
instance, when she traveled to America for the first time in 1958 the
loose gray sheath and matching turban with which she swathed herself
for her famous lunch with Marilyn Monroe, Arthur Miller and Carson
McCullers was called "Sober Truth." The affect no doubt was accentuated
by the pallor of her face, powdered white, and the darkly made-up eyes
which she attended to the very end.[89]

Isak Dinesen died in 1962, of emaciation. She did it exactly the way
she had chosen—growing lighter and lighter until finally she floated
upward and away, and disappeared, carrying with her a profound originality that had prospered in isolation. No Bloomsbury or Paris sustained
her. She found a way to live almost entirely on her own.

Isak Dinesen was a masterful teller of tales. So was Franz Kafka. He wrote three novels, but, often as not, it's the fables and parables for which he is celebrated. Born in 1883, a year after Virginia Woolf, Kafka spent the brief time allotted him in Prague, living with his parents until he was thirty-two; studying Judaism with a passion his father had long since set aside; frequently making, then breaking engagements to eager young women; fathering a son he never knew; suffering seven years from tuberculosis, which took his life at forty-one. Not until he was desperately ill did Kafka quit his job at the Workers' Accident Insurance Institute, a bondage that brought him insight as well as aggravation. From this experience came a dark and prescient view of the marketplace and what it would do the ordinary people who keep it going. The narrator comments in "The Metamorphosis":

> They fulfilled to the uttermost all that the world demands of poor people, the father fetched breakfast for the small clerks in the bank, the mother devoted her energy to making underwear for strangers, the sister trotted to and fro behind the counter at the behest of customers, but more than this they had not the strength to do.

Kafka wrote about the weird, the woebegone, the eccentrically sad. His stories are peopled with men turned suddenly into insects; hunger artists for whom fasting in carnival cages is more than a living, it's a peculiar, prideful act of creativity; creatures who burrow beneath the earth in anxious solitude. From these characters flow the deep foreboding that has come to be called Kafkaesque. The narrator in "The Burrow" speaks:

> And what trust can I really put in him? Can I trust one whom I have had under my eyes just as fully when I can't see him, and the moss covering separates us? It is comparatively easy to trust anyone if you are supervising him or at least can supervise him; perhaps it is possible even to trust someone at a distance; but completely to trust someone outside the burrow when you are inside the burrow, that is, in a different world, that, it seems to me, is impossible.

> I shall dig a wide and carefully constructed trench in the direction of the noise and not cease from digging until, independent of all theories, I find the real cause of the noise. Then I shall eradicate

it, if that is within my power, and if it is not, at least I shall know the truth. That truth will bring me either peace or despair, but whether the one or the other, it will be beyond doubt or question.

Why have I been spared for so long, only to be delivered to such terrors now? Compared with this, what are all the petty dangers in brooding over which I have spent my life!

Kafka was no creator of beautiful language like Woolf or Proust, or arresting ideas like Forster. No. Instead, Kafka generated tension. He built it up, sentence by sentence, detail by detail, repetitious and tendentious, until he snared the reader in a web of anxiety. Some see in his work a premonition of Hitler and Stalin. (Indeed, his three sisters would die in German concentration camps, one at Auschwitz.) Others divine the definitive shape of bureaucracy as hegemonic monster. John Updike said that Kafka projected onto all authority his fear of an all-powerful father, who made a success in the wholesale clothing business and looked askance at the literary bent of his "sensitive only son."[90]

But Kafka moved steadily forward, turning from the necessary writing he had to do at the office—tracts such as "On Mandatory Insurance in the Construction Industry"—to tales that would make him emblematic of the terror-ridden twentieth century. In his weird characters—the insect whose exhausted family is happy and relieved when he is dead; the hunger artist who endures humiliation to keep his act going; the worrying burrower, impervious to the peace he craves—we see ourselves.

It was a lively, disputatious session that John Cheever, Lillian Hellman, Yevgeny Yevtushenko and a few others had in 1972 trying to decide what is the most significant novel of the twentieth century. Their conclusion: *Doctor Zhivago*.[91] Artistically, one might take issue with them, though Boris Pasternak's book has many lovely moments. But in terms of the sweep of history, he certainly dealt with one of the pivotal events of the past hundred years: the Russian Revolution of October, 1917.

It can be argued that the age turned on World War II with its ghastly Holocaust. Certainly this was the crime of the century as Susan Sontag has said and the most memorable writing that flowed from it was a diary written by a child in Amsterdam named Anne Frank. But the rise of Marxism and its fall constituted the most important intellectual dissension, the most far-reaching break in patterns of thought, of the epoch, both in its beginning and in its end.[92] It was against the destructive energy of Marxism that Pasternak honed his genius.

Boris Pasternak, an intellectual's son, grew up with the likes of Tolstoy and Rachmaninoff in the house. As a young man, he was torn between music and literature, but chose poetry when "his idol, Alexander Scriabin, listened to his composition and gave him a left-handed compliment—that he had a good ear."[93] Pasternak endured long years living in a writers' colony near Moscow, producing poetry and translations of Shakespeare and Goethe that were highly respected by his literary peers but not widely known outside Russia. Then, at sixty-seven, three years before his death in 1960, he brought forth *Doctor Zhivago*, a book he'd been writing since 1948.[94]

Describing *Doctor Zhivago* as "a novel of the moral breakdown of the twentieth century," Yevtushenko told the story of how it reached the west despite the vicious and vituperative efforts of Soviet censors. Pasternak, he related, managed to get the manuscript to a publisher in Italy with these instructions: Believe only messages written in French. When the Soviet propaganda machine began to rev up against him, as he had feared it would, Pasternak wired his publisher to stop publication, but the telegram was in transliterated Russian. The publisher understood perfectly. He halted nothing. Instead he gave *Doctor Zhivago* to the world.[95]

Though Pasternak won the Nobel Prize a year later, in 1958—the Soviets forced him to refuse it—his preeminent work, except for some poems, could not be read in his own country for another thirty years. By then Mikhail Gorbachev thought it advantageous to permit Russians to have *Doctor Zhivago*.

What they found was a mature novel of considerable beauty that recalled its author's early years as a philosophy student in Marburg:

> But all the time, life, one, immense, identical throughout its innumerable combinations and transformations, fills the universe and is continually reborn. You are anxious about whether you will rise from the dead or not. But you rose from the dead when you were born and you didn't notice it.

> However far back you go in your memory, it is always in some external, active manifestation of yourself that you come across your identity—in the work of your hands, in your family, in other

people . . . . You in others—this is your soul. This is what you are. This is what your consciousness has breathed and lived on and enjoyed throughout your life—your soul, your immortality, your life in others. And what does it matter to you if later on that is called your memory? This will be you—the you that enters the future and becomes a part of it.

Pasternak invested his characters with his own strong sense of life's purpose. This is especially true of Lara, drawn after Olga Ivinskaya, a twice-married beauty who fell in love with Pasternak when he was fifty-six and she was over twenty years younger. She described it as "a meeting with God." Olga paid for the affair with a prison sentence, probably levied against her to punish and pressure Pasternak whom Stalin considered anti-Soviet. She was pregnant at the time with Pasternak's child, but suffered a miscarriage.[96]

After the death of Stalin, Olga was released. She moved into a small house in the writers' colony where Pasternak lived and became his literary agent. Days he spent with her and nights he was at home with his wife and family. But Pasternak died in 1960. It wasn't long before Olga was arrested again for "smuggling foreign currency—the royalties she collected for Pasternak from the West—" and returned to a labor camp. It was then that Olga wrote to Soviet leader Nikita Khrushchev pleading for release and pointing out how she had cooperated with the authorities in their zeal to curb Pasternak. "I did everything in my power to avoid a misfortune, but it was beyond my capacity to neutralize everything at once," she wrote on March 10, 1961, adding, the *New York Times* reported, that she "tried to cancel the writer's meetings with foreigners, worked closely with the Central Committee to try and delay publication in the West of 'Doctor Zhivago' . . . and dissuaded Pasternak from leaving the Soviet Union after he was forced to turn down the Nobel Prize he won in 1958."[97]

Olga served half of an-eight year sentence, then lived in limbo until Gorbachev granted her rehabilitation in 1988, the year *Doctor Zhivago* finally appeared in the former Soviet Union. She died seven years later, at eighty-three, leaving behind a bitter battle between her heirs and Pasternak's over his papers which were taken from her apartment when she was arrested the second time.[98]

It was a rough life, made more distasteful by being forced to inform on Pasternak, but Olga achieved apotheosis as Pasternak's Lara:

For a moment she [Lara] rediscovered the purpose of her life.

She was here on earth to grasp the meaning of its wild enchantment and to call each thing by its right name, or, if this were not
within her power, to give birth out of love for life to successors
who would do it in her place.

While Pasternak doesn't hesitate to denounce the rhetoric of the
revolution as "so unimaginative and second-rate," it is the love story of
Lara and Yurii that carries the novel, a love always emanating from the
unified field of human experience.

Oh, what a love it was, utterly free, unique, like nothing else on
earth! Their thoughts were like other people's songs . . . . Never,
never, even in their moments of richest and wildest happiness,
were they unaware of a sublime joy in the total design of the
universe, a feeling that they themselves were a part of that whole,
an element in the beauty of the cosmos.

And this from Lara when Yurii died:

"Your going—my end. Again something big, irreparable, the
riddle of life, the riddle of death, the enchantment of genius, the
enchantment of unadorned beauty—yes, yes, these things were
ours."

Such an understanding filled her now, a dark, indistinct knowledge of death, preparedness for death, a preparedness that
removed all feeling of helplessness in its presence. It was as if
she had lived twenty lives and lost Yurii countless times, and had
accumulated such experience of the heart in this domain that
everything she felt and did beside this coffin was exactly right
and to the point.

Lowering her head, she withdrew into memories, reflections,
conjectures. She escaped into them, sank into them, as though
carried forward for a time, for a few hours, into some future that
she might not live to see, a future that aged her by several
decades, a future where she was an old woman. In her thoughts
she seemed to touch the very bottom of her unhappiness.
That future Lara did not live to see.

One day Larisa Feodorovna went out and did not come back. She must have been arrested in the street at that time. She vanished without a trace and probably died somewhere, forgotten as a nameless number on a list that afterwards got mislaid, in one of the innumerable mixed or women's concentration camps in the north.

All that beauty and spirit extinguished in ugly anonymity. No one to mourn for Lara. Nothing speaks with more terrifying clarity of the brutal Soviet state than her final disappearance.

With the publication of *Doctor Zhivago*, the Kremlin erupted in rage. Those who had never read the book railed against it anyway in the public press. "Workers letters" were prepared the better to fuel the scandal. Pasternak—contented by now with his second wife Zinaida—had "never participated in a single political battle, [but he] ended up in the middle of one, to his own surprise."[99]

To the apparatchik mind, *Doctor Zhivago* had to be counterrevolutionary because it put a love story ahead of history, it elevated Yurii and Lara above the Communist system. "They were used to the theory and practice of turning people into cogs in a state machine. This apologia not of the state but of the human soul had to seem alien and heretical to them."[100]

The irony is that Nikita Khrushchev read *Doctor Zhivago* after Pasternak had died and found nothing counterrevolutionary in it. "'I was tricked . . .' [he] said. 'Then why not publish the novel?' [asked a journalist]. 'They set the whole propaganda machine against it,' Khrushchev sighed. 'It's all too fresh in people's minds . . . Give us some time and we'll publish it.' Khrushchev didn't have time to do it, and Brezhnev didn't dare."[101]

Pasternak was not one of those Russians (like Gorbachev) who yearned for the West. Nor was he limited by Russian nationalism. Yevtushenko described him as both Slavophile and Westernizer. But his emphasis always returned to the soul which allied him forever with the deepest reaches of Russian life. He said so himself: "The soul is leaving the West—it has nothing to do there."[102]

Isaiah Berlin observed this of Pasternak: "[His] passionate, almost obsessive, desire to be thought a Russian writer with roots deep in Russian soil was particularly evident in his negative feelings towards his

Jewish origins . . . . He spoke to me as a believing, if idiosyncratic Christian." And he was at heart a traditionalist. Though steeped in Proust and Joyce's *Ulysses*, Pasternak had little connection to the art of his day or to contemporaries such as Stravinsky or Eliot. As Berlin noted, "Picasso and Matisse, Braque and Bonnard, Klee and Mondrian, seemed to mean as little to [him] as Kandinsky or Malevich . . . . [He] seemed basically untouched by the modern movement . . . ." Berlin also remembered Pasternak's great capacity for conversation. "The only other person who seems to me to have talked as he talked was Virginia Woolf, who . . . made one's mind race as he did, and obliterated one's normal vision of reality in the same exhilarating and, at times terrifying way." Pasternak always knew he was standing in the shadow of all time to come. "How much courage is needed," he wrote, "to play for the centuries."[103]

Like Pasternak, Nadine Gordimer has been tied to historic and cataclysmic events. Where Pasternak endured the Bolsheviks, wrote about them, and suffered at their hands, Gordimer has devoted her life to chronicling apartheid in South Africa. "[A] writer is 'selected' by his subject," she once observed . . . "his subject being the consciousness of his own era."[104]

It took a while for the times to express themselves through Nadine Gordimer. Born in 1923 in Springs, a small, gold-mining town in the Transvaal, she first cast about a bit, playing golf, sipping gin with RAF pilots at the nearby air station, learning first aid and nursing, and living the ornamental, modestly useful life of a well-born young woman before she found her way to writing, at twenty-eight.[105] Where Pasternak was a philosopher, Gordimer has been a politician, joining the African National Congress in 1990, metamorphosing from liberal to radical and back to liberal again. Where he was a poet, she might have been a brilliant essayist if the short story and novel had not claimed her. Where he put love ahead of history, her characters carry always an interpretation of politics and eventful oppressions.

"The fact that I've lived, was born into, a highly politicized society has meant that political meaning has come out of these lives," she said to a *New York Times* interviewer. "I . . . have always been looking for the concealed side." Extolling writing from the third world, "she argues that fiction from these charged circumstances carries an authentic edge; it can bear the weight of rhetoric without 'breaking the spell of the imagination' more readily than contemporary Western fiction because the politics is woven into the very fabric of daily life."[106]

Gordimer's prose does not always succeed. It works least well, said reviewer Caryl Phillips, "when she attempts to comment directly on the South African situation, creating characters, black or white, who are forever in danger of becoming little more than vessels to convey their creator's thoughts and observations." But it is Gordimer's powers of observation that carry her (not intuition—leave that to Pasternak). It is her merciless command of detail that brings her prose to life. In the view of some critics her short stories, taut and stretched over excellent bone structure, tend to be stronger than her novels.[107] They radiate elegance and irony.

Consider *Jump and Other Stories*, a superb collection of contrasts— between worlds that think themselves settled and spheres of chaos, between one person's belief and another's deception, between naive white women of decent intention and third world men who use them. Gordimer writes of suburban houses walled by bristling razor wire (prison architecture, she calls it); a fresh-faced man who jogs foolishly into a black township and is shielded from bad trouble by an African woman with the look of a churchgoer; a principled social-working woman who takes some black youths to her house for lunch and realizes that in mere months they'll be on the streets with guns.

And there's Sylvie of "Safe House," an affluent woman with a husband frequently away, whose car breaks down and she has to take a bus (the first bus she's been on in thirty years) back to her house in a suburb of Johannesburg. On the ride she meets a man who accompanies her home:

And wondering, now, no doubt, whether it was possible that this man off the bus really could be living in the suburb of large houses hidden by trees where she lived, or whether he had left the bus to follow her, and was to be feared, although he was white, in this city where so much was to be feared. It was true that he had picked one of his maze of trails about the city and suburbs in order to walk with her—an impulse like any of the impulses with which he had to fill in the days of his disconnection from consecutive action. The unexpected was his means of survival. To be Underground is to have a go at living without consequences.

So she drew him round, and murmuring casual thanks, he joined her. Now they were walking together. At one of the pillared entrances in white battlements topped with black iron spikes she pressed the button of an intercom panel and spoke. The flats of a stage set, the wide polished wooden gates slid back electronically. Trees, her trees led up to and overflowed the roof of the spread wings of the house. Small dogs jumped about her. Sprinklers arched rainbows over lawns. She called out in the joyous soprano used to summon faithful servants, and ice and fruit juice were brought onto a shaded terrace. Behind him the colours of Persian carpets, paintings and bowls of flowers blurred in the deep perspective of one of those huge rooms used for parties.

But Harry (the name he uses) is not what she supposes:

In his cell, he wondered—an aside from his preoccupation with the trial, and the exhilaration, after all, of being once again with his comrades, the fellow accused—he wondered whether she had recognized him. But it was unlikely she would follow reports of political trials. Come to think of it, there were no newspapers to be seen around her house, that house where she thought herself safe among trees, safe from the threat of him and his kind, safe from the present."

So Gordimer, a genius of cautionary tales, reminds us once again that we often protect against the wrong things.

There is no protection for those who people the world of Toni Morrison. She writes about American apartheid and the cruel legacy of slavery. Born Chloe Anthony Wofford, a ship welder's daughter, in the rust belt of Ohio, she tells her stories with such radiant, searing insight that her work commanded the Nobel Prize for Literature in 1993.[108]

Reared in a family where tales of ghosts and dreams were freely related, Morrison was the first in her kindergarten class to read. Nonetheless she was cleaning the houses of white people by the time she was thirteen.

Morrison escaped that fate at Howard University where she studied hard and ran for sorority queen. She also earned a masters from Cornell. Drawing on the novels of Virginia Woolf and Faulkner, she did her thesis on their treatment of suicide. Howard lured her back to teach, and there her students included Stokely Carmichael and Claude Brown who later wrote *Manchild in the Promised Land*.

She married an architecture student, Harold Morrison, and had two sons, but it didn't work and they parted after five years. Toni Morrison began writing, she said, to ward off "melancholy." Then came the opportunity to join a publisher in Syracuse as a textbook editor. Random House bought the company and moved Morrison to New York, where she shepherded the writing of Angela Davis among others. Years later the State University of New York offered her a professorship. She accepted, and later moved to Princeton.

By then Morrison's novels had long since been winning the National Book Critics Circle Award (for *Song of Solomon* and *Beloved*) as well as the Pulitzer Prize (also for *Beloved* which was based on a true story she uncovered while editing *The Black Book* for Random House.)

Toni Morrison's characters live lives so brutal they make dying seem easy. In *Beloved*, they say as much themselves:

"Was it hard? I hope she didn't die hard."
Sethe shook her head. "Soft as cream. Being alive was the hard part."

And there's this echo of agony:

Walking through it [Sethe's house] a wave of grief soaked him so thoroughly he wanted to cry . . . . Paul D looked at the spot where the grief had soaked him. The red [a strange light] was gone but a kind of weeping clung to the air where it had been."

Paul D appears from the past. To Sethe, who has not seen him in eighteen years, he is a Godsend.

What she knew was that the responsibility for her breasts, at last, was in somebody else's hands. Would there be a little space, she wondered, a little time, some way to hold off eventfulness, to push busyness into the corners of the room and just stand there a minute or two, naked from shoulder blade to waist, relieved of the weight of her breasts, smelling the stolen milk again and the pleasure of baking bread? Maybe this one time she could stop dead still in the middle of a cooking meal—not even leave the stove—and feel the hurt her back ought to. Trust things and remember things because the last of the Sweet Home men was there to catch her if she sank?

Paul D, however, has weaknesses, impossible to overlook:

> But maybe a man was nothing but a man, which is what Baby Suggs [Sethe's mother-in-law] always said. They encouraged you to put some of your weight in their hands and soon as you felt how light and lovely that was, they studied your scars and tribulations, after which they did what he had done: ran her children out and tore up the house . . . .
> "A man ain't nothing but a man," said Baby Suggs. "But a son? Well now, that's *somebody*."

Sethe's own two sons do not turn out so well. When the stakes are high and it really counts, they run out on their mother, leaving her to bitter isolation. There is a daughter named Denver who stays, but peace she can find only in fantasy.

> In that bower, closed off from the hurt of the hurt world, Denver's imagination produced its own hunger and its own food, which she badly needed because loneliness wore her out. *Wore her out*. Veiled and protected by the live green walls, she felt ripe and clear, and salvation was as easy as a wish.

Salvation seems to lie in the strange girl, Beloved. Denver (like Sethe) is obsessed with her:

> Beloved got up and lay down on the bed. Their quietness boomed about on the walls like birds in panic. Finally Denver's breath steadied against the threat of an unbearable loss.

Morrison dispenses her wisdom through Baby Suggs, holy, Sethe's sainted mother-in-law:

> Before 124 and everybody in it had closed down, veiled over and shut away, before it had become the plaything of spirits and the home of the chafed, 124 had been a cheerful, buzzing house

where Baby Suggs, holy, loved, cautioned, fed, chastised and
soothed. Where not one but two pots simmered on the stove;
where the lamp burned all night long. Strangers rested there
while children tried on their shoes. Messages were left there, for
whoever needed them was sure to stop in one day soon. Talk was
low and to the point—for Baby Suggs, holy, didn't approve of
extra. "Everything depends on knowing how much," she said,
and "Good is knowing when to stop."

Accepting no title of honor before her name, but allowing a small
caress after it, she became an unchurched preacher, one who visited pulpits and opened her great heart to all who could use it. In
winter and fall she carried it to AME's and Baptists, Holinesses
and Sanctified, the Church of the Redeemer and the Redeemed.
Uncalled, unrobed, unanointed, she let her great heart beat in
their presence. When warm weather came, Baby Suggs, holy,
followed by every black man, woman and child who could make
it through, took her great heart to the Clearing—a wide-open
place cut deep in the woods nobody knew for what at the end of
a path known only to deer and whoever cleared the land in the
first place. In the heat of every Saturday afternoon, she sat in the
Clearing while the people waited among the trees.

After situating herself on a huge flat-sided rock, Baby Suggs
bowed her head and prayed silently. The company watched her
from the trees. They knew she was ready when she put her stick
down. Then she shouted, "Let the children come!" and they ran
from the trees toward her.

"Let your mothers hear you laugh," she told them, and the woods
rang. The adults looked on and could not help smiling.

"Then let the grown men come," she shouted. They stepped out
one by one from among the trees.

"Let your wives and your children see you dance," she told them,
and groundlife shuddered under their feet.

Finally she called the women to her. "Cry," she told them. "For the living and the dead. Just cry." And without covering their eyes, the women let loose.

It started that way: laughing children, dancing men, crying women and then it got mixed up. Women stopped crying and danced; men sat down and cried; children danced, women laughed, children cried until, exhausted and riven, all and each lay about the clearing damp and gasping for breath. In the silence that followed, Baby Suggs, holy, offered up to them her great big heart.

She did not tell them to clean up their lives or to go and sin no more. She did not tell them they were the blessed of the earth, its inheriting meek or glorybound poor.

She told them that the only grace they could have was the grace they could imagine. That if they could not see it, they would not have it

For all her spirit, Baby Suggs cannot keep her great big heart from breaking, from giving up and giving in to a slow, indifferent departure. After she's gone Beloved arrives, and the house that had burst with life, then shrunk from death, glows with the surreal light that so disturbed Paul D.

Paul D delivers in the end. He returns to Sethe, walks right in again to her circle of personal horror:

Paul D sits down in the rocking chair and examines the quilt patched in carnival colors. His hands are limp between his knees. There are too many things to feel about this woman. His head hurts. Suddenly he remembered Sixo trying to describe what he felt about the Thirty-Mile Woman. "She is a friend of my mind. She gather me, man. The pieces I am, she gather them and give them back to me in all the right order. It's good, you know, when you got a woman who is a friend of your mind."

Louise Cowan, a professor of literature, said that Beloved, the girl, embodies the guilt of slavery that must be acknowledged, given its due, and then "disremembered." In capturing those years of reawakening and torment after the Civil War, Toni Morrison bridges a continental divide in the American psyche, between national ideals and awful actuality. There is a sin at the core of the culture, it's been said, and Morrison brings her readers as close as any writer can to collective redemption.

William Faulkner has been called America's foremost writer of the twentieth century. Certainly Louise Cowan believes that. (I don't. I would go instead for Wharton.) Awarded the Nobel Prize in 1950, Faulkner has been compared to Balzac,[109] but he himself said that the most formative influences on his work were Melville, Dostoevski, Conrad, and the Old Testament. (Indeed his titles are steeped in Biblical resonance: *If I Forget Thee, Jerusalem; Go Down, Moses and Other Stories; Absalom, Absalom!*)

Whatever the provenance, his was a brutal world. Faulkner's Mississippi in the first half of this century was toxic with resentment and the bitterness of loss. Defeat clotted the air, suffocating decent human sentiment.

Faulkner got away from Mississippi for awhile. He spent some time in Paris and developed a feeling for art. He saw the work of Rodin, Matisse and Picasso, and he fell in love with the luminosity of Cezanne.

In 1918 he pretended to be British so he could enlist in the Royal Air Force in Toronto. But the war ended before he got out of training.

Faulkner, however, was no expatriate. He returned to his home state and enrolled at the University of Mississippi where his father was assistant secretary. Faulkner even pledged a fraternity. From there, his own ground, later evoked as Yoknapatawpha County, his work would grow.

Marriage to his childhood sweetheart (already divorced from what had seemed a better prospect) did not deter Faulkner from frequent affairs, including a long liaison with Meta Carpenter, assistant to Howard Hawks, the movie director. For him and others Faulkner wrote a number of screenplays to make money, including Hawks' *To Have and Have Not*, based on a novel by Hemingway and starring Humphrey Bogart and Lauren Bacall.

Faulkner's first novel, *Soldiers' Pay*, appeared in 1925 and his mother was so appalled by its sexual content she told him he would be best off leaving the country. His father refused to read the book. *Sanctuary* followed four years later, and this time it was Faulkner's publisher who was shocked. There were many months before he worked up the courage to bring it out and only then because he thought it might make some money.

Sanctuary was indeed a big seller, and, compounding its success, Paramount produced it as a movie. (By then Faulkner had begun writing scripts for Hollywood.) Intrinsic in *Sanctuary* were all the seeds of Faulkner's genius, fertilized by his despair.

Has there ever been a baby more clearly doomed than the one described in *Sanctuary*?

> It [the child] lay in a sort of drugged immobility, like the children which beggars on Paris streets carry, its pinched face slick with faint moisture, its hair a damp whisper of shadow across its gaunt, veined skull, a thin crescent of white showing beneath its lead-colored eyelids.

Light in August followed in 1932 with characters who are just as desolate:

> She was a waitress in a small, dingy, back street restaurant in town. Even a casual adult glance could tell that she would never see thirty again. But to Joe she probably did not look more than seventeen, too, because of her smallness. She was not only not tall, she was slight, almost childlike. But the adult look saw the smallness was not due to any natural slenderness but to some inner corruption of the spirit itself: a slenderness which had never been young, in not one of whose curves anything youthful had ever lived or lingered.

Both books are sunk in wretched gloom and lacerating acts of violation. Faulkner doesn't just write a rape, but a rape with a corncob. His Joe Christmas doesn't commit mere murder, he practically hacks a woman's head off. But there is a difference. The characters of *Light in August*, however degraded and sickening, are capable of salvation. In *Sanctuary*, with few exceptions, this is far from true.

Faulkner, like Proust, created an atmosphere that is palpable, only his is tawdry where Proust's is elegant. Like Morrison, Faulkner dealt with the rough edges of American life and showed them to be closer to the core than many would like to admit. He lacked her lyricism and her gift for pulling poetry from the vernacular of ordinary people. Instead Faulkner's strength lay in his narrative power. Enormously influential among Latin American magical realists, his stories called the nation to the absolution that only can come from intimate acquaintance with its own shadow.

Who would have guessed in the luscious days of Proust or the harsh, high moment of Faulkner that the twentieth century at the end would reach back two hundred years to reclaim the "genius of measure, decorum and irony"—Jane Austen.[110] Lionel Trilling spotted the trend as early as the 1950s when he wrote that "her very name is a charged one."[111]

By 1973, when the women's movement was in full sail along with the counter-culture, Trilling offered a course on Jane Austen at Columbia University, bitter scene of campus protests, and was deluged with applicants. There was an "almost hysterical moral urgency" about it, he related.[112]

What did they want? Was it manners and order as some supposed when *Sense and Sensibility* hit the screen and the best-seller list in 1995? By then, yes, that would have been part of it. Exhausted and debilitated by the social convulsions that commenced in the sixties, people no doubt wanted relief and release from constant unguided confrontation with each other.

But this was not likely the case in 1973, much less 1957. Some convincing answers can be found in Trilling, at least for women. The first lies in Emma: "The extraordinary thing about Emma," wrote Trilling, "is that she has a moral life as a man has a moral life. And she doesn't have it as a special instance, as an example of a new kind of woman, which is the way George Eliot's Dorothea Brooke has her moral life, but quite as a matter of course, as a given quality of nature . . . . Women in fiction only rarely have the peculiar reality of the moral life that self-love bestows. Most commonly they exist in a moonlike way, shining by the reflected moral light of men. They are 'convincing' or 'real' and sometimes 'delightful,' but they seldom exist as men exist—as genuine moral destinies."[113]

A moral life! Of course, this would be supremely important to women. It was one reason they rallied to Lillian Hellman in the 1970s and especially to "Julia," the film made from one of her stories. Julia and Hellman, in those harrowing days before World War II, had moral lives. Hellman smuggled money into Germany by train to help Julia in her work for the resistance.

But back to Emma: Trilling noted that Emma saw no need for self-effacement. "She is 'Emma, never loth to be first,' loving pre-eminence and praise, loving power and frank to say so." Moreover, she hopes to become "more acquainted with herself," as Austen wrote. What a modern woman she is and "how thoroughly she confirms [the judgment] that Jane Austen is the first truly modern novelist of England."[114] Even more subtly, Trilling cites a nineteenth century critic who suggested that Austen's mind was "saturated" with a "Platonic idea"—the idea of "intelligent love," based on "the giving and receiving of knowledge, the active formation of another's character, or the more passive growth under another's guidance." The Platonic idea holds this, he said, as "the truest and strongest foundation of love."[115] Wasn't this the love of Edith Wharton and Walter Berry, of Leonard and Virginia Woolf, and the love that Margaret Schlegel wanted with Mr. Wilcox in *Howards End*? Wouldn't this kind of love hold a powerful attraction for late twentieth century women? No wonder they flocked to Jane Austen.

But there is something more, something that would have no appeal for university students of the counter-culture but that certainly speaks to those struggling with the sober last days of the twentieth century. Harold Bloom understood it when he wrote that Anne Elliot of Austen's last novel, *Persuasion* (a "perfect novel" he called it), was "a more problematic being [than other Austen heroines], tinged with a new sadness concerning life's limits."[116]

Trilling elaborated on this point: "What we may call Jane Austen's first or basic irony," he said, "is the recognition of the fact that spirit is not free, that it is conditioned, that it is limited by circumstances. This, as everyone knows from childhood on, is indeed an anomaly. Her next and consequent irony has reference to the fact that only by reason of this anomaly does spirit have virtue and meaning."[117]

So it wasn't just the yearning for social stability or civility in manners that sent film-goers hurrying to *Sense and Sensibility* and *Persuasion* in the mid-1990s. It was a wish to find dignity and significance in lives that are circumscribed.

Jane Austen's life was circumscribed too. Living in her father's parsonage with no room of her own for working, she covered her page with a blotter whenever she heard the approach of family or visitors. "She never travelled," observed Virginia Woolf, "she never drove through London in an omnibus or had luncheon in a shop by herself."[118]

"Had she lived a few more years only," wrote Woolf, "all that would have altered. She would have stayed in London, dined out, lunched out, met famous people, made new friends, read, travelled, and carried back to the quiet country cottage a hoard of observations to feast upon at leisure." And, of course, to incorporate into her work. Given a longer life, "she would have been the forerunner of Henry James and Proust . . . ."[119]

As it was, Jane Austen produced six immortal novels before she died at forty-two. And she became the forerunner by one hundred years or more of Virginia Woolf, Edith Wharton, Isak Dinesen, Toni Morrison and Nadine Gordimer. Wharton, of course, mastered the novel of manners, but Woolf's poetic vision; Dinesen's gothic sensibility; Morrison's tragic earthiness and Gordimer's terse, politically charged realism bear little resemblance to the elegant portraits composed by Jane Austen. Yet Jane Austen led the way. She proved that a woman could be a writer of the first rank.

It is due in part to her that the twentieth century belongs to women writers and especially to Virginia Woolf—not as a fixture of Bloomsbury, not as a champion of feminists, not even as a novelist, but as someone who thought deeply about life and transposed those thoughts into a poet's prose. She took the torch of Jane Austen and delivered it, much enhanced, to today's generation of literary women.

Chapter
Seven

George Gershwin
   George Gershwin was emblematic of those who gave the world musical theatre and created a new, distinctly American art form.

By Popular Demand: Musical Theater

Helen pushed her way out during the applause.
She desired to be alone. The music summed up
to her all that had happened or could happen
in her career. She read it as a tangible
statement, which could never be superceded.
The notes meant this and that to her, and they
could have no other meaning, and life could
have no other meaning.

E.M. Forster

The past hundred years have not called forth classical music in the way that the eighteenth and nineteenth centuries did, though certainly there have been moments of magic. Nurtured by the long, post-Napoleon peace that Metternich and Castlereagh gave Europe with a only a few interruptions, music flourished after 1820, elaborating on well loved themes, romanticizing the past and preparing the soil for the emergence of sounds wholly new and disruptive.

Gustav Mahler, mostly a man of the nineteenth century, maintained the old, elegant order while foretelling the harsh tone that lay ahead. Indifferent to his Jewish roots, he converted to Catholicism just two months before being put in charge of the Vienna Opera. Some call it pragmatic, but his Second Symphony (known as *Resurrection*, completed a few years before his turning to Rome) certainly attests to strong spiritual feeling.

Mahler's life was triumphant, but laced with difficulty. In the midst of major conducting assignments in Prague, Budapest, Hamburg, London, and New York as well as Vienna, he remained preoccupied with death and at one point consulted Freud for help. His wife, Alma, caused him great distress when she struck up an affair with architect Walter

Gropius, founder of the Bauhaus. But none of it daunted Mahler. He made music germinal enough to reach into the twentieth century and inspire the likes of Schoenberg.[1]

Claude Debussy, praised as the true heir of Chopin, brought to the piano a gracefulness of feeling no less exquisite because it was based on a scale of six whole tones that looked ahead to harmonies never heard before. He created melodies both sophisticated and beguiling, ripe with riches, drenched in loveliness, blessed by the utter absence of strain.

If Debussy set Impressionist paintings to music, with color shimmering in the sunlight, quintessentially French, as some have said, then Sergei Rachmaninoff was the Cézanne of the orchestra. Just as Cézanne, with his powerful sense of form, could not be contained by France, so Rachmaninoff transcended his native Russia, which he left after the revolution, to become the lyric voice of the age, beloved in a way that most twentieth century composers are not. Even so, just as Cézanne molded his own landscape into a universal statement, rendering it with Voltairean vigor, Rachmaninoff drew upon the depths of Russia, from Tchaikovsky to Tolstoy to the Orthodox Christian chant, to create beauty so lustrous that it kept alive the idea of romance when all evidence to support it had been extinguished by tragedies too radical for human assimilation.

Rachmaninoff did not influence the composers of his time in the way that Cézanne reached beyond his death in 1906 to shape the work of Picasso and Matisse, but he gathered the glories of his heritage into a lasting gift. Cézanne was an artist of projection, Rachmaninoff of recollection. Both were indispensable creators of their times.

No one brought more gravitas to the era than Jean Sibelius who never forsook the romantic impulse. He too proved that deeply indigenous music could soar to universal significance. Finland was his great love, and it was in the folk songs of the Finnish people that he found his strength. These he translated into seven symphonies of sonorous splendor. Verging at times on the dissonance of the day, his work returned always to a call for truth. With unfailing, dramatic flair, he discovered in sound a cosmic order of coherence and joy.

But it was a structure he could not sustain. By the time he was sixty-four, Sibelius had written his last, seventh symphony. Time and again he tried for an eighth, only to destroy the work and lapse once more into silence. Almost three more decades he lived, but, like Brancusi, he had exhausted his inner resources in a punishing quest for internal unity, which can be a wellspring of power. But, as Margaret Thatcher and

Virginia Woolf learned, the strain of such striving also can bring an end too soon to creative life.

"At the close of World War I," wrote Carl Schorske, "Maurice Ravel recorded in *Le Valse* the violent death of the nineteenth century world. [It was a] frantic *danse macabre* . . . a fantastic whirl of destiny . . . . The concentric elements became eccentric, disengaged from the whole, thus transforming harmony into cacophony."[2]

Certainly *La Valse* is on the edge, replete with rapture and disintegration, anxiety and expectation, then, finally, frenzy. Ravel permitted himself to feel the panic implicit in that moment when one world vanished and another took terrifying shape as responsible people stood aside, helpless to intervene.

Yet this is the same Ravel who wrote the radiant *Pavane for a Dead Princess*. This is the same Ravel who produced the robust sexuality of *Bolero*. This is the same Ravel whose piano compositions are compared to those of Debussy in their delicacy and tact.

It has been said that Ravel was not an experimental musician. He didn't have to be. Ravel allowed his times to flow through him, expressing themselves in utmost modernity that resonated still with the romantic impulse. No matter how harried, his work couldn't help being voluptuous and lyrical.

Igor Stravinsky presided over the new epoch, a complex presence. Born in 1882, the same year as Virginia Woolf and James Joyce, he stormed into the twentieth century as a creator of ballets. For Diaghilev he hit three homes runs: *The Firebird, Petrushka,* and *The Rite of Spring* which was staged by a neophyte choreographer named Vaclav Nijinsky, one of the greatest dancers of all time.

The audience went wild over *The Rite of Spring*, as well it might. Bracing as a brisk morning in March, it exudes new life with an agony of longing.

In this work, Stravinsky strove, as always, for the Apollonian principle. It is his steadfast embrace of reason that has caused him to be considered the finest composer of the age. Stravinsky embodies the rationalist ethic that made its way from the Enlightenment to its final denouement in the twentieth century.

That did not keep him from the depths of human experience. His *Symphony of Psalms* is profound, ominous. It imagines much that might require divine protection. It's like a requiem, only death lies ahead, not behind.

Nor did reason preclude in Stravinsky the nerve to experiment. He turned for the first time to twelve-tone composition when he was sixty-nine. Apollonian he may have been, and anti-romantic, but he knew how to keep himself alive.

Then there's Dmitri Shostakovich, who never left Russia, as Stravinsky and Rachmaninoff did, both eventually for America. Shostakovich endured the days of Stalin, sometimes in favor, sometimes not. He learned to hunker down and deliver his music in heavy disguise so no one could tell what he was saying, if anything, about the Bolshevik state. Even then he was criticized as too far removed from "Soviet reality."[3] Despite constant strain, he turned out fifteen symphonies full of foreboding and shrill poignancy, soaring at times to unexpected elegance.

Béla Bartok was as wedded to his own Hungary as Sibelius was to Finland. Bartok too fell in love with folk songs, but unlike Sibelius, he felt isolated, even in his own land. Not for him were the sounds of earlier eras. Bartok was compelled to push tonal music as far as it would go. Melody he discarded and replaced with tones of harsh intensity that pierce to the bone. His work is dark and riddled with tension—like the twentieth century. Yet it goes deep into the earth, and from unseen roots it soars into the stratosphere of disharmony, beyond worldly arrangements. His notes are discordant, but true.

And what of the truth of Arnold Schoenberg? He went searching for it in grating, twelve-note compositions that seduce the intellect but leave the heart untouched except to agitate the emotions with atonal anxiety. Snapping the mainsails of the highly strung, Schoenberg brought the century home to people who knew that there were no safe harbors.

And no one understood that better than he did. Born Jewish in Vienna, deserted at one point by his wife who ran off with a young painter (she later came back and the painter committed suicide), Schoenberg converted in time to Lutheranism. But in 1933, as Hitler was hatching the Nazi horror, he renewed his old faith which meant he had to leave Europe for the United States.

Unable to bear his own interpretation of the times, Schoenberg turned later, while living in California, not only to tonal pieces of his own but also to orchestrating Brahms and Bach, reinvigorating the German tradition he had so willfully shattered.[4] Thus even Arnold Schoenberg could not work on the edge forever.

John Cage could. But there are reasons for that: If Schoenberg was perfect for the age of psychoanalysis, his pupil, Cage, announced the arrival of Prozac. His is the music of repose, the modern world made habitable. Often working on prepared piano (with bolts, weather stripping and other objects inside, between the strings, generating sounds never associated with Steinway), Cage produced his art through random selection. The results, though sometimes frenetic, could also be charming, even soothing, foretelling a strange and surprising peace.

But these were not the sounds that captured the allegiance of the era. How could they, descending as they did into a hodgepodge of approaches, heavily influenced by totalitarian politics and marked by the "gradual disappearance of large . . . forms like the oratorio and the grand symphony and the lack of a common musical language"? It all pointed toward the end of literacy in music and a desperate need for fresh inspiration.[5]

In the midst of this disintegration, however, new tunes burst forth to enchant a growing and devoted public. Though many of the century's great composers came eventually to America—Mahler (for three seasons of conducting), Rachmaninoff, Stravinsky, Bartok and Schoenberg—it was other immigrants, or children of immigrants, who set the world singing in a different key. They made New York the center of musical theater.

Few of them had any training in composition. Some needed help to orchestrate their scores. One (Bob Merrill, who wrote the lyrics for *Funny Girl*) created his tunes on a toy xylophone.[6]

The most emblematic figure of Broadway's golden age of musical theater is George Gershwin. Born in Brooklyn in 1898, the son of Russian-Jewish immigrants, he grew up on the Lower East Side and never finished high school. Yet the artistry he produced was so compelling Leonard Bernstein called Gershwin "one of the true authentic geniuses" of American music. "Time and history," said Bernstein, "may even show him to be the truest and most authentic of his time and place."

Gershwin's father was forever trying a new small business from bakeries to restaurants to bookmaking. He liked to live within walking distance of his work, so the family moved frequently—twenty-eight times before George was eighteen.

By then he had studied piano, written his first song, and taken accounting to please his mother who thought this would be a good profession for him. But numbers, his biographer Charles Schwartz relates, were not for George. Notes were. Gershwin was only fifteen when he asked his mother to let him leave school and go to work as a pianist and song plugger at Remick's, the music publisher in Tin Pan Alley. She said yes, and he was off—a child rushing to a racy world—to record piano rolls and play at "parties, nightclubs, and theatres."

Before long one of Gershwin's songs was published. This led to his getting a number into Sigmund Romberg's latest revue—a coup. Before long, Gershwin was ready to leave Remick's and follow his idol, Jerome Kern, to Broadway. En route, he turned down a job transcribing songs for Irving Berlin and instead produced his own work for Tin Pan Alley's most important music publishing firm.

Gershwin's first Broadway musical opened in 1919, when he was twenty-one. It was *La, La, Lucille,* and it didn't do badly. But it couldn't compare in impact with "Swanee," his first real hit song, performed that same year in a show of Al Jolson's. "Swanee" made George Gershwin rich.

Then *Lady be Good* (with "Fascinating Rhythm") appeared in 1924, followed by *Funny Face* ("My One and Only" and "S'Wonderful") in 1927. Both involved collaboration with George's brother Ira and dancing by a brother-sister team named Fred and Adele Astaire. The years brought other sensations: *Oh, Kay!* ("Someone to Watch Over Me") with Gertrude Lawrence; *Rosalie* ("How Long Has This Been Going On?" and "The Man I Love"); *Show Girl* ("Liza,"); *Strike Up the Band* ("I've Got a Crush on You" and "Soon,"); and *Girl Crazy* ("Bidin' My Time," "Boy! What Love Has Done to Me!" "But Not for Me," "Embraceable You," and "I Got Rhythm,") with Ethel Merman and Ginger Rogers.

Lady Be Good was so successful that George earned enough from it and other shows to buy a five-story town house near Riverside Drive. His parents lived there. So did his brother Ira with his wife, plus another brother and a sister. The house was always overflowing with people, so George took a couple of rooms in a nearby hotel where he could work quietly.

Gershwin was never satisfied to think of himself as merely a tune-smith. Though only marginally acquainted with matters of theory and counterpoint, he set about at the age of twenty-five to write an orchestral piece ambitious enough to draw upon Liszt, Chopin, Tchaikovsky, and Debussy. Envisioned for jazz band and piano, the work was intended, said Gershwin, to refute certain misconceptions about jazz: that it "had to be in strict time," or it "had to cling to dance rhythms." What resulted was *Rhapsody in Blue.*

The basic idea for *Rhapsody* came to Gershwin while he was on a train to Boston. "It was on the train," he said, "with its steely rhythms, its rattle-ty bang that is often so stimulating to a composer . . . . I frequently hear music in the very heart of noise."[7]

With Gershwin at the piano, *Rhapsody* was performed by Paul Whiteman, who assembled a distinguished list of patrons for the concert including Sergei Rachmaninoff, Fritz Kreisler, Jascha Heifetz, Leopold Stokowski, Heywood Broun, Frank Crowninshield, and Gilbert Seldes. Greeted by wild applause, *Rhapsody in Blue* prompted Leonard Bernstein to say, years later, of its young composer, "I don't think there has been such an inspired melodist on this earth since Tchaikovsky . . . ."[8]

Bernstein recognized the deficiencies of *Rhapsody*: "The *Rhapsody* . . . ." he wrote, is ". . . a string of separate paragraphs stuck together— with a thin paste of flour and water . . . . I find that the themes, or tunes, or whatever you want to call them, in the *Rhapsody* are terrific . . . . Your *Rhapsody in Blue* is not a real composition in the sense that whatever happens in it must seem inevitable, or even pretty inevitable. You can cut out parts of it without affecting the whole in any way except to make it shorter. You can remove any of these stuck-together sections and the piece still goes on as bravely as before. You can even interchange these sections with one another and no harm is done . . . . It's still the *Rhapsody in Blue*."[9]

Gershwin pushed on to a second orchestral piece, *Concerto in F*, which premiered at Carnegie Hall. For this he had to learn what a "concerto" was. So he bought a text book on orchestration to guide him. Next came *An American in Paris*, which he went to France to write. There he met a number of eminent composers, from Prokofiev to Ravel with whom he wanted to study. Most of them (though not Prokofiev) praised his work and encouraged him to continue in the symphonic vein he yearned to pursue.

Gershwin also considered studying with Schoenberg when both were in Hollywood, but it never came about. He did work on his musicianship with others. And he assembled a notable art collection—Gauguin, Rouault, Kandinsky, Léger, and Picasso among others—as well as painting portraits himself.

Women were important to Gershwin, but he seldom stayed in love for long. He did plead with Paulette Goddard to leave her husband, Charles Chaplin, and marry him, but she said no. Some have observed that Gershwin was drawn to women who were safely wedded to other men.

Gershwin could be obsessed with himself, and certainly he had his detractors. Oscar Levant once observed, "An evening with Gershwin was a Gershwin evening. There were recurrent, lengthy references to his piano playing, his composing, his conducting, his painting—. . . monologues . . . which George's audiences absorbed with the fascinating attentiveness of a Storm-trooper listening to one of Hitler's well-modulated fireside chats."[10]

Of course, it must be admitted that when Gershwin was at a party, many of the guests expected him to perform at the piano and they welcomed his music. It must be admitted too that in his opera, *Porgy and Bess*, Gershwin fulfilled his dream of serious composing, even including some of the atonality he admired so much in Alban Berg. Duke Ellington may have criticized Gershwin for writing a "white" *Porgy*, but once again the young man from Tin Pan Alley took an art form of which he knew little and made it rapturous. He also wrote with great respect for the black experience and with full recognition, as he said, that "[a]ll modern jazz . . . came directly from Africa."[11]

The Great Depression sent Broadway into desperate straits, but Hollywood did well, offering an oasis to talent such as Jerome Kern, Irving Berlin and the Gershwin brothers. One of George and Ira's earliest movies was *Shall We Dance* with Fred Astaire and Ginger Rogers. It was full of treasures such as "Let's Call the Whole Thing Off," "They Can't Take That Away from Me," "They All Laughed," and "Slap That Bass." This was followed by another Fred Astaire film (*A Damsel in Distress* with Joan Fontaine) featuring "A Foggy Day" and "Nice Work If You Can Get It."

Then, shocking as a chill in July, death came unannounced to George Gershwin, after surgery for a brain tumor. At thirty-eight, he left in progress "Love Walked In" and "Love is Here to Stay" as well as a body of work now known as the primary classics of musical theater.

George Gershwin was an immigrant's son who gave Americans music that was quintessentially their own. He captured the country in the 1920s and 1930s, emitting the same reckless bravura, insisting later on sober hope. Gershwin's romantic imagination soared brightly and briefly, proving to Americans that they could withstand anything, even the plunge from high exaltation to sudden loss. After all, 'they can't take that away from me.'

Cole Porter, seven years older than Gershwin, was the scion of a solid, Midwestern family with roots deep in the earth of Peru, Indiana. His great-grandfather settled there and built a respectable estate from farming and merchandising. His son—Cole Porter's strong-willed and dominating grandfather—left for gold-rush California, only to return to Peru successful enough to launch businesses and land ventures in several states. When his adored daughter Kate married a druggist, J. O. Cole continued running everything as if his unprepossessing son-in-law had never entered the family. Kate liked her husband's interest in poetry and literature, but her father and her son remained the critical men in her life.

Young Cole Porter, his mother's only child (she lost two others), enraged his grandfather when he went away to Worcester Academy in Massachusetts, then to Yale. Instead of training to take over the family empire as his grandfather wished, Cole, once in college, wrote over three hundred songs at his own upright piano, including "Bull Dog," which is sung still at Yale games. He joined the Whiffenpoofs and put together musical productions that foretold the magic to come.

But J. O. Cole, who had not spoken to his daughter for two years after she permitted her son to go to Worcester, still saw a legal, not musical, career for his grandson. At the patriarch's insistence, Porter went to Harvard Law School where his house-mate was Dean Acheson. But law interested him not at all. So without telling his grandfather, he switched to Arts and Sciences. Here Cole had the full support of his mother, who had done all she could to encourage him at the piano, often joining him in songs of surprisingly irreverent wit for a proper woman of Indiana.

Music, of course, it would have to be. Like Gershwin, Cole Porter was very young (only twenty-five) when his first show appeared on Broadway. *See America First* was panned as O.K. for Yale, but not New York. Even so, it was a beginning, though Porter would not be back for three years.

In 1917, while war was ravaging Europe, he sailed for France, a zither outfitted with a small piano keyboard strapped to his back. There he did volunteer work distributing food. He also met Linda Lee Thomas, a banker's daughter from Louisville, Kentucky, who had married, then divorced, the philandering heir of a publishing family. She was elegant and wealthy with notable friends ranging from George Bernard Shaw to John Galsworthy, Winston Churchill, and Bernard Berenson. Several years older than Cole, Linda Thomas was the epitome of sophistication, glamour, and taste. She and Cole took to each other right away. He was drawn to her beauty and her lavish way of life, she to his talent.

When they decided to be married, Porter returned to the U.S. to entreat his grandfather to allow him to receive income from a trust set up with real estate holdings in Kentucky and West Virginia. Failing this, Cole hoped J. O. would be willing to reinstate his allowance at $500 a month. (His grandfather had cut it to $100, apparently to express his displeasure at Porter's lack of professional direction.) J. O. said no, but Cole's mother, Kate, agreed to help.

There was another fortunate result of the trip back to America. On the boat Porter met a producer who was planning a Broadway revue called *Hitchy-Koo of 1919*. He asked Cole to write the score. From this association came his first hit song, "Old-Fashioned Garden" as well as a contract with the music publishing house that brought out the work of Gershwin, Jerome Kern, Richard Rodgers, Kurt Weill, and Sigmund Romberg.

Still, it was Linda's money that financed their life together, at least until J. O. died four years later. Then Cole came into a substantial inheritance. The Porters had a house in Paris and spent several summers in a villa at Cap d'Antibes, where Sara and Gerald Murphy (the painter whose family ran Mark Cross) were guests. Next they took a palazzo in Venice, which Porter finally had to leave after a police raid found Italian boys dressed in Linda's fancy clothes (she was away) cavorting for Cole and some of his friends. One of the boys was the son of the police chief, so the incident was hushed up quickly, but Cole knew he couldn't stay in Venice.

The question arises: how did Linda cope with Cole's homosexuality? The answer is: with complete acceptance. In his wife, Porter had found a version of his mother. In Linda he had "an indulgent . . . totally giving, older, rich woman," very much like Kate.

Linda ran their various households with flair and grace. Her parties not only generated a circle of fascinating friends, they gave Cole a chance to present his songs to the right people as he entertained guests at the piano. Porter never had to hustle in Tin Pan Alley. He used his social life to promote his work, subtly and stylishly.

Linda believed totally in Cole Porter as a composer. She encouraged him to write serious music, and she tried to interest Diaghilev in doing a ballet by her husband, or Stravinsky in teaching him harmony and composition, or Shaw, Galsworthy, and Arnold Bennett in writing a libretto Porter could turn into an opera. But nothing came of these overtures. Cole did study briefly in Paris, but without much effect. He never orchestrated any of his own songs. Nor did he ever succeed at the large-scale pieces that lifted Gershwin into a class all his own, though he did write a jazz ballet called *Within the Quota* for a Swedish company, with libretto, costumes, and scenery by Gerald Murphy.

The truth was that Porter's gifts lay elsewhere. It was Cole Porter who revolutionized the lyrics of American musical theater, lacing them with language that was bright, witty, sophisticated and endlessly inventive. No number better exemplifies the Porter approach than "My Heart Belongs to Daddy" from *Leave It to Me* of 1938.

> While tearing off
> A game of golf
> I may make a play for the caddie.
> But when I do
> I don't follow through,
> 'Cause my heart belongs to Daddy.
>
> If I invite
> A boy, some night,
> To dine on my fine finnan haddie,
> I just adore his asking for more,
> But my heart belongs to Daddy.

This was the song that made Mary Martin a star. She performed it with a strip tease and won herself an audience forevermore. (It was quite an apotheosis for Martin. She showed up for her audition looking like a frightened girl who belonged back in Texas behind the counter of a ten-cent store. Yet Porter himself called her try-out that day the finest he had ever heard.) *Leave It to Me* also featured Sophie Tucker and introduced Gene Kelly to Broadway.

By then Cole Porter was well established as a key figure of the musical stage, both in New York and London. Already his successes were classics: *Paris*, with "Let's Do It, Let's Fall in Love," from 1928, the Broadway triumph that sent his career soaring; Wake Up and Dream, with "I've Got a Crush on You," "Looking at You," and "What Is This Thing Called Love?" a year later; followed by *Fifty Million Frenchmen* ("You Do Something to Me"); *The New Yorkers* ("Love for Sale," banned on American radio); *Gay Divorce* ("Night and Day" and "After You, Who?") with Fred Astaire; *Anything Goes* ("I Get a Kick Out of You," "You're the

Top," "Blow, Gabriel, Blow," and, of course, "Anything Goes") with
Ethel Merman; *Jubilee* ("Begin the Beguine," "Just One of Those
Things," and "Why Shouldn't I?). With the book by Moss Hart; *Red, Hot
and Blue!* ("Down in the Depths," "It's De-Lovely," and "Ridin' High,"
with Ethel Merman, Jimmy Durante, and Bob Hope); and *You Never
Know* ("At Long Last, Love).

Porter was celebrated for his words, but his music also could
enchant. His secret? Follow the great Jewish composers—Irving Berlin,
Jerome Kern, George Gershwin—and write Jewish melodies, in a key
that shifts from major to minor. This Cole explained to Richard Rodgers,
who thought he was joking. But Rodgers hummed "Night and Day,"
"Begin the Beguine," "Love for Sale," "I Love Paris," and "My Heart
Belongs to Daddy," and discovered that Porter, the Yalie WASP from
Indiana, had indeed embraced the sounds of European Jews.

The most important women in Cole's life in those years were his
mother, Kate, whose support in the beginning he never forgot, and Linda,
a stabilizing presence. Every opening night, according to Schwartz, she
was there, always with the same gift to commemorate the occasion—an
elegant cigarette case, sometimes leather, sometimes gold or silver, often
"studded with precious stones." Taken together, the collection bespoke a
lifelong devotion to his work.

Like Gershwin, Irving Berlin, and Jerome Kern, Porter moved to
Hollywood during the 1930s. There he quickly became the same domi-
nant force he was on Broadway. First he wrote *Born to Dance* ("Easy to
Love" and "I've Got You Under My Skin") with Eleanor Powell and
Jimmy Stewart. Then came a film version of *Anything Goes*, also with
Ethel Merman; plus a film of *Rosalie* ("In the Still of the Night") first
done for Broadway by Gershwin.

Porter loved Hollywood and resolved to live there at least four to six
months a year. But Los Angeles did not work for Linda. She disliked the
drunken abandon of social life among movie people, and especially she
worried that Cole's sudden sexual flamboyance would bring him trouble.
He had long had an appetite for sailors, truck drivers, and other rough-
hewn types, but in New York he had operated more discreetly, often
through pimps. The glitz of Hollywood galvanized in him a whole new
modus operandi, and Linda cautioned her husband against recklessness.
Cole agreed to restrain himself, but didn't.

Pushed too far, perhaps, Linda left for Paris. There she stayed until a
catastrophe sent her rushing back to Cole. Visiting friends at Oyster Bay,

he had ridden a high-spirited horse (against the advice of the groom—he was not much for warnings). The horse had reared, then fallen on its side, pinning Cole's leg to the ground, then, falling again, had crushed the other one as well.

The doctors recommended amputation, but Linda implored them to do nothing until she reached New York. Once there she insisted that Cole's legs be saved. This was accomplished, but at the price of more than thirty operations and constant pain for the rest of his life.

Porter returned to song writing, and *Leave It to Me* was his first Broadway show after the accident. Prolific as always, he created works for stage and screen, writing numbers such as "But In the Morning, No," "Do I Love You?" "Friendship," "Dream Dancing," "So Near and Yet So Far," "You'd Be So Nice to Come Home To," "Ev'ry Time We Say Goodbye," and "I Love You."

In the years between 1948 and 1960 came some of Cole Porter's finest productions: *Kiss Me, Kate* ("Another Op'nin', Another Show," "Why Can't You Behave?" "Wunderbar," "So in Love," "I Hate Men," "Too Darn Hot," "Always True to You in My Fashion," and "Brush Up Your Shakespeare"), a musical version of Shakespeare's *Taming of the Shrew*, made into a film with Kathryn Grayson, Howard Keel, Ann Miller, and Keenan Wynne; *Can-Can* ("C'est Magnifique," "I Am in Love," "It's All Right with Me," and "I Love Paris"); and the scintillating film *High Society* ("True Love" and "Well, Did You Evah?") with Bing Crosby, Grace Kelly, Frank Sinatra, Celeste Holm, and Louis Armstrong.

It's an amazing output for a man rarely free of physical distress which turned finally to emotional turmoil. In 1951 Porter had to be hospitalized for electric-shock treatments.

A few years later Cole Porter's world began to disintegrate. His mother died. So did Linda, after a siege of illness. She was keenly missed, especially when Cole had to have his right leg amputated close to the hip and Linda wasn't there to intercede for him and lift his spirits. To honor her, Cole had horticulturists develop a Linda Porter rose.

Cole spent his last years drinking too much, dyeing his hair, listening to the soap opera *Stella Dallas* on the radio, and grieving for lost glories. He died in 1964, having established himself as a song writer of unparalleled style and sophistication.

Gershwin had elegance, Porter had wit, and Irving Berlin had soul. He created some of the most memorable music of the epoch—"White

Christmas," "Easter Parade," "Always," and "God Bless America." No more trained in composition than Gershwin or Porter, limited to just one key, as Phil Hanry and Dave Laing comment, Berlin blessed his audiences with tunes so simple and words so rich that they became mainstays of the national culture.

Irving Berlin was born in Russia in 1888. His name then was Israel Baline. He was not yet five when his family moved to the United States and settled on New York's lower East Side where his father inspected poultry for kosher kitchens and painted houses. At fourteen Berlin (as he would become) left home to earn a living, working as a song plugger and also as a singing waiter at the Pelham café. There he began writing songs, progressing steadily from a music-publishing contract to various revues to his spectacular "Alexander's Ragtime Band," written for a show put together by a club of George M. Cohan's.

After World War I, during which he performed his own "Oh How I Hate to Get Up in the Morning" on Broadway, Berlin started a publishing company, buying back his earlier copyrights. Next he built a theater, the Music Box, where he staged many of his own revues.

From Ragtime his music moved to the ballad, and he became a master of the form. Especially poignant is the song he wrote after the death of his first wife, Dorothy Goetz, in 1912—"When I Lost You." Dorothy caught typhoid fever honeymooning with her new husband in Cuba and died only five months after the wedding.[12]

Berlin didn't remarry for fourteen years. Then he met Ellin Mackay, a friend of Linda Porter. Mackay was the daughter of an Irish-Catholic immigrant called "Bonanza" who made a fortune in Nevada silver and became so prominent he even entertained the Prince of Wales at his house on Long Island. Berlin's marriage, undertaken without the blessing of the father of the bride, elevated him to high social circles, though to some of them he never stopped being an outsider. But none of that sapped his energies. Still the melodies flowed, including "Always," written for Ellin. Theirs was a famously successful union, which lasted sixty-two years.

"Blue Skies," created to celebrate the birth of his daughter, Mary Ellin, was such a sensation when Al Jolson introduced it in *The Jazz Singer* that Berlin gravitated more and more toward the movies. He wrote "Cheek to Cheek" and "Isn't This a Lovely Day" for Fred Astaire and Ginger Rogers in *Top Hat*, as well as "Let's Face the Music and Dance" for *Follow the Fleet* and "Change Partners," for *Carefree*, both introduced by the redoubtable Astaire.

Ever ready with a patriotic effort, Berlin did *This Is the Army* during World War II, as both a revue and a film. He took it to American troops all over the world. Once the fighting was over, he scored his greatest theatrical triumph, *Annie Get Your Gun*, a veritable showcase for Ethel Merman, which featured "There's No Business Like Show Business," "I got Lost in His Arms," "They Say It's Wonderful," "I got the Sun in the Morning," "You Can't Get a Man with a Gun," and "The Girl That I Marry." Merman returned with Berlin to Broadway in *Call Me Madam*, where it seemed she was born to sing "The Hostess with the Mostess on the Ball," "It's a Lovely Day Today," and You're Just In Love."

Irving Berlin lived to be over one hundred. Reclusive at the end, possessed by his old recurring depression and obsessed with protecting the rights to his songs, he put a distance between himself and the world that loved him. But no one could separate the hearts of Americans from the music he gave them, music that buoyed their lives with the possibility of joy.

Nobody brought more artistry to musical theater than Jerome Kern. He was the great connector of Broadway to the European operetta tradition. And it was he who accomplished the decisive break with that tradition in *Show Boat* in 1927. Based on a novel by Edna Ferber, with lyrics by Oscar Hammerstein, *Show Boat* was "the first wholly integrated musical with an American subject," Hardy and Laing point out. Featuring songs such as "Bill," "Ol' Man River" (written for Paul Robeson), and "Can't Help Loving That Man of Mine," it was a sensitive exploration of black music and culture.

Jerome Kern had spent years preparing himself for *Show Boat*. Born to a prosperous business family in New York, he studied piano and composition both there and in Germany. After writing tunes in England for awhile, he returned home and worked (like Gershwin and Berlin) as a song plugger, then a rehearsal pianist. Success came quickly to Kern, as it had to Berlin and Gershwin. At twenty, Kern's "How'd You Like to Spoon with Me?" appeared in an English operetta. In the next few years he supplied some twenty songs to European productions, including "They Didn't Believe Me."

In time he turned to the New York stage and joined forces with Guy Bolton and P.G. Wodehouse to write musical comedies about the lives of contemporary Americans, not the costume dramas audiences were accustomed to seeing. Before long he established himself as an innovator of the theater.

Kern had many collaborators, but none worked better with him than Oscar Hammerstein. After their triumph in *Show Boat*, they did two more musicals for Broadway (one of them included "All the Things You Are") and then, in Hollywood, "The Folks Who Live on the Hill" (in *High Wide and Handsome*) and "The Last Time I Saw Paris" (for the film version of *Lady Be Good*).

There were other lyricists: Kern worked with Otto Harbach on "Smoke Gets in Your Eyes"; with Dorothy Fields on "The Way You Look Tonight"; with Johnny Mercer on "You Were Never Lovelier," "Dearly Beloved," and I'm Old-Fashioned"; and with Ira Gershwin to produce "Long Ago and Far Away"—all for the movies.

When Rodgers and Hammerstein set out to produce *Annie Get Your Gun*, they first wanted Jerome Kern and Dorothy Fields to do the score. But Kern died, in 1945, so the assignment went instead to Irving Berlin who achieved with it his finest moment on Broadway. Kern need have no regrets. He had already written himself into musical history as the man who turned operetta into theater.

Certainly Gershwin had a flair for music, but so did Richard Rodgers. His songs are among the most durable of the American canon. Cole Porter once said, "The word for Dick Rodgers' melodies . . . is holy. For Jerome Kern, sentimental. For Irving Berlin, simplicity."[13] Working with two wildly different lyricists, Lorenz Hart—as sophisticated as Porter—and Oscar Hammerstein—whose words are as beautiful as Berlin's—Rodgers created classics so radiant they resonate still wherever there's romance.

Rodgers, the second son of a Russian-Jewish doctor, grew up in upper-middle-class New York in what is now Harlem. He lived in a contentious family with his mother's parents also a part of the household. His grandfather Levy was Orthodox, while his grandmother was an atheist with strong opinions on everything. The oldest son, Mortimer, was bar mitzvahed. Richard, never a believer, was not. He did, however, inherit his parents' passion for music. His mother would play Broadway songs on the piano and his father would sing. Richard played too, and for him the piano became a refuge from the complicated personalities around him.

By the time he was fifteen, Rodgers knew his life would be in musical theatre. That year he wrote songs for an amateur benefit show at the Plaza Hotel in which he not only played the piano but also conducted a five-piece orchestra. Next came Columbia University where he participated in musical revues, just as Cole Porter had done at Yale. Rodgers later transferred to the Institute of Musical Art, which would become the Juilliard School of Music, and found there the perfect atmosphere for his temperament: Averse to competition (unlike Gershwin and Berlin), he shrank from conflict and worked best among people who were warm and congenial. Though his path to Broadway had about it the assurance of destiny he felt sufficiently uncertain at one point, having done thirty amateur productions with nothing to show for them, to consider selling baby clothes. A call to do a show for the Theater Guild changed that.

By then Rodgers had already encountered the literary Lorenz Hart. They met when Rodgers was seventeen and Hart twenty-four. Hart was from a German-Jewish immigrant family and also was a product of Columbia, where he had studied journalism. The two teamed up immediately, and from their collaboration came some of the great standards of American music—their first hit, "Manhattan," and "Mountain Greenery "(both for revues); "A Blue Room" (*The Girl Friend*); "Thou Swell" and "My Heart Stood Still" (*A Connecticut Yankee*); "You Took Advantage of Me" (*Present Arms*); "With a Song in My Heart" (*Spring Is Here*); "Ten Cents a Dance" (*Simple Simon*); "My Funny Valentine," "Where or When," and "The Lady Is a Tramp" (*Babes in Arms*, choreographed by George Balanchine); and "Bewitched, Bothered, and Bewildered (*Pal Joey* with Gene Kelly). They also wrote "Blue Moon," which a Hollywood producer unwisely rejected.[14]

In 1925, Rodgers and Hart took a grand tour of Europe. They met the Cole Porters in Venice, and more importantly, on the ship home, Rodgers ran into the Feiners, whom he had known as a child from summers on Long Island. They were traveling with their daughter, Dorothy, who was about to enter Wellesley. Dorothy, gifted with a fine eye for art and elegant interiors, was drawn to Richard and he to her. They were married five years later.

Rodgers's marriage to Dorothy produced two daughters and moved much more smoothly than his partnership with Larry Hart. Their songs flowed fluently, with Rodgers most often writing the music first and Hart following with lyrics. But it was not easy dealing with Larry Hart. Where Rodgers was relentlessly hard working, Hart spent a great deal of time drinking and depressed, terrified that his mother would find out he was gay.[15]

It could be trying prying lyrics out of Larry Hart. When the two were writing *By Jupiter*, Hart checked into Doctors Hospital to dry out.

Rodgers followed him there, took a guest room, got Steinway to send over an upright piano, and together they ground out the songs. It was a nightmare.

Hart was functioning so badly that he failed to recognize a critical opportunity and refused to do a show based on Lynn Riggs' *Green Grow the Lilacs*, complaining that it was not suitable material for the stage. Jerome Kern also said no to *Lilacs*, arguing that Westerns would not work in the theater. So Rodgers turned to Oscar Hammerstein II, who had already achieved considerable success as a lyricist with Rudolf Friml (*Rose Marie*), Sigmund Romberg (*Desert Song*), and most notably, Kern in *Show Boat*. But Hammerstein had not had a hit on Broadway in over a decade, so he welcomed the new collaboration.

With an opera-impresario grandfather and a dad who was a theater-manager, Hammerstein had been drawn naturally to show business. He tried law school at Columbia but quickly abandoned it to take a backstage job with an uncle who later steered him in the direction of the group that brought forth Rose Marie.

Like Rodgers, Hammerstein discovered the love of his life, another interior designed named Dorothy, on a boat trip to Europe. This Dorothy was from Australia. Both she and Oscar were already married, each with two children. They left their respective mates to wed, have a son of their own, and move to a farm in Bucks County, Pennsylvania, where they sheltered several offspring of friends during World War II.

Rodgers found working with Hammerstein entirely different from his experience with Larry Hart. Hammerstein liked to write the lyrics first. He also did the book. This allowed him, according to William Hyland, to "shape the overall concept of the musical . . . ." The two of them would meet to thrash out the basic plot of a show, then repair to their separate places to produce the words and music. This was quite a change for Rodgers, who was accustomed to spending long hours secluded with Hart to create their songs. Reportedly he was amazed when Hammerstein delivered his lyrics on time and in finished form.

Hammerstein was dependable, but he was also meticulous and slow. It took him three weeks to write the words to "Oh, What a Beautiful Mornin'." Then he took them to Rodgers's house in Connecticut where the tune was turned out in ten minutes. Unlike Gershwin, Berlin or Porter, Rodgers had some grasp of composition. He could "write a complete piano-vocal version of his songs," said his biographer William Hyland, and the numbers usually "emerged from a show almost exactly as he wanted [them . . .] presented in the sheet music." A master of the waltz ("The Most Beautiful Girl in the World," "Falling in Love With Love"), less influenced by jazz or ragtime than Gershwin and Berlin, Rodgers thought in terms of shows, not single songs. He was quintessentially a man of the theater.

The first Rodgers and Hammerstein collaboration transformed *Green Grow the Lilacs* into *Oklahoma!* It was a breakthrough musical with choreography by Agnes De Mille embedded in the dramatic flow of the story and songs that celebrated the pleasures of country life: "Oh What a Beautiful Morning," "Surrey with the Fringe on Top," and "People Will Say We're in Love," as well as the spirited title song.

Soon after the opening of *Oklahoma!* in 1943 Larry Hart died, leaving Rodgers free to pursue an association with Oscar Hammerstein that lasted eighteen years and produced work radiant with beauty, refinement and emotion. Born during a time of world cataclysm, their partnership grew to reflect the optimism and energy of post-war America. With unfailing charm, they never hesitated to nudge their audiences toward racial and ethnic acceptance. Certainly this was a theme of *South Pacific* ("You've Got to Be Carefully Taught," "Some Enchanted Evening," "Bali Hi," "I'm Gonna Wash That Man Right Outta My Hair," and "Younger Than Springtime") with Mary Martin and Enzio Pinza; *The King and I* ("Getting to Know You," "Shall We Dance," and "Hello, Young Lovers") with Yul Brynner and Gertrude Lawrence; and *Flower Drum Song* ("I Enjoy Being a Girl" and "Love, Look Away").

The pair established a business organization known for being tough if not brutal. This was due mainly to Rodgers, cold and distant, the one who actually liked office work. His determination to dominate the details of their operation put considerable strain on relations with Hammerstein, but they managed to keep their partnership on track. Together they produced many of their own shows and also the work of others, such as Irving Berlin's *Annie Get Your Gun*. Their efforts earned them both a fortune.

Ill health dogged Richard Rodgers. He had to have surgery for cancer of the jaw when he was fifty-three. Two years later he was hospitalized for depression which never really left him and which in fact he had had for years. One of his daughters felt that her father lived with an undercurrent of sadness, but this was seldom apparent to his friends, who saw only the maker of radiant music.

Rodgers and Hammerstein did some of their most moving work in *Carousel* ("If I Loved You," and "You'll Never Walk Alone"—it was

Rodgers's favorite show) and *The Sound of Music* ("How Do You Solve a Problem Like Maria?" "Edelweiss," "My Favorite Things," "Do-Re-Me," and "Climb Ev'ry Mountain"), with Mary Martin on stage and Julie Andrews on film, their last show together. Hammerstein died of stomach cancer while the production was still playing in New York. Before the end, the pair had a farewell lunch at the Oak Room of the Plaza Hotel.

Rodgers tried to continue, creating his own words for *No Strings* and writing *Do I Hear a Waltz* with Stephen Sondheim. (This collaboration did not go well. Nor did an effort by Rodgers to do *On a Clear Day You Can See Forever* with Alan Jay Lerner. Rodgers eventually withdrew from the show and Lerner finished it with Burton Lane.) There were other projects with other people, but Rodgers belonged with Larry Hart or Oscar Hammerstein. Those two partnerships illuminated the musical stage and carried the emotions of millions.

Alan Jay Lerner and Frederick Loewe, Hardy and Laing claim, are the "stylistic heirs of Rodgers and Hammerstein." They too created shows that were more than music. They were experiences, rich in texture and character. Who doesn't treasure Eliza Doolittle and Henry Higgins (played by Julie Andrews and Rex Harrison) in *My Fair Lady*? Or the songs that expressed their world and their subtle combat: "Why Can't a Woman Be More Like a Man?" "On the Street Where you Live," "Show Me," "Wouldn't It be Loverly," "The Rain in Spain," "Ascot Opening Day," and "I've Grown Accustomed to Her Face"? *My Fair Lady* was based on Shaw's *Pygmalion*, which Rodgers and Hammerstein had once considered for a musical, but discarded.

It took a while for Lerner and Loewe to find each other. Loewe, the son of a Viennese tenor, was a piano soloist with the Berlin Symphony Orchestra by the time he was thirteen. He came to America at twenty-four to pursue a piano career that never materialized. He took unlikely jobs around the country, even working at one point as a cow puncher, and finally landed in New York where he tried putting together a musical. The show failed, so Loewe played a restaurant piano until 1942, when he met a Juilliard-and-Harvard graduate named Alan Jay Lerner. Born to an affluent New York family, Lerner had been writing for radio while waiting for a break.

After an initial flop, the two of them burst forth with *Brigadoon*, one of the most lilting, romantic musicals ever written. Set in a misty fantasy high in the Scottish hills, *Brigadoon* blooms with sound surrounding words that seem like poetry: "Almost Like Being in Love," "Come to Me, Bend to Me," "I'll Go Home with Bonnie Jean," and "From This Day On."

Next came *Paint Your Wagon*, a tale of the California Gold Rush, with "I Talk to the Trees" and "They Call the Wind Maria," followed, later, by the scintillating film *Gigi*. Based on a novella by Colette and featuring Leslie Caron, Louis Jourdan, Maurice Chevalier and Hermione Gingold, it sparkles with gentle sophistication. "The Night They Invented Champagne," "Thank Heaven for Little Girls," "I'm Glad I'm Not Young Anymore," "Yes, I Remember It Well," and "Gigi"—all are delectable evocations of youth and a certain age in Paris.

Their last show together, *Camelot*, brought Julie Andrews back to Broadway, along with Richard Burton and Robert Goulet to sing "If Ever I would Leave You," "What Do the Simple Folk Do?" and "How To Handle a Woman." (Vanessa Redgrave and Richard Harris took the leading roles in the film.) It's clear from a reading of the lyrics that while some may say Alan Jay Lerner was another Oscar Hammerstein, actually he was closer to Larry Hart. Though not as worldly as Hart, Lerner's words have the same intricate and clever construction, much also like Cole Porter's. All this is clear in "The Simple Joys of Maidenhood," sung by Guenevere.

> Where are the simple joys of maidenhood?
> Where are all those adoring, daring boys?
> Where's the knight pining so for me
> He leaps to death in woe for me?
> Oh, where are a maiden's simple joys?
>
> Shall I have the normal life a maiden should?
> Shall I never be rescued in the wood?
> And shall true knights not tilt for me
> And let their blood be spilt for me?
> Oh, where are the simple joys of maidenhood?
>
> Shall I never be disputed for
> Or on any minstrel's lips?
> Never have my face recruited for,
> Launching countless ships?

Where are the simple joys of maidenhood?
Are those sweet, gentle pleasures gone for good?
Shall a feud not begin for me?
Shall kith not kill their kin for me?
Oh, where are the trivial joys,
Or less convivial joys?
Where are the simple joys of maidenhood?

Lerner and Loewe dissolved their partnership in 1962. Loewe retired, and Lerner indulged himself in politics, helping to plan the famous party for John F. Kennedy where Marilyn Monroe sang "Happy Birthday." Though addicted to drugs prescribed by a society doctor who gave shots of Methedrine and vitamins, Lerner plunged into new projects, doing *On a Clear Day You Can See Forever* with Burton Lane and *Coco* with André Previn. But never did he match the magic he had made with Frederick Loewe. Together they reigned over the mid-years of the century.

Frank Loesser, son of a New York piano teacher, was once a reporter as well as a pianist. He turned to show business in time and wrote many songs that became mainstays ("Baby It's Cold Outside" and "Spring Will Be a Little Late This Year"), but his reputation rests primarily on two shows for Broadway: *Guys and Dolls* and *The Most Happy Fella*.

Drawn from a series of stories by Damon Runyon, *Guys and Dolls* mates a young woman from the Salvation Army with a gambler both rakish and appealing. Their music has made its way into the American memory: "I've Never Been in Love Before," "If I Were a Bell," "I'll Know When My Love Comes Along," and "Sit Down You're Rocking the Boat."

Loesser did the book as well the words and music for *The Most Happy Fella*, an operatic *tour de force* set in Napa Valley. Lovelier songs have never been heard on Broadway: "Joey" and "My Heart Is So Full of You," along with the lively "Standing on the Corner."

While Frank Loesser cannot be numbered among the giants of musical theater and film, he made a contribution in the 1940s and 1950s that is solid, lyrical, and lasting.

The full and robust vitality that had fueled musical theater began to dwindle in the sixties, its best energies spent except for a few solitary sensations such as *Funny Girl* (music by Jule Styne and lyrics by Bob

Merrill) and Jerry Herman's *Hello Dolly*. (He also did *Mame* and *La Cage aux Folles*.) However, a fantastic resurgence occurred in 1968 with *Hair*, a "tribal love-rock" happening by Galt MacDermot, Gerome Ragni, and James Rado. Announcing the arrival of the Age of Aquarius, they delivered a startlingly trenchant commentary on their tumultuous decade, then disappeared along with the anti-war movement. It wasn't long before the country turned to *Godspell*, Stephen Schwartz's explication of St. Matthew, which prophesied the turning to religion that lay ahead. But first came *Chorus Line* by Marvin Hamlisch and Edward Kleban, a show about striving and the limits of achievement.

America produced only one more great song writer before century's end: Stephen Sondheim. Son of a New York dress manufacturer (it's striking how, with only a few exceptions—Cole Porter, Frederick Loewe—most of the great Broadway songsters were born in New York), Sondheim was drawn to musical theatre by Oscar Hammerstein II, a neighbor and father figure in Bucks County Pennsylvania, where Steve lived with his mother, a dress designer, after his parents were divorced. Foxy Sondheim was a woman of aggressive talent and careless mothering. She caused her son pain and confusion by adopting toward him an approach so seductive that she took to holding his hand in the theatre and asking him to mix her drinks. "What she did to Stephen was unforgivable," said Susan Blanchard, Dorothy Hammerstein's daughter. "When he was still a preadolescent she would have house parties in her farm with everyone drunk out of their minds. You didn't dare walk into a bedroom."[17]

Before the divorce, Sondheim's parents, both working in their fashion business, had little time for their son. He spent weekdays in prekindergarten, then grade-school, playing afterwards with children in his building on Central Park West. His Saturdays were occupied by an all-day program in the park. Household help provided supervision but little sense of family. In an atmosphere too distant, and then too close, Sondheim grew to be a boy who was "brittle, competitive, and sarcastic." Or so said his friend, Jamie Hammerstein, Oscar's son.

Sondheim had no religious life as a child, no bar mitzvah, and never saw the inside of a synagogue until he was nineteen. When his father remarried and had two more sons, the boys did not know Stephen was their half-brother for years though they saw him from time to time. Sondheim moved in with his father in New York when he was a freshman at Williams.

There he set out to major in English, editing the campus magazine,

The Purple Cow, with Stephen Birmingham. But this changed when
Sondheim started working on college shows (like Cole Porter and
Richard Rodgers). Struck with admiration for Tchaikovsky,
Rachmaninoff, Prokofiev, Aaron Copeland, and Ravel, he steeped himself
in music.

Like most of his predecessors on Broadway, Sondheim began writing
music while very young. He was twenty-seven when the first big moment
came: Leonard Bernstein asked him to write the lyrics for *West Side
Story*. Together they created "Maria" and "Tonight."

Next came the lyrics for *Gypsy* with Jule Styne as composer ("Small
World" and "Everything's Coming Up Roses") and, on his own,
Sondheim wrote both words and music for *A Funny Thing Happened on
the Way to the Forum*, *Company* ("Side by Side by Side," and "Being
Alive"), and *Follies* ("I'm Still Here"). But it was with *A Little Night
Music* ("Send in the Clowns"), based on Ingmar Bergman's film, *Smiles
of a Summer Night*, that Sondheim really arrived. It was then that
Leonard Bernstein called him "the most important force in the American
musical theatre."

Sondheim had a few flops: The worst was *Anyone Can Whistle* with
Angela Lansbury. The show took on psychiatry, corruption in politics,
sexual stereotypes, racism, Madison Avenue, the military-industrial
complex, and the boredom of convention. It was more burdens than any
theatrical effort could carry. However, the production brought a new presence to Sondheim's life: the actress Lee Remick. The two of them were
drawn to each other even though she was married and he was gay.
Remick would have left her husband for Sondheim, but things never got
that far.

Sondheim also spent some time with Nancy Berg, a super-model,
and there were one or two other women, including Mary Rodgers, daughter of Richard, who was in love with him. They had an engagement, but it
didn't work. "He was terrified," said Mary, "not of giving love, but having to get it."

His sexual nature was difficult for Sondheim, who felt that being gay
complicated his life. He had a brief affair with a guy on the administrative staff of *Do I Hear a Waltz*, a show Sondheim did with Richard
Rodgers. By then Rodgers was drinking a lot and hard to work with.
Besides, Sondheim did not like being limited to lyrics only. He had won
a prize some years before that had enabled him to study music with a dis-
ciple of Schoenberg. He learned composition, theory, and harmony, and

he took great delight in the musical side of theatre, ignoring the obvious truth that his true talent was for words. He was in fact called "the new Cole Porter."

Unlike Cole Porter, also gay, Sondheim did find a great love. He was in his sixties when young Peter Jones arrived from Denver for a meeting with the great man. Jones, like so many others, hoped to study with Sondheim, to learn from him. Immediately they were drawn to each other, and Stephen invited Peter to his country house in Connecticut for a weekend. Sondheim broke his ankle, and the two of them fell in love. In January, 1994, they exchanged wedding rings. Sometimes the relationship worked. Sometimes it didn't, and Peter, feeling overwhelmed, sought consolation elsewhere. They stopped wearing their rings, but much that was valuable to them returned.

By the time he met Peter, Sondheim had already done *Pacific Overtures* and *Sweeney Todd* as well as the revue, *Side by Side By Sondheim* and *Sunday in the Park with George*, a luminous exploration of Georges Seurat's painting, *A Sunday Afternoon on the Island of La Grande Jatte*. Those who have ever fretted about what they're going to do next saw themselves in this show. Sondheim captured perfectly the anxiety of the creative life, then came into his maturity with *Into the Woods*, a composite of fairy tales that are really about life, as fairy tales always are. In this work he develops a philosophy for enduring.

Sondheim was in London when his mother died, at ninety-five. He did not return for her funeral, and he never stopped hating her. The final rupture had occurred when Foxy was about to have a pacemaker installed. Overdramatizing it to herself as "open-heart surgery," she wrote to Stephen the night before that "the only regret I have in life is giving you birth." Apparently believing she would not survive and feeling a sense of urgency if not malice, she had it hand-delivered. Sondheim was livid. He responded with a blistering three-page letter, explaining why he didn't want to see her anymore, though he would continue to support her.

At forty-nine, Sondheim himself had a heart attack, but he recovered through a regimen of exercise and careful eating, something he had never pursued before. Indeed, drugs had been a part of his life. He used cocaine, and tried mescaline and acid. He usually worked with liquor and marijuana, which helped, he said, when he needed to drift. But they were useless when he had to have precision.

It has been said that Stephen Sondheim is a "Hart in search of a Rodgers." It's true that Sondheim is no melodist. But his words make up for it. His words speak for all those who are groping their way to meaning.

By the 1980s musical theater had moved to Europe where *Les Misérables* and *Miss Saigon*, both by Alain Boublil and Claude-Michel Schonberg, revived the operatic tradition of the nineteenth century and shaped it for a popular audience. New York soon learned to look to London for imported shows that would keep Broadway alive. Nobody had more impact at this point than Andrew Lloyd Webber. With Tim Rice writing lyrics, he had already astonished audiences with *Joseph and the Amazing Technicolor Dreamcoat* followed by *Jesus Christ Superstar.*

Andrew Lloyd Webber (born, like Sondheim, on March 22, but eighteen years later) came from a musical family. His father, Bill, started giving organ recitals in London when he was ten and later became music director at All Saints, then at Central Hall, Westminster, a Methodist church. He taught composition and harmony at the Royal College of Music and yearned to be a composer himself, but his other commitments left little time for writing music. Andrew's success was hard sometimes for his father to take. Bill once said to his son, "If you ever write a song as good as 'Some Enchanted Evening,' I'll tell you . . . ." But never did he say a word.

Then there was Andrew's mother, Jean, who taught piano, and his brother, Julian, today considered the finest cellist in Britain.

Andrew's family assumed he would become an historian, but instead he left Oxford and moved back home to pursue song writing. His father advised against study in a conservatory, fearing that Andrew would lose his gift for melody in an atmosphere saturated with twelve-tone composition.

By this time Tim Rice, determined to be a pop star, had left the solicitor's office where he was working and joined a record company. He was three years older and far better acquainted in the popular-music world than Lloyd Webber when they met, but Andrew's family, livelier than his own upper-middle-class household (his father was a business executive), was fascinating to Rice. He moved in with the Lloyd Webbers and began with Andrew, then only seventeen, to write songs. In time, the *Daily Mail* forecast that they would be the next Rodgers and Hammerstein.

Joseph and the Amazing Technicolor Dreamcoat they wrote as a commissioned piece for a prep school. Later it was performed at Central Hall, Bill's church. Then, padded with reprises, it opened in Brooklyn. Back in Britain Joseph was embraced by Father Martin Sullivan as a means of getting young people to church. So intent was Sullivan on this mission that once he amazed his congregation by parachuting into St. Paul's from the top of the dome.

Lloyd Webber was twenty-two when he had his first big success: *Jesus Christ Superstar*. With lyrics by Tim Rice, this rock opera was first developed in a recording studio where the title song was produced and became a hit single. Father Sullivan was willing to open the show at St. Paul's until the *Daily Express* dreamed up the story that John Lennon of the Beatles had been asked to play Christ and wanted his wife, Yoko Ono, to portray Mary Magdalene. By the time these rumors had been dispelled, the chance to premiere *Superstar* at the cathedral had evaporated.

That may be just as well, because *Jesus Christ Superstar* posed a question that might have been discomfiting to the Anglican hierarchy: Was Jesus Christ really God?

Just as *Superstar* was taking off, Lloyd Webber met sixteen-year-old Sarah Hugill, daughter of a conservative research chemist who insisted that she wait until her eighteenth birthday to marry. This she agreed to do. Then Sarah became Lloyd Webber's wife and also his assistant, organizing their houses—in London and Wiltshire—and his burgeoning business interests. (Lloyd Webber was a millionaire at twenty-five.)

The question was: What would be the next move? Tim Rice was determined that they would do a show about Eva Peron. So obsessed did he become with her that he took Jane McIntosh, whom he later married, on a research trip to Buenos Aries right after they met. The two of them even named their first daughter Eva.

Lloyd Webber resisted, pleading no interest in Eva Peron. Instead he insisted on pursuing *Jeeves* with Alan Ayckbourn. Based on stories by P.G. Wodehouse, *Jeeves* was a flop. It sent Lloyd Webber scurrying back to Tim Rice and *Evita*.

Rice idolized Eva. Lloyd Webber was repelled by her. Nonetheless he made her wonderful. He made her so wonderful that Tim Rice fell in love not only with *Evita*, but with the actress who first played her in London, Elaine Paige, and managed, at least for awhile, to maintain relationships both with her and his wife. Recorded before it was staged, *Evita* was immediately acclaimed as an opera. Lloyd Webber had taken musical theater and returned it to its pre-operetta origins, with all spoken dialogue banished. After *Evita*, he had to be recognized as a composer of importance.

This was not always easy for critics, some of whom charged Lloyd

Webber with appropriating the melodies of others. He was said to be writing in the vein of Richard Strauss, Offenbach, Prokofiev, Puccini, Jerome Kern, and Frederick Loewe. Sometimes there were similarities, but never outright plagiarism.

The truth is that Lloyd Webber brought back the musical that audiences could leave singing. He also knew how to enhance his songs with body mikes, synthesizers and bass amplifiers. He took a tired art form, reinvigorated it with inspiration from the past and made it contemporary all over again.

After *Evita*, Lloyd Webber turned to an unexpected lyricist: T.S. Eliot. From Eliot's *Old Possum Book of Practical Cats* he fashioned his own show, *Cats*, with a major assist from Trevor Nunn, who wrote the lyrics for "Memory." (Nunn's version won out over Tim Rice's, no small matter since there was a lot of money to be made on that song.)

Cats, a stupendous success, brought more to Lloyd Webber than money: a saucy soprano named Sarah Brightman showed up to audition and got the role of Jemima. She didn't catch Lloyd Webber's attention right away, but in time he was fatally drawn to her pure, clear voice, just as Tim Rice had been to Elaine Paige's. Awkward though it was, Lloyd Webber left his wife, Sarah I, with whom he had two children, to marry Sarah II.

For Brightman, and to honor his father who had died, Lloyd Webber wrote *Requiem* (with the poignant "Pie Jesu") which premiered at St. Thomas Episcopal Church in New York and two months later at Westminster Abbey in London. This was an effort to do something serious after *Starlight Express*, a *tour de force* on roller skates that echoed the technical prowess of *Cats*, and *Song and Dance*, which had some stunning music ("Tell Me on a Sunday" and "The Last Man in My Life") but was still a minor work.

By this time Andrew Lloyd Webber had become a businessman of considerable note, having bought the Palace Theatre and consolidated his holdings in the Really Useful Group, which later would be taken public, then private again; then a third would be sold to Polygram—all in hugely profitable transactions. The company held the rights to all Lloyd Webber's work and, in time, it franchised productions of his shows all over the world. At one point it even had in its employ Prince Edward, whose working name is Edward Windsor.

Like Gershwin and Richard Rodgers, Andrew became an art collector, specializing in Pre-Raphaelite painting. His country estate, Sydmonton, was a center of creative activity as he tried out all his shows in the chapel there and also made it the setting for an arts festival. He had even bought a house in Oxfordshire for his former wife, putting it in the name of their children. There was no doubt Andrew Lloyd Webber had made it. Now he was ready for the next artistic breakthrough.

It came to Lloyd Webber when he was in New York, browsing in a second-hand book store. He came across a novel from 1910, Gaston Leroux's *Le Fantome de l'opéra*, which had been made into a silent movie with Lon Chaney and later a talkie with Claude Raines. Lloyd Webber saw right away the possibilities for his own kind of revival. He asked Alan Jay Lerner to write the lyrics, but ill health forced him to withdraw. Casting about for somebody else, Lloyd Webber came finally to Charles Hart, twenty-four, a London songwriter just getting started. The role of Christine, of course, was shaped for Sarah Brightman.

Andrew Lloyd Webber's *Phantom of the Opera* was a luminous triumph, certainly his strongest creation, with songs that became widely loved: "All I Ask of You," "The Music of the Night," "Angel of Music," "Think of Me," and "Wishing You Were Somehow Here Again." Though he took his usual beating from the critics, Lloyd Webber won a permanent place in musical history.

But there was trouble with the leading lady. Often on the road alone, Sarah Brightman tumbled into bed with other men. Not one to be obsessed with sex, Lloyd Webber overlooked it as long as she was discreet. But the moment came when the situation no longer could be ignored. Also, Lloyd Webber was becoming a public figure of importance, about to be knighted as well as ushered into the House of Lords. He could not live with Brightman's indifference to her role as suitable wife and hostess.

So the end came. Brightman continued to perform Andrew Lloyd Webber's music in concerts on both sides of the Atlantic, but their marriage was over. Lloyd Webber lost no time finding and wedding Madeleine Gurdon, a brigadier general's daughter who was a businesswoman and expert equestrian. (Curiously, she reminded him of his first wife.) Andrew installed twenty horses at Sydmonton and learned to ride. A designer and marketer of country-style clothes, Madeleine tidied up her husband's appearance and urged him to stress the business side of himself. Together they settled into a life of prominence and had three children.

Lloyd Webber's last memorable work was *Aspects of Love*. Based on a slender novel by David Garnett of Bloomsbury (he married Vanessa Bell's daughter, having years before conducted an affair with the girl's father, Duncan Grant), the show, though convoluted in plot, had glorious music—"Love Changes Everything," "Seeing Is Believing," "A Memory of a Happy Moment," "The First Man You Remember," and "Anything but Lonely." Billed as an effort at intimacy instead of the megamusical, it did brilliantly in London, as Lloyd Webber's things always did (at one point he had six shows running simultaneously in the West End), but was less well received in New York. Even so, it's a score of great style and elegance.

There have been other efforts since then: *Sunset Boulevard* made a big splash, but was ultimately disappointing without a single song worth recalling. Not even Glenn Close in the New York production could bring the show to life. *Whistle Down the Wind* had an opening number that, according to Michael Walsh, "skirted brazenly close to the principal theme of John Williams's score for *Jurassic Park*."

The problem was that Andrew Lloyd Webber, by the time he was fifty, had run out of creative steam. He tried diverting himself with a weekly newspaper column called "In Matters of Taste," and he joined with some friends to buy a $40,000 gelding racehorse which he named Frank Rich after the *New York Times* theater critic whom he loathed (and for good reason: Rich had been merciless to Lloyd Webber). He bought a Blue-Period Picasso for $29 million at Sotheby's, also a Canaletto, and he explored the idea of building a gallery for his collection on London's South Bank near Royal Festival Hall, with Richard Rogers as architect.

But like Brancusi and Sibelius, Lloyd Webber saw his creative energy ebb too soon. Why? With Brancusi the problem was striving too hard for saintliness, which inhibited the life forces necessary to fuel the growth of art. Similarly, Sibelius cramped his own style, stamped out his own complexity, in a relentless quest for the One, the unified response. For Lloyd Webber the problem was different: He allowed the affairs of business to overtake him, curbing the flow of his ample spirit into the constraints of bottom-line thinking.

In 1996, the *London Times* estimated Lloyd Webber's net worth at more than $1 billion, with *Phantom* alone having grossed $1.5 billion by late 1995, more than *Jurassic Park* or *E.T.* ". . . At any given moment in the 1990s," wrote Walsh, "more than half the tickets sold on Broadway were for Lloyd Webber productions."

Evita, at last, after years of contention, was made into a movie with

Madonna, but Lloyd Webber could not get his other shows produced on film, except for *Jesus Christ Superstar* in 1973, which somehow missed its moment. The megamusical was over, as he had said, and apparently his creative years were over too, though that could always change.

With Lloyd Webber went the great age of musical theater. What was left were revivals, and there have been plenty of those, both in New York and London: Rodgers and Hart's *On Your Toes*; Rodgers and Hammerstein's *Oklahoma!*, *Carousel*, *The King and I*, and *The Sound of Music*; Cole Porter's *Can-Can*, *High Society*, and *Kiss Me Kate*; Gershwin's *Girl Crazy* (renamed *Crazy for You*) and *Strike Up the Band*; Kern and Hammerstein's *Show Boat*; Loesser's *Guys and Dolls*; Berlin's *Annie Get Your Gun*; and Sondheim's *Follies* (in Millburn, New Jersey), *A Funny Thing Happened on the Way to the Forum*, *Gypsy*, *A Little Night Music,* and *Sweeney Todd*.

These shows have returned to the stage because audiences cannot let them go. They have become the classics of an art form invented in America, refurbished in Britain and woven into the lives of people all over the world.

Chapter
Eight

Ingmar Bergman
 Ingmar Bergman has taken film to its deepest maturity. Son of a Lutheran pastor, he rebelled against the church, then suffused his work with startling insights of the spirit.

How Film Captured the Spirit of the Century

There is always some name, some face
which sheds a radiance, which lights up
her pavements and makes it possible for
her to replenish her dreams.
Virginia Woolf

The twentieth century brought forth another great popular artistic achievement—film. Part technology, part theater, part painting, part music, and sometimes part dance, film gave a voice to the drama and aspirations of ordinary lives. The movies produced stars that guided the dreams of audiences everywhere. But above all film belonged to directors. It was they who made a story sing.

The foremost pioneer director of the age was David Wark Griffith. Born in Kentucky in 1875 to a veteran colonel of the Civil War known as "Roaring Jake" Griffith (he died of a long festering battle wound when the boy was still a small child), D. W. left home at twenty to work as an actor with touring stock companies. He wrote a play himself, but it fizzled in Washington.

That was when Griffith turned to film, an infant industry just moving from saloons to nickelodeons with silent pictures designed for mass entertainment.[1] Griffith got a job writing and acting with the Edison Company, and later with Biograph, which made him a director.

In the four hundred films he directed for Biograph, Griffith stopped the slavish adherence to theater that had dominated movie-making and embraced instead a variety of shots—close-up, medium, and long. In editing, he learned to cross-cut between scenes, and the stress he placed on subtlety in acting greatly improved the overwrought techniques of the prevailing melodrama.

In time, Griffith grew tired of Biograph's reluctance to venture into feature films. Finally he left to form his own production company. The result, in 1915, was his twelve-reel masterpiece, *The Birth of a Nation*. This film is hardly attuned to decent sensibilities in its treatment of race during Reconstruction. As Andrew Sarris said, "Griffith never freed himself from the most rampant prejudices of his childhood. His greatest limitation is that he became urban without becoming cosmopolitan."

Even so, this picture shines in the strength of its Civil War battle scenes, with shots of the war dead grim enough to move audiences of any era. The frames are elegantly composed, especially those with Lincoln conducting the business of America from a simple table at the right of an otherwise darkened screen. There is great narrative power, even with no spoken dialogue. Subtitles carry the action, and pictures dramatize it in a way that pulls the viewer into the emotion of every moment.

There were other successes, many of them with the actress Lillian Gish who appeared in *Birth of a Nation*, but their collaboration came to an end eventually and Griffith lamented, "I never had a day's luck after Lillian left me."[2] In fact, he never had any luck after the advent of sound. Griffith did make two talkies, including *Abraham Lincoln* with Walter Huston, but he never stopped grieving for the loss of silent film. "Give us back our beauty," he cried.

A new kind of beauty had arrived, however, bringing a bracing realism that Griffith could not absorb. Wedded still to Victorian sentiment, he was overwhelmed by the Jazz Age. His high moment after *Birth of a Nation* lasted little more than five years. Then began the long decline. At war with the growing studio system and unsuccessful as an independent producer, Griffith spent his last two decades drinking and womanizing, his creativity killed, perhaps, by a festering wound suffered in the civil wars of early Hollywood, a wound that immobilized him and made him unable to adapt to changing technology and challenging times.

He died, his life long since finished, in the Hollywood Knickerbocker Hotel.

Just as D. W. Griffith's life was beginning to crumble, another director a world away was coming to the fore: Sergei Eisenstein, like Griffith, got his start in the theater but quickly found his way to film. Son of a successful German-Jewish architect and engineer, deserted as a child by his Russian mother, Eisenstein studied architecture himself, but after a stint in the Red Army and a fling in experimental drama, he made his first full-length movie, *Strike*, followed by three others, including

Battleship Potemkin, and immediately became the most celebrated film maker in the Soviet Union.[3]

An avowed propagandist for the Bolsheviks, Eisenstein was a master of montage, juxtaposing one image with another, and, later, images with sound, to create a dramatic effect that would glorify the national myths of the Marxist regime. In some ways it worked. In other ways it didn't. The use of montage in *Battleship Potemkin*, about a failed revolution in Odessa in 1905, generated a remarkable sense of action. But also cut in the cross-cutting was emotional involvement. Feeling got lost.

Even so, *Potemkin* won for Eisenstein world-wide recognition. In 1930 he traveled to Hollywood to bask a bit in his celebrity. Paramount offered him a contract, but no projects ever materialized, though he did write a script for *An American Tragedy* by Theodore Dreiser. David O. Selznick rejected it, however, though he pronounced himself much moved by the work. So Eisenstein pursued an epic documentary in Mexico with the writer Upton Sinclair. It remained unfinished, but the material was edited later by other film makers into as many as three separate projects.

Eisenstein, homosexual but married to a woman determinedly loyal to him, returned home to find a grim culture, imprisoned by Stalin. Montage was now in disrepute, so he struggled to make movies that would satisfy the state without violating his own standards. *Bezhin Meadow*, about a boy who, it was said, had been murdered for reporting his father to the police, so irritated the authorities that Eisenstein had to apologize to them for his "individualistic illusion."[4]

Nonetheless, he was allowed to make another movie as long as he stuck to a historic theme. He told the story of Alexander Nevsky, a thirteenth-century figure who fought invading Teutons. Prokofiev did the music. Though Eisenstein tried hard to create an independent work of art, some still criticized him for tacking too closely to the state. Certainly he did please the powers in the Kremlin with the first part of *Ivan the Terrible*, which won the Stalin Prize. The second part, a picture of Ivan as a mad man, was less well received and was not released for another twelve years.

Before *Ivan* he had a fling at opera, directing Wagner's *Walküre* at the Bolshoi Theatre. (Stalin had thought this would please the Nazis who were his allies at the time, but they overlooked Eisenstein's German father to complain about his Jewish heritage.)

By this time film no longer worked for Eisenstein. Increasingly ill and isolated, he died at fifty of a heart attack, in 1948—the same year as Griffith. "I think he knew that once he made the second part of *Ivan* he would never be allowed to make another film," said Naum Kleiman, director of the Film Museum in Moscow.[5] Then too, he feared execution by Stalin. Denounced during his life as not Marxist enough, criticized today as too cozy with the state, Eisenstein, in spite of everything, still stands as the dominant figure of Soviet film.

Griffith and Eisenstein were great early innovators of silent film, but the ranking genius of the genre was Charlie Chaplin. The child of music-hall performers in London, he saw his family fall into desperate straits after his father died of alcoholism and his mother, her singing career in shambles, went mad and had to be hospitalized. After living for a time in various orphanages, Charlie, at ten, went to work with a dance and comic act. Nine years later he joined Fred Karno's Speechless Comedians, where, along with Stan Laurel, he learned the classic sketches in mime that soon became staples of one-reelers on film.

Chaplin toured the United States as the star of a Karno ensemble and was spotted by Mack Sennett's Keystone film company which offered him not only a contract but also entrée into a world in which he could fully realize himself. By 1914 he had created the character that would project him into the hearts of movie-goers in a way achieved by no one else. Charlie Chaplin's tramp, thrown together by chance for a scene in *Kids Auto Races*, brought accumulated pathos, hardship, and suffering to the screen and made it a means of emotional release for millions.

Chaplin quickly became his own director as well as writer. But even then he felt constrained by the rapid pace of Keystone films and left before long to seek greater freedom at other companies. He needed room for his little tramp to breathe and time to convey his wisdom of timid hope in the face of unbearable odds. Finally Chaplin built his own Lone Star studio and founded United Artists with D.W. Griffith, Mary Pickford, and Douglas Fairbanks. In these settings he created a world on film suffused with the agony of the immigrant and the strain of daily striving.[6]

Once in Hollywood, Chaplin felt little strain himself. He accomplished enormous early success, his income jumping from $150 a week at Keystone (through 1914) to $1250 a week at Essanay (1915) to Mutual ($670,000 a year) to a multimillion plus contract at First National. World famous before he was thirty, Chaplin used his acclaim over the years to attract ever younger women. After his first two marriages failed, he wed the actress Paulette Goddard (also beloved by Gershwin), who starred in Chaplin's films, *Modern Times* and *The Great Dictator*. That lasted nine years.

Then followed others, one of whom accused Chaplin of getting her pregnant. A blood test proved he was not the father of her baby girl, but she won her lawsuit for support nonetheless. Chaplin found stability with Eugene O'Neill's daughter Oona, a New York debutante who had once dated J.D. Salinger and Orson Welles. She gave up her hopes of a movie career to marry Chaplin when she was eighteen and he fifty-four. Estranged from her father, she found what she needed in Charlie. The actress Joan Collins noted that Oona "catered to him with an almost geishalike deference," but it became clear on the sets of his later films, when he looked to Oona for approval after every take, that he depended on her opinion and her approval.[7] Together they had eight children, and when he died, she spent the last years of her life drinking too much and grieving for him.

Chaplin was slow to embrace sound. He held out as long as he could, making *City Lights*, his masterpiece, in 1931. In this story, the tramp falls in love with a blind, blonde beauty, a seller of flowers. He enters a boxing match to help her pay the rent on the rooms she shares with her grandmother. Then he saves a millionaire from suicide and gets the money from him to pay for eye surgery for the young woman in Vienna. Afterwards, she can see. With astonishment she realizes that the man who has meant so much to her, whom she supposed to be wealthy, is a tramp.

After one more silent film, *Modern Times*, a scathing critique of the machine age, Chaplin moved to motion pictures that talked. And he had a lot to say. In *The Great Dictator*, he excoriated Hitler, ridiculing him as the Phooey of Ptomania, Adenoid Hynkel. Chaplin plays both Hynkel and a Jewish barber. As the Phooey, he has some lovely silent moments dancing down sidewalks, tossing a globe of the world in the air. (Of course, it bursts.)

Chaplin's portrayal of Der Führer calls to mind Stanley Kubrick's *Dr. Strangelove* almost thirty years later. Both are forceful anti-war films, and both use heavy satire to achieve their purposes. Chaplin, however, reveals idealistic yearnings never glimpsed in Strangelove. In the end the barber, masquerading as the Führer, gives a magnificent speech that echos the theme of *Modern Times*.

His plea for more feeling and less cold cynicism did not set well with the henchmen of McCarthyism, poised in the early 1950s to poison American life. For years the FBI had been convinced Chaplin was a Communist. Agents had collected endless data on him and it was they who had pushed Joan Barry, clearly a disturbed young woman, into filing the paternity suit that was instrumental in destroying Chaplin's reputation. His movie, *Monsieur Verdoux*, about a bank clerk laid off during the Depression who feels he is forced to earn a living by becoming a bluebeard, wooing women then killing them, did not help Chaplin with the authorities, especially not when they saw his scene in court when he declared that arms dealers were far more effective at taking lives than he was.

When Charlie and Oona sailed to London and the premiere of *Limelight*, a lyrical film about a comedian at the end of his creative life who is drawn to a ballet dancer on the cusp of hers, the Justice Department refused to let him return to the country. Rather than contest the ruling, the Chaplins settled in Switzerland where most of their children were born. So mortified was Oona by the actions of her government that she renounced her American citizenship and became a British subject.[8]

Oona and Charlie Chaplin returned to Hollywood in 1972 when he received an honorary Oscar. Not long after that he was knighted by Queen Elizabeth II. Chaplin died on Christmas Day, 1977. Twenty years later the U.S. Postal Service issued a stamp in his honor.

Charlie Chaplin brought sophistication to slapstick and proved it could be artful. He worked with empathy for his audience and social sensitivity to his times. He staked out high territory in film that few others ever attained. As Andrew Sarris noted, Chaplin was absorbed into every world culture, where he was known as "Charlie," "Charlot," "Carlino," "Carlos," and "Carlitos." He was, it can be argued, the greatest genius ever to work in film.

Where Charlie Chaplin was never far from the shadow of himself, his dark side, Buster Keaton exuded innocence. Chaplin's tramp was poignant to the point of tragedy. Keaton's character was bland, blank, ever calm in the face of threatening fortune. He responded to trouble with resourcefulness and bravery, but no one was more surprised than he was when he prevailed.

Keaton was born in Kansas to parents who were appearing in a medicine show. It was Harry Houdini who gave young Joseph Francis his nickname, Buster. He joined the family act when he was three, and by five he was a star acrobat. There he stayed for almost twenty years, then moved to New York to work with Fatty Arbuckle at Comique film studios.

Keaton found an angel in his brother-in-law, Joseph Schenck. Together they went to Hollywood, and produced films for distribution by MGM. Then Schenck switched to United Artists (Chaplin's company) and Keaton had no choice but to go along too. By then most of his major films had been accomplished, among them the celebrated *Sherlock Jr.*, a beguiling look at the fantasies of a young man who operates a movie house.

He did create one great picture at UA: *The General*, a Civil War story told, like *Birth of a Nation*, from the standpoint of the South. Set in the West, near Chattanooga, it involves spectacular trains, one locomotive chasing another, with Keaton performing desperate acts of daring while his lady tosses impediments onto the track.

Not long after that, impediments appeared in Keaton's path that he could not overcome. His brother-in-law cut off financial support and dispatched him to MGM, where he floundered on a salary, shorn of all creative control of his work. Among the casualties of this new arrangement were not only his art but his marriage. Divorced by his wife and fired by MGM, he sank into alcoholism, reduced to the role of gagman and bit-part actor.

Keaton lived like this another thirty-three years, and died at seventy-one, having just appeared in *A Funny Thing Happened on the Way to the Forum*. He may have suffered excruciating losses, but never did he give up.

Silent film had no more sensitive artist than Abel Gance. Inventive he could be, bringing the triptych (three simultaneous images) to film, in *Napoléon*, but the deep pleasure of his work lies in its sheer beauty and feeling. *La Roue*, the story of a railroad engineer who rescues a young girl after a train wreck, adopts her, then falls in love with her, is resplendent with radiant lighting, rich symbolism, and dramatic tension.

Gance grew up in France. He worked for a solicitor, but spent as much time as he could in the library, reading Racine, Rimbaud, Omar Khayyam, and Edgar Allan Poe. Clearly a romantic, he did some acting and wrote screenplays which were snapped up by the French film industry. Before long he wanted to direct.

Abel Gance was thrilled by the new. He used distorting lenses to portray a sense of fantasy. He also was resourceful, shooting two features at the same time, on the same location, with the same cast. The company wanted two movies. The company got two movies.

World War I so disturbed Gance that he made *J'Accuse!*, a film in which the dead return to ask if their sacrifice was justified. He's been chided for recruiting troops on leave to play the vanquished soldiers just before they were obliged to march into the fiery furnace of Verdun, but the film does have power.

Gabriel de Gravase, an actress in *La Roue*, said this about Abel Gance: "What actor wouldn't want to make pictures with this innovator, this marvelous director, this perfectionist, who obtains the most impressive lighting one can get in photography and does it all with simple means, which are available to every director. Indicating, thinking, playing, living each role with each player. He is not merely the author of the scenario, the cutter, the chief mechanic, the electrician, the cameraman— he is everything: the heart and soul of the film."

Another giant of the silent era was Sweden's Victor Sjostrom, who directed fine pictures in Hollywood (where he called himself Seastrom) as well as at home. His father, married to a former actress, was in the lumber business. The family moved to New York when Victor was only seven months old. His mother died young. The boy grew unhappy with her replacement and a dad who displayed an alarming streak of authoritarianism. So he returned to Sweden to live with his Uncle Victor, an actor.

It was the perfect household for young Victor, who adored acting and did well at it, running his own theatre company before he was asked to join a film studio. There he switched to directing and became the foremost master of Swedish cinema. The height of his artistry can be seen in *The Phantom Carriage*, a Dickens'-*Christmas-Carol*-like story in which David Holm is forced to review his life with the driver of the phantom carriage who works for Death. The last person to die on New Year's Eve must assume the duty of the driver for the next year, and Holm is about to become that man. Nearby, a nurse also is dying. She sends for David Holm, and the intertwining of their lives creates a mood of foreboding that anticipates expressionism in German films of the 1920s[9] and the magical realism that arose in literature in the last decades of the century, especially in the work of Gabriel García Márquez and Isabel Allende.

Next came Hollywood, where Sjostrom made *The Divine Woman* with Greta Garbo as well as *The Scarlet Letter* and *The Wind* with Lillian Gish. Those were happy years, but the coming of sound sent him back to Sweden, where he did only two more films, then returned to acting along with serving as artistic adviser to a film organization. It was Sjostrom who played Professor Borg, the crusty, difficult, eminent academician who is transformed by memory and the shadow of death in Ingmar Bergman's *Wild Strawberries*. Bergman wrote this of Sjostrom's last scene in the movie: "[His] face shone with secretive light, as if reflected from another reality. His features became suddenly mild, almost effete. His look was open, smiling, tender. It was like a miracle." Three years later, Sjostrom himself was dead.

Eisenstein refined montage and made it his own. F.W. Murnau, the other strongly influential director of the silent era, showed film makers how to work with a moving camera.[10] The greatest German expressionist of his day, Murnau (born Friedrich Wilhelm Plumpe) was a poet of the cinema. From his study of art history and literature at the University of Heidelberg, he imbibed a dramatic sense of composition which he infused with baroque taste. So clearly gifted was he in student plays that Max Reinhardt offered to train him for free at his school in Berlin.

When World War I erupted in 1914, Murnau served in the infantry on the Eastern front before transferring to the air force. Then he landed at Verdun, and survived there when few he knew did.

After the war, Murnau immersed himself in film. One of the most memorable of those years was *The Last Laugh*, a study of pathos and lost identity in which an old hotel doorman of appealing pride is forced out of his splendid uniform and into a menial retirement job tending the men's lavatory. He stoops under the weight of his humiliation, but his back straightens when he puts on a uniform, lifted from the hotel, with the same epaulettes he had loved, to wear home each day and keep face before his family and neighbors. But he is found out finally, as he learns when he returns to his apartment one evening to see all the ladies of the building hanging out their windows, laughing at him. And so he slumps once more, never, it would seem to lift his head again. But an unexpected legacy from an eccentric American millionaire who died in his arms in the wash room turns his slow death into rejuvenated life, and he does indeed have the last laugh. It's a splendid film, composed with elegance, shot with style, and warmly felt.

Murnau was another who went to Hollywood, and there, finding release perhaps for his nature as a homosexual, he brought forth one of the most beautiful works of silent film—*Sunrise: A Song of Two Humans*. About trust, temptation, weakness and redemption, with love betrayed, deep wrong forgiven, and love regained, it brings to full fruition the intensity of the German Gothic. *Sunrise* was not a success in its day. That can only be because people were not ready for the moral seriousness of Murnau's art.

Just as he was coming into his own as a film maker of high aesthetic achievement, Murnau was killed in an automobile accident in California. He was only forty-two.

For passion, suffused with religious longing, no one surpassed Carl Dreyer. From a desolate childhood (the illegitimate son of a maid and a Swedish factory-owner in Copenhagen, he was adopted by cold, Lutheran parents) he distilled feelings of loneliness and futility into films that radiate spiritual composure.

Dreyer didn't find his way immediately to movies. First he worked as a journalist, doing theater and film reviews and covering the court house. Next came screen writing, followed, at thirty, by his first directing assignment. Drawing on Sjostrom and Griffith, Dreyer developed one of the richest dramatic talents ever seen in the cinematic arts.

Nowhere is it more movingly realized than in *The Passion of Joan of Arc*, one of the last silent pictures, shot in 1928 in France. Filmed almost entirely in closeups—faces against stark white architecture, like a Richard Avedon photograph—the camera moves relentlessly from one grim visage to another as the bloodless French clergy sit in judgment on Joan, played by Maria Falconetti, a classical beauty of startling emotional power. This was her only film. She went mad and never made any more.

Though a masterpiece, *Joan of Arc* did not succeed at the box office. Neither did a subsequent effort. As a result, Dreyer, in his prime at forty-three, was all but barred from his art. Colleagues considered him a despot whose projects rarely worked, though he was hardly more difficult to deal with than many of his peers.

After knocking about the world, from Britain to France to Somalia, pursuing ideas that never came to fruition, Dreyer went back to Denmark and journalism. Finally, during World War II, he got a chance to film *Day of Wrath*. But it was taken by some as a comment on Nazi persecution of the Jews, which forced him to flee to safety in Sweden. After the war he returned to Copenhagen and scraped together enough money running a movie house to make *The Word*. It, like *Day of Wrath*, was a meditation on the religious life.

One more film, *Gertrud*, followed, but it too took a long time germinating. Dreyer died in 1968, having just raised the funds from the Danish government and Italian state television to create a life of Christ. His last two decades were harder than they should have been for such a luminous director. *Joan of Arc* alone should have assured him all the work he ever could want.

Erich von Stroheim lived for excess. He shot too much film, spent too much money, and invented a pretentious lineage for himself. But his exaggerations were matched by the brilliance of his work. His movies may have been more melodrama than art, but they had something to say.

Stroheim grew up in Vienna, the son of a German-Jewish merchant and a mother from Prague. At twenty-four he went to the United States where he presented himself as an aristocrat of military background. (He had been a soldier for awhile, but not in so splendid a style as he implied.) At other times he masqueraded as a German university graduate, though there is no evidence this was true.

What was true was Stroheim became a Catholic in Hollywood and also an actor, playing bit parts in *Birth of a Nation* and other films by Griffith. He styled himself for roles as an evil Prussian officer during the anti-German years of World War I. But what he really wanted was to direct. Finally his chance came, and he used it shaping characters like those in Zola, characters ruled by destiny.

Stroheim's most memorable creations were McTeague and his wife Trina in *Greed*, a silent film based on a novel by Frank Norris that, incredibly, he shot to run eight hours or more. The studio—Metro-Goldwyn-Mayer—cut the movie to a quarter of its original length. Set in California, it's the story of an ordinary man named McTeague whose mother is very ambitious for him. She sends him to study dentistry with a man who turns out to be a charlatan. McTeague gains no acceptable credentials, but he starts a practice anyway. He also marries a young woman who has just won $5,000 in the lottery. Her cousin, Marcus, also interested in Trina, grows angry that he missed the opportunity to wed her himself and enjoy the benefits of her unexpected dowry. He confronts Mac and demands some of the $5,000. McTeague replies that it isn't his to give.

Trina becomes more and more stingy, hoarding her gold pieces and polishing each one as if it were a jewel. When her mother writes, requesting $50, Trina takes the money from her husband but declines to send it, reasoning that if her mother really needs help she'll write again.

Mac receives an official letter telling him that he can no longer work as a dentist without a proper license. (Marcus probably tipped off the authorities.) He says he won't stop because of a piece of paper, and Trina urges him to make as much money as he can before it's all over.

But it is over, very soon. No patients come any longer. Trina starts carving toys to make a living. None of her lottery funds, of course, can be touched. Mac goes to work in a surgical-instrument factory, but he gets fired. Trina goes on, polishing her coins, more obsessed than ever.

Defeated, Mac leaves. Then she takes a job scrubbing floors in a kindergarten. He returns, saying he hasn't eaten in days. Trina won't let him in. Again, Mac leaves. But he comes back and in a fury kills Trina, takes the $5,000, and heads for Death Valley.

Marcus joins a posse to track down McTeague. They find him in the desert. Mac murders Marcus, then realizes that he is handcuffed to him and there's no way to release himself. He too will die in the searing heat. The $5,000 can save neither of them any more than the money protected Trina.

It is a large statement about the destructiveness of greed, and the strength of Stroheim's talent. But his own extravagance undid him. Studios couldn't tolerate his arrogant overruns in cost and footage. He returned to acting, appearing once with Greta Garbo, and late in his life, with Gloria Swanson as her butler and former husband in *Sunset Boulevard*.

Some say Stroheim was cynical, others that he looked askance at innocence and set out always to shatter it and reveal the ugliness underneath. Sometimes he was right. Innocence did indeed mask evil. And no one exposed it more mercilessly than Erich von Stroheim, who was born with a knowing heart.

Jean Renoir also must be credited with acute artistic insight. Known for "poetic realism," his films of the 1930s expressed the hollowness of Europe in a society that could not right itself as it lurched from one conflagration to another.

Where his father, Auguste Renoir, the Impressionist painter, lavished on his work the utmost in uncomplicated loveliness, Jean created films that were as brittle as they were beautiful. Reared in a family where everybody posed for the master, with and without clothes, Jean married his father's last model, Catherine Hessling, then built around her a series of films designed to evoke an aura of sado-masochistic fantasy.

That changed in time with *A Day in the Country*, a feature cut short by the shortage of money but as a result no less appealing in its romantic tribute to Impressionist painting. Based on a short story by de Maupassant,[11] the ending has a twist—not unusual for Renoir—that points the way to other, not so bucolic work.

The Grand Illusion, starring Erich von Stroheim, was as strong an anti-war film as has ever been made. Pitting the old world against the new, aristocracy against the merit of common accomplishment, it explores the lives of French officers in a German prison camp during World War I. The commander (Stroheim) spots among his charges a French officer of his own upper class and treats him respectfully, only to have to shoot him when the Frenchman engineers the escape of two compatriots by playing the flute, with elegance and insolence, to distract the guards. The German commander, ever loyal to a fellow gentleman, aims for the leg, but misses and hits the stomach instead. The Frenchman yields up his life, explaining that "for us, to die in war is a good solution." Their class, he well knows, will be finished after the armistice, no matter who wins. The future belongs to a couple of lesser military men of France who escape to the farmhouse of a German woman, then to Switzerland.

Two years later, in 1939, with France quaking in the shadow of Germany, Renoir did *The Rules of the Game* and played in it himself. Billed as "an entertainment, not social criticism," it nonetheless draws a scathing picture of French society, stuck in its own decadence, not sure what it believes in, if anything, except the protection of its own interests. Influenced by Mozart,[12] Renoir creates an orderly household of weekend guests, playing by rigid rules, who march to tragedy without recourse to reason, much less honest emotion.

The French were disturbed by *The Rules of the Game* and received it badly. Renoir left for California, where he made five fiction films (though he never stopped being baffled by the studio system) and one for the Office of War Information. He traveled to Europe and India for other movies and wrote a biography of his father as well as his own memoirs. The books tell a story that seldom occurs, of a son who succeeded in art quite as much as his father.

Like Murnau, Ernst Lubitsch worked as an actor in Max Reinhardt's theatre. The son of a Jewish tailor, he went on to become the Cole Porter of German and American film—a debonaire sophisticate too cynical to be much moved or hurt by love.

Lubitsch spent his early years directing and acting in silent movies, in which he played a slapstick assistant in a clothing store. From a base of Jewish comedy he expanded his spoofs to operettas and Shakespeare. Costume dramas followed, grandly set but always amusing.

Then Lubitsch left Berlin for Los Angeles, where he moved gracefully from silent film to sound, luxuriating in the new possibilities with sleek, splashy productions such as *The Merry Widow*, starring Jeanette MacDonald and Maurice Chevalier. But his most scintillating work of the period was *Trouble in Paradise*, which opens in Venice, bristling with wit and wicked innuendo. As amoral as *Monsieur Verdoux* (which uses amorality to make a moral point), this movie has no message as Chaplin's did. It merely celebrates a peculiar tie that binds two thieves together in mutual, sexual understanding.

Unlike Renoir, Lubitsch, with his big cigars and thick German accent, worked his way into the inside of Hollywood, becoming director of production at Paramount, where he antagonized other film makers with excessive, obsessive oversight. He also made *The Shop Around the Corner*, an exquisite story of love letters that lose their illusions, acquire faces, and burst into passion despite the resistance and amazement of the two who wrote them. Written originally as a play and set in specialty store called Matuschek & Co. in Budapest, this picture has a delicacy unusual for Lubitsch. Starring James Stewart and Margaret Sullavan, it glows with expectation and gentle irony from the moment the pair agree, by letter of course, to meet in a café. They'll know each other by red carnations, his in his lapel, hers as a bookmark in a copy of *Anna Karenina*.

It takes longer than that encounter for these two, who both work at Matuschek in a state of mutual antagonism, to understand what they have together. But the unfolding of this epistolary relationship, based on correspondence celebrating literature and love that begins always with "Dear Friend," is so affecting it's been remade twice, as *The Good Old Summertime* with Judy Garland singing in 1949 and *You've Got Mail* by Nora Ephron with Tom Hanks and Meg Ryan in 1998. (This film showed that Ephron's love affair with New York is delirious enough to surpass Woody Allen's.) *The Shop Around the Corner* also was done as a musical play, *She Loves Me*, first produced in 1964 and then revived in 1993.

Lubitsch returned to his broader comic form in *To Be or Not to Be* in 1942, with Carole Lombard and Jack Benny playing a theatrical husband and wife in Warsaw on the brink of war. Robert Stack is a young aviator who undoes Benny night after night by exiting from a center seat near the front just as the actor is beginning the famous soliloquy from Hamlet, "To Be or Not to Be." Stack is leaving to rendezvous with Lombard in her dressing room. But it is not jealousy that flusters Benny. It is the thought that somebody has walked out on him.

Working with their Polish acting company, in and out of disguise, Lombard and Benny flummox the Gestapo and even the Führer. In her work for the resistance, she picks up a secret message in a book store: It's a photograph of an enemy professor with identification and instructions on the back stuck, naturally, in *Anna Karenina*. Like *The Great Dictator* by Chaplin, *To Be or Not to Be* is a sly indictment of Nazis and all tyrants. Remade in 1983 by Anne Bancroft and Mel Brooks, it was Ernst Lubitsch's statement against the terror that had overtaken his own country.

Along with Murnau and Lubitsch, Fritz Lang is considered a giant of German silent cinema. Like his father, Lang set out to study architecture, but gravitated instead to painting. He served in the Austrian army during World War I, and after a serious wound, began writing scripts while convalescing. After the war, his ambition took him to Berlin, where he wrote and acted in films and then proved himself as a director. He also married a prominent screenwriter and novelist, Thea von Harbou.

Few films have been more monumental in style or intention than *Metropolis*. Set in an architectural construct of overbearing dimensions, this film explores the same theme as Chaplin's *Modern Times*, which followed ten years later—the fatal, forced collaboration of man and machine. Like Chaplin, Lang shows scores of people marching to work through a tunnel. They descend below a proscenium of Art Deco grandeur into a world of harsh, hard subterranean labor. Presiding over everything is John Masterman, the richest man in Metropolis, the brain of the city. John Masterman has a son Eric who surveys his father's domain and is horrified. "What shall it profit a man if he gain the whole world but lose his soul?" he asks, adding "Isn't that from some ancient religion?"

Machines without a soul lead to revolution. Slogans are in the air: "God is power! God is love!" A mad scientist—another forerunner of Dr. Strangelove—creates a woman robot called "Efficiency." He also pursues mechanical men who will never tire and never make mistakes. In the midst of a true Tower of Babel, Mary, an angelic figure, appears. She calls for a mediator between the brain and the hands. That mediator, properly understood, is the heart. Eric is drawn to Mary, and eventually John Masterman is won over to a more humane dispensation. It may sound contrived, but Lang, like Chaplin, had an important point to make and he went to considerable lengths to give it dramatic force.

A later film, *The Last Will of Dr. Mabuse*, affronted Nazi censors, and Lang was summoned to see Joseph Goebbels, the Minister of Propaganda and controller of all national culture. Instead of chastising Lang, Goebbels offered to make him head of German film. Lang refused, and left instead for exile in California, leaving behind his wife who sympathized with the Hitler regime.

Once in Hollywood, Lang's work took on an entirely different style. Becoming a master of *film noir*, he made movies such as *The Big Heat*, in which Glenn Ford and Gloria Grahame suffer mightily at the hands of bad crooks and worse cops. Shot from a pessimist's view of the world, it has the narrative power of a fine novel. Though shorn of Lang's earlier, German pretensions, it retains still his stark sense of rectitude.

Where Lang worked from a moral imagination, Josef von Sternberg was a pure sensualist. A true child of his native Viennese appetites, he grew up there and in New York, where he acquired an American taste for gamesmanship. It was not the rules of the game that interested him, as they did Renoir. It was the spirit of play that impelled his art into realms of fantasy.

Sternberg started out as an apprentice to a millinery shop, a position settled on by his parents. It didn't suit him at all, so he ran away from home and took a job with a repairman in the motion picture business. In time he made his way to the World Film Corporation in New Jersey, where he moved through a series of assignments, patching films and shipping them, until he rose to become the chief executive's top assistant. Sternberg made training films during World War I and served as a signal corps photographer in Washington. Then he returned to World Film only to leave and go out on his own to write and edit silent movies and work as assistant director. Before long he landed in Hollywood, where Chaplin saw his first work as a director, *The Salvation Hunters*, steeped in camera movement like Murnau's, not the montage of Eisenstein, and pronounced Sternberg a genius.

Sternberg built his greatest pictures around a single presence: Marlene Dietrich. He discovered her in Berlin's cabaret world and brought her to glory in *The Blue Angel*, his only German-made film. That same year, 1930, Sternberg took Dietrich to Hollywood where together they did films for Paramount. The first, *Morocco*, involved Dietrich with Gary Cooper as a Foreign Legionnaire in North Africa. He meets her in a night club where she is singing, clad in her trademark white tie, top hat and tails, all sultry insolence. Later Dietrich says to Cooper, "There's a Foreign Legion of women, too, only they don't wear uniforms, but they are just as brave."

Sophisticated like Lubitsch, but with a rich mix of exotica, Sternberg is a creator of atmosphere. In *Shanghai Express*, he places Dietrich on a train heading into Chinese civil war territory. She runs into a military doctor she had known and loved before. By now she is Shanghai Lily, a woman of sardonic experience. ("It took more than one man to change my name to Shanghai Lily," she advises the doctor.) The train is seized by Chinese rebels who hold the doctor captive and also Shanghai Lily. They escape finally and rediscover each other. It's a romance seen through the mists of murky history and ironic wit. But the most important relationship of the movie is that between Sternberg and his star. Together they make magic.

The 1930s also brought *The Scarlet Empress*, a *tour de force* in which Dietrich plays Catherine II. In a Russia built on "ignorance, violence, fear and aggression," as Sternberg says in the opening titles, he creates a world of elegant intrigue in which Sophie Frederica (renamed Catherine by the reigning czarina) out-maneuvers her dim, befuddled husband and takes his place as the next ruler of the land. With fantastic style she rallies the army and becomes not only empress but also the most celebrated woman of her day. It's probably Sternberg's best film and one of the last that he made with Marlene Dietrich.

When their collaboration came to an end, he struggled through other projects only to be fired from Paramount by Lubitsch. Then came other, lesser films, such as *Jet Pilot* with John Wayne and Janet Leigh, a commercial movie about a woman Soviet pilot (also a spy) who is shot down near an American air base and assigned to the supervision of John Wayne, who of course falls in love with her while trying to find out what she and Moscow know about fighter technology. He uses her. She uses him. But they wind up together, emblematic still of the Sternberg worldly humor.

There was another German actress whom Sternberg offered to take to Hollywood, but she stayed behind to become the most bitterly controversial film maker of the century—Hitler's documentarian, Leni Riefenstahl.

Widely acknowledged as the most important woman director in the history of cinema, Riefenstahl nonetheless stands forever accused because she put her genius at the service of pure evil. That she didn't know the true nature of Hitler, as she claims, may mitigate the case, but it took great powers of self-absorption to miss the horror that was welling up in Germany, soon to engulf all of Europe.

Of course, in joining the rush to the Third Reich, Riefenstahl was accompanied by countless business and professional people, including Daimler-Benz, which used slave labor—often Jewish—to manufacture tanks, trucks, and aircraft engines for the war, their regular employees having been pressed into the armed forces. For this company, as for many bankers, lawyers, scientists, and musicians, working with Hitler was a matter of opportunism. For the maker of the Führer's favorite Mercedes, it was a profitable arrangement.[13] Hence it could be said that Leni Riefenstahl got caught up in a fever that was sweeping the civilized echelons of Germany, spreading contamination where there should have been horrified resistence.

Leni Riefenstahl was born to a comfortable, middle-class, Berlin family in 1902. Her father had a plumbing business prosperous enough to provide two houses, servants, and a chauffeur. He wanted his daughter to be a classical artist, and indeed she did study painting. He also kept her strictly supervised, forbidding her to date or to go out alone until she was twenty-one. Vowing, understandably, to become independent, Leni took dancing lessons without telling her father, and later, having broken free of family constraints, she became a dancer, but injured her knee. Turning then to film, she established herself as an actress of considerable reputation in the heroic mountain movies that were the Westerns of Germany. This she accomplished by sending her photograph to Arnold Fanck, the foremost director of the genre. He was so taken with Leni that he promised to write his next picture for her.

And so he did. Riefenstahl starred in her first silent film and quickly soared to fame. "Germany's Garbo" they called her. As Richard Corliss relates, she played in "seven Fanck adventures, climbing mountains barefoot, enduring avalanches, crossing deep crevasses on a rickety ladder, radiating alpine glamour." Her frequent co-star was Luis Trenker, the top mountain leading man. When she tumbled into bed with him for a one-night stand, Fanck, clearly enamored of Leni, was so upset he tried to kill himself. Fanck was taken off the picture and Riefenstahl finished it herself, demonstrating from that early moment her gift for directing.

She also attracted the furious jealousy of Trenker, who later betrayed her.

It was not the only time the aftermath of love led to treachery for Riefenstahl. She also had an affair with Hans Schneeberger, Fanck's cameraman (work was the place she usually found her men; there was no time to look elsewhere), who taught her how to ski, then turned against her. Her infatuation with Schneeberger was among the reasons she refused Josef von Sternberg's offer to go to Hollywood.

Riefenstahl married only once. She chose an army major named Peter Jacobs whom she met on a train. Though unfaithful to her, he did help with some of her films. They parted after the war, when Leni's plunge into poverty put too great a strain on both of them. Other men came along, however. Even in her eighties she was living with Horst Kessner, forty years younger than she was.[14]

Even so, Richard Corliss, a journalist, has pointed out that what mattered to Leni was "not so much the men in her past but the man in her." "I have a man's way of thinking," she said, "but a woman's way of feeling . . . . I have a great organizing talent. I can do a cost estimate, tell camera people what to do, organize film material."

She also was an innovator of motion pictures, handling close-ups and lighting in a way that was fresh and highly creative. All this became clear in *The Blue Light*, which she directed in 1932. By then there was sound, Frank Deford points out, but she used it sparingly. So successful was *The Blue Light* that it won the gold medal at the Venice Biennale.

Extreme experience is what Riefenstahl sought, and she made a film in Greenland to find it. "This high-striving woman was eager to get away from the ordinary, the messiness of the mundane," wrote John Simon. "If a yearning for extremes is part of the fascist spirit, then Riefenstahl was ripe for fascism."

Certainly fascism was ready for her. Adolph Hitler was quick to respond when Riefenstahl wrote to him requesting a meeting. She had seen him at a rally and been overwhelmed by his presence, John Simon relates. "I had an almost apocalyptic vision that I was never able to forget," she recalled later . . . . "I felt quite paralyzed." She was not so incapacitated, however, that she did not pursue Hitler immediately, just as she had Arnold Fanck.

They became friends though, apparently, not lovers. Riefenstahl began visiting Hitler, sometimes taking her parents along. In time she created a salon for his circle at her Berlin house. She and the actress wife of Luftwaffe chief Hermann Goring were called "the DuBarrys of the

Nazi Empire." So great was Leni's rapport with the German dictator that when Mussolini summoned her to see him in 1936, Il Duce sent a message to Hitler through Riefenstahl: "You can tell the Führer," he is reported to have said, "that whatever happens with Austria I will not interfere in Austria's internal affairs." Riefenstahl passed this along to Hitler as soon as she returned home. It, of course, smoothed the way for the Nazis's march to Vienna.[15]

By then other atrocities were already well underway: In 1933, the Nazis, elected by only 44 percent of the popular vote, barred Jews from the civil service as well as the professions and German universities. The next year brought the "Night of the Long Knives" when the entire command of the SA storm troopers was wiped out. Then followed, in 1935, the Nuremberg Laws which began officially a brutal regime for the Jewish community.

In the midst of the mounting terror, Riefenstahl was implored by Hitler to document on film his Nuremberg rally of 1933. She hastily threw together a short work called *Victory of Faith*, but it became dated by Nazi upheavals too soon ever to be shown.

Then came the call to film the extravaganza Hitler planned for Nuremberg in 1934. One and a half million people were mustered for a display of fealty that would establish the Reich conclusively as master of Germany and as a force to be respected if not feared throughout Europe. To make sure the film conveyed the supreme power of the moment, Albert Speer was commissioned as architect of the rally. He created an enormous site just outside the city and took the stadium where Nazi war criminals would be hung in 1946 and made of it an imperial space.[16]

Whatever Riefenstahl wanted, she got. Speer built her an elevator on a flagpole so she could put drama into her overhead shots. A plane also was put at her disposal. She deployed forty-nine cameramen, some on roller skates, who captured perspectives never seen before on film. When sound problems spoiled some of the speeches, leaders of the Nazi regime delivered them again for her, later, in a studio, with the set designed by Speer. All told, Riefenstahl gathered over sixty hours of material which she edited during the next year to two hours.

Riefenstahl was convinced that Hitler "did not want a political film; he wanted an artistic film."[17] And indeed that may be true. Goebbels, Susan Sontag emphasises, was much taken with the aesthetic aspect of political ideas. Politics, he said, is "the highest and most comprehensive art there is, and we who shape modern German policy feel ourselves to be artists . . . the task of art [being] to form, to give shape, to remove the diseased and create freedom for the healthy"—certainly a disquieting pronouncement. "It takes imagination," he continued "to grant life to the innermost purpose and innermost constitution of a new world."

This Riefenstahl surely accomplished. Her film, *Triumph of the Will*, has been called a masterpiece. Hitler himself declared it a "totally unique and incomparable glorification of the power and beauty of our movement." "And so," said Sontag, "it is."

Triumph of the Will starts with solemnity and builds slowly, inexorably. The titles announce, "Twenty years after the outbreak of world war—sixteen years after Germany's crucifixion—nineteen months after the beginning of Germany's rebirth—Adolph Hitler flew—to Nuremberg." And there, amidst the clouds, deceiving with loveliness, his plane appears, bearing from Berlin the leaders of the Third Reich.

The Führer descends in a manner both careful and deliberate. He is greeted by throngs of people—men, women, children—brightly smiling, extending their arms and chorusing as if in a massed choir, "Heil Hitler! Heil Hitler!" Then come his lieutenants: Rudolph Hess, Heinrich Himmler, Joseph Goebbels.

Their motorcade rolls grandly down the streets through a sea of white handkerchiefs, waving in welcome. Arms reach out through windows, stretching to the sky in elegant, baroque buildings bedecked with flags. Hitler stands in his automobile, in profile, watchful, gauging the allegiance of the crowd, saluting, but without a smile. The officers of the Reich enter an edifice in slow motion. Then, suddenly, Hitler appears above in a window, like the Pope, or Evita and Peron.

That done, the Führer and his party make their way to the stadium, and the speeches begin. Hess speaks directly to his boss: "My Führer, around you are the flags and banners of our national socialism . . . . Only when these banners are in tatters will mankind fully understand the real greatness of our time . . . . You were the symbol of our victory." Then, fervor mounting, Hess addresses the assembled, throbbing throng: "The party is Hitler. Hitler, however, is Germany, just as Germany is Hitler. Heil Hitler! Heil Hitler! Heil victory! Heil victory! Heil victory!"

Others are heard from, but none are more ominous than Streicher, who warns, "A people that does not guard the purity of its race must perish."

In the crowded stadium are row upon row of soldiers, Teutonic, swastikas on their arms, just above the elbow. Military faces appear in close-up, each telling the part of Germany he comes from. Titles on the screen pronounce them "One people—one Führer—one Reich!" Next the camera catches the gleaming, open mouth of a trumpet, and a child playing a kettle drum with the gravitas of an old man. Blonde boys perform in their own band. More boys, in knee sox and short pants, stand on tip-toe to see. A leader declares, "At your command, my Führer, German youth faces you."

The Führer faces them, and here is what he says: "You are flesh of our flesh and blood of our blood . . . . Our future is Germany. Our today is Germany. Our past is Germany . . . . Though the older generation may be unstable, the younger generation is with us body and soul . . . . We must eliminate those who prove unworthy . . . and therefore are no part of us."

He meant, perhaps, the hapless officers of the SA who had been fatally terminated only weeks before. The rank and file still remained, and there they stood, hearing their fate, as if they hadn't grasped it already. But the response was what Hitler came to Nuremberg to hear and Riefenstahl came to capture on film: Soldiers processed in a torch-light parade, their commander vowing to the Führer, "We shall obey your orders alone."

Susan Sontag has written tellingly about *Triumph of the Will*: "The relations of domination and enslavement take the form of a characteristic pageantry: the massing of groups of people; the turning of people into things; the multiplication or replication of things; and the grouping of people/things around an all-powerful, hypnotic leader-figure or force. The fascist dramaturgy centers on the orgiastic transactions between mighty forces and their puppets, uniformly garbed and shown in ever swelling numbers . . . . Fascist art glorifies surrender, it exalts mindless-ness, it glamorizes death."

Richard Corliss called *Triumph of the Will* "a newsreel raised to romantic myth." Brian Winston noted that it deified Hitler, "a political boss" whom 56 percent of the voters had refused to approve. All this is true. It is also the case that in *Triumph of the Will* Leni Riefenstahl created a work so powerful, so astounding in its zeal to overwhelm that it compels admiration that cannot help but be accompanied by revulsion, given all that we know about what would follow.

Riefenstahl's reputation rests on two documentary works: *Triumph of the Will* and *Olympia*, shot at the 1936 Berlin Games and called "the greatest sports film ever made." For these two efforts, wrote Richard Corliss, "Riefenstahl deserves to be classed with D.W. Griffith, Sergei Eisenstein, and Orson Welles as one of cinema's great innovator artists."

The Olympics of 1936 were held in an atmosphere of strain and fore-boding. Five months before, Hitler had marched into the Rhineland. There was talk in Britain of boycotting the games, but Harold Abrahams, the gold-medal winner of 1924 mythologized in *Chariots of Fire*, led the campaign to go to Germany. In the end, over twice as many athletes as had participated in Los Angeles four years before turned up in Berlin.

Eager to impress the world, Hitler, once again, denied Riefenstahl nothing in her mounting of the movie. She placed cameras in balloons, on a truck that ran on tracks beside the sprinters, and underwater to capture the divers, using equipment that could change exposure from above to below the surface of the pool. She used night filters and telephoto lenses, and when the light was too dim for the pole vaulters to be shot properly, she had them do it all over again, after the games had ended.

The prologue begins in Athens at the Temple of Zeus where a beautiful young man starts the run to Berlin, bearing the torch of the Olympiad. Riefenstahl was there, of course, filming everything and also making news herself. The *New York Times* reported that she was drawn to an especially well-built athlete, and exclaiming, "He looks like a Greek god," she offered to take him to Berlin in her plane and help him break into the movies. There was nothing to this but professional interest, she explained to the press.[18] The prologue features not only male nudes but women as well, and Riefenstahl, splendid at thirty-three, is among them.

Once in the Berlin stadium there is only one star—Jesse Owens, the magnificent black American. Owens sprints, and wins. Owens jumps, and sets a world record. Owens is the triumphant figure of 1936. He dominates the Olympics, and Riefenstahl celebrates him with every shot in which he appears.

She shows the shadow of a discus thrower, in slow motion. Athletes compete from Japan and Poland. Over it all hovers the after-knowledge that in only a few years these elegant young men will be at war, with each other.

During the games, Leni was quite taken with Glenn Morris, the American decathlon champion, and she made of him a romantic conquest. But there can't have been a lot of time for love. She had 250 miles of film to edit and the process took two years. Once finished, she had a work of art that won the Venice Film Festival of 1938, beating Walt Disney's *Snow White*. British and American delegates walked out in protest, complaining that *Olympia* was a documentary, not a feature. But Stalin sent Riefenstahl a note of praise, and Mussolini asked her to make a film for him. Hitler observed his forty-ninth birthday with a world premier of *Olympia*.

Riefenstahl made much of insisting that Geobbels was wildly jealous of her, feared her influence over Hitler, and tried to destroy her. The story goes that in 1937 he announced at a social gathering that he and his wife could no longer remain in the room because a person of non-Aryan ancestry was there. It was Riefenstahl he meant. Riefenstahl, he said, was only three-fourths Aryan. This claim was disputed by Hitler, who declared, "It is I who will decide who is a Jew and who is not." The Führer summoned a photographer and ordered Goebbels to meet them at Leni's house, where her family also was told to be present. The photographer snapped pictures of Hitler and Goebbels chatting with the Riefenstahls. Thus the rumors were countered.

Whenever, during their conversations, Leni tried to bring up Hitler's animus toward Jews, she said he simply cut her off. God and the Messiah he would discuss, but not that.

It was in this atmosphere that Riefenstahl set forth for the United States in 1938 to tout *Olympia*. The reception was not good. Kristallnacht had occurred just days before she docked in New York. When journalists met her at the boat and asked about the horror of broken glass all over her country, she recalled telling them that "it couldn't be true, because in the American newspapers on the ship I had read so many lies about Germany."[19]

She would not learn the truth until she returned home. Meanwhile, her U.S. tour was marred by members of the American Jewish Congress and the Jewish Labor Committee who announced they would picket any theater that showed *Olympia*. In Hollywood, though Walt Disney received her, the Anti-Nazi League for Defense of American Democracy distributed leaflets calling Riefenstahl the "head of the Nazi film industry." The league took out an ad in movie trade papers urging the film industry to "close its doors to all Nazi agents."[20]

Riefenstahl insisted that her trip was "absolutely private" and she had "no official orders to carry out." (How Germanic of her to think in terms of "orders".) "I never held an official position in Germany," she argued. "I am an independent artist."[21]

This illusion she carried with her back to Europe. Landing in France, she complained that two detectives hired by the Anti-Nazi League had followed her all over Hollywood. They got in her way when she was walking and were "actually rude to me a couple of times."[22]

Life would grow worse than rude in the days ahead. War erupted and Riefenstahl saw less of Hitler, though he did confide to her at one point that he would like to turn over the government to others when victory was won and devote himself instead to making movies with her. "If brilliantly done," he said, "motion pictures could change the world." That would never be. Not only had Hitler doomed himself, he also had put an end to Riefenstahl's film career through his own association with her.

Riefenstahl had a brief stint in Poland, where she accompanied invading German forces as a correspondent with her own camera team. But the sight of dead bodies so sickened her that she retreated to Austria and Czechoslovakia. There she spent the rest of the war working on the film *Tiefland*.

Tiefland took more than fifteen years to complete. Four years went into the shooting. Then the French government confiscated Riefenstahl's rushes and kept them for a decade. Other problems surfaced in connection with the work: In 1982, a filmmaker named Nina Gladitz did a documentary in which she charged that Riefenstahl had used gypsies from a concentration camp near Salzburg as extras in *Tiefland* (which required Spaniards, but none could be found in Germany during the war), then knowingly returned them to certain death. Riefenstahl sued. At the trial, a witness, who had been thirteen at the time, testified that he told Leni about the gas chambers and she promised to intercede for the gypsies, but nothing ever happened. Many of them were executed as soon as the filming was over.[23]

Taking the stand on her own behalf, Riefenstahl, then eighty-two, insisted that she had never visited that concentration camp herself and had no idea of the fate that awaited people there. She reminded the court that she had faced similar allegations in 1949 and defeated them.[24] Riefenstahl lost in her effort to force Gladitz to eliminate all reference to the matter from the film, but prevailed in getting the court to order that the documentary could not include the supposition that Leni had made "empty promises" to the gypsies that they would not be sent to death. The ruling said that neither side had proved its case.[25]

When the war was over, life changed drastically for Riefenstahl. She was thrown out of her Austrian villa by "a hard-boiled Boston Irishman who did not even know who she was . . . ." The lakeside house was turned into a rest center for the Rainbow Division. "Baby," she recalled an American saying to her, "I've been going to the movies a long time and I never heard of you." Reportedly, Riefenstahl wept as she told this story.[26]

There was much else to weep about, but it could have been worse. The U.S. investigated Riefenstahl and denazified her right away. But then she fell into the hands of the French who put her in prison, and then an insane asylum. Finally they too denazified her only to turn her over to the Germans. What followed was such vitriol that Leni filed fifty libel cases, which she claimed she won. The West Berlin denazification court, Deford relates, pronounced that Riefenstahl engaged in "no political activity in support of the Nazi regime which would warrant punishment . . . . No relationships were established that went beyond what is necessary for the execution of her artistic undertakings . . . . No close or even intimate relationships with Hitler existed."

This was refuted by the publication in 1947 of Eva Braun's diary which described a vivid affair between Riefenstahl and Hitler. But the diary was proved to be a hoax. And the perpetrator? Luis Trenker, Leni's jealous co-star in the mountain movies of twenty years before.

Despite her exoneration, Leni was cut off from filmmaking, except for a few sports documentaries. She lived with her mother in Munich, in a single room with no kitchen or bath, working, finally, as a freelance photographer for *Stern* magazine and other publications. From time to time there were film offers, but always they fell through.

There was some relief in 1954 when Jean Cocteau advanced her work at the Cannes Film Festival, and in 1959 she was honored along with Josef von Sternberg at the Venice Film Festival.

Leni persisted in her pursuit of film and photography and was drawn in time to Africa, which she said, "means more to me than any country." (Still, it was extreme experience that attracted her.) Then she read Hemingway's *The Green Hills of Africa* and knew she had to go to the Sudan. There she created a book of 126 glorious color photographs of the Nuba people. Even in this effort she could not escape her work being characterized as fascist. Here's what Susan Sontag wrote: "Riefenstahl strongly recalls fascist rhetoric when she celebrates the ways the Nuba are exalted and unified by the physical ordeals of their wrestling matches, in which the 'heaving and straining' Nuba men, 'huge muscles bulging,' throw one another to the ground—fighting not for material prizes but 'for the renewal of the sacred vitality of the tribe.'" Maybe so. But they are superb photographs nonetheless. And Richard Grenier had a point when he said if Riefenstahl's work with the Nuba, among whom she lived for six months, makes her a practitioner of the "fascist aesthetic," then the sculpture of Michelangelo and the Greeks must be fascist also.

At seventy-two, Riefenstahl enrolled in scuba diving classes, claiming she was twenty years younger to meet the age requirement. What followed was *Coral Gardens*, a book of color photographs taken in the Indian Ocean, the Caribbean, and the Red Sea. This too was acclaimed as a work of genius. She also made an underwater film in the Maldives, and at ninety-five she was still pursuing deep sea videos.[27]

The year Leni turned ninety-five, in 1997, a gallery in Hamburg held the first exhibit of her work in Germany since the war. The show included color photographs and clips from her old black-and-white movies. Public officials stayed away because Riefenstahl was still controversial. "In the very ambiguity of the role she played during the Nazi era," wrote Frank Deford, "she reminds Germans of themselves."

Her art also has been exhibited in Japan and Italy, though protesters turned up in Milan. And in the United States, Riefenstahl's films are frequently shown. A retrospective at the Telluride Festival in Colorado in 1974 did much to rehabilitate her, even in the face of clamorous dissension. She still will not allow *Triumph of the Will* to be screened in Germany, even though students might find it edifying. "The film has a strong effect," she said. "If young people see it, maybe they will get too enthusiastic about it in the wrong way and not understand the difference between art and history."[28]

Even so, Riefenstahl's art and her history are still vivid in her own mind. "She can sit in front of an editing machine," noted Janet Maslin, "and recall exactly how each shot in one of her films was achieved, right down to the color filter and the brand of the camera."[29]

And still she cannot comprehend the trouble the films for Hitler caused her. "I absolutely cannot imagine that I did anything unjust," she said. "What crime did I commit?"[30] Why, she wondered, should she have declined the opportunity to do *Triumph of the Will*? "I still don't know why I should have turned it down when Hitler was wooed by foreign statesmen and not even his worst critics dared to predict his subsequent atrocities."[31] What's more, she pointed out, "If I had been an American, English, or Russian and had been given an order from Churchill, Roosevelt, or Stalin to make a film about flying or about a Moscow party rally, I would have done it too and to the best of my ability as an artist."[32] (Orders again. One of her cameramen, according to Deford, made the same observation; so evidently she had gone to some effort to get this line set.) "I didn't know about the concentration camps until I was under arrest with the Seventh Army," she insisted. "I always admitted that yes, in the beginning, I was fascinated by Hitler. I never denied that. But I had no idea what Hitler was doing."

And there were strong incentives not to know: "I could work!" she exulted. "I was free!"[33] Then too, she admitted, "I was always isolated and living for my work." Riefenstahl loved beauty, and it became a fixation: "I am fascinated by what is beautiful, strong, healthy, what is living," she said. "I seek harmony . . . ." But beauty betrayed her, not admitting into her conscious life the possibility of imperfection. Harmony imposed limitations that enhanced her art but blinded her as a person.[34]

It was "the willful blindness of the total narcissist,"[35] said Molly Haskell, and that may well be true. Then too, there was something profoundly German about Riefenstahl that caused her to be swept up in events and refuse to go to Hollywood when she had the chance. Like many of her countrymen, she too followed orders. (Hitler called her "my perfect German woman.") In orders she thought she found, paradoxically, artistic freedom. But instead she was ensnared by her time and her place and her drive for harmony that could not acknowledge the world as it was, even when that world was sinking into hell.

If Riefenstahl's genius was ill used, in the service of evil, Orson Welles saw his own genius come to early fruition, then struggle for years thereafter to express itself. Born in Kenosha, Wisconsin, to parents who died when he was still a child, Welles was considered a prodigy. A local newspaper headlined him as "Cartoonist, Actor, Poet and only 10."[36] At the Todd School in Illinois, Welles bloomed as a dramatist, staging and performing in plays, especially Shakespeare. He left there at sixteen to become an actor with the Gate Theater in Dublin. Next came New York, where he joined John Houseman to direct plays for the New York Federal Theater. That folded, so together they formed the Mercury Theater in 1937.

Welles also pursued radio, presenting the classics for general audiences. It was there that he had his first sensation: a Halloween adaptation of *The War of the Worlds* by H.G. Wells. It electrified millions of Americans who believed that Martians truly had invaded the planet and the end was near.

But it was all leading to his first, most celebrated film: *Citizen Kane*. Made when Welles was only twenty-five, it chronicles the life of Charles Foster Kane (played by Welles), unlikely heir to a vast fortune who immerses himself in a newspaper he finds among his many holdings and builds it into a popular bonanza, pushing crime and low culture while espousing the principles of a populist. With eyes on the White House, he marries the president's niece, has a son, grows bored, takes up with a salesgirl which precipitates his losing a race for governor, weds her after his wife and child are killed in an auto accident, and seeks to launch his new bride as an opera singer. But she doesn't have the voice to sustain the life he tries to create for her, and he doesn't have the love in him to keep her happy. She leaves. Much else is lost as well, and Kane dies broken and deserted at his fantasy castle called Xanadu.

Citizen Kane is a rich, aromatic, baroque masterpiece, drenched in exaggerated detail from the dizzying heights and debilitating lows of a useful life turned suddenly eccentric and grotesque. It's a picture that might have been made in *fin de siècle* Vienna.

Seeing himself in *Citizen Kane*, William Randolph Hearst, fabled czar of yellow journalism, tried everything to keep the film from being distributed and forbade its mention in any of his newspapers. But that only stimulated interest in the show. It opened in New York in 1941 to full houses, though it did less well elsewhere in the U.S. and in England.

Citizen Kane was so astounding that it colored the rest of Orson Welles's life, setting expectations at a level too high ever to attain again.[37] Not only did he revolutionize film in *Kane*, deploying deep focus photography better than anybody had ever done before, he also leveled a moral indictment at the megalomania of America's business elite, where too often responsibility gets lost in hubris.

Next came *The Magnificent Ambersons*, based on a novel by Booth Tarkington, who was a friend of Welles's father. Orson in fact was the model for George in the book. Directing the film, Welles drew George's parents to resemble his own mother and dad, just as Tarkington had.

The picture opens with a witty exposition on gentlemen's fashions of 1873, then quietly reveals the elegant house with the grand staircase where the Ambersons hold court and dominate the community. The years pass. George grows to young manhood. Eugene Morgan, inventor of the Morgan motor car, returns with love still alive for George's mother and some trenchant observations on the social changes that lie ahead: "Man's mind will be changed in subtle ways by the automobile," he says. Echoing Chaplin and Lang, Welles offers a telling juxtaposition between the horseless carriage created by Gene and a lyrical horse-drawn sleigh. There is no doubt where lies the poetry of life.

Later, when electric lines appear overhead and industry overtakes the town, Welles observes of the new scene, "It befouled itself and darkened the sky."

There are those who prefer *The Magnificent Ambersons* to *Citizen Kane*. One of them is Andrew Sarris who argues that "*Amberson* is to *Kane* what *The Marriage of Figaro* is to *Don Giovanni*, what *Anna Karenina* is to *War and Peace*, and what *Uncle Vanya* is to *The Cherry Orchard*. . . . . *Ambersons* is subtler and deeper than the more expansive and spectacular *Kane*." Sarris quotes André Bazin, saying he "suggested that Welles reversed the usual order by creating his baroque work (*Kane*) first and his classical work (*Ambersons*) second." Both of them have a point.

A sensibility such as Welles's required Shakespeare, and he knew it. Welles did *Macbeth* in 1948 and, four years later, *Othello*. The picture opens with tragic arabesques against a dark, bloodless sky. Orson Welles as Othello is being carried to his grave. Like Fritz Lang, Welles makes impressive use of architecture, shadowing Desdemona and the Moor on the wall. And with unsurpassed flair for the dramatic, he uses the camera to achieve great depth of emotive perception. Later, in the elegant *Chimes at Midnight*, Welles explored King Henry IV, Prince Hal and Falstaff, whom he played. With John Gielgud, Jeanne Moreau and Ralph Richardson's voice reading from Holinshed's *Chronicles*, this film collects Shakespeare's life of Falstaff from *Henry IV* (both parts), *The Merry Wives of Windsor*, Henry V, and *Richard II*. Pauline Kael pronounced it a great film despite technical problems due to lack of money.[38] She was right.

By the time Orson Welles directed and acted in *Touch of Evil*, with Janet Leigh, Charlton Heston, and Marlene Dietrich, he was enormous, at about four hundred pounds. This made him all the more menacing as a crooked police captain in a drama set on the U.S.-Mexico border. Janet Leigh is newly married to an Hispanic government official who's chairman of the Pan American Narcotics Commission.

They collide with the captain, and the result is an engrossing tale that survived pedestrian editing by Universal to become an enormous influence on French New Wave film makers Jean-Luc Godard and François Truffaut and reverberate later in Curtis Hanson's *L.A. Confidential* and John Sayles's *Lone Star*. So distressed was Welles by the heavy-handedness of the studio that he wrote a fifty-eight-page memo outlining what must be done to make the picture right. That memo came to light in the 1990s and guided a reworking of the film to conform to Welles' original thinking. Robert Wise, who directed *Touch of Evil*, said this is the only film to which Welles brought the kind of concentration that he gave to *Citizen Kane.*[39]

Scattered attention was a problem for Welles. According to Wise, who edited *Citizen Kane,* "self-indulgence and lack of self-discipline [destroyed Welles] after he made his start . . . . He directed *Ambersons* by day and acted at night in *Journey into Fear.* How can you do that at the same time?"[40]

You can't. So Welles led a frenetic life, unable to keep to studio hours or studio anything, enraging his boss at Columbia with the film, *The Lady from Shanghai,* with his then (estranged) wife Rita Hayworth, who had to cut her magnificent hair and dye it blonde for the role. Before long he was banned from the steady financial support of the studios and forced to scramble for money to produce his work, usually in acting assignments. His career declined prematurely, and he made only two theatrical movies during the last seventeen years of his life.

Sarris condemns myths that "entomb Welles as a burned-out prodigy, a wastrel, an unappreciated visionary, a trickster, a Renaissance man for all media—cinema, theatre, radio, television; an egomaniac, a compulsive storyteller right out of 'The Ancient Mariner,' a persecuted liberal and New Dealer without portfolio, a failed newspaper columnist, a huckster, a public clown, a martyr to Hollywood philistinism, a raging sexist, a baroque mannerist, a man who scared a nation, a twentieth century incarnation of Sigmund Freud's *Leonardo da Vinci,* and an Oedipally crippled artist congenitally inhibited from finishing his projects." But Sarris concedes that Welles was "all these things and more."

Orson Welles died in 1985, at seventy, leaving behind one of the great legacies of American cinema. He was not the only director to burn brightly, then flicker for years in an art that uses up talent too voraciously. Of course, Welles, like Stroheim, contributed to his own troubles through extravagance and lack of discipline. Nonetheless, Welles brought power and intellect to the screen and made of his films a mirror of his own imposing personality.

Like Sternberg, Max Ophuls was a cynical romantic, and like Sternberg, he proved that this need not be an oxymoron. It's been said that some wear cynicism like a tourniquet, to stop the bleeding. This was true of Max Ophuls.

Ophuls was born Max Oppenheimer, the son of prosperous Jewish parents, in Germany. The name Ophuls he adopted when he joined the theater in 1919 so as not to embarrass his father, the proprietor of a prominent department store. After ten years working as a stage director, Ophuls moved to Berlin to take up a film career just as sound was coming in. In 1933, the year Hitler came to power, he and his family fled to France (did Leni Riefenstahl not notice this?), and seven years later they were forced to move again, this time to California, where Ophuls took not only his wife and son but also his mistress.[41]

It took a long time to break into Hollywood. The war was over before Douglas Fairbanks, Jr. gave Ophuls a chance to direct *The Exile*. Then John Houseman helped with an assignment to oversee *Letter from an Unknown Woman*. Finally, after two more films, Ophuls returned to France, where he created a quartet of works, marked by brilliant camera movement, including the sad, but scintillating *Madame de . . .*

The story turns on a pair of earrings that a general (Charles Boyer) gives to his wife. She sells them to pay some debts. Later, she tells her husband she lost the earrings at the opera. There's a big to-do about theft. The loss is even written up in the newspaper. Hearing rumors of chicanery in the midst of music, the purchasing jeweler returns the earrings to the general, who says nothing to his wife. Instead, he gives the earrings to a departing mistress, who turns them over to a casino in Constantinople in order to indulge herself in more gambling.

Then the general's wife meets a baron (Vittorio De Sica) and is strongly attracted to him. As it happens, the baron has come into possession of the earrings. The general buys them back, then gives them to a niece who has just had a baby. The niece sells them to the jeweler to save her husband from bankruptcy. The general's wife trades some diamonds, emeralds and other pieces to the jeweler to get them back. Finally, the general challenges the baron to a dual. His wife insists on attending, but she has a bad heart and dies during the encounter, leaving the earrings to her saint.

It's an exhausting plot, just as the duplicity and the absence of true caring can be exhausting in marriage. Ophuls was a master of psychological complexity. Especially he explored the damage done by narcissism, by those incapable of love. Some say his films are too frothy to be serious. But style does not rule out penetrating analysis. Ophuls excelled at both.

The Golden Age of Hollywood brought forth three great directors: Howard Hawks, Alfred Hitchcock, and John Ford. They grew up in the studio system. (Hitchcock transferred there from brilliant beginnings in Britain). Pressed to produce movies that would entertain audiences and make money, they called themselves craftsmen, never artists, but, as Vincent Prothro observed, "The art rose out of the craft. They were so good the work became art."[42]

Called by his biographer, Joseph McBride, "the most versatile of all great American directors," Howard Hawks was born to a wealthy family that owned paper mills. His grandfather started the business. His father and his uncle continued it. When Hawks was two, his parents moved from Indiana to Wisconsin, then on to California eight years later in search of a climate that would benefit his mother's health. They lived in Pasadena, where Hawks' father became vice president of a hotel company. They also had an orange grove in Glendora. Hawks went away to Exeter and became a tennis champion, then on to Cornell to study mechanical engineering. (His brothers went to Yale, his son to Princeton.)

Not yet twenty, Hawks raced cars, driving a Mercedes given him by his grandfather. He even built a racer that won the Indianapolis 500. One summer he worked at Famous Players-Lasky Studio (then the production arm of Paramount) in the prop department. He got to know Douglas Fairbanks and Mary Pickford at the height of their courtship, and Mary made him her property man. Once, when her director was drunk and couldn't work, Hawks filled in and made some scenes for Mary. She liked them.

Hawks was a flight trainer in Texas during World War I before serving in France. He became famous in his squadron when Mary Pickford showed up for a bond drive and he, a private, got to show her around.

After the war, Hawks worked in an aircraft factory, then moved on to Hollywood where he found a job with Cecil B. DeMille in props. By chance, he got to know Irving Thalberg, production head at Metro-Goldwyn, who was a neighbor. Often they talked movies. When a top official of Paramount wanted to make forty films, Thalberg recommended that Hawks buy the stories and hire actors and directors, Joseph McBride relates. "At that time," Hawks explained, "all stories for pictures were written just for pictures, and the writers weren't too hot. But I went out and bought two Zane Greys, two Joseph Conrads, two Rex Beaches, two Jack Londons—you name it, I bought 'em . . . . That was the most successful year Paramount ever had."

Those were silent films, so Hawks wrote the titles for them, until he got sick of it and found some newspapermen to write them instead. When sound came, he, like John Ford, quickly grasped that dialogue should not be overdone. Even so, he continued to believe that good writing made a movie last. He worked with Hemingway, Faulkner, Ben Hecht, and Charles MacArthur. And it paid off. Hawks's films have endured.

Hawks has been called "the only American director who knows how to draw a moral." His morality, though acted out in an atmosphere of overarching rules, was embedded in how people treated each other. As Joseph McBride pointed out, "Hawks' films almost always deal with a tightly knit group of professionals trying to perform a difficult task together while upholding their own rigorously defined code of conduct . . . . [That code required] professional skill, group loyalty, and self-respect . . . . Not even the strongest characters in Hawks's films can function effectively outside the group . . . ."

But in these men—played through the years by John Wayne, Humphrey Bogart, Cary Grant, and Gary Cooper—Hawks also explored the male and female principles in a single psyche. His heroes, John Belton proposes, individuate by incorporating the feminine side of themselves.

As for female characters, Hawks gravitated toward strong, sophisticated, independent women played by Lauren Bacall, Carole Lombard, Rosalind Russell, Angie Dickinson, and Katharine Hepburn. They deal with men as equals, and they don't hide their sexuality behind a protective coating of coquetry. They expect a lot from life, and they're prepared to deliver in return. In his conception of women, Hawks foretold the last decades of the century.

One of his most spirited women was Katharine Hepburn in *Bringing Up Baby*, which Pauline Kael has called "the American movies' closest equivalent to Restoration comedy."[43] Hepburn plays an heiress with a dog named George and a leopard named Baby. She meets a paleontologist (Cary Grant) who's just discovered the missing bone for his brontosaurus. George captures the bone, and Hepburn captures Grant, though not without causing him plenty of worry that she's made of trouble for him and his dinosaur. It's a lively farce, and it proves that Hawks really could do anything.

Then there was the young Lauren Bacall, a new discovery when Hawks featured her opposite Humphrey Bogart in *To Have and Have Not*. Based on the book by Hemingway, with a screenplay by Faulkner plus one other, this is a story set in Martinique in 1940 after the fall of France. Bogart plays Harry Morgan, an American who runs a fishing boat. Pressed by the Free French to rescue one of their compatriots and bring him to the island, Bogart takes on the assignment, mainly because he wants to collect some cash to help Bacall get a plane home.

Bacall—"Slim" to him—he met when she stopped by his hotel room to ask, "Anybody got a match?" It seems she landed in Martinique having traveled there from Brazil, then Trinidad, and stayed because she had run out of money. Cool enough to take a slap from the Gestapo without blinking (Bogie is impressed), she refuses the air ticket to stay in Fort de France because she doesn't want to leave him. A night club hires her to sing with Hoagy Carmichael, and Bogart is smitten further when he hears her deep, sultry voice.

By movie's end Bogart has agreed to get another De Gaulle patriot off Devil's Island and back to Martinique where he will be central to the resistance. "Slim," as daring as anybody, joins him on the mission.

Hawks's own favorite among his pictures was *Scarface*. Made in 1932 for Howard Hughes and written by Ben Hecht, it was the story of the criminal booze business. Hawks and Hecht envisioned it as the Borgia family transplanted to Chicago, with Al Capone as Borgia with a Lucretia-like sister. Starring Paul Muni and Boris Karloff, it's a stylish gangster film with guys in dressing gowns and a hit man whistling the sextet from *Lucia di Lammermoor* as a prelude to murder.

Hawks was no saint himself. David Thomson has called him a "chronic liar and compartmentalizer, a secretive rogue, a stealthy dandy, and a ruinous womanizer." But he made thoughtful movies, with a flair for the modern, and for that he deserves to be remembered.

Alfred Hitchcock, genius of the thriller, was born in London in 1899 to a Catholic family. His father ran a grocery store. After studying with the Jesuits at St. Ignatius College he got his start in British film studios as an artist and set designer, working up to writer, assistant director, and, finally, director. He came early to the fore, bringing to silent pictures a combination of German camera moves and Russian montage that generated excitement and awe. With the advent of sound, he created the first British talkie, *Blackmail*, followed by spy classics such as *The 39 Steps, The Lady Vanishes*, and *The Man Who Knew Too Much*. Then, in the bloom of a booming career, he moved to Hollywood at the invitation of David O. Selznick to film *Rebecca*, an aromatic Gothic melodrama.

Rebecca was based on the novel by Daphne du Maurier with a screenplay by Robert Sherwood plus one other. Joan Fontaine plays a young woman traveling in the south of France with an obnoxious, social-climbing American dowager. She meets an English nobleman named

Maxim de Winter (Laurence Olivier), who's stricken still, it appears, by the drowning death of his wife, the beautiful Rebecca, a year before. Olivier marries Fontaine and takes her back to Manderley, his imposing country house, where she's intimidated by the grim, resentful housekeeper, who adored the first Mrs. De Winter.

Every scene is full of foreboding, as Fontaine searches for the real Rebecca, then struggles to be rid of her. But Rebecca is a mystery, a stubborn, extravagant presence, revealed in the end to have been a woman of heedless affairs, hated by her husband, who prefers an empty arrangement to the dishonor of divorce. (One of those later loves is played by George Sanders, who tries to get de Winter charged with murder when he cannot collect a bribe for silence.)

De Winter, as it turns out, did not murder his wife in the film as he did in the novel. The censors insisted that Rebecca die instead from striking her head in a fall after her husband had struck her in anger. The cool de Winter is exonerated of all blame and united finally in warmest love with his new bride. Enraged and defeated, the housekeeper sets fire to Manderley, sending all that remains of Rebecca up in smoke.

Lifeboat followed in 1944. With a script by John Steinbeck, it's a story of survival in the face of evil both subtle and ambiguous, but evil. Tallulah Bankhead, a mink-coated journalist, confronts a Communist crewman on a lifeboat after their ship has been sunk by German fire. Fascinated, she is filming everything. Repelled, he hurls her camera into the ocean. Others clamber aboard: a wealthy industrialist, a nurse, a woman with a baby that is dead but she takes a while to realize it, more crewmen, and, finally, a Nazi captain whose U-boat went down.

Intense debate ensues: Should the Nazi be tossed into the sea? No, argues Bankhead. That's not right. She translates German for him and insists that he be put in charge of the boat, since he's the only one with any knowledge of how to get them to Bermuda. In time she prevails over the one who's assumed leadership of the hapless vessel, the Communist crewman, with whom she spars with the hostile energy of mutual attraction.

The German captain reveals that he does indeed speak English. He also lets it slip that he's not as nice a guy as some have supposed. He pushes a crew member who's lost part of his leg to gangrene (William Bendix), overboard, explaining that the crewman was crippled and starving, so, of course, the Nazi solution was to end his life. The German also admits that while everybody else has been desperately hungry and parched he, all along, has had water and food tablets, taken from his boat before it went down. His passengers turn ugly and mob-like. They beat the captain senseless and send him to a wet and salty grave.

Those who are left come upon a Nazi supply ship at last. But it is blown up by an American war vessel right behind. As the lifeboat group awaits rescue, another Nazi is pulled from the ocean. He has a gun. They take it from him. He asks, "Aren't you going to kill me?" They wonder in response, "What kind of person says that?"

Lifeboat has dramatic problems. Sometimes it is too pedantic and heavily symbolic. Nonetheless, it's an arresting use of film to make a philosophical point about the true nature of human beings.

Hitchcock turned from the war to Freudian analysis to make *Spellbound* in 1945. With a screenplay by Ben Hecht and a dream sequence by Salvadore Dali, he created a love story set in a psychiatric hospital in Vermont. There Ingrid Bergman plays a cool, science-absorbed doctor who's drawn immediately to the clinic's new director (Gregory Peck). When he turns out to be an amnesiac who believes he killed the real incoming chief executive, Bergman sets out to cure him and to solve the crime. There are those who disparage this film, including Pauline Kael and Andrew Sarris,[44] and perhaps the guilt-complex-based-on-childhood-trauma theme does seem a little overdrawn, but not by much. These concepts are still the stuff of our lives and conversation, and Bergman and Peck could not be more engaging.

Ingrid Bergman also starred in *Notorious*, and again Ben Hecht wrote the script. It begins in Miami in 1946 with the trial of a Nazi for treason. He goes to prison where he kills himself with a poison pill. His daughter (Bergman) goes to Brazil to track down Alex Sebastien (Claude Raines), a mysterious businessman up to no good who knew her father and used to be in love with her. He falls for her again when an American agent (Cary Grant) puts her in his path so she can investigate what's going on in his house.

The secret—uranium ore—is in the wine cellar. Grant and Bergman discover it when she, having married Raines, steals the key. Her husband realizes she is working for the U.S. government and puts poison in her coffee, just a little at a time, so she will sicken gradually and die. Grant, of course, arrives in time to effect a rescue. Raines is left to the mercy of his Nazi colleagues. Intricate and psychological, *Notorious* points the way to the great films to come. Hitchcock's most memorable pictures were made between 1950 and 1960. They began with *Strangers on a Train*. Ominous in black-and-white, the film crafts an amazing trajectory from a chance meeting in a railroad car to a harrowing resolution of madness and murder on a carousel out of control.

Bruno (Robert Walker), disturbed scion of an important family, proposes to Guy (Farley Granger), a tennis star who wants to marry a senator's daughter (Ruth Roman) if he can just get out of his tired marriage to a music store clerk, that he, Bruno, will kill Guy's wife if Guy in turn will take out Bruno's father. Then motivation will be missing, and neither crime will be solved. It doesn't occur to Guy that the stranger is serious until he gets word that his wife is indeed dead.

It's the sort of intricate plot that Hitchcock adored. He would film many others (*North by Northwest, Rear Window*), but none would be more effective than *Vertigo*, another story of insanity, or what looks like insanity. Jimmy Stewart plays a retired police detective. Implored by a friend who fears his wife (Kim Novak) is possessed by an unknown spirit, to follow her and figure out what's wrong, Stewart sets forth on a tour of San Francisco that takes him from the Legion of Honor Museum to the ocean front. He moves in the wake of ravishing Kim Novak, apparently obsessed by Carlotta Valdez, her great-grandmother who went mad and killed herself when her child was taken from her by a lover.

The picture evolves with tantalizing twists that reveal Novak to be someone other than the friend's wife, someone completely sane. It's part of a Hitchcock genre that relied on well-constructed stories. "For Hitchcock's direction is very much a function of screenwriting," said Andrew Sarris. "He collaborated throughout his career with his wife, Alma Reville, on the continuity of his films." As usual, *Vertigo* leaves the audience lost in ambivalence. The "moral uneasiness at the end of all Hitchcock films," Sarris noted, "is profoundly original."

The decade concluded with *Psycho* in 1960, as chilling a film as has ever been made. The scene of Janet Leigh being slashed to death in the shower is impossible to forget. And, of course, the killer is not only deranged, but unspeakably odd. It was the beginning of Hitchcock's weird period, when he seemed to forget his credo that suspense is superior to shock.[45] Even so, *Psycho* was a financial bonanza, reportedly earning its director, who had a percentage of the gross, over $20 million. It was remade in 1998.

Hitchcock also succeeded on television, with two different series that bore his name. And there was a Hitchcock magazine of mystery articles. He also became Sir Alfred, no small honor for a defector to America. But most of all, he reigned over the elegant thriller, a master of suspense and sophistication.

The most celebrated American director of them all has been John Ford, winner of six Oscars and four New York Film Critics Awards, a record unmatched in the history of Hollywood. He was Orson Welles' favorite American director, and Ingmar Bergman called him the best in the world. To Frank Capra he was king of the profession.

"Ford has been called the greatest stylist in American film," said his biographer, Ronald Davis, "but the essence of his style remained simplicity." The secret, Ford confided, is not in the camera. "The secret," he said, "is in people's faces, their eye expression, their movements." A director, he explained, is "more like an architect" than an author. A director puts "a pre-designed composition on film." To accomplish this, Ford would spend as much as six months planning a project, then shoot it in five weeks. And he rarely used more footage than he wanted to see in the final cut. So editors found that their work had already been done for them. It was all in his original design, revised only to admit spontaneity from his performers.

The Western was Ford's special achievement, though it was not for Westerns that he won his Academy Awards. Even so, he loved them. "Is there anything more beautiful than a long shot of a man riding a horse well, or a horse racing free across a plain?" he asked. The American West was a fit place for heros, and Ford took the Hegelian view that a hero was necessary "to bring a new world into existence." But unlike Hawks, Ford rarely explored the feminine side of his male characters. Most of the time, they were relentlessly manly, without emotion and seldom with strong ties to women. And they were public people, acting always in full view of the world, with no inner lives of their own, much less inner conflicts.

Yet Ford himself was riven with conflict, and it was conflict rooted in the Irish Catholic repression with which he grew up. It was the experience of living in an immigrant family in Maine that gave John Ford, born Sean Aloysius O'Freeney, his sense of always being an outsider. (Even at the height of his acclaim in Hollywood, he shunned social life and never once turned up at the Oscar ceremonies where he was honored.) Ford's parents came from Galway. Once in Portland, his father opened his own restaurant and saloon and became a Democratic ward boss, meeting new immigrants at the dock, getting them jobs, bringing them into the party machinery, and holding political meetings at his place.

Young Jack, the thirteenth child in the family, was devoutly Catholic and deeply involved in the rituals of the church. Like most of the men he knew, he learned from the worship of Mary to put his mother, and later his wife, as well as the heroines in his pictures, on a pedestal, beyond the reach of the appetites. And like other Irishmen, he would find relief from matriarchy in masculine pursuits. But where for some the outlet was politics, the military, or the priesthood, for Jack it would be his drinking pals, and he would drink far too much, trying to overcome his ancestral sense of guilt and melancholy. His tender heart he would wrap in an irascible personality. Few would know the feeling behind the difficult facade.

Excluded in Protestant Maine or not, Ford succeeded on the high school football team. He wanted to go to Annapolis but failed the entrance exam. The University of Maine offered him an athletic scholarship which he accepted. But when he realized that studies in agriculture were required, he never showed up for registration. Instead he waited tables for awhile, then left for California to follow his older brother, Francis Freeney (by now Francis Ford), who had become an actor in New York, then Hollywood, after doing a stint in the Spanish-American War as well as in the circus.

By the time Jack got to Los Angeles, his brother had moved into directing silent two-reelers. Frank got Jack (who also changed his name to Ford) a job at Universal, where he dug ditches, did stunts, and finally got a chance to act. He even appeared in *Birth of a Nation* as one of the Klansmen. D.W. Griffith was his hero. "D.W. was the only one then who took the time for little details," said Ford.

The opportunity to direct came early to Jack Ford. It was only another year before he made his first two-reeler, *The Tornado*. He also wrote it and acted in it. Twenty Westerns followed, starring Harry Carey. But his silent masterpiece was *The Iron Horse*, about the building of the first intercontinental railroad in America. After this film, Ford was considered a director of real promise.

In 1920, Ford married Mary McBryde Smith, daughter of a member of the New York Stock Exchange and a nurse during World War I. A Protestant from the old Southern aristocracy, she belonged to the Daughters of the American Revolution and the Daughters of the Confederacy. It would not be a happy union. Both would drench their tension in alcohol. So, in time, would their two children. Ford was simply not geared up for married attachment. As Ronald Davis put it, he was "fearful of intimacy, mistrustful of love, ashamed of sex, [and] more comfortable with a celibate life."

All this could be seen in his movies, where he rarely achieved a satisfying portrayal of love between the sexes. "Like many fine artists—Herman Melville for instance—his true feeling was for the man-man or man-men relationship." So said screenwriter Dudley Nichols.

Ford's great admiration for Griffith gave way to reverence for Murnau after a trip to Germany where he met the master of expressionism and shadow. In time, Ford learned to synthesize the moving camera of Murnau with Eisenstein's montage.[46] Before long, he discovered someone else who would be increasingly important to him: Marion Michael Morrison, called Duke, a football player at the University of Southern California, turned up as a property boy on one of Ford's films. He stayed, and became John Wayne, one of Ford's biggest stars and in many ways a son to him. Ronald Davis suggests that John Wayne on screen was the man John Ford yearned to be.[47]

Stagecoach, a film Ford based on a story in *Colliers* magazine, rescued Wayne's floundering career in 1939 and moved the Western from the studio to Monument Valley on the Arizona-Utah border. There, with magnificent desert landscapes even in black and white, Ford created on film the mythic American West. In *Stagecoach* he told his favorite story, according to Ronald Davis, of "outcasts in times of danger mustering the strength to slay the monster that threatens the community that rejects them." John Wayne, tough but compassionate as a fugitive named Ringo, soared to importance after this picture. But he wasn't the true star of *Stagecoach*. "I think you can say that the real star of my Westerns has always been the land," Ford said.[48]

Ford's first three sound pictures were flops financially, but in 1935 he created the film that established him as a director of artistry and strength: *The Informer*. Based on a novel about the republican movement in Ireland, it had, according to Sarris, "an allegorical parallel with the Passion Play." The Biblical references are clear in the opening titles: "Then Judas repented himself and cast down the thirty pieces of silver—and departed." Betrayal comes early as Frankie McPhillips of the IRA sneaks into Dublin to visit his mother and sister but is surprised at their house and killed by British police informed of his whereabouts by a good friend who covets the 20-pound reward.

The friend is found out and sentenced to die at a court of inquiry held at one a.m. in an ammunition dump. The camera pans from face to face as IRA men, drawn and disturbed, in their caps and trenchcoats, sit in judgment of one of their own. The dramatic tension recalls Carl Dreyer's *Joan of Arc*. The informer escapes and dashes finally into a Catholic church where McPhillips's mother is praying. He begs her to forgive him. This she does, saying that he didn't know what he was doing. The informer stretches his arms into a crucifix, collapses and dies.

From this work flowed not only an Oscar and a New York Film Critics Award but also the chance to make other movies drawn from literary works, including Sean O'Casey's *The Plough* and the *Stars* and Maxwell Anderson's *Mary of Scotland*.

This last film was momentous for Ford because he fell in love with the star—Katharine Hepburn. They had an affair, but Ford was too serious a Catholic to divorce his wife for the new love. Hepburn understood, and backed off. They remained friends, Ronald Davis relates, and years later she said to his grandson, "He's terribly tough and arrogant, but he's truly sensitive. You can see the sensitivity in his hands . . . . Nobody has a career that lasts with the distinction of his who hasn't traveled his own trail. Most people have about a fifteen-year product that is of any interest; they never refill the reservoir . . . . He has the artistic point of view of an old Renaissance craftsman. He just could do it, without a lot of conversation. He had great faith in his work, and he had marvelous general knowledge of what was thrilling, what was beautiful, what was original, and what moved."

Hepburn felt that Ford was a lot like Spencer Tracy. Both were Irish. Both had great dramatic gifts. But they viewed life through a prism of pain. In sadness, Ford stayed with Mary, but spent as little time with her as possible. He bought a yacht, which he named the Araner after the islands off the coast of Ireland, and there he would retreat with his men friends as soon as he finished a picture. There he would drink, trying to ward off the terror of idleness, the fear of life without work. Once back on the set, the drinking usually would stop. Nor would he permit alcohol for anybody else involved in a picture he was shooting.

Ford could be tyrannical. Often he picked out one person to abuse with hostile teasing. Some became so disturbed they refused to work with him again. He also had a disconcerting appearance. Geraldine Page described him like this: "Mr. Ford affects army fatigues as a way of dress with a hat cocked way over on one side, and he has a habit of having a very used handkerchief in his pocket, which he takes out and twists, and puts in the corner of his mouth and sucks on while he's talking. It gets wet with saliva about four inches down . . . . The visual image of him is so revolting that you have to remember the wonderful things he's done."[49]

And wonderful things he certainly did accomplish. Foremost among them was *The Grapes of Wrath*, adapted from Steinbeck's novel. To create a set, Ford and the designer studied the paintings of Thomas Hart Benton. With Henry Fonda in the lead, and "Red River Valley" for theme music, *The Grapes of Wrath* has been called Ford's "greatest critical triumph" and the film that transformed him, Sarris asserts, "from a story-teller of the screen to America's cinematic poet laureate." As Gene Kelly said, "The end of the frontier was in that picture." So was searing black and white cinematography with light and shadow drenching every shot in dramatic tension

Like *The Grapes of Wrath, How Green Was My Valley* (one of Ford's most lyrical films) deals with social injustice—in this case a manage-ment-labor dispute—and the disruption it causes in family life. Only by chance did Ford make this movie. It had been assigned to William Wyler, who had planned to shoot it in Wales in technicolor. But Wyler was sum-moned to another project and Ford took up where he left off, except that Wales was no longer possible in 1941 with German bombs threatening Britain. So the picture was shot in Hollywood on the set of a Welsh coal-mining village that resembles Murnau's *Sunrise* in its shadowed, romantic intensity.[50]

How Green Was My Valley involved a family that reminded Ford of his own when he was growing up. Roddy McDowall plays Huw, a young boy in a large coal-mining family, presided over by Ivor, a patriarch who reads a chapter of the Bible aloud almost daily. ("Father, give us a chapter," his sons say.) Wages are cut. A strike ensues. Walter Pidgeon, playing a newly arrived minister, observes darkly, "Something has gone out of this valley that may never be replaced." He's right. Once the strike ends, some are found to be redundant. Huw's two older brothers are laid off. Too highly paid to compete with other, more desperate men, they leave for America, but their sister, Angharad (Maureen O'Hara), stoically marries the son of the mine owner. (She's really drawn instead to the new minister.)

The pastor becomes equally important to Huw when he is injured in a fall. He helps the boy walk again and tells him about prayer: "Prayer," says the minister, "is another name for good, clear, direct thinking."

More trouble comes when a resentful servant of Angharad spreads the word that she intends to divorce her husband because she's in love with the pastor. (It's a moment that calls to mind the gossips in *The Last Laugh*.) In a fit of sanctimonious agitation, the deacons of the church want to discipline Angharad, but the minister chastens them. Pointing out that none of their imaginings are true, he resigns. Angharad would like to leave with him, but he says no, he has nothing to offer her. So O'Hara, unfilled in love, becomes John Ford's definitive heroine, Ronald Davis says, a feminine counterpart to John Wayne.

The final blow falls when the mine collapses, killing Ivor. Desolation is all about, but the spirit of the family regenerates itself. The brothers, gone to America, reappear in the closing moments. So does another brother, killed in an earlier mining accident. And Ivor. Then comes Angharad, fresh again and hopeful. For Ford, said Andrew Sarris, "there is an unbroken chain of feelings between the living and the dead. Hence the epilogue of *How Green Was My Valley* reunites a family fragmented by death and departures. Ford's ghosts are not the memory images imparted to Victor Sjostrom's old professor in Ingmar Bergman's *Wild Strawberries* (1957), but mystical incarnations of an unchanging world beyond the valley of death."

Ford was named best director by the Academy and the New York Film Critics in 1940 for *The Grapes of Wrath* and in 1941 for *How Green Was My Valley*, which won best picture over Orson Welles's *Citizen Kane*. That was a sound decision. *Citizen Kane* has baroque audacity. But *How Green Was My Valley* has soul.

World War II brought Ford some years of deep satisfaction. Stationed in Washington, he ran a naval field photographic unit which worked under the aegis of the Office of Strategic Services (forerunner of the CIA) to do films and photographs for the record and for propaganda. One of his first projects was a filmed report on the military installation at the Panama Canal, done to show Roosevelt what was going on there. Then he went to Hawaii, to document the aftermath of Pearl Harbor.

From there the wake of battle gave way to the war itself. When the U.S. intercepted Japan's plans to attack Midway, to Midway Ford was sent. He filmed the rampage of June 4-6, 1942, from a tower, taking a wound in the arm himself and catching the moment the flag was raised, at eight a.m., as usual, despite bombs falling everywhere. Undeterred, Ford flew the footage to Los Angeles to get a print, then on to Washington for secret screening, only to return to L.A. to edit, away from navy censors, with an armed guard outside the door. Dudley Nichols wrote a script. Henry Fonda plus two others did the voice-over. The finished film was rushed to President Roosevelt who approved it. In September, *The Battle of Midway* was distributed to theaters all across the country. It demonstrated to Americans that their troops had won a pivotal victory and taken control of the central Pacific. It also reassured them that they might after all win the war against Japan.

The *Battle of Midway* won an Oscar in 1942 for best documentary short subject. It was actually propaganda, in the way that Eisenstein and Riefenstahl did propaganda, though she never admitted it. The difference, of course, is the cause. Eisenstein, like millions of Russians, had reason to believe in the revolution at first, though it turned cruelly against him. Riefenstahl believed in Hitler when there was mounting evidence that he would do unspeakable, if unpredictable harm. Ford was on the right side of a terrible war. His films were critical to the morale of the home front.

Another Ford effort, edited from the footage he shot at Pearl Harbor, became a film called *December 7th*. It won the Academy Award for best documentary of 1943. Since then it's been criticized for implying that all Japanese-Americans were spies.

John Ford's unit covered the North African invasion. He photographed air raids over Burma and China, and supervised coverage of the D-Day landing. He also crossed the Rhine with the Allies at Remagen. After the war he became a rear admiral with the naval reserve, and he used a big fee from Louis B. Mayer for directing another war film called *They Were Expendable* to build a retreat and retirement community for the 180 men who had served with him. A sign at the entrance said, "NO WOMEN EXCEPT ON VISITOR'S DAY."

No sooner was the war over than the House Un-American Activities Committee (the Un-American Committee, Lillian Hellman called it) revved up, in 1947, and began looking for Communists in Hollywood. John Wayne became a spokesman for the militant right-wing, but Ford tried not to take sides though he was growing increasingly conservative. He finally spoke up when Cecil B. DeMille got the board of the Directors Guild to approve a loyalty oath while Joseph Mankiewicz, the president, was in Europe. Mankiewicz returned and opposed the move, so DeMille tried to get him thrown out as president, calling him a leftist. Ford was offended. He may have been conservative, but he didn't think a loyalty oath was fair or decent. At a meeting of the Guild, Ford lambasted DeMille and moved that he and the board resign. They did. And Mankiewicz won a big vote of confidence.

Unfortunately, only five days elapsed before Mankiewicz turned around and asked guild members to sign the oath voluntarily. Explaining that he had signed it himself, he argued it would help dispel the "misconception" that clouded the industry. But the misconception continued, and festered. More hearings were held in Washington. Distinguished artists named names of friends who had once been associated with Communist organizations. It was an ugly moment in American life, and it lasted until the end of the decade.[51]

During those years, Ford returned to the Western, and he turned often to painters and sculptors to discover the atmosphere he wanted. For *She Wore a Yellow Ribbon*, he studied the work of Frederic Remington and recreated some of those compositions on the screen. For *The Searchers*, his model was Charles M. Russell. Funded by Jock Whitney, this was another Monument Valley movie starring John Wayne as Ethan Edwards, a Confederate soldier who returns from the Civil War having let the woman he loves marry his brother. The family is massacred by Comanche and the two daughters abducted. One is killed. Edwards spends the next seven years looking for the other, Debbie, played by Natalie Wood. He is driven mainly by hatred for the Indians and by lust for revenge.

When he finds her, Debbie has grown up to be an Indian squaw. He's tempted to kill her since she is now no longer white, but relents when he realizes how much she looks like her mother. He also accepts his nephew, who is adopted and part Indian.

The Searchers is one of Ford's most aesthetically beautiful films. The door of a teepee frames the sandy countryside, revealed again later through a hole in the craggy cliffs. The yellow-brown of the land is repeated in the floor of the house, and again in the bricks of the wall. Using the shades of the earth, Ford showed himself to be a landscape painter of the West. And no shot is sadder than the last one when Wayne can be watched through the open door of the house, walking away. The story of *The Searchers*, said Ford "is the tragedy of the loner."

A few years before, Ford took a break from Westerns to make *The Quiet Man*, with John Wayne as Sean Thornton, an American looking for his roots in Ireland. He is recognized by a priest as a prizefighter who quit boxing after he killed a man in the ring. The priest promises to keep Sean's secret, but encourages him not to shrink from a fight with Will, the bullying brother of Mary Kate (Maureen O'Hara) who has become the American's wife. High-spirited and strong-minded, Mary Kate is determined to wrest from her brother the 350 pounds he promised as her dowry, and she wants her husband to get it for her. He resists, blaming her for putting too much emphasis on money.

But it is not money that drives Mary Kate as much as pride. Once Sean takes on her brother, decisively, she is delighted to help toss the coins aside and return home to fix dinner.

In this film Ford proves once again that he has the most exquisite color sense of anyone who ever made movies. Where *The Searchers* glories in earthy terra cottas, *The Quiet Man* is graced by blue. A radiant blue adorns Mary Kate's blouse, the table cloth, and the dishes on the sideboard, as well as men's shirts and tweed jackets, creating the possibility of beauty and calm. *The Quiet Man* earned Ford another Oscar.

Ford made his last film at seventy-two and died seven years later. Since then he has been likened to Walt Whitman, Mark Twain, William Faulkner, Charles Ives and William Butler Yeats. John Ford truly was a poet of the screen. He loved books. He was a student of the Civil War. And he made sure his work was informed by the visual arts. He brought to filmmaking a literary sensibility which gave him staying power as well as astonishing success.

Since World War II, no one has contributed more to serious film than Ingmar Bergman. Some say his work is too grim and closed in upon itself, but it has such depth that even David Thomson, a critic of his early pictures, admits that Bergman "showed the way to a cinema of the inner life."

Bergman was born in Sweden to a Lutheran pastor and his wife. As a child he loved the performing arts and spent his time playing in a puppet theatre and making movies of his own. Like Carl Dreyer, also of the Scandinavian, Lutheran north, he was chafed by his parents's stern morality. Finally Bergman rebelled, at nineteen, and ran away from home to become a stage director. He didn't take long to succeed. By 1944 he was running the Helsingborg City Theater and in subsequent years he headed playhouses all over the country including the Royal Dramatic Theater in Stockholm. It was there he found the magnificent company of actors and actresses who became his professional family, appearing in many of his films.

Even in his most intense years of filmmaking, Bergman still made time for the stage. When he was eighty he still pursued live drama, doing a play about his old mentor Victor Sjostrom. Theater, explained Bergman, "is like a loyal wife, film is the great adventure, the costly and demanding mistress."[52]

As for wives, Bergman married six times and had a child by Liv Ullmann, a luminous presence in his pictures. (The relationship didn't last, but the collaboration later was resumed: she directed the film made from his script, *Private Confessions*, in 1998.)[53] If Lutheran orthodoxy meant little to him, the faith of his father still resonated in his mind. Many of Bergman's films explore religion: *Virgin Spring* and *The Seventh Seal* are medieval in their quest for the reverent life. In *Wild Strawberries*, two young men debate the existence of God. *Fanny and Alexander* features a cruel bishop (Bergman's father?), but the light-hearted family at the center of the story makes sure the children say their prayers at night.

The bishop was not Bergman's only brutal father-figure. His early work is replete with them, and often in those years he wrote the screen-play himself. It was not until his tenth film, *Summer Interlude* in 1951, that Bergman found his professional footing. Four years later, *Smiles of a Summer Night*, the elegant weekend-in-the-country comedy that became the basis for Stephen Sondheim's *A Little Night Music*, brought him to the attention of an international audience. Both deal with the ephemeral nature of love.

At that point Bergman's work turned inward, in a search for the psychological core of human life wherein resides the soul. *Wild Strawberries*, said to evoke the spirit of Ibsen, showcases Victor Sjostrom as Dr. Isak Borg, an aging professor about to receive an honorary degree. But it is no time for rejoicing. Dr. Borg is visited by a dream of death, which reminds him that a doctor's first duty is to ask for forgiveness. Like Parsifal confronted by his sins, Dr. Borg recollects lost years, and a wife who tells him he's cold beyond bearing and he doesn't really care what she does. His punishment? Loneliness.

Dr. Borg stands in a generational line of icy people stretching from his mother to his son, Evald, who resents his father's refusal to help him by canceling a debt. Evald's wife, Marianne, drives with her father-in-law to the university where the honor is to be conferred. She announces that she is pregnant and her husband doesn't want the baby but she's determined to have it anyway. Moved by her insistence on life and his son's remote resignation to the deadening of his heart, Dr. Borg forgives the debt and finds himself transformed. He had long been a man of some decency: A filling station owner attests to the professor's kindness. But it had been superficial, and reserved for people distant from him. What was needed was generosity toward those close at hand. This he finally achieves.

Bergman turned to medieval Sweden of the fourteenth century in *The Seventh Seal*, a powerful search for God in which a knight, just returned from a lost decade in the Crusades, plays chess with death to win a reprieve so he might find the final answers before his end. It puts one in mind of *The Phantom Carriage*, by another Swede, Victor Sjostrom.

The fourteenth century surfaced again in *Virgin Spring*, where Bergman explores a Christianity so intense it cannot avoid colliding with the ugly vulgarity of the world, a vulgarity that turns bestial and violent. It begins at the family table, arrayed like the Last Supper. Because it's Good Friday, the mother, in medieval headdress, mortifies her flesh, pouring hot wax onto the inside of her wrist. Her daughter, Karin, whom she adores, she sends off to church on horseback to deliver candles to the Virgin Mary. But on the way the girl meets a horrifying fate: she is raped and murdered. Her father, one of the most splendid, commanding Vikings ever to appear on screen, manages to kill the rapists who happen into his house by chance. But he too must mortify the flesh. He wrestles a birch tree to the ground, then flails himself with its branches, pouring hot water on the wounds.

He and his wife set forth to find their daughter, and they do, dead as they had feared. The father rails at God, then promises to build a church with his own hands on the spot where she died. A spring flows from the earth near the girl who lies ravaged. Her mother uses it to cleanse the lifeless face. A young woman servant, who in her jealousy had prayed for Karin's destruction, also washes herself in the spring water. So, like Sjostrom's *Phantom Carriage*, *Virgin Spring* brings redemption as well as sin.

Bergman's work grew so dark that he became known as a gloomy prophet, foretelling only desolation. *Persona*, a study of deep psychological intensity in which a nurse (Bibi Andersson) appropriates the personality of her patient, an acclaimed actress who has retreated into silence, (Liv Ullmann) is a masterpiece of the form. So is *Cries and Whispers*, another Ullmann film, set in a feminine community of three sisters and suffused with an astonishing grasp of the female psyche. But this period grew tired in *Scenes from a Marriage*, which even Ullmann could not save from tedium. But all that he stripped away in 1982 to make the iridescent *Fanny and Alexander*. Both written and directed by Bergman, every frame is radiant, bathed in bright, white light. Echoing the magical realism of Gabriel García Márquez, the script has great elegance of language and idea. "Swarms of ghosts, spirits," are invoked. So is philosophy: "Everything is alive. Everything is God or God's thought, not only goodness but also cruelty." From there the audience is transported to a rapturous and vivid Christmas one can but dream about. The year is 1907. The Ekdahl family, theatrical and charismatic, is about to celebrate the season.

Deeply intelligent, with references to Hamlet and Strindberg, the story is told. The leader of the family acting troupe dies, leaving two offspring, Fanny and Alexander, and their beautiful mother, also an actress. She marries the bishop, whose love for her and the children is "strong and harsh." Indeed it is harsh, if it can be called love at all. But the bishop dies in a fire and the Ekdahl family is reunited, mostly under one roof. Joy reigns, restored for good. That's because the Ekdahls have a capacity for happiness, no matter what.

Woody Allen has called Ingmar Bergman "the greatest film artist . . . since the invention of the motion picture camera." That is close to true, though of course there have been others. But none fill the heart in quite the way he does. Bergman brought to the screen the deepest yearnings of humankind and made them rich with the possibility of fulfillment.

Akira Kurosawa brought Japanese cinema to the West with *Rashomon*, which won the Venice Film Festival in 1951 as well as an Oscar for best foreign-language movie. This picture, as carefully composed as a haiku, revolves around high tension and a question of truth. A medieval nobleman, leading his beautiful wife through the woods on a horse, is killed, by a bandit. Or is he? There are four versions of what happened in the forest that day, including one from the demure wife, who deals some surprises of her own. As Kurosawa said of his characters, they have a "sinful need for flattering falsehood [and] cannot survive without lies to make them feel they are better people than they really are."[54]

Kurosawa was born in Tokyo in 1910, the son of an athletic director at a military institute who once had been an officer himself. He traced his lineage back to an eleventh century samurai. Kurosawa's mother was from a family that had prospered in business. The youngest of eight children, Kurosawa suffered from epilepsy as a child. That did not prevent him, however, from responding to painting at an early age, encouraged by a teacher. Movies he got to know through a brother who fell out of favor with their father, left home, and worked as a silent-film operator until the advent of talkies robbed him of his job. Distraught, the brother committed suicide.

Though Kurosawa was deeply touched by Abel Gance's *La Roue*, he didn't turn to film until after some time at a school of Western art. But he couldn't make a living at painting so he did projects for magazines and cookbooks instead. Finally, answering an ad for apprentice assistant directors at production studio, he met the man who would show him his destiny—Kajiro Yamamoto, the foremost film director then working in Japan.

After drenching himself in the aesthetic of traditional Japan in a hungry quest for beauty during the trauma of World War II, Kurosawa's cravings turned to realism. Influenced by the films of Roberto Rossellini and Vittorio De Sica, he made pictures about right-wing atrocities in Japan and an alcoholic doctor working in the slums of Tokyo.[55]

He married an actress and also fell in love with Western images, especially the films of John Ford. Hollywood reciprocated the esteem. Kurosawa's masterpiece, *Seven Samurai*, was drawn upon for *The Magnificent Seven*, and Rashomon inspired *The Outrage*. Yojimbo became *A Fistful of Dollars* and then *The Last Man Standing*. Kurosawa won an honorary Oscar, presented by Steven Spielberg and George Lucas, who readily admitted that parts of *Star Wars* had been adapted from *The Hidden Fortress*.

Kurosawa didn't make movies like most directors. He rehearsed his actors for days, even weeks, then shot the scenes in sequence, striving to capture a complete performance. At the end of each day on the set, he would edit the rushes together, which gave him a rough assembly already in hand by the time filming was completed.

Kurosawa based his work on a clear-eyed look at life. "To be an artist," he said, "means never to avert one's eyes." He recalled his brother saying to him, "If you shut your eyes to a frightening sight, you end up being frightened. If you look at everything straight on, there is nothing to be afraid of."[56]

Kurosawa did fear failure. When critics began to dismiss him as old-fashioned and finished, he believed them and tried to end his own life in 1971. But then came a blazing comeback with remarkable epics such as *Ran*, a feast of spectacle and dramatic power based on Shakespeare's *King Lear*. Though he made only six films in the last twenty-eight years of his life, Kurosawa was restored to the realm of memorable twentieth century directors.

Another master of the golden age of Japanese film that flourished in the

1950s was Kenji Mizoguchi. He was twelve years older than Kurosawa and less adept at presenting himself to the West. Yet he knew American and European work, and especially he admired Murnau's *Sunrise*.

Like Kurosawa, Mizoguchi was born in Tokyo, and like Kurosawa he studied painting. He did layout for newspapers before finding his way to the studio of the New School, where he worked as an assistant, then directed movies himself. Here melodrama was the preferred genre, but outside this circle, Mizoguchi made everything from detective and ghost stories to comedies.

Mizoguchi is best known in the U.S. for *Ugetsu*, a haunting film about two potters and their wives in the midst of war. One longs to be a samurai, the other to expand the reach of his ceramics business. They leave to accomplish their ambitions, while their wives stay behind, wracked with worry and foreboding. Their fears are justified. One woman is raped and the other killed.

The samurai comes upon his wife, eventually, in a brothel. The potter falls in with a mysterious woman who wants to marry him. She is actually a ghost who cannot hold his interest indefinitely. He returns home to find his wife gone, then in the room with him, another ghostly presence, and finally gone again, forever.

Ugetsu is a work of great beauty and restraint. It alone puts Mizoguchi in the upper ranks of world cinema.

Japan produced another great director in Yasujiro Ozu, who found a way to make ordinary families in his country resonate all over the world. Turning early to cinema, he worked first as an assistant cameraman at Shochiku Films, began creating his own movies at twenty-four, and then spent his entire career at that same studio. Bored with conventional Japanese fare, he studied Chaplin and Lubutsch and found in their work a way to bring comic vitality to his own pictures.

Ozu is best known for his studies of middle-class life in modern Japan, as the generations struggle to shed and preserve the old ways. It was one of these movies, *Tokyo Story*, that first brought Ozu recognition in the West. Elegantly composed, with each shot a work of art, this is the story of an older couple who leave their small town to visit their grown children in Tokyo.

Their son, a pediatrician (but only in the suburbs, his father discovers sadly) is preoccupied with his patients and must cancel a sight-seeing tour. Their daughter, a beautician, is busy with her work and her husband.

Only Noriko, the wife of a son lost in World War II eight years before, makes an effort for them. Her mother-in-law urges her to cut loose from the past and remarry.

After a noisy, unsatisfactory stay at a spa, where the children send their parents to avoid having to entertain them in Tokyo, the couple returns home where she becomes ill and dies. The family gathers for a tearful farewell, only to have the married daughter issue quick requests afterwards for a sash and kimono of her mother's that she wants. Everybody returns to Tokyo except Noriko, who stays a few days more and reveals her own shadow: There are days, she says, when she doesn't even think of her dead husband, and her serene demeanor belies the fear she feels of the loneliness that may lie ahead. Her father-in-law, alone now himself except for a younger daughter who lives with him, affirms Noriko as a kind and honest woman. He gives her his wife's watch as a remembrance.

Ozu died at sixty, having created a body of work that was universal in its grasp of human emotion.

The 1960s brought the New Wave, and with it came new techniques such as "ultrarapid cutting, hand-held cameras, zoom lenses, dramatic use of slow motion, helicopter shooting, brief flashes lasting only a fraction of a second, and freeze-frame endings."[57] No one gave more grace to this frenetic period than François Truffaut, who learned motion pictures working as a critic in Paris and then as a researcher for Roberto Rossellini. His break came when he met Madeleine Morgenstern, the daughter of an important French movie distributor. Their encounter in Venice in 1956, when he was covering the film festival, led to his first production, backed by her father, and also to their marriage.

Ever youthful, ever enraptured by film, Truffaut established his reputation with *The 400 Blows*, an autobiographical work about his troubled boyhood, when he was an illegitimate child, unwanted by his mother and stepfather, who spent time in reform school for petty theft. (It won him the Cannes prize for best director when he was only twenty-seven.) Later, after years of work kept hectic to avoid depression, Truffaut paid tribute to the art of cinema in *Day for Night*, which he dedicated to Lillian and Dorothy Gish.

Not only did Truffaut direct *Day for Night*, he also played in it a character meant to be him, and wrote the screenplay with two others. It's an off-camera look at the myriad of details involved in making a movie, details sometimes involving difficult personalities who must be brought around, no matter how. At one point in the film, Julie (Jacqueline Bisset, who became Truffaut's lover, the usual thing for his leading ladies), star of the picture within a picture, declares she cannot continue without country butter in an old-fashioned tub. Butter like that cannot be found, so Truffaut sends for blocks of commercial product and presses them into a mold, just as she wanted. Never does he tell her she's crazy and to get a grip. There's no time for therapy. He simply delivers the butter. And Julie appears to shoot the scene.

Julie is a Hollywood star who has married her doctor who brought her back from a breakdown. He left his family for her. He leaves Julie on location where she has a one-night stand with her co-star Alphonse (Jean-Pierre Léaud) to keep him from leaving the show out of despondency because his girlfriend has deserted him for the stunt man. But all that is incidental to keeping the project on schedule. "Making a film is like a stage coach ride in the Old West," says Truffaut. "First you hope for a good trip. Then you simply want to reach your destination." Or, reiterated later, "Before starting, I hope to make a fine movie. The problems begin . . . and I aim lower! I hope to make the movie . . . period!"

There are other observations from other characters: "I'd drop a guy for a film. I'd never drop a film for a guy." Alphonse sees it differently: "Life is more important than film," he insists. But Truffaut speaks for himself (and John Ford) when he admits, "People like you and me are only happy in our work."

Day for Night offers an irresistible montage of filmmaking and how it's done, how the illusion is created. A car-crash scene in which Pamela (Julie's character) is killed at night is shot in broad daylight—"day for night" or "nuit Américaine" in film talk. Death itself intrudes on the picture when Alexander (Jean-Pierre Aumont) dies in a real auto accident. The insurance company won't put up the money to have his scenes shot again with another actor, so a stand-in must be used for the climactic moment, on a street covered with manufactured snow, when Alexander is gunned down by his son, enraged because his father has fallen in love with the boy's bride, Pamela.

Finally the film is finished. The company parts. "Unemployment bureau here we come," shouts a member of the crew. A props man is interviewed for television. Everything went smoothly, he assures. He hopes everyone enjoys seeing the film as much as they enjoyed making it.

Apparently Truffaut did not enjoy it as much as he needed to. His

New Wave had long since spent itself upon the beach. He withdrew from movie making for a couple of years, but returned, to direct more pictures, none as successful as before, and also to appear in Steven Spielberg's *Close Encounters of the Third Kind*. Truffaut died young, at fifty-two, of a brain tumor, having had a daughter with the actress Fanny Ardant during the last year of his life. (Ardant starred in his final film, *Confidentially Yours*, as well as in *The Woman Next Door*. Truffaut and Madeleine Morgenstern, with whom he had two daughters, had long since divorced. She remained a friend, however, and became an executor of his estate.)

Truffaut worshiped Jean Renoir, who once hired him for a theatrical production, and also Alfred Hitchcock, with whom he did a book-long interview. But Truffaut was more whimsical than Renoir, more spontaneous than Hitchcock. Truffaut created a new kind of film and made it lyrical.[58]

The New Wave produced another giant: Jean-Luc Godard. Born in 1930 to an upper middle-class French family, he studied in Switzerland and became a Swiss citizen during World War II only to return to Paris to attend the Sorbonne and then write for magazines on cinema and the arts. He fell in love with Hollywood movies and in time began to pursue his own work, creating screenplays and, finally, his own features.

Like Orson Welles, Godard's most memorable full-length film was his very first: *Breathless*, which appeared in 1959. There on the streets of Paris, Jean-Paul Belmondo, as Michel, pursues Patricia (played by Jean Seberg), an American who hawks the *Herald Tribune* and hopes for a job as a reporter. Having coffee with a journalist who promises to help her, she languidly observes, "I don't know if I'm not free because I'm unhappy or unhappy because I'm not free."

Her bondage is to some internal disconnection from the world. Even so, she responds with delight when she returns home to find Belmondo waiting for her in her bed. A lanky, sexy guy, with the habit of rubbing his thumb across his full-bodied lips, back and forth, he completes the seduction with a minimum of effort without telling her that he has just shot a policeman on the highway where he was racing heedlessly along in a stolen car.

She gets pregnant. He gets deeper into trouble as his photograph appears in the paper with a caption naming him as the chief suspect in the killing of the cop. She says she cares for him nonetheless. Then, as they are hiding out in a friend's apartment, with Mozart's clarinet concerto to console them, she leaves abruptly, stops at a phone down the street, calls a police officer who has been questioning her, and turns her lover in. Returning to tell Belmondo what she has done, Seberg explains that she wanted to see if she really loved him or not.

Belmondo goes out to get some money being dropped off by an old associate in thievery and is gunned down by the police. His long legs run the length of the block before he drops, at last, to die. Seberg runs to him, more in curiosity than regret. Belmondo is heard to mutter, "You really are . . . ." His voice trails off. What did he say? she asks. Someone supplies the answer: "You really are a little bitch." The movie ends with Seberg rubbing her thumb across her lips and wondering what it means.

François Truffaut did the initial outline for *Breathless* based on an item he saw in a newspaper. However, it was not the story but the style that made *Breathless* such a major influence on American directors in the 1960s, as Pauline Kael has noted. Shot in black and white, with fast jump cutting, it took the gangster movie to a level of insouciance never contemplated, even by Bogart.[59]

Godard could not sustain his creative core, though he lasted longer than Truffaut. Veering off into leftist politics, he joined forces with a compatriot to film essays on ideology, including *Letter to Jane*, a caustic commentary on Jane Fonda in Vietnam. He tried video art as well and turned again in time to the kind of cinema that had made him a marvel of modernity. But the critical insights eluded him. His talent depended on the exuberance of youth. It did not mature into wisdom.

Besieged by war, Italian filmmakers rallied to give the world a new kind of cinema called Neo-Realism. Luchino Visconti foretold the movement with *Ossessione*, shot in 1942 and based on *The Postman Always Rings Twice*, a novel by James Cain. There could not have been a more unlikely leader of the rush to real locations and gritty, greedy characters than Visconti, a wealthy, homosexual aristocrat who embraced the high arts of Europe, directing both opera and theatre as well as movies.

Visconti's films are relatively few, but they spanned many years and some of his best pictures came later. *Rocco and his Brothers*, shot when he was fifty-four, chronicles the disintegration of a peasant family of five sons and their mother who leave the olive trees of Sicily after the father dies. They move to Milan where Rosaria, the matriarch, demands that her boys bring home money every evening to maintain their small apartment with beds lined up along the wall for each one of them. She has dreamed of getting away from the enslavement of the land and living an urban life.

Milan is not easy. One brother marries a women Rosaria doesn't like and has a child. Blessedly they have their own place to live. Another, Ciro, works in a factory, while Rocco gets a job with a dry cleaner. Luca, the youngest, stays at home. Simone becomes a boxer. Primitive and dangerous, he is drawn to a Nadia, a prostitute, who disappears without explaining that she must serve a brief stay in prison for some small offense. Once released, she runs into Rocco, and they fall in love. Under his influence, she renounces her old life and starts typing school. Simone hears of it and plummets into rage. Taking along his gang of thugs, he tracks the couple down, rapes her in front of everybody, then beats up Rocco whose response is surprising: He tells Nadia that she must go back to Simone because clearly he cannot cope without her. Nadia, of course, is horrified. But Rocco is a saint. He has purity. He has simplicity. Insight, however, eludes him.

Rocco is pressed to enter the boxing ring, where he proves to be a finer fighter than Simone who takes no care of himself. Simone does have Nadia living with him in the family apartment, causing his mother great agitation. Finally, Nadia can take no more. She goes back to the carnal world where Simone seeks her out, begging her to return to him. She professes only hate and contempt, which drives him to murder her. When Rocco hears what has happened, he wails like an animal. Too much good, he understands too late, can bring forth evil.

In *The Leopard*, drawn from the novel by Giuseppe Tomasi di Lampedusa, Visconti explores the response of an aging Italian prince (played by Burt Lancaster) to revolutionary changes all around him. Set in the 1860s, it describes a moment when power passes ineluctably from the old aristocracy to a corrupt, new parvenue culture. Trying to preserve as much as he can, he urges his nephew to do something unheard-of for someone of their station: run for office. "Don't you see," says the Prince, "things must change in order to remain the same."

Visconti was drawn to film by Jean Renoir, whom he met through Coco Chanel in 1935. Renoir also introduced him to leftist politics, surging then in France. Having absorbed the germinal lessons of his life, Visconti returned to Fascist Italy and began a career in pictures that would chronicle the social history of his time with immediacy and narrative power.

Roberto Rossellini was born in Rome in 1906, the same year as

Visconti. Son of a wealthy building contractor, he grew up spoiled and self-indulgent. As a young man Rossellini pursued "fast cars, fast women, and cocaine." He "borrowed money shamelessly without the least intention of repaying it," and he neglected to pay his servants, apparently thinking they were lucky to be working for such a great man.[60]

Rossellini ran through his inheritance, then turned accidentally to film through friends who already were working under the patronage of Mussolini's oldest son, a devotee of the movies. Vittorio Mussolini created an atmosphere that was relatively open and tolerant, far from the situation in which Leni Riefenstahl worked in Hitler's Germany.

Rossellini was thirty-eight when he made *Open City*, a brutal story of the Italian capital under the boot of Germany. Shot in 1944, right after the liberation, this movie was put together by a group of friends, including Federico Fellini, then a young journalist, who helped with the script. Engrossingly realistic—indeed, Rossellini was part of Visconti's New Realism—*Open City* was filmed on bits and pieces of stock financed by $25,000 the director was able to raise. But it wasn't enough. He and his star, Anna Magnani, had to sell their clothes to pay for the rest.[61]

What resulted was an account of that world, related with documentary persuasion and in many cases with amateur actor simply drawn from the street. It is peopled by resistance workers who endure torture, women who love and (sometimes) betray them, a Catholic priest who protects them, and young boys who mount clandestine operations of their own and whistle encouragement to the priest as he faces a German firing squad. It is a time of food rationing, black markets, and curfews; of weddings interrupted by fascists and pregnancies ended by bullets, one of which fells also an expectant mother, played by the magnificent Magnani.

With help from Fellini on the script, he also did *Paisan*, a series of six vignettes about the progress of Allied troops up the Italian peninsula. Though Rossellini preferred it to *Open City*, he was wrong. The make-do actors manage far less well than in the earlier film, and some scenes are allowed to run much too long.

There is a lovely moment when a Catholic chaplain encounters some monks in a monastery and they debate the fate of two allied colleagues of the cloth, one Protestant, the other Jewish. Their souls are doomed, said the Italian fathers. The chaplain did not agree, but he was moved nonetheless by the serenity of spirit he found in that small, devout community.

Rossellini cared about the politics of his country and the place of

Italy in the post-war world. Calling himself a moral film maker, he was a devoted Catholic who for years seldom failed to give his films a spiritual dimension. But he alienated many in the church when he left Anna Magnani for Ingrid Bergman, who also paid a high price for deserting her husband and daughter to marry the Italian director and bear him three children.

Then began a series of Rossellini pictures starring Bergman. The first, *Stromboli*, is as static as *Open City* is captivating. Bergman plays a Lithuanian refugee who finds herself in Italy after World War II. She marries a man she's barely met who takes her to live in his fishing village on an island best known, if at all, for its volcano.

But Bergman erupts before the volcano does. Maddened by the stultification of her life, she pleads with a priest for consolation. He counsels patience. Her husband grows unreasoningly jealous. He beats her and locks her in her room with the door nailed shut. Bergman yells to a passer-by in a boat, who rescues her through a window. She sets forth on foot to make her way past the agitated volcano to the other side of the island where she hopes to escape in a motor launch. It's a harrowing journey and all we know of it is this: Bergman, the cool skeptic, cries out to God for help.

Roberto Rossellini was intimidated by Ingrid Bergman. Awed by her beauty, which he certainly captured on film, he had trouble evoking from her the kind of performance she proved in other venues, after their divorce, she could give. Rossellini did far better work with Anna Magnani. She spoke his language. She embodied his philosophy.

After the Bergman years, Rossellini made a number of unsuccessful films in languages and cultures he did not know, "believing he could simply parachute into a place and start filming," an attitude stretching back to his playboy years. Then he turned increasingly to documentary, to history, and to television where the scripts with which he had to work were tightly disciplined.[62] To these he brought great craftsmanship, but, like Godard, his genius was concentrated in the bloom of youth.

A few years older than Rossellini and Visconti, Vittorio de Sica echoed their New-Realistic look at 1940s Italy in his early work, but not before he had spent several years acting, first as a child, then as a gallant romantic star, a role he continued to play in films such as *Madame D . . .* by Max Ophuls. Not turning to movie-making until he was thirty-nine, De Sica made good use of non-professional actors to create portraits of everyday people that resonated with conviction.

Nowhere was his Neo-Realism better realized than in *The Bicycle Thief*. Shot in 1948, this sad story of Italy in the wake of Mussolini is built around Antonio, a man on the edge of unemployment who is offered a job as a poster hanger, but only if he has a bicycle. That, however, he does not have. To raise money for this necessary purchase, his wife gathers up the sheets and sells them. Antonio gets the job, but one day, as he is plastering a poster to an outside wall, a man steals his precious bicycle, only a few feet away, and races off with it.

Antonio spends the rest of the movie searching for parts (stolen vehicles are always broken down, he's told), and, at one point, he chases a man on a bicycle, certain it is his. Desperation overtakes him, and finally he steals a bicycle himself, only to be caught and humiliated in front of his young son. It's heartbreaking. And it leaves no doubt that De Sica is a master of pathos and subdued emotion. As he said, "There are no small events when it comes to the poor."[63]

By the time he was seventy, De Sica had strayed from his earlier black-and-white discipline to create an elegant, and haunting, feature— *The Garden of the Finzi-Continis*. This is a depiction of upper-middle-class life in Italy from 1938 to 1943. With opening sequences bathed in the radiant light of high morning, blonde and sumptuous, like Bergman's *Fanny and Alexander*, this film follows a group of young people, dressed in sporting white, as they bicycle through the countryside near Ferrara, play tennis at the Finzi-Continis, fall in love, resist love, all in a world of idyllic loveliness.

Important work, splendid marriages, and promising children should lie ahead for them. But their perfection is soon to be devastated. Anti-Semitic laws have just been passed ruling that Jews may not marry Aryans, attend state schools, have obituaries or servants, or play at the racket club. Giorgio, a young Jewish man is kicked out of the library by an official who knows his father. The father tries to be understanding, always understanding: The official has a family, he reminds his son. "All Italy has family," the boy replies. A bitter observation.

Giorgio leaves for Grenoble to take money to his brother. There he hears about Dachau. But hope is not yet extinguished. He returns home and declares his love for Micol Finzi-Contini, who says she feels for him, but not that way. It is too late for them in any case. Six months later, the gestapo comes for the Finzi-Continis. They descend the staircase, their household staff huddled to one side. Micol runs into Giorgio's father at the collecting center and learns that her former suitor and his mother have escaped.

The Garden of the Finzi-Continis is an elegy for a graceful moment, when life had form and substance and the possibility of beauty. De Sica took the Neo-Realism of twenty-five years before and converted it into a work of art. He died three years later.

Federico Fellini was no Neo-Realist. Though that was the atmosphere in which he got his start, he gravitated in time toward highly personal cinema, based on vivid memories and ecstatic dreams. Born in Rimini, he became enthralled by Rome and used it as a locus at which to explore the high life of the last half of the century as well as his own fantasies. Fellini's films, said Orson Welles, "are a small-town boy's dream of the big city. His sophistication works because it's the creation of someone who doesn't have it."

Fellini did have a gift for cartoons and comedy gags, both of which he pursued along with radio writing before finding his way to screenplays, working often with Rossellini. At twenty-three he married the actress Giulietta Masina, who starred in some of his most successful pictures, including *La Strada*, which may be Fellini's masterpiece. Playing a Chaplinesque waif with an "artichoke look" who is sold by her impoverished mother for ten thousand lire to a brute of a character (Anthony Quinn), she becomes a clownish counterpoint to his road-side act as a strong man who breaks a chain around his chest with the muscular force of an ignorant giant. Brutalized by him, playing a trumpet to keep herself alive, ever waving tearful goodbyes from the back of their truck to people who have shown her kindness, she is a picture of poignant innocence, left finally to die by a hard partner who takes too long to know what he has in her.

Never was modern Rome more complicated or compelling than in *La Dolci Vita*, directed and partly written by Fellini. Featuring Marcello Mastroianni as a reporter, it opens with a statue of Jesus being carried by helicopter over ancient ruins. Sunbathers wave from the roof of a resort hotel. Before long Mastroianni goes to cover the arrival by plane of a Swedish film star played by Anita Eckberg. "Paparazzi" are there too. (It was with this film that the term entered the language.) Eckberg tours Santa Maria's, dressed in black and white, like a priest. Next she appears entirely in white, her elegant bosom anything but ecclesiastical, dancing with Mastroianni to "Arrivederci, Roma," and then strolling outside, into the fountain, dress and all. Fully suited up, he follows her, in one of the most sensual scenes ever put on film.

The movie moves on to a miracle: Some children have seen the Madonna. It's a media circus, of course. A person dies. A priest intones the last blessing. A paparazzo crosses himself, then snaps a photo, foreshadowing that moment, just after midnight, in Paris, when a photographer would take the pulse, then the picture, of Princess Diana, dying in a smashed Mercedes.

Orson Welles charged that Fellini showed "dangerous signs of being a superlative artist with little to say." That may be so, in the pictures other than the poignant, deeply affecting *La Strada*. But Fellini created images that live in the mind, deeply resonate of a certain moment when the twentieth century sought to revive itself through personal discovery.

Michelangelo Antonioni went for startling effect, and usually he achieved it. Born in Ferrara, he studied business and economics at the University of Bologna (following the lead of a girlfriend), then worked as a film critic. He edited Cinema until the fascists decided he was too left-wing, and he also pursued movies himself, crafting a script for Rossellini, among others. Moving on to his own projects, Antonioni became a prophet of social breakdown, as David Thomson has observed.

Antonioni has been forever contemporary as Geoffrey Nowell-Smith observes. Even his later work has about it the edge of the immediate. *Blowup*, done in 1966 when Antonioni was fifty-four, brings to life the vivid London of those years when Vanessa Redgrave was shockingly young and beautiful with hair and brows an unexpected pale brown. She dominates the picture as David Hemmings, playing a photographer, follows her and a male companion in a park, shooting pictures of them. She shows up at his house, demanding the film. He says no. There are other shots on the reel he needs.

Redgrave stays for an afternoon of flirtation and manipulation. He teaches her to smoke against the beat of the music. She takes off her top and waits for him in a hallway, her long arms draped across her breasts. Not yet the great actress of the age, Redgrave nonetheless is an electrifying presence.

The photographs, once blown up, reveal a mystery: As Redgrave embraces what must be her lover, having pulled him several steps in her direction, she glances toward shrubbery nearby, where a face can be seen in the bushes. Hemmings races back to the park and finds a man dead beneath the branches. By this time it is night. He returns the next day to get a shot of the corpse, but the dead man is gone.

The movie concludes abruptly, whimsically, in a way not altogether satisfying. *Blowup* tantalizes, then ends, just as one thinks it's about to begin.

Zabriskie Point was Antonioni's dissection of the sixties in America. It features an assistant professor of history who gets arrested; a student rally replete with bloodshed; a guy who escapes to the Arizona desert in a pink plane; a girl who drives in an old beat-up car to meet him there; ominous developers, plotting outrage in real estate; and a huge, fiery explosion in the end, as a TV set, a refrigerator, and an oversized package of wonder bread erupt from the demolition of a house on a hill to fill the pastel sky with the endless debris of U.S. living. Pauline Kael called it embarrassing.[64] She was right.

Even so, Antonioni ranks high among Italian filmmakers. He knew how to capture the moment and make it memorable. Anyone who wants to study the middle decades of the twentieth century would do well to consult his work.

Bernardo Bertolucci, a generation younger than Antonioni and the New Realists, can be shocking or enchanting. But he has seldom failed to fascinate. From a family of artists, he is the son of a fabled Italian poet and the brother of a film director like himself. At twenty-one, Bertolucci won a prize for a first work of poetry, but then moved quickly into movies. By the time he was thirty he had begun to achieve some recognition, and in 1973, *Last Tango in Paris* established him as a film maker of importance and audacity. *Tango* created a scandal wherever it went, but it earned millions in the United States and was one of Italy's most successful pictures even though an order had been issued to destroy it.

Two Francis Bacon paintings boxed in the credits, raw and desperate, foretell the rough, bestial, brilliant performance by Marlon Brando as an American who meets Maria Schneider while she's looking for a Paris apartment. They rendezvous often in that nearly empty apartment and tumble into sex kept primitive and coarse (though erotic) by Brando's insistence on no names, no life stories, no mutual exchange of any kind.

Brando runs a hotel that was owned by his wife before she used a razor to kill herself in the bathtub. He's distraught, but recovers sufficiently to take Schneider to a lounge where there's a tango contest. They join in the dance. He asks her to live with him. She says no, she'd rather end it. He chases her to the apartment where she shoots him, repeating (as if rehearsing for the police), I don't know his name. I don't know who he is.

Bertolucci turned to Asian themes with *The Last Emperor*, story of the forlorn boy born to preside over the twilight of the Qing dynasty in Peking, but imprisoned on his throne by Japanese invaders and forced to serve their purposes only to spend ten years later being "reeducated" by the Chinese Communists (the film won nine Oscars), and *Little Buddha*, about another boy destined for a life different from the one that seemed laid out for him.

This only child, named Jesse, lives with his parents in Seattle. They are startled when a Buddhist monk from Tibet arrives at their house and gradually reveals to them that he believes their son to be the reincarnation of his revered teacher who died a year before Jesse entered the world. The priest persuades the couple to allow the boy to travel to a monastery in Bhutan for spiritual tests. Together with his dad, he sets out from Seattle.

Jesse is given a book, *The Story of Little Buddha—Prince Siddhartha*. It's the story of a young man who grows up in Nepal, protected by his powerful father from knowledge of old age, illness, death, pain, and poverty. But Siddhartha discovers these horrors, accidentally, while outside the palace gates. Shocked, he leaves his wife and new baby to go out among humankind. Thus begins his "long journey of awakening," in which he learns "the middle way . . . . the great truth . . . he would teach to the world."

Siddhartha, the story goes, "achieved the great calm that precedes detachment from emotions. He had reached beyond himself. He was beyond joy or pain, separate from judgment, able to remember that he had been a girl, a dolphin, a tree, a monkey. He remembered his first birth and the millions after that. He could see beyond the universe. Siddhartha had seen the ultimate reality of all things. He had understood that every movement in the universe is an effect provoked by a cause. He knew there was no salvation without compassion for every other being. From that moment on Siddhartha was called the Buddha, the awakened one."

Two other candidates appear—a boy and a girl. All three of them are found to possess holy incarnations.

In his taste for Asia and the exotic, Bertolucci moved far afield from the raw carnality of *Last Tango in Paris* and created impressive beauty. But it is for the earlier effort, animated by the genius of Marlon Brando, that he will mainly be remembered.

The Italian imagination, transplanted to America, continues today in the work of Martin Scorsese. Heir of *film noir*, born to the art of the street, he is considered one of the foremost directors of the last decades of the century.

Scorsese grew up in New York's Little Italy, the son of parents from Sicilian immigrant families who worked in the garment industry. There was an interlude in Queens, where people had yards and trees, but that came to an end when his parents fell out with the landlord and had to move back to Martin's grandparents' place on Elizabeth Street before getting their own apartment. There he stayed, too asthmatic to play stickball with his friends from St. Patrick's School, enthralled by movies and television, resentful of tourists who came to stare at tenement life. (Scorsese would organize make-believe gang fights to shock them, then laugh in their wake.)[65]

Scorsese went to Cathedral College of the Immaculate Conception in Queens with the thought of becoming a priest. But his grades were not good, nor was his Latin. So he changed to Cardinal Hayes High School in the Bronx, taking the subway there every day. These were his first experiences since the age of eight outside the confines of Little Italy. He didn't do well enough to get into Fordham, but he was accepted at New York University where he studied film (and later taught) and shot his first movie as a sophomore.

Scorsese left home in 1965 to marry Larraine Marie Brennan, an actress he met at NYU. They moved into a flat in Jersey City and had a baby girl named Catherine after his mother, whom he revered. Trouble came when Larraine began pressuring Martin to earn a living which he could not yet accomplish working in movies. Yet filmmaking was what he was determined to do. The marriage ended, and Scorsese lived with Sandy Weintraub in Hollywood for four years.

He also plunged ever deeper into films, some of which his father helped finance. Later, once he was successful, Scorsese returned the kindness by moving his parents to a high rise on Gramercy Park.

Scorsese's work was marked by the hard streets of his upbringing. One of his first movies, in fact, was called *Mean Streets*. It was also his first with Robert De Niro, who grew up only a few blocks from Scorsese, but in a middle-class, artistic setting; so the two had never met before. Shot in his old Italian-American neighborhood as well as in Hollywood, it was hailed by Pauline Kael in the *New Yorker* as "a true original of our period, a triumph of personal filmmaking." She later called it "the best American movie of 1973."[66]

Mean Streets dealt with both crime and the church, two institutions excruciatingly familiar to Scorsese. "I was raised with them, the gangsters and the priests," he said. "And now, as an artist, in a way, I'm both a gangster and a priest."[67] The movie made it hard for him to go back to Little Italy. People there were not pleased with the way he portrayed their community.

Three years later came *Taxi Driver*, also with De Niro. A searing exploration of New York at night, the film presents De Niro as a John Hinkley kind of character who tracks a presidential candidate with psychopathic precision only to wind up a hero in the end. Conceived in the dark inspiration of *film noir*, it's a powerful look at the edge of life, over which one falls forever into the certitude of doom. ". . . [A]t the same time as giving this accurate picture of Italian-Americans," said Scorsese, "I was trying to make a kind of homage to the Warner Brothers gangster films."

Scorsese was not immune to Hollywood's drug culture or to cocaine which made him high and manic. A crisis came at the Telluride Film Festival in Colorado. There he had a violent reaction to his asthma medication together with other prescription drugs and bad coke. He knew then he had to change.

At that point Scorsese was divorced for the second time and living with Isabella Rossellini, daughter of Ingrid Bergman and Roberto Rossellini. ("Sandy Wentraub," wrote Peter Biskind, "joked that he was sleeping his way through the daughters of his favorite directors.") He took time out during the shooting of his next picture, *Raging Bull*, to marry her in Rome. They stayed together less than five years. When Isabella began moving from journalism to her spectacular career as a model as well as to acting, Scorsese reacted badly. "He wanted me to spend life between the cookstove and the kids," she told *Time* magazine.[68]

Raging Bull is probably Scorsese's most highly regarded picture. Based on the boxing career of Jake La Motta, who fought Sugar Ray Robinson in two matches three weeks apart in 1943, it is the story of brute passion disciplined to express itself in violence of directed cruelty. It's also a story of defeat, for La Motta, and for Scorsese who had hoped to win an Oscar for this movie. "When I lost for *Raging Bull*," he confided, "that's when I realized what my place in the system would be, if I did survive at all—on the outside looking in."[69]

Scorsese did survive, and he turned at times to other sources, making

The Last Temptation of Christ (hugely controversial) from the novel by
Nikos Kazantzakis; *The Age of Innocence* (a departure into elegance),
drawing upon Edith Wharton; and *Kundun*, about the Dalai Lama, which
Scorsese felt was misunderstood by critics. ". . . [T]here's a certain kind
of film that you can make," he said, "where the texture of it, the rhythm
of it, is like music. They just didn't get it."[70]

But Scorsese hardly remained an outsider. Today he's widely
acknowledged as one of the finest filmmakers working in America.

Woody Allen has been called the true descendant of Charlie Chaplin.
Like Chaplin, he writes, directs, and stars in his own movies. And like
Chaplin, he plays a little guy, anxious and vulnerable.[71] Allen does not
have Chaplin's range or depth, but he brings to his own character and to
others who populate his films such acute observations that his work will
be a lasting guide to how bright, neurotic New Yorkers lived in the last
years of the century.

New York, of course, is where Allen Stewart Konigsberg was born.
He dropped out of New York University and City College on his way to
becoming Woody Allen. Before his widely discussed marriage to Soon-
Yi Previn, there were two much earlier wives: Harlen Rosen and Louise
Lasser, who appeared in some of his first movies. But before that Allen
wrote jokes for Sid Caesar's television show and performed himself in
nightclubs. Then he turned to screenwriting and it wasn't long before he
was acting and directing as well.

Where Scorsese had to struggle to raise money for his films, Allen
was blessed not only with funding, first from United Artists, then Orion,
and later Tri-Star Pictures, but also creative control of his projects. He
aspired to work with a tightly knit production family—like Ingmar
Bergman—and he did. But all that unraveled in the late 1990s as his
pictures, which once had grossed $40 million in the U.S. (*Hannah and
Her Sisters* in 1986) fell to earning $6.3 million domestically (*Mighty
Aphrodite* in 1995) or sometimes $9.7 million (*Everyone Says I Love You*
in 1996). Since a Woody Allen movie was usually budgeted at $20
million or so, that clearly had to change. With Sweetland Films, an independent company fueled by European investors, financing his work,
Allen began paring away longtime producers, cinematographers, and
crew members, many of whom had already taken pay cuts, and replacing
them with less expensive people. He also changed from a New York to a
Hollywood agent, hoping, it was reported, to attract more acting assign-

ments, which can be lucrative.[72]

Part of the problem can be traced to Allen's messy breakup with Mia Farrow when he was charged in court with pursuing her adopted daughter, Soon-Yi, and behaving inappropriately with the other children. That's when his relations with Tri-Star began to founder. "One of the reasons studios loved being in business with Woody, and were happy to break even" observed an associate, "was that surely he was one of the world's great directors and there was a public relations value of being in business with him. [But when reports of his affair with Soon Yi started to surface] that value was diluted. People weren't knocking down the doors to do business with him."[73]

Woody Allen may be personally irresponsible, but behind a camera, or in front of it, he has undeniable genius. His most celebrated film, *Annie Hall*, has a command of language and idea, laced with astonishing wit, seldom seen in films. Those who say that words don't matter should listen closely to Woody Allen, who won three Oscars for this movie: screenplay, direction and best picture. Like John Ford, he was not at the ceremony. He chose instead to spend the evening in New York, playing Dixieland clarinet.

He also has been lucky in his leading ladies. Diane Keaton, to whom he was close, brought fantastic style to *Annie Hall*, which may even have been named for her (Keaton's real name is Diane Hall), as well as *Manhattan Murder Mystery*, *Sleeper* and *Love and Death*. Then came Mia Farrow (not so lucky in the end) who reigned in *A Midsummer Night's Sex Comedy*, *Zelig*, *Broadway Danny Rose*, *The Purple Rose of Cairo*, *Hannah and Her Sisters*, *Radio Days*, *September*, *Another Woman*, "Oedipus Wrecks" from *New York Stories*, *Crimes and Misdemeanors*, *Alice*, *Shadows and Fog*, and *Husbands and Wives*, released just as her court battle with Allen was ablaze in the headlines.

Allen took a beating from critics and journalists for *Deconstructing Harry*, about a writer who enrages family, friends, and lovers by putting them in his books. It's been called one of his angriest films.[74] Certainly he does wrestle with the difficulties artists have negotiating life. Maureen Dowd called it "a clinical document, an anthology of unexamined prejudices, a tiresome Manhattan whine . . . told from the point of view of a weaselly, overcivilized, undermoralized, terminally psychoanalyzed terminator."[75] Margo Jefferson admits that *Deconstructing Harry* "does have an emotional edge. But if anyone tries to tell you that this makes it a genuinely deep or brave movie, be afraid."[76]

Deep and brave it is not, but *Deconstructing Harry* is wildly funny. Witness: the scene where Harry (Woody Allen), his young son, a prostitute in hot pants, and a friend with cardiac problems are rolling down the road, on their way to see Harry receive an award from his school (reminiscent of Bergman's *Wild Strawberries*), all singing "When the Red, Red Robin Comes Bob-Bob-Bobbin' Along." Harry had begged each to come with him because he dreaded having no one with whom to share his honor. Together they form an unlikely community that's nonetheless resonate of modern America.

"Life is more important than films," said Alphonse in Truffaut's *Day for Night*. For Woody Allen, life is the price to be paid for art. David Thomson has even suggested that "his indefatigable unconscious mind knew he needed trouble and disruption." Whatever brought about his lapse from even loosely delineated norms, Woody Allen stands nonetheless as the most expressive filmmaker of his times.

Expressive of his times Woody Allen certainly is, but he shows none of the passion so prevalent in the early years of film to change the age and make it more amenable to human habitation. Before mid-century, movies often began with titles that declared a serious purpose. Sometimes it was imposed by industry censors, as was the case with Howard Hawks's *Scarface*, which issued an indictment of gang rule in this country and asked what the government was going to do about it.

But often the sentiments were sincerely meant, especially in the vivid speeches of the 1930s such as Ronald Coleman's closing declaration of integrity in *Arrowsmith* (1931), based on the novel by Sinclair Lewis and directed by John Ford. There were other statements just as fervent, Sarris notes: "Edward G. Robinson's in *Five Star Final* (1931), Walter Huston's in *Law and Order* (1932), John Barrymore's in *Topaz* (1933), Paul Muni's in *The Life of Emile Zola* (1937), Robert Donat's in *The Citadel* (1938), and of course . . . James Stewart's veritable flood of rhetoric in *Mr. Smith Goes to Washington* (1939)." Then there was the "we-the-people . . . populist manifesto" at the close of Ford's *The Grapes of Wrath* (born of Steinbeck's novel), which surely compares with Chaplin's exhortation to peace that concludes *The Great Dictator*.

A sense of social responsibility extended to what some directors were willing to do on film. Howard Hawks refused to direct a plot that involved attempted suicide because he didn't believe in it. He did depict flights that amounted to unavoidable suicide in *Dawn Patrol*, but those he saw as a case of wartime heroism.

In the past three decades there have been some directors who have worked from a moral base—George Lucas extolled good over evil in *Star Wars*; Steven Spielberg told an important story of decency during the Holocaust in *Schindler's List*, and again, in *Amistad*, he portrayed a lawyer of strong character who defended slaves on trial for an uprising at sea—but mainly the past few years have depended on history and literature, presented by Merchant and Ivory among others, for films of true distinction.

Charles Silver of the Film Study Center at the Museum of Modern Art has pointed out that some of the finest filmmakers have had nineteenth century sensibilities. Griffith, he notes, read Dickens and was a student of the Civil War (as was John Ford). Welles had a nineteenth century turn of mind, and Renoir was looking back to his father's day. They made pictures about nineteenth century values. But what, asked Silver, are twentieth century values?

That may be something filmmakers feel they cannot settle, but actually they have much to contribute to the answer. A survey of motion pictures of the past eighty years makes clear the influence of this art form. Fashions may change. Technologies may change. But genius endures and always has the power to move the emotions and energize the spirit.

Chapter
Nine

Václav Havel

Václav Havel, president of the Czech Republic and leader of the Velvet Revolution that freed his nation from the Communists, is leading Central Europe through limbo to a future that is sane, humane and worthy of the suffering of the century.

The Age of Limbo

*Now is life very solid or very shifting? I am
haunted by the two contradictions. This has gone
on forever; goes down to the bottom of the world—
this moment I stand on. Also it is transitory, flying,
diaphanous. I shall pass like a cloud on the waves.
Perhaps it may be that though we change, one
flying after another, so quick, so quick, yet we are
somehow successive and continuous we human
beings. We show the light through.*

Virginia Woolf

When did the twentieth century begin to run out of steam? Certainly the ebbing of creative energy has been apparent since the 1970s. Solitary performers there have been, but the groundswells of culture that elevate a people gave way years ago, leaving convulsive reaction that ushered in the age of limbo.

Sen. Daniel Patrick Moynihan has said that the twentieth century began in 1914 in Sarajevo with the assassination of Austrian Archduke Franz Ferdinand. He also lamented that the twentieth century ended there with destruction of much that we had fought for over the lifetimes of six generations.

It is widely assumed that the modern world coincides with the twentieth century, but by 1914 the modern impetus was already over in the view of Rebecca West. ". . . I realize," she wrote, "that when Alexander and Draga [the king and queen of Serbia] fell from that balcony [brutally murdered in 1903], the whole of the modern world fell with them. It took some time to reach the ground and break its neck, but its fall started then."[1]

But Rebecca West may have misproclaimed the crash, placing it too early. It seems to me that the modern world plunged to its destruction during the Great Depression of the 1930s, and it hit the ground, for Americans at least, in the 1960s with the Kennedy and King assassinations and the Vietnam War. Since then art has dissolved into minimalism, science has turned to the tiniest quanta which at any given moment may or may not exist; and statecraft has become no less inexact as nations struggle to understand themselves in a global atmosphere growing daily more intrusive. We're groping in an empty era, void of definition, on the cusp of something more substantial.

The moment is so nondescript it has no name except "post-modern." This epithet is applied to everything from the Bosnian War (no formal military forces any more, just "armies and peoples [that are] indistinguishable") to the collapse of the Mexican peso (marked by the speed with which investors over the world pulled out of all emerging markets). It even has surfaced in Tarot cards that are "multicultural, non hierarchical, nonthreatening, almost user-friendly."[2]

Post-modernism finds its clearest expression in architecture. Here the post-modern draws on the vocabulary of earlier styles, especially the classical. It refutes the notion of buildings as spare, pared-down, functional boxes. And while it may not rejoice in ornament as Louis Sullivan did, it does adorn itself with arches, domes and sensuous shapes. Post-modern architecture embraces the curve, not just the angle. Thus it restores the feminine to the landscape of cities.

Late twentieth-century architecture looked back to earlier styles for good reason. It began to realize that, with the exception of Frank Lloyd Wright, I.M. Pei, Frank Gehry, and a few others, the modern was not going to hold up against Classical, Gothic, Baroque or Renaissance building or their later versions in Georgian, Federal, Victorian or Beaux-Arts styles, not to mention the lovely creations of Asia. Too much had been eliminated. Some debilitating inhibition had taken hold, banishing the sensual and the exuberant. Unable to create a widely accessible style, modern architecture became like ballet and the violin, also the plays of Noel Coward: you mustn't try any of them unless you're very, very good. Hence the style flourished only in the hands of a few masters. It was never able to create whole villages, whole districts, where everyone follows a common vision as a matter of course, not as coercion.

Especially disturbing has been the failure of modern architecture to create much fine religious building. With few exceptions—Frank Lloyd Wright's Unity Temple in Illinois, Philip Johnson's Roofless Church in Indiana, Le Corbusier's chapel at Ronchamp or Breuer's at St. John's Abbey in Minnesota, among others—there is little to compare with the Gothic cathedrals, Christopher Wren's churches, Baroque Rome, the temples of Kyoto or the missions of the American Southwest. Louise Nevelson did a lovely chapel at Saint Peter's in New York and of course there's the Rothko Chapel in Houston and Matisse's at Vence. But they are primarily interior art, not architecture.

And why the emphasis on chapels in the twentieth century? Where are the great ecclesiastical structures? Their absence has to reflect on the spiritual state of the age itself. While the last years of the century saw a surge of fundamentalism and a great awakening of sorts, they did not produce anything approaching a Chartres. The failure has to be in the energy of the inspiration.

Lorin Hollander, the pianist, pointed out that the great cathedral builders were not relying on engineering alone. It was not their ability to build a Gothic arch that created their soaring sanctuaries. They *knew* something. As Heine put it, they had convictions where only opinions reign among the moderns.[4] And the post-moderns? Here we find a desperate wish to recapture the eloquence of the past.

Actually, the twentieth century has seen the construction of some sacred spaces. They are the museums and performing halls that have arisen from Los Angeles to Paris to Bilbao to Shanghai. They mark the only moment when there has been sufficient aggregation of talent and money to build something monumental. They are saying that the epoch, burdened by a history both ugly and brutal, is seeking salvation in beauty.

Post-modern literature, like architecture, is in search of treasures from the past. But where classicism is the preferred idiom in architecture, post-modern writers have a taste for the Gothic, for the mind of the Middle Ages. And seldom do they shrink from mystery or mysticism. Their work is rich in symbols and a symbiosis between loveliness and dread. They understand the Jungian shadow, the dark side of personality, and the need to incorporate it into respectable lives.

Science is not without hopeful, post-modern interpretations. Indeed, Václav Havel, president of the Czech Republic, sees in science a source of reassurance. "The 'anthropic cosmological principle,'" he said, "brings us to an idea, perhaps as old as humanity itself, that we are not at all just an accidental anomaly, the microscopic caprice of a tiny particle whirling in the endless depths of the universe. Instead, we are mysteriously connected to the universe, we are mirrored in it, just as the entire evolution of the universe is mirrored in us."[5] We are not accidents of random selection. We are meant to be here, just as Stuart Kauffman, the biochemist, insists.

There is more. It deals with the Gaia hypothesis: "The 'Gaia hypothesis,'" Havel explained, "brings together proof that the dense network of mutual interactions between the organic and inorganic portions of Earth's surface form a single system, a kind of mega-organism, a living planet, Gaia . . . . According to the Gaia hypothesis, we are parts of a greater whole . . . .This awareness endows us with the capacity for self-transcendence."[6] Here again, we are an integral aspect of all that is, and that knowledge elevates us beyond the limits of our own beings.

In politics it has not gone as well. For a politician to be labeled post-modern is not a compliment. Disraeli has been called "the prototypical post-modern politician, driven only by ambition, endlessly reinventing himself and famous for little apart from being famous."[7]

Post-modern journalism has fared no better. It's been dismissed as obsessed with image, the appearance of things and nothing more. All too often this is true.

Moreover, through the media the post-modern has invaded popular philosophy and rendered objective reality obsolete. "Post-modernists now place quotation marks around words like 'reality,'" wrote one observer. "Throughout our culture, the old notions of 'truth' and 'knowledge' are in danger of being replaced by the new ones of 'opinion,' 'perception' and 'credibility.'"[8]

Gertrude Himmelfarb is no more sanguine. Post-modern scholarship, especially deconstruction, she stressed, has given itself up to relativism and "aporia," which she describes as "difference, discontinuity, disparity, contradiction . . . perversity, opacity, obscurity, anarchy, chaos." Current historians, she said, are striving to be "imaginative," "inventive" and "creative" rather than accurate. "[T]he result," wrote her reviewer, "is a blurring of the lines between history and fiction . . . . The suggestion that all historical tests are 'indeterminate and contradictory, paradoxical and ironic, rhetorical and metaphoric' tends to create a state of affairs in which any event, even the Holocaust, can be deconstructed and relativized."[9]

The case grows even more serious in *Post-Modernism and the Social Sciences*, where Marie Rosenau "maintains that skeptical post-modernists react against modernism (the quest for certainty and universal truth) by arguing that 'the post-modern age is one of fragmentation, disintegration . . . absence of moral parameters . . . .'"[10]

Modernism as a search for universal truth: Certainly this can be seen in Mondrian's resolute devotion to essential things and Kandinsky's journey toward the spiritual in art. It reached its fullest flowering in the perfection of Brancusi. Barnett Newman's *Stations of the Cross* also bespeaks the same yearning (as does much of Rothko), while Miro and Malevich seem definitely to have arrived at an intuition of Pure Consciousness which they elaborated from physics into metaphysics, pointing to a metaphor for the age. Mies van der Rohe and Le Corbusier tried for extreme unity in their work, and looked for support to the natural order.

Modernism's problem was that it went too far, paring away beauty, mystery, elegance and finally imagination itself. Proportion was lost, and human scale. An excess of clarity led to a loss of the sensual and then to an ascetic ethic.

Where does Picasso fit in the modern world? The answer is: he doesn't. One major museum director maintained that Picasso was not really modern at all. Léger, he said, that prophet of the machine, was the first modern painter. Picasso was an Old Master.

But if Picasso at times looked backward to classicism, as an Old Master might, it was only to look forward again and far ahead to the post-modern era. He leapt over decades, skipping the modern impulse altogether.

"Modernism," said Barnaby Fitzgerald, an artist, "means you can break the rules. The post-modern rejects the new, sets its face against the new."[11] Picasso, of course, did break the rules, with cubism and much that followed. Moreover it's hard to argue that he was not aligned with the new. But universal truth, so important to modernism, hardly enthralled him, and fragmentation and disintegration certainly characterize his later work. Even so, post-modernism cannot contain Picasso. Nothing can.

Peter Berger, a sociologist, summed up the post-modern moment in his comments about the "deconstruction of the self": The post-modern self, he observed, has nothing at the core; it exists merely as a social (not a spiritual) being.[12] Berger, like Himmelfarb, saw the post-modern as close to spiritual nihilism, drained of essential juices, beyond redemption. And there are aspects of the culture that support this view. But in literature and architecture, the post-modern, when it works, is rich and deeply resonant. If artists are indeed their time, as Martha Graham said, then *their* post-modernism—at least that of writers and architects—may well be telling us that something deeply integrative is underway. Picasso's fragments are about to reassemble themselves in a whole new configuration with implications reaching deep into human experience.

Limbo will not last forever.

Nobody understands the post-modern predicament better than Václav Havel. No one knows better than he does the limits of the Enlightenment. He had much time to think about such things during long stretches in prison for affronting the Soviet puppets in Prague.

There is something poignant about Prague, Budapest, Warsaw and the other great cities of Central Europe, isolated for forty-four years while the Western half of the continent not only regained its wealth and composure, but also re-created itself as a whole new political entity. The great divide that developed only reenforced the psychological predicament of Central Europe: always to be the shadow of the continent. Poland, Hungary, the former Czechoslovakia and the others have been made to carry the dark side of the European people. Theirs was the wild emotion, the black chaos, while reason and light were assigned to the West.[13]

But suddenly, in the closing days of 1989, the Iron Curtain lifted. Havel, the playwright, understood his cue and presented the greatest production of his career—the velvet revolution of then Czechoslovakia.

It was accomplished with astonishing speed, improvisation and merriness, reported Timothy Garton Ash. And Havel was "at once director, playwright, stage-manager and leading actor in this, his greatest play." The action took place primarily in the Magic Lantern Theatre, where Havel and his compatriots in the highly ad hoc Civic Forum holed up in dressing rooms 10 and 11 to plot their strategy. Once rehearsed, they would mount the narrow stairway to the stage itself for their daily press briefing. It is here that the Forum would present its "latest communique, programmatic statement or negotiating position."[14]

And who were these revolutionaries of the Forum? Twenty years before they had been "journalists, academics, politicians, lawyers, but now they [came] here from their jobs as stokers, window-cleaners, clerks or, at best, banned writers. Sometimes they [had] to leave a meeting to go and stoke up their boilers. A few of them [came] straight from prison, whence they [had] been released under the pressure of popular protest." But, renewed by the warm spirit of the theatre that frosty but animated autumn, they became actors as accomplished as any in Havel's professional company. Indeed, when the crowds thronged finally in Wenceslas Square, what they shouted was "Long live the actors! Long live the students!" to honor those who had started the uprising in the first place.[15]

For this moment Havel had prepared with the care of a theologian. He believed in the importance of words.

Only six weeks earlier he had talked about words at the German Booksellers' Association: "In the beginning was the Word," he quoted, "and the word was with God, and the Word was God." From this declaration of Christian belief Havel leapt to a discussion of language and the perversion of meaning. He cited "socialism." In its name civil wars were fought, and for the betterment of ordinary citizens. But before long secret police were mustered, totalitarian governments fortified, and prisons filled—all to protect "socialism." What had started out as a pro-people word was then used to repress and imprison millions for its own sake. Havel wanted none of this. He was determined his revolution would speak with clarity and commitment to its own truth.[16]

Already Havel had moved beyond post-modern relativism if in fact he ever had paused there. Drawing on Martin Heidegger's idea of Being—the "whole of existence," beyond technology and rationalism— and adding a bit of Beckett and Kafka, he created his own "language of democracy."[17]

Even so, clarity had not been a habit with Havel. He had long been accustomed to writing on several simultaneous levels. His play *Temptation*, for example, was ostensibly a parody of Faust. But what it was really saying is, you have to take sides, you can't sit out the crisis or straddle the fence.

Havel sat out nothing. Always he was a full participant in his times. When he became president of his country, Milan Kundera, the Czech writer, wondered provocatively what happens when an artist's life itself becomes the work of art. There is a danger, he said, that the creative work gets lost. And the person could be damaged as well. "The work of art that a life becomes is not identical with that life," he said, "it may even be hostile to it." Moreover, "there is no unity between a man's character and his destiny, the one is always victim of the other."[18]

Will Havel the artist or Havel the human being suffer at the hands of Havel the politician? Not necessarily, in spite of Kundera's forebodings. Another observer noted that the Czech president is primarily a man of politics and a brilliant essayist before he is a brilliant playwright. There are signs this may be true. Certainly his insistence on merging thought with action testifies to his wish to be the integrating personality that he himself has said must be summoned.

When Havel spoke to the U.S. Congress in February, 1990, he

invoked the Founding Fathers of America as intellectuals who assumed responsibility for public affairs and did not hide behind a desire for personal independence. He might have been speaking of himself. Havel, in fact, is one of a number of intellectuals who came to the fore as Eastern Europe was defying the Soviets: Landsbergis in Lithuania was a music professor, De Maiziera in the former East Germany a violinist, Jozsef Antall in Hungary a one-time teacher and librarian and his colleague Arpad Goncz a playwright, Croatia's Franjo Tudjman was a historian as well as a general, and President Zhelyu Zhelev of Bulgaria was a dissident philosopher. They were instrumental in freeing their countries from the certainty of servitude. They had no way of knowing that limbo lay ahead.

As for the modern world, to my mind it reached its pinnacle in the 1920s, surely the most wildly creative decade of the twentieth century. The Bauhaus flourished in Germany, oblivious to the catastrophe to come. Modern to the core, Walter Gropius, Paul Klee, Wassily Kandinsky and others sought to unify the arts.[19] Painting, weaving, architecture, photography, sculpture, furniture, printing and bookbinding, metalworking, stained glass, theatre, dance, pottery—the Bauhaus embraced all of these and made of them a statement of the twentieth century aesthetic: lean, intellectual, geometric, functional, abstract, at once simple and complex, the bare bones of the universe made elegant and lively.

An occasional visitor in Germany during the 1920s was the Russian, El Lissitzky. He would travel from Moscow to edit a journal in Berlin, publish some lithographs or design a gallery in Hanover,[20] or exchange ideas in Düsseldorf where he met Moholy-Nagy of Hungary who later joined the Bauhaus.

Lissitzky was spreading the word about a remarkable movement called the Russian Avant-Garde. Torn between art for its own sake and art in the service of the state, its members supported the 1917 Revolution only to be brutally suppressed by it. They were far too vibrant and unconventional not to threaten Lenin. One was sent to a labor camp, others died young, some left the country and a few, no doubt with a painful sense of self-violation, disguised their work in accepted styles. But not before they had created a whole new aesthetic, mystical and worldly.

They found soul in geometry and vast reverberations in the square or the triangle. Some of them shunned the sphere. "[T]he sphere," wrote Lissitzky, "is the crystal of the universe, but we cannot do anything with it . . . since that is the final state (death); that is why we concentrate on the elements of the cube, which can always be reassembled and destroyed at will (life)."[21] Ironically, to reassemble and destroy at will became the dominant intention of the regime consolidating power in Russia. Only its leadership thrived on death, not life.

The Russian Avant-Garde included many women, some of them highly gifted if tinged by tragedy. Liubov Popova died at thirty-five after catching scarlet fever from her child and Olga Rozanova was dead of diphtheria at thirty-two before the high moment of the 1920s had even begun. Luckier was Natalia Goncharova who fled with her artist-lover to Paris before the revolution and lived a long, productive life. Recognized early, her work was seen in the 1913 Post-Impressionist show organized in London by Bloomsbury's Roger Fry.

Notoriety the Russian Avant-Garde certainly achieved, but still these artists worked largely in isolation, separated much of the time from the main currents of Europe. This may explain their great originality. As Haydn said, "I was cut off from the world, and so I had to become original."

While the Russian Avant-Garde struggled to survive, France bloomed. Picasso and Léger held forth in Paris. So did Mondrian, having just created the Dutch de Stijl group (which also abhorred the circle) in Holland. And there was Brancusi, like Mondrian a purist. And Matisse, ever enamored of lyrical, sensuous curves.

Picasso and Matisse drew often on elemental Asian and African motifs while Mondrian threw away everything but line and primary color. Brancusi sought sacred form and found it. Léger made the machine age elegant.

Some soared. Some dug deeply beneath the surface of the psyche. It was a moment so rich that French museums seldom saw reason to acquire outside their own country.

And in England, of course, there was Bloomsbury, reigned over by Virginia Woolf and Vanessa Bell with John Maynard Keynes garnering his own kind of glory. Together they and their compatriots produced unforgettable literature, economics, painting, and criticism. They also left behind letters, diaries and artifacts of a creative community that still inspires with its capacity for pleasure and life-long devotion.

The 1920s were overtaken by depression and war, and the century never recovered. The New York School of Abstract Expressionism was one of the few transcendent achievements in the years that followed. Pop

Art, Color Field painting, Minimalism, Conceptualism and the rest were marked by individual brilliance (Lichtenstein, Rauschenberg, Ellsworth Kelly) but not the kind of sustained fruition that creates a great culture, as the Impressionists did at the turn of the last century. To see how impotent painting has become in the Age of Limbo one had only to go to the Venice Biennale or the Whitney Biennial of the early 1990s. There artistic insight had degenerated into political and sexual fury.

Even so, apart from the fever of the last years of the century, Willem de Kooning, old, infirm and some would say demented, painted canvases of radiant loveliness. Ribbons of color, from the sunshine side of the spectrum, delicate yet vibrant, wave in the final breeze of an extraordinary life force. These pictures prove that creativity doesn't come always from the mind. It springs from another place.

In literature politics has produced some of the more lasting work of the post-war period. Elegant language, whose proper cargo is wisdom, has endured limbo on the strength of Boris Pasternak, Nadine Gordimer, Toni Morrison, and others who have used their gifts to illumine unspeakable wrongs.

Perhaps the most intuitive response to limbo has come from science. While orthodox practitioners carry on, sometimes spectacularly, pursuing the particulars of the Big Bang or the secrets of human genetics, others, especially in physics, are reaching out with admirable imagination to become the metaphor for the age, supplementing the creation story with the dream of the Unified Field which might be conceived of as Pure Consciousness. Once physics grew at the expense of philosophy. Now cosmologists have become the newest philosophers, leading the search for the origin of life and the nature of God. "Either theology is pure nonsense, a subject with no content," wrote Frank Tipler in his book *The Physics of Immortality*, "or else theology must ultimately become a branch of physics."[22]

Theology may never become a branch of physics, but science, even so, continues its embrace of religion (confirming the worst fears of some mentioned in Chapter Four), and it's finding an appreciative public. In 1995 the Templeton Prize for Progress in Religion—$1 million—went to Paul Davies, a mathematical physicist from Australia whose works include *The Mind of God*, an inquiry into "the origin of the universe, order in nature and the nature of human consciousness." Davies was the third physicist to be so honored in a lineup that included Mother Teresa;

Billy Graham; Lord Jakobovits, former chief rabbi of Britain and the Commonwealth; and neo-conservative Catholic scholar Michael Novak.[23] So science and religion are joining forces against limbo.

That doesn't mean all is cozy. Science and religion are about to collide over the Human Genome Project, a $3 billion effort (headed at one time by Dr. James Watson of Chapter Four) at the National Institutes of Health. Its mission is to discover the 100,000 genes that encode human life. Researchers are identifying the genes that cause a predisposition to a myriad of disorders from Huntingdon's disease and osteoporosis to cancers of the colon, breast and ovaries to diabetes, heart disease and mental illness.

What certainly will develop is a raging debate over how to use this explosive knowledge. Some theologians fear that suffering is about to disappear forever, thwarting God's rigorous plan for human instruction. But really, they needn't be concerned. People will always find a way to suffer. If they can't grieve over the early death of a spouse through war or childbirth, they'll try divorce. If they can't wear themselves down with long treks over wild, frontier territory, they'll embrace corporate moves from city to city, suppressing the need for community. And so on. Divine Intention that human beings learn through adversity is not likely to be overcome, even by post-modern science.

But still there is agonizing. Some worry that doctors someday will be able to detect susceptibility to critical illnesses in the womb. Should that fetus then be aborted? Or might genetic intervention someday make it possible to eliminate the prospect of serious disease for that person-in-progress? There are those who fear the answer may be yes. Stanley Hauerwas, a theology professor at Duke University Divinity School, deplored such a possibility, pointing out that "you can't eliminate retardation without eliminating the retarded."[24]

Quite so. But why would he insist that some unlucky people be retarded? To permit those who are normal to feel the satisfaction of helping? But surely there will be other opportunities for compassion. There's no need for the cruelty that would sentence some to conditions that could be averted.

Then there's the question of routine genetic testing. Would this be a good thing? Especially if there's little that can be done by doctors about a potentially adverse result but much that can be done by employers or insurance companies to punish those with worrisome mutations?[25]

Probably widespread genetic testing should await the ability of medical science to help those with bad reports.

Jessica Tuchman Mathews has framed many of the pertinent questions about genetics: "What will it mean for society when every child enters the world with hundreds of 'pre-existing conditions'? What will it mean for religion when innate characteristics become a matter of choice? . . . Should prospective employers and insurers have access to an individual's genetic profile? What about prospective spouses? . . . How will we cope with decades of enormous uncertainty as scientists sort out the interactions of the resulting genetic propensities with the environment?"[26]

And what about the amazing case of Dolly, the cloned sheep in Scotland? Chances are she will lead to great breakhroughs in pharmaceuticals and animal husbandry. But will she change the conception of humans? Cloning a person is already illegal in Britain and several other European nations as well as California, though scientists point out that the practice is almost impossible to police. Some, including Laurence Tribe of Harvard, argue that a ban on cloning would violate an individual's right to reproductive freedom.[27] Others feel a moral aversion to the idea, and their intuition should be heeded.

Once again, as if in reaction to what Havel has called "the first atheistic civilization in the history of humankind,"[28] science is pointing the way back to philosophy and theology, a journey strongly recommended by Pope John Paul II, who issued an encyclical in 1998 calling for faith and reason to work together against the "philosophy of nothing" spawned by the New Age. With the logic of Aquinas, the Pope stressed the importance of rigorous philosophy to keep the church from "withering into myth or superstition." He also urged that scientists not shrink from the great moral questions of the day, including questions arising from their own discoveries.[29]

In spite of their phenomenal discoveries, scientists are hardly working with the full force of their times behind them any more than Virginia Woolf was. Post-modern critics seem bent on destroying science and denying its accomplishments. Congress called an end to the superconducting super collider, not caring if it might mean the death knell for American physics, and now the reaction to advanced technology can be seen on all sides, beginning with the quest for alternative medicine.

Now the opposition comes not just from "religious fundamentalists who are the traditional foes of science," wrote physicist Robert Park, "but

[from] serious academics and writers who regard themselves as intellectuals." Standards formulated for teaching history in the mid-1990s made no mention of science, he lamented, except "in a list of professions from which women have been systematically excluded" and as a costly byproduct (weapons research) of the Cold War. Post-modern hostility to science has led to a renewed passion for magic, said Park, citing the National Institutes of Health's interest in "various magical cures, from 'Lokota medicine wheels' to 'mental healing at a distance,' as though they deserve serious attention."[30] He refused to concede that such methods may have value in the *art* of healing, but of course he is right in insisting that they are not science.

The truth is not that science is dead (it isn't) but that the Enlightenment has overreached itself. And as Carlos Fuentes observed, "reason that knows not its limits is a form of madness."[31] So the resurgence of magic should be neither surprising nor alarming. Properly understood, it is a reaching beyond the strictures of logic to rediscover irrational sense.

"Sleight-of-hand and escape artists, spiritualists and mediums appear whenever society feels powerless or overwhelmed," explained Dr. Lionel Tiger, an anthropologist. George Rosenbaum, a market research executive, added that society is "hungry for simple belief systems." He pointed to the "disaffection with traditional religions and [the] growing appeal of mysticism" as manifestations of the struggle to accommodate "huge leaps in technology and a revolution in the ethnic and social fabric of life."[32]

So technological and social changes are accentuating the age of limbo and calling forth in response a taste for magic, including the "magical realism" of writers such as Toni Morrison, Gabriel García Márquez, and Isabel Allende. Limbo, it seems, can be attributed in part to unassimilated transformations.

As the century slouched to a close, it was marked by an obsession with values—not principles, not ethics, not standards, but values. Unlike truths, values are inherently subjective. Dr. Frederick Wilhelmsen, a professor of philosophy and politics at the University of Dallas, said that prior to 1900 nobody used the word "value" except in economics. It was unheard of by Plato, Aristotle and Aquinas. They spoke in terms of principles, virtues, reasoned conclusions.[33]

The word "value," he explained, stems from subjectivist thinking that developed among German idealists who saw values as a projection of one's own understanding of the world. Thus values were divorced from reality. The West's substitution of "values" for "the good," he further observed, demonstrates a gradual abandonment of objective reality as a criterion for judgment. And why not, when so much is surreal anyway?

So "values" is a weak word born of post-modern limbo where nothing is as it seems. Friendships, marriages, standards and work dance in and out of existence, like particles, bubbling up from the quantum realm for awhile and then returning.

No wonder some philosophers see in physics a flight forever from first principles. It will take life beyond limbo to reconcile the quantum realm with objective reality, to move from "values" to something more substantial.

So concerned were some at century's end to impose control on life they began to see it as a drama, directed by human will. They revived the word "scenario" from the Nixon era and added to it the notion that any situation will "play out" in true narrative style. As Shakespeare said, "The play's the thing in which we catch the conscience of the king"— and all else as well, thus bringing order, however artificial, to complex circumstances.

But not everything can be ascribed to human will. Some feel forces in the world that cause them to believe events are "driven." They are market-driven, advertiser-driven, or politically driven. It's intoxicating to those who see themselves as shapers of experience. They are the ones for whom the word "driven" is most compelling. To them it has come to signify a "triumph of the will," as Leni Riefenstahl called her famous film for Hitler, and it is a high form of hubris.

Journalists have taken the cycle of the seasons and turned it into a frenetic round of "news cycles," truncated, unnatural and thoughtless. What once brought the comfort of rhythmically recurring heat and cold, leaves and branches, now brings only fabricated vignettes, playing themselves out in 24-hour snippets, spun like sugar to prevent insulin shock. And why must public business be spun into fruit loops of fantasy? To keep the play going.

And not just going, but "going forward." This phrase, so prevalent in business, is designed to obliterate the past, to insist on optimism as a discipline. Optimism, after all, is the preferred antidote to fear. And fear there was after storms in Asia threatened to sweep across Latin America, spreading "moral hazards," which might attend the bailing out of imprudent bankers but which really bespoke anxiety about the random retribution global markets can deliver. Perhaps a little liturgy deploring "moral hazards" would keep bad trouble at bay. Meanwhile leaders of the developed world began to talk of a new financial "architecture," an edifice to shelter established interests from treacherous, fickle flows of capital and collapsing currencies.

The atmosphere grew if not dark then uncertain. It prompted a look for light, a quest for the reassurance of color. A biography of the Bundy brothers, McGeorge and William, was called *The Color of Truth*. A television commercial referred to "the color of trust." And politicians continued to search for "defining moments." But there were few to be found. Because the sickness of the late twentieth century is the loss of authenticity, the loss of defining essences. The echo of the void can be heard in the language.[34]

You could tell the Age of Limbo was at hand when the times turned turbulent. Peter Drucker warned us this was coming in 1980.[35] He could not have been more prescient. Within ten years new technology (in the last great creative spurt of the century) and the pressures of world trade were forcing drastic disciplines on corporations. Desperate, they reached back to an early concept of Drucker's—people as cost centers—to justify a wave of reductions that shell-shocked Americans. They called it "downsizing" and recalled with praise Joseph Schumpeter's idea of "creative destruction."

By the nineties work, sometimes at two or three jobs, had become so demanding that people could not tolerate any commitments beyond job and family. Once famous as volunteers, they stopped joining charitable organizations and withdrew from community life. They were even bowling alone.[36]

The problem at century's end, according to Drucker, was the erosion of basic ideas that had sustained the previous three hundred years. First came *laissez-faire* in the 1770s, the liberal dream of Adam Smith, and it lasted until 1873, when the "Vienna stock market crash and short-lived panics in Paris, London, Frankfurt and New York" brought forth a new kind of politics. Formulated in response to the Industrial Revolution, it relied on "security and protection." "Within ten years of the Vienna crash," wrote Drucker, "German Chancellor Otto Von Bismarck had invented national health insurance and compulsory old-age insurance. Within twenty years Marxist socialists had become the largest political party in every major country of continental Europe."[37] In the United States the Interstate Commerce Commission was created to regulate the railroads (a marked departure from the unrestricted market), and anti-trust laws were born along with state statutes governing securities.

The 1880s saw the rise of the populists and the first anti-business movement in the U.S. Then followed Teddy Roosevelt's progressive initiative which sought to strengthen the federal government as a counter-vailing power to corporations. His dispensation, augmented by Franklin Roosevelt's New Deal and Lyndon Johnson's Great Society endured until the late 1960s and early seventies, the period, said Drucker, in which the twentieth century came to an early end. The Enlightenment in govern-ment began to fade, he argued, as faith in collective action gave way to utter bewilderment. Even politicians on the left, from Bill Clinton to François Mitterand to Boris Yeltsin, started casting about for market, not centralized, solutions. "The period 1968-73," observed Drucker, "is a divide fully comparable to 1873. Whereas 1873 marked the end of *laissez-faire*, 1973 marked the end of the era in which government was the 'pro-gressive' cause, the instrument embodying the principles of the Enlightenment. The 'oil shock,' the floated dollar, and the student rebellions across the West set us adrift from the century in which we had lived."[38]

As Rebecca West would say, it took a while for the modern economy to hit ground and break its neck. It happened finally with the rule of Britain's Margaret Thatcher in the 1980s, and was confirmed in the U.S. when Republicans took control of Congress in 1994. Since then it has been apparent that the economic giant of the twentieth century, John Maynard Keynes, has become obsolete.[39] No longer can a government expect to control its national economy through Keynesian methods of managing money, credit and interest rates. The system is too fluid now, the borders too porous, one market too blurred with another, for the kind of stimulus favored by Keynes not to be dissipated. Indeed, the Reagan tax cuts of the early 1980s failed to stimulate the economy in the way that had been expected because Americans spent the money on imported goods.[40]

The new day becomes even more apparent when we realize that raw materials have been uncoupled from industry, which relies more heavily on innovation and design than on components. Manufacturing has become uncoupled from labor, as the robot and other technologies have soared. The "real" economy of goods and services has become uncoupled from the money economy.[41] This became clear when the American GDP grew, but Wall Street, fearing inflation and higher interest rates, despaired. Then, in a turnabout, investment managers cheered when a company laid off thousands of workers. It was the triumph of Schumpeter.

Today investment and facilities turn up anywhere in the world where wages and skills are advantageous, dictating trade patterns instead of following them. Currency exchanges and financial transactions call their own tune, quite apart from production.[42] In short, the autonomous nation-state, on which the Keynesian approach depended, has eroded and with it has gone the confidence with which workers in developed nations once greeted the morning.

The creative task of the next century, which Drucker said has long since begun, will be to devise new forms of security as Bismarck did over one hundred years ago.[43] It won't do simply to declare these times "Darwinian" as one chief executive did[44] and let it go at that. Even more crucial will be the kind of innovation that can propel the world economy into a wholly new golden age.

A sure sign of limbo in the mid-1990s has been the ascendancy of the message. Politicians are frantic to stay "on message." Attorney Johnnie Cochran urged the jury in the first, criminal O.J. Simpson trial to "send a message" to the Los Angeles Police Department. The Nobel Committee dispatched a message to France and China, both testing nuclear weapons, when it awarded the Peace Prize for 1995 to Joseph Rotblat, a physicist who worked on the first atom bomb at Los Alamos, then spent much of his life opposing strategic weapons.

Certainly this was a worthwhile thing to do. And France and China should have been made to feel the disapproval of the world. And apparently they did. They conducted their last nuclear tests in 1996.

But whenever the prize is awarded for anything except extraordinary individual achievement, it loses a certain influence, the influence born of the power of personal example. And justice cannot be done if it's applied to too many issues at once. Certainly racism in the L. A. Police Department is important, but it was not the issue that cried out for justice in that criminal trial. The issue that cried out for justice was two brutal murders. But the message often obscures the true issue. That's what it's intended to do.

The cult of the messenger began with a Canadian named Marshall

McLuhan who wrote a book in 1967 called *The Medium is the Message*.[45] Though he produced a brilliant explication of the electronic age, some of his most provocative insights have suffered from drastic reduction. So obsessed have people become with media they can't imagine any other, richer interpretation. Significant occasions that might best be understood as deep experiences are seen instead as prepackaged messages.

Former Alabama Governor George Wallace was among the first to pick up McLuhanism. Running for president on the American Party ticket in 1968, he urged voters to "send them a message in Washington." But the victor that year, Richard Nixon, had an attorney general, John Mitchell, who still believed in action. "Watch what we do," he advised, "not what we say."

While that smacked of deception, at least Mitchell, for all his glaring deficiencies, assumed responsibility for *doing* something. That gave way twenty-five years later to members of government determined not to "step on the message," to be sure everybody is "singing from the same sheet of music." Gone too often today is the intention, much less the expectation, of accomplishing anything.

Contrast today's apostles of the message with former Prime Minister Margaret Thatcher, who called herself a "conviction politician." Certainly that's a far stronger thing to be than merely "on message." In spite of her efforts, and those of Ronald Reagan, the whole of Western culture has been infected with the cult of the messenger. Among the casualties have been objective truth and individual attainment. Doesn't sending a "signal" or a "message" imply something contrived, something crafted by a crafty person and transmitted to the public? Doesn't it ignore the truth that leadership rests finally on something intrinsic to leaders themselves, something larger and deeper than a "message"?

Now everything and everybody stand for something else, a distortion of symbolism. Nothing and no one stand on their own. We have a new syllogism foretold by McLuhan: The medium is the message. The person is the medium. Therefore the person is the message. And only the message. Much has been lost to limbo.

In American politics, limbo has been marked by a loss of intellectual poise and a rush to the fringes of thought, as if extreme positions would bring release. As the new millennium approaches nothing would be more helpful than a revival of moderation. It's important to honor the person who takes the middle ground, and holds the middle ground, yielding neither to the right nor to the left, acknowledging the strengths of both, beguiled by the blandishments of neither. It's absurd to castigate voices of the sane center as dull, uninspired, devoid of the passion of politics. They, after all, are the cornerstone of civil society.

Moderation took a beating during the presidencies of Nixon, Ford and Carter. All three were men of the middle, but they were history's holding action while the right wing gathered its forces. Then began the fall from fashion of centrists who were suddenly despised by Republicans in the same way white liberals had come to be loathed by African Americans.

So off into the wilderness went the left-and-right-of-center while the new conservatives presided over the pauper's burial of liberalism itself. Gone was tact in political discourse. Gone was that fine distinction between public and private life. Gone was the honorable effort to gloss over differences. Raw emotion, as tasteless as possible, was the order of the hour. Subjects once confined to the gynecologist's office became the stuff of national debate. Agonizing issues of race were exacerbated.

It started as a justifiable reaction by conservatives to the excesses of liberalism. But conservatives went too far. They developed an alarming tolerance for intolerance. Suddenly anything could be said and it was acceptable. Then, predictably, came a counterreaction and a plea for renewed delicacy, but this effort was overtaken by political correctness.

What was urgently needed by century's end was an understanding of moderation. Few seemed to know, for example, that moderation is not the same thing as pragmatism. A pragmatist is interested in what works. A moderate seeks the golden mean of Aristotle. Both are useful, but moderation has the higher claim.

What was needed also was the passion of the centrist—a passion for justice and moral order, a passion for civility, which is not the absence of passion as some suppose. It is the sublimation of passion to the demands of creativity. It is the necessary condition for the return of genius.[46]

Also lost in the age of limbo has been a sense of history, at least in the United States. Too many Americans have no acquaintance with the past, which, according to Frederick Turner, "breaks the shackles of the present in order to create the future."[47]

A woman who conducted tours through the White House reported that freshmen in Congress, elected in the Republican sweep of 1994, had no notion of Dolley Madison or Abigail Adams or the signing of the bills that created Lyndon Johnson's War on Poverty much less Franklin Roosevelt's New Deal. In flailing against Medicare, Medicaid and help for the poor, they were eager to destroy the work of four generations without the slightest idea where it came from or why, or what conditions might reassert themselves after the bloodletting. They believed, the guide said, that American history began with Ronald Reagan.

The trouble lay not in the trite contention that those who are ignorant of the past are condemned to repeat it. It's doubtful that the same circumstances present themselves twice in the great flow of human affairs even though cycles certainly can be discerned over time. Hence Bosnia was not Vietnam all over again. There was no reason to fear, as many did, automatic over-extension, or that other banality, a quagmire.

All the same, history can instruct through analogy. That's one reason for studying it, but not the main reason. We study history mainly to stabilize our minds, compose our emotions and harmonize our spirits with those of generations that have gone before. We study history to civilize our passions and fulfill ourselves as people of the ever renewing national covenant. We study history for a sense of continuity and grace so that we might be ballast in the boat of our own times.

Though Americans were alarmingly rootless by century's end, there were encouraging signs of real interest in the past, including literature as well as history. "Sense and Sensibility" was not only a successful film; it also appeared on the *New York Times* paperback best-seller list. One observer noted that movie makers started turning to Jane Austen and Shakespeare because they had identified a niche called "chick flicks"— that is, films for women. If that was the case, it hardly negated the effort. Women are people, after all, and active agents in the world, and they've certainly saved the culture more than once.

But during the 1990s, the aura of earlier eras held little appeal for members of Congress. Their utter lack of respect for those who struggled to bring them to their own moment resulted in a legislative body that had lost its powers of deliberation. The genius of statecraft must wait now for the past to reassert itself and break the shackles of the present limbo.

The cultural deprivation of the last years of the century could be seen in the void on Broadway which had to be filled with revivals. It also was evident in the unexpected turning to Magritte. Not only did the Metropolitan Museum showcase his work, Magritte's eerie, Surrealist vision also surfaced in the sets of "The Barber of Seville" at the Dallas

Opera and "A Midsummer Night's Dream" in New York as well as in a slide presentation by Dr. Joe Goldstein, a Nobel Prize winner, at Southwestern Medical School.

Surrealists emerged in Paris in the 1920s, that most fecund of decades, to declare the ascendancy of the dream. "Their allegiances derived from literature, from medicine, from psychoanalysis, and from the ideology of political revolution. 'Beauty must be convulsive,' wrote their chief spokesman, poet and critic Andre Bréton, 'or it will cease to be.'"[48]

Beauty scarcely had a speaking part in the work of Magritte. He was a man off-balance, a prophet of deep disequilibrium, looking to dreams to restore a ruptured world. Small wonder he seemed suddenly so pertinent in the mid-1990s, when "surreal" became the watchword, replacing "unreal," by which was meant experience exaggerated beyond belief, for good or ill. But "surreal" had come to mean weird. It described the perceptive apparatus of an uncertain people, making do with unreasonable facsimiles of real life.[49]

At the same moment, there were certain weddings in America that exuded an aura distinctly Pre-Raphaelite, as if something sensual and true were trying to break through. The scene in its factual exactitude, shorn of all pretty conventions of painting, is what the Pre-Raphaelites tried to give. Medieval in tone, the Pre-Raphaelites considered nature, as John Ruskin would put it, the embodiment of moral truth.[50] That these American brides in their scrumptious simplicity should reach for the English aesthetic of 100 years ago suggests a wish for honest loveliness in a culture gone phony.

Those were spring and summer brides. There were others, in winter, who turned to the High Renaissance and the Edwardians for inspiration. They too unconsciously were seeking to shore up their own uncertain time with the texture and elegance of a more solid epoch.

There were other signs of the culture struggling to right itself. By reviving the songs of World War II, Andrea Marcovicci, a torch singer, helped her audiences recover the strengths of that era. Sprinkling her C.D.s with the poems of Edna St. Vincent Millay, she scored a triumph of style, intelligence and taste. Not for her the vocal perfection of Ella Fitzgerald or Karen Akers. Marcovicci has achieved an artistry so hard won, so moving, that some have likened her to Frank Sinatra, the true sound of two generations. Only Marcovicci is more complex, as she would have to be to represent her own moment with such startling fidelity.

She is grappling with the deficiencies of the age. And she is using the past to break the shackles of the present.

Where Marcovicci addresses a dream world, Tammy Wynette sang for those who no longer believe in romance, if they ever did. Marcovicci's women are forever falling in love. Wynette's are committed —for better or worse, usually worse—and they're trying to find a way to see it through. Tammy Wynette's songs tell little stories, of waitresses in bar rooms yearning for a man to "take me to your world"; of mothers coping with the pain of D.I.V.O.R.C.E. (Andrew Lloyd Webber picked up on this number in *Starlight Express* with U.N.C.O.U.P.L.E.D.); of wives relying on "good lovin'" to "keep the home together." These situations are less complicated than Marcovicci's: Feminine dependence is clear.[51]

And, of course, when Tammy Wynette died, in 1998, her signature song, "Stand By Your Man," had caught hold of the culture. Political wives from Colorado to Georgia to Washington, D.C. were loyally, publicly supporting their husbands as they confessed to unfortunate affairs.

"Stand By Your Man" was first recorded in 1968, two years before the Women's Liberation Movement began its urgent effort to transform male-female relations. At twenty-five, Wynette already had done quite a lot to liberate herself, having left the husband she married eight years before and with whom she lived in dreary poverty to rear three little girls on her own as a hairdresser. With as much courage and spunk as Betty Friedan ever could wish, Wynette had made her way to Nashville and sung herself into a recording contract.

Success came quickly and lasted a long time. Fans responded to Tammy Wynette's elemental power. Close to the earth, she sang of life as it really was and celebrated a kind of womanly nobility. She gave meaning to lives that otherwise might have been unbearable. Presenting the hard truth that feminists were fighting to revolutionize, or avoid, she reminded those who did flee into intellect or spirit of all they had renounced.

Tammy Wynette renounced nothing. Possessed by Hera, she married relentlessly, five times, and had four children, acquiring two more who belonged to her last husband, George Richey. Touring, she used to say, was "a great escape." And, one could imagine, there was plenty to escape from.

One thing she could never leave behind was bad health. Several abdominal surgeries sent her eventually to the Betty Ford Clinic to conquer an addiction to prescription painkillers.

Her life was not good for her voice. The amazing strength in the upper register held up only through her thirties. When she did "Stand By Your Man" on the television show *Capitol* in 1986, other singers backed Wynette on the telling title words where eighteen years before she had belted them out with such authority no one could match her. But she had developed an artistry that more than made up for the loss of youth. Her hair shorter, her clothes more chic, she created an elegant recollection of her early triumph.

Tammy Wynette did not manage to stand by her man until the last twenty years of her life, but that may be because she had such trouble determining who her man really was. The husband of her teen marriage was doomed to fade when she grew up. So was the song writer/hotel clerk in Nashville who could not withstand the competition of country star George Jones. He should have been the one, and would have been had he not wrecked their life together with drugs and drinking. For a brief moment, she flirted with other worlds, first with Burt Reynolds, whom she did not marry, then with a real estate man in Nashville, whom she did. It lasted only forty-four days. She turned finally to George Richey, who became her manager, which is what she had needed all along.

Turbulence, success, and setbacks did not sever Tammy Wynette's essential connection to her times. Anybody who wants to understand American women in the last three decades of the century must listen to her.

Less successful in coping with the culture has been Michael Jackson whose concerts, at his zenith in the 1980s, seemed to elicit from his young fans not sexual excitement but a yearning for Armageddon and a final release from the tension of limbo. He has used historical gimmicks, such as pulling Excalibur from the stone, but he has given no real thought to Arthur and hence has failed to create the resonance that Jackie Kennedy accomplished when she evoked Camelot to characterize her husband's brief reign at the White House. Jackson's gifts have been tossed about by the seas of limbo, unguided by any serious navigation, where Jackie Kennedy Onassis survived much to become the most emblematic American woman of the century, surpassed only by Eleanor Roosevelt, the greatest woman of American history.

Jackie Kennedy was an introvert in a relentlessly gregarious family that mirrored a nation obsessed with outgoingness. She kept her composure in politics, which has driven lesser women to the bottle and worse. She transformed a difficult marriage to a dazzling young president into a union that illumined the world.[52]

She overcame an unlikely second marriage from which she got more than money. She got the name that would free her from premature sainthood. As Jackie O., tarnished yet burnished by the Greek experience, she truly came into her own. And through the turmoil of those years, she reared two children to responsible adulthood, though one would die tragically.

She was famous for bringing the arts to the White House, both as historical restorer and as impresario of fabulous performances. Her greatest gift, however, was for the language. Indeed, she might have been a fine writer had circumstances been different. But writing, no matter what the subject, would have forced her to reveal herself as writers always do. That was unthinkable. So editing suited her better.

When Jackie Onassis died, her son, John Kennedy, Jr., reported that she was "surrounded by her friends and family and her books and the people and things that she loved." In the end, it was books, more than art objects, that held her heart.

Much has been made of the paradox of this intensely private, dramatically public woman. But actually there is no paradox at all. Jackie Onassis was in every way a public figure, but she understood in the European sense the difference between public and private life.

Richard Sennett explained it well in *The Fall of Public Man*. Writing about London and Paris in the seventeenth and eighteenth centuries, he pointed out that ordinary people in those days had a rich public life. When they went to the theatre, they didn't simply sit and watch. They hooted. They hissed. If they wished, they mounted the stage themselves and participated in the show. Women wore grand hats adorned with their husband's vocation—a small ship, perhaps, for someone in maritime trade. Private clothes were looser. In fact they were negligée.[53]

That critical distinction now is gone. There is no public life any longer. Utterly lost are intelligent argument, spirited debate, satisfying ritual (except at funerals). In their place is private life, exposed in a way that is unseemly and destructive. Jackie Onassis grasped this completely. For her, public life was a work of art, designed to support and enrich civil society. Private life was to be kept to one's self. She thought carefully about how she lived, and she knew the value of simplicity. As once was said of Edith Wharton she, "fought her way through to some kind of choice."

At century's end another feminine presence startled the world with her power to bear the projections of the era. Diana, Princess of Wales, carried the hopes and anxieties of women everywhere. They relied on her resiliency, her moxie, her style. In her life they found their own lives, in her failure, their own failures, in her survival their own struggle to survive. Then suddenly, on August 31, 1997, when she didn't survive a car crash in Paris, it was devastating to millions who had searched for their own fate in her's.[54]

It is not unusual for people to try to clarify their feelings through figures larger than themselves. In the Middle Ages it was through the saints. Then kings and queens. Then heads of government. And more recently, through sports and movie stars. With Diana they returned to royalty to find an idol, but Diana was more than a princess. For women she embodied the aspirations of the age—to be one's own person in a way that does not exclude motherhood or men.

Diana was a woman of her time, of our time. She couldn't conform to eighteenth century ideas of monarchy. Some insist that she should have understood the sexual habits of royalty. Mistresses are well represented in the annals of British kings. Wives do their duty and carry on. But Diana could not. She was too sensitive, her feelings too deep as well as too close to the surface. And she was too proud for that kind of arrangement not to do her serious harm.

She turned against herself in a fit of bulimic gorging and purging, seeking nourishment, then distrusting it. And she turned against her husband in affairs that brought her more hurt. Her story is not unlike that of women all over the industrialized world, struggling to make sense of modern life, when the old disciplines had given way to agonizing opportunity.

Even after her divorce, Diana continued to live in the realm of a queen who, one observer said, can move through a garden party and expend less energy than Calvin Coolidge. A retentive personality, unable to give or to take, Elizabeth II practices an economy of emotion that must have been punishing for the princess with the overflowing feelings.

That same queen gave Britain a son similarly restrained by debilitating inhibitions that burst their boundaries from time to time, usually with Camilla Parker Bowles, a divorced horsewoman. It is she who has been his constant love. But just as the British were about to write off Diana and accept Camilla as Charles' morganatic wife, Diana died. All the fresh vivacity that captivated the world, and the admirable savvy and spunk that enabled her to win a $23 million settlement from the Crown of England, suddenly dissolved to reveal what she always was and had to be—a tragic heroine.

The day she died, Diana told a London journalist that she planned to withdraw from public life within three months. But she had made this proclamation at least once before. There was no real possibility of retreat. She had constructed herself as a public person, painfully, with little education and no one close to help her. She couldn't walk away from the self she had created at enormous personal cost.

She was surely well named—for Diana, goddess of the hunt and of childbirth, one unto herself. But she was also Apollonian, both sacred and profane. She loved the high life, but she was drawn to human suffering. Had she lived, she would have been forced by her own nature to integrate the two into a more complex maturity.

Both sensual and compassionate, she went straight for the essential issues, instinctively. She didn't intellectualize them. Without knowing it, she followed the dictum of the Zen abbot who said, "Don't think about the answer. Go out and become the answer." That's what Diana, who yearned to be "Queen of Hearts," was trying, imperfectly, to do when her own heart, unable to get enough blood, enough nourishment, gave out in a Paris hospital in the early hours of a dark summer dawn.

Then followed a funeral that has been called "more Medieval than modern."[55] It returned the world to the seed-bed of the century.

Diana, Jackie, Tammy. All three came young to glory, then died too soon. Tammy Wynette sprang from the earth, Princess Diana from the spirit, and Jackie Onassis stood for authenticity. Tammy taught women how to live with faithless men and therein find meaning. Jackie did. Diana could not, even to serve the monarchy. Tammy and Jackie did not expect much of men. Diana, a generation younger, did.

As the age that began in Sarajevo drew to a close, negotiators, exhausted from the agonizing effort to end the Bosnian War, concluded that peace was more important than justice, that it mattered more to be normal than moral.[56] But normalcy couldn't last. The Balkans erupted again, in Kosovo, bringing a bloody end to a hundred years of horror. Debilitated by the Great Depression, demoralized by the Holocaust and Stalin's labor camps, dispirited by the Cold War and its denouement in the former and present Yugoslavia, the epoch ended where it had begun, as Moynihan noted, in a despondent state of listless ambiguity.

The decomposition evident since the 1960s no doubt will be compost for a new age.[57] And there is every reason for hope. As Louise Cowan said, "After we get through the violence we're going toward a greater sense of community, a more feminine society, the end of the age of dynamic growth and [the beginning of] a society that perfects itself instead of inventing new things."[58]

No doubt invention will go on, technology will continue its amazing trajectory, but not as the primary instrument of transformation. That will occur on a deeper level, as creativity—which has its origins always in the community, whether it's a pueblo, a Gothic cathedral, or the thinking of Freud—springs forth once more to engender human harmony. Beauty will indeed save the world, as Dostoevsky predicted, and the twenty-first century, as Malraux prophesied, "will be spiritual or it will not be."[59] Faith in the essential rightness of the universe will endure, having been tempered, one must hope, by adversity into wisdom. But adversity cannot do its saving work unless the faith holds. That is the lesson of the twentieth century. May it sustain the genius of the next generation as it struggles free from limbo to create the age to come.

Endnotes

CHAPTER ONE

[1] John Darnton, "50 Years After War, Historians See Era's End," *New York Times* 7 May 1995. See also Eugene D. Genovese, "The Squandered Century," *The New Republic* 17 Apr. 1995: 38. This review of *The Age of Extremes: A History of the World, 1914-1991* by Eric Hobsbawn notes that an estimated 187 million people—as many as 10 percent of the population of 1990—"were killed or allowed to die by human decision" between 1914 and 1990. In "The Charms of NATO," *New York Review of Books* 15 Jan. 1998, Václav Havel put the figure at 200 million people who died in wars or concentration camps during the twentieth century. See also "When Children Are Soldiers," *New York Times* 5 July 1998.

[2] Gustav Niebuhr, "Unitarians Striking Chord of Spirituality: Church's Shift Mirrors a Trend in Society," *New York Times* 8 Dec. 1996.

[3] I am indebted for this insight to Thomas Moore, author of *The Care of the Soul*.

[4] Daniel Cattau, "Episcopal diocese's office is exorcized," *Dallas Morning News* 10 Oct. 1993.

[5] Barbara Tuchman, *A Distant Mirror: The Calamitous 14th Century* (New York: Alfred A. Knopf, 1978). Quotations are from front flap of jacket and p. 112.

[6] Richard Bernstein, "The Inquisition: A Spanish Model for a Final Solution," *New York Times* 23 Aug. 1995. See also Richard L. Kagan, "Article of Faith?" *New York Times Book Review* 27 Aug. 1995: 15-16.

[7] John F. Burns, "With Old Skills and New, India Battles the Plague," *New York Times* 29 Sept. 1994. See also "Return of the Plague," *New York Times* 29 Sept. 1994.

[8] Factual information and quotations from Tuchman, 112-115, 123-125.

[9] Malcolm Godwin, *Angels: An Endangered Species* (New York: Simon & Schuster) 32. Timothy Jones, "Rumors of Angels," *Christianity Today* 5 Apr. 1993: 18-22. Nancy Gibbs, "Angels Among Us," *Time Magazine* 27 Dec. 1993: 56-65. "The counter-attack of God," *The Economist* 8 July 1995: 19-21.

[10] Karen Armstrong, *A History of God: The 4000-Year Quest of Judaism, Christianity and Islam* (New York: Alfred A. Knopf, 1993) 3, 29. See also Angela Tilby, *Soul: God, Self and the New Cosmology* (New York: Doubleday) 99.

[11] C.G. Jung, *Modern Man in Search of a Soul* (San Diego: Harcourt Brace Jovanovich, 1933).

[12] Peter Steinfels, "Witch Trial Held in New England," *New York Times* 1 May 1996. The controversy, apparently, stemmed more from real estate than spiritualism.

[13] Marlise Simons, "France Under the Spell of Druids?" *New York Times* 30 Apr. 1996.

[14] John Horgan, *The End of Science: Facing the Limits of Knowledge in the Twilight of the Scientific Age* (Reading, Mass.: Helix-Addison-Wesley, 1996) 132.

[15] Malcolm Waldrop, *Complexity: The Emerging Science at the Edge of Order and Chaos* (New York: Simon & Schuster, 1992) 120-125, 133.

[16] Michael J. Behe, "Darwin Under the Microscope," *New York Times* 29 Oct. 1996.

[17] Horgan 173.

[18] Francis Fukuyama, *The End of History and the Last Man* (New York: Avon Books, 1992) xi-xxiii. See also Horgan 64, 71-76, 149.

[19] Horgan 14-15, 23-24, 57-58, 62-63.

[20] G.K. Chesterton, *Saint Thomas Aquinas: "The Dumb Ox"* (New York: Doubleday, 1956). Quotations from Chesterton in this and following paragraphs from pp. 24-27, 32-33.

[21] Tilby 149.

[22] Quotations by Dr. Schubert Ogden are from a telephone interview in 1994.

[23] Tuchman front flap of jacket.

CHAPTER TWO

In my discussion of the life, writing, and influence of Sigmund Freud, I am indebted to Peter Gay, *Freud: A Life for Our Time* (New York: Anchor-Doubleday, 1989). Unless otherwise attributed, information and quotations pertaining to Freud's life refer to this excellent study.

[1] Agnes de Mille, "Measuring the Steps of a Giant," *New York Times* 7 Apr. 1991.
[2] This is from a speech by Ada Louise Huxtable in Dallas in 1976. The Martha Graham quote is from "The Shape of Achievement, In the Artist's Own Words," *New York Times* 7 Apr. 1991.
[3] Anna Kisselgoff, "Martha Graham Dies at 96; A Revolution in Dance," *New York Times* 2 Apr. 1991.
[4] Harold Bloom, *The Western Canon* (New York: Harcourt Brace, 1994) 373, 375.
[5] Carl E. Schorske, *Fin-de-Siècle Vienna* (New York: Alfred A. Knopf, 1980) 4-5.
[6] Frederic Morton, *A Nervous Splendor* (Boston: Little, Brown, 1979) 219-235. I have drawn on his account of the relationship and suicide of Prince Rudolf and Mary Vetsera.
[7] Schorske 67, 118.
[8] Bryan Gilliam, "For Bruckner, a Vague Nazi Aura Persists," *New York Times* 20 Oct. 1996.
[9] Schorske 116-120, 133-146.
[10] Paul Gray, "The Assault on Freud," *Time* 29 Nov. 1993: 47.
[11] Irvin Molotsky, "Freud Show Delayed Amid Criticism," *New York Times* 6 Dec. 1995. Dinitia Smith, "Freud May Be Dead, But His Critics Still Kick," *New York Times* 10 Dec. 1995.
[12] Quoted in Clark 4.
[13] Lee Cullum. Interview with Robert Coles for KERA-TV and KDTN-TV, the public television stations in Dallas-Fort Worth, 1992.
[14] Clark 12.
[15] Sigmund Freud, *Civilization and Its Discontents*, trans. James Strachey (New York: W.W. Norton, 1961) 11, 19, 23, 28
[16] Ernest Becker, *The Denial of Death* (New York: The Free Press, 1973) 204.
[17] This came from a conversation with Thomas Moore at the Dallas Institute for Humanities and Culture in 1993.
[18] Arthur Miller, *Timebends, A Life* (New York: Harper & Row, 1987) 321.
[19] C.G. Jung, "Crazy Times," *New York Times* 19 Nov. 1993. This is an unpublished letter, dated 12 Nov. 1959 from Jung to Ruth Topping, a Chicago social worker.
[20] Clark 116. Harold Bloom has insisted that Freud found psychoanalysis thoroughly manifested in Shakespeare (2-3, 25, 331-394).
[21] As cited in C.G. Jung, *Modern Man in Search of a Soul* (San Diego: Harcourt Brace Jovanovich) 56.
[22] Quoted in Jung 67.
[23] Jung 73.
[24] Emily Yoffe, "How the Soul Is Sold," *New York Times Magazine* 23 Apr. 1995: 47.

CHAPTER THREE

I am indebted to several biographies in my discussion of major statesmen. A primary source in this chapter for the life and career of Theodore Roosevelt is William Henry Harbaugh, *Power and Responsibility: The Life and Times of Theodore Roosevelt* (New York: Farrar, Straus and Cudahy, 1961); of Franklin Delano Roosevelt, Doris Kearns Goodwin, *No Ordinary Time: Franklin and Eleanor Roosevelt: The Home Front in World War* (New York: Simon & Schuster, 1994); of Gandhi, Judith M. Brown, *Gandhi: A Prisoner of Hope* (New Haven: Yale UP, 1989); of Zhou Enlai, Han Suyin, *Eldest Son: Zhou Enlai and the Making of Modern China, 1898-1976* (New York: Hill and Wang, 1994); of Mikhail Gorbachev, Dusko Doder and Louise Branson, *Gorbachev, Heretic in the Kremlin* (New York: Penguin Books, 1991); of Winston Churchill, John Charmley, *Churchill: The End of Glory* (New York: Harcourt

Brace, 1993); and of Nelson Mandela, his autobiography, *Long Walk to Freedom* (Boston: Little, Brown, 1994). Unless otherwise attributed, information and quotations concerning these figures refer to these studies.

[1] Harbaugh is citing the view of Sir Bernard Pares.
[2] George Kennan, "The Balkan Crises: 1913 and 1993," *Introduction to The Other Balkan Wars* (Washington, D.C.: Carnegie Endowment, 1993) 3.
[3] Quoted in Timothy Egan, "Pacific Chiefs to meet where 2 worlds mix," *New York Times* 5 Nov. 1993.
[4] Michael J. Sandel, "America's Search for a New Public Philosophy," *Atlantic Monthly* 3 Mar. 1996: 60-62.
[5] Richard Hofstadter, *The American Political Tradition* (New York: Vintage Books, 1957) 220-233.
[6] Quoted in Hofstadter 222.
[7] Michael Lind, "The Southern Coup," *New Republic* 19 June 1995: 23.
[8] Hofstadter 210, 229. TR became obsessed with cultivating an "extreme militaristic masculine persona" after being "ridiculed as a 'Jane Dandy' and an 'Oscar Wilde' because of his 'Harvard-bred dandyism.'" See Tom Lutz, "Macho Men: Exploring Harvard's role in the construction of the late-19th-century manly ideal," *New York Times Book Review* 5 Jan. 1997.
[9] Quoted in Harbaugh 461-462.
[10] John Kenneth Galbraith, *The Great Crash 1929* (New York: Time, 1962) viii, 67, 144.
[11] Galbraith, Great Crash 9-12, 25-26, 48.
[12] Galbraith 74, 87-88, 100, 145.
[13] Quoted in Hofstadter 315.
[14] Hofstadter 315-316. Remark concerning FDR's temperament is from Geoffrey C. Ward, *A First-Class Temperament: The Emergence of Franklin Roosevelt* (New York: Harper and Row, 1989).
[15] Ray Choiniere and David Keirsey, *Presidential Temperament* (Del Mar, CA: Prometheus Nemesis, INTJ Books, 1992.) In this study they outlined four basic types: artisan, guardian, rationalist and idealist. Guardians (twenty of them have become president, including George Washington, Woodrow Wilson, Harry Truman, Jimmy Carter and George Bush) conserve communities and institutions and protect against loss. Rationals (8 presidents) are divided into two groups: architectural engineers of government (Thomas Jefferson, James Madison and Abraham Lincoln) who pursue their own inspiration (381) with utmost faith in logic and reason, and organizers (John and John Quincy Adams, Ulysses S. Grant, Herbert Hoover and Dwight Eisenhower) who take charge and push an enterprise toward well-defined results.(15-32, 157-169, 371-384.) There have been no idealist presidents, though Choiniere and Keirsey point out that Eleanor Roosevelt exerted enormous influence while her husband was in the White House. She is said to have been instrumental in conceiving his great, lasting domestic contribution, Social Security (493-534).
[16] Choiniere and Keirsey 76. According to the authors, "player artisans," such as Ronald Reagan, love excitement and the game. They perform with energy and flair. "Operator artisans," including the Roosevelts, Andrew Jackson, Lyndon Johnson, John F. Kennedy, and Bill Clinton, are masters at manipulation and maneuver. All artisans believe they live charmed lives and indeed do have nine lives if not more. This explains Franklin Roosevelt's remarkable resilience (see 15-32.).
[17] Hofstadter 316-317, 332, 328.
[18] Goodwin 45-46. See also Isaiah Berlin, *Personal Impressions* (New York: Viking, 1981) 11.
[19] Hofstadter 333-334.
[20] Goodwin 42.
[21] Berlin 10-12.
[22] Goodwin 43-45.
[23] Alistair Horne, "Tougher Than George C. Scott," *New York Times Book Review* 10 Dec. 1995: 9. See also Goodwin 51-52.
[24] Goodwin 102-104.
[25] William J. vanden Heuvel, "The Holocaust Was No Secret: Churchill knew. We all knew, and couldn't do anything about it —except win the war." *New York Times Magazine* 22 Dec. 1996.
[26] Hoftsadter 348.
[27] Choiniere and Keirsey 80.
[28] Theodore Draper, "Neoconservative History," *New York Review of Books* 16 Jan. 1986.
[29] It should be understood that in taking a vow of celibacy, Gandhi was acting within the Hindu tradition which values sexual pleasures but advises abstinence for those who would liberate their souls from continual rebirth and be united with the Supreme Being. See Raleigh Trevelyan, "One Nation

Under Many Gods," rev. of *In Light of India* and *A Tale of Two Gardens* by Octavio Paz" *New York Times Book Review*, 30 Mar. 1997: 25+.

[30] Quoted in Brown 146-147.

[31] Harrison Salisbury, *The New Emperors* (New York: Avon Books, 1992) 346.

[32] Richard Nixon, *In the Arena* (New York: Pocket Books, 1990) 4.

[33] Quoted in Nixon 4.

[34] Salisbury 471. See also Han Suyin 17-22.

[35] Han Suyin 101-103; and Salisbury 471.

[36] Salisbury 286, 287.

[37] Henry Kissinger, *The White House Years* (Boston: Little, Brown and Company, 1979) 1064-1065.

[38] Jung Chang, *Wild Swans* (New York: Doubleday Anchor Books, 1992) 220-222.

[39] Nicholas Eberstadt, "The Great Leap Backward: The story behind Mao's policies of the late 1950s, which led to the starvation of tens of millions," *New York Times Book Review* 16 Feb. 1997: 6-7.

[40] Jung Chang 275-276.

[41] Jung Chang 276. See also Han Suyin 311-313.

[42] Jung Chang 276.

[43] Mao's method, wrote Jung Chang, was to break the health of the person whom he wished to eliminate. Then he had no blood on his hands, no blame. Medications and their withdrawal were used to kill (391-392).

[44] Salisbury 265-275.

[45] Salisbury 312.

[46] Kissinger, *White House Years* 1059 (unnumbered note).

[47] Salisbury 130. The *Economist* magazine wrote that Mao "was responsible for the deaths of more of his compatriots than Stalin" (17 Aug. 1996: 18-19).

[48] David Remnick, "The First and the Last: Lenin revealed, and buried by Gorbachev," *New Yorker* 18 Nov. 1996: 122.

[49] See Bill Keller, "The Art of the Possible," *New York Times Book Review* 20 Oct. 1996. See also Abraham Brumberg, "Yesterday's Hero," *New York Times Book Review* 7 July 1996.

[50] Doder and Branson 13-14. See also Jack F. Matlock, Jr., "Gorbachev: Lingering Mysteries," *New York Review of Books* 19 Dec. 1996.

[51] Nicholas Henderson, "Their Man in Washington: Anatoly Dobrynin examines the motives and miscalculations of the cold war," *New York Times Book Review* 10 Sept. 1995: 11.

[52] David Remnick, "Gorbachev's Last Hurrah," *New Yorker* 11 Mar. 1996: 80.

[53] Alessandra Stanley, "Neither Ridicule Nor Rancor Halts Gorbachev Election Bid," *New York Times* 17 May 1996. See also Alessandra Stanley, "Communist Struggles for Support as Rivals Back Yeltsin," *New York Times* 20 June 1996.

[54] Remnick 74.

[55] Doder and Branson 416.

[56] This thought I gained from a discussion of Jane Jacobs's book, *Systems of Survival* (New York: Random House, 1992) in a television interview I did with her in May, 1993 for KERA-TV and KDTN-TV the PBS stations in Dallas-Fort Worth.

[57] William Manchester, *The Last Lion, Winston Spencer Churchill, Alone, 1932-1940* (Boston: Little Brown 1988) 664.

[58] Corelli Barnett, *The Collapse of British Power* (Atlantic Highlands, NJ: Humanities Press International, 1972) 10-15.

[59] Margaret Thatcher, *The Downing Street Years* (New York: Harper Collins, 1993) 5.

[60] Quoted as epigraph in Larry Collins and Dominique Lapierre, *Freedom at Midnight* (New York: Avon, 1975).

[61] Charmley 18. Teddy Roosevelt also was affected by Darwinism, and like Churchill he applied it to nations (Harbaugh 62, 99).

[62] Winston Churchill, *History of the English-Speaking Peoples* (New York: Barnes & Noble, 1995) 430.

[63] Charmley 85. The full quote by Sir. Charles Hobhouse was "He really is a spoilt child endowed by chance with the brain of a genius."

[64] Berlin 2-3, 6.

[65] Berlin 3.

[66] Berlin 4, 12-13.

[67] Berlin 14-16.

[68] Churchill was named First Lord of the Admiralty in Chamberlain's war cabinet in 1939 after Germany invaded Poland. He also was asked to preside over the all-important Military

Coordination Committee.

[69] Lee Cullum interview with Margaret Thatcher for KERA-TV and KDTN-TV, the PBS affiliates in Dallas-Fort Worth, Mar. 1991. Thatcher served as prime minister of Britain from 1979 to 1990.

[70] Richard W. Stevenson, "The Pain of British Privatization Has Yielded a String of Successes," *New York Times* 22 Feb. 1994.

[71] "The Thatcher Legacy: the immortal remains of Margaret Thatcher," *Economist* 22 Oct. 1993: 67.

[72] Hugo Young, *The Iron Lady* (New York: Noonday Press-Farrar, Straus and Giroux, 1989) 83-91.

[73] Thatcher 452, 461.

[74] Henry Kissinger, "The Right to be Right." Rev. of *The Downing Street Years*, by Margaret Thatcher, *New York Times Book Review* 14 Nov. 1993.

[75] Seymour Martin Lipset, "Political Renewal on the Left: A Comparative Perspective," *Progressive Policy Institute*, January, 1990.

[76] Thatcher 533.

[77] Youssef M Ibrahim, "Mandela Ends Triumphant Visit to Britain," *New York Times* 13 July 1996.

[78] Sebastian Mallaby, "Father of His Country: A closer look at the man who brought majority rule to South Africa," *New York Times Book Review* 1 Mar. 1998.

[79] Thatcher 532.

[80] See Anthony Lewis, "Mandela the Pol," *New York Times Magazine* 23 Mar. 1997: 43, 45.

CHAPTER FOUR

I am especially indebted to the following two books for information about the life and career of Albert Einstein and of Andrei Sakharov: Abraham Pais, *'Subtle is the Lord—': The Science and the Life of Albert Einstein* (Oxford: Oxford UP, 1982); and Andrei Sakharov, *Memoirs*, trans. Richard Lourie. (New York: Alfred A. Knopf, 1990).

[1] Holroyd, Michael. *Bernard Shaw: The Lure of Fantasy* (Volume 3, 1918-1950), New York: Random House, 1991, pp. 219-220. Holroyd gives a wonderful account of that evening in London when Einstein was honored. I am indebted to him for these passages on that occasion which was recorded and broadcast by the BBC. The transcript can be found in the BBC Archives, 921-SHA. Shaw discussed the remarks he planned for Einstein in a letter to John Reith; see Bernard Shaw, *Collected Letters, 1926-1950*, ed. Dan H. Laurence (New York: Viking, 1988) 211-212.

[2] Tom Siegfried, "Fickle equation now finds universe finite," *Dallas Morning News* 16 June 1991.

[3] Science writer Dick Teresi called Hubble possibly "the most important astronomer since Galileo. Perhaps since Copernicus. He made two great discoveries: (1) The universe is bigger than anyone thought. (2) It's getting bigger all the time." Hubble's work, Teresi wrote, "has fueled cosmology for more than 60 years"; "The Cosmic Egoist, A life of Edwin Hubble, who had one eye on the universe and the other on himself," *New York Times Book Review* 3 Sept. 1995: 1, 21.

[4] Siegfried; see also John Noble Wilford, "Big Bang's Defenders Weigh Fudge Factor, A Blunder of Einstein's, As Fix for New Crisis," *New York Times* 1 Nov. 1994; and Wilford, "Finding on Universe's Age Poses New Cosmic Puzzle," *New York Times* 27 Oct. 1994.

[5] "New Data Hint that Universe May Be Bigger Than Thought," *New York Times* 15 Feb. 1997. See also Wilford, "Scientists, Once Starry-Eyed. Get Clearer View of Universe," *New York Times* 7 Apr. 1997; Wilford, "New Data Suggest Universe Will Expand Forever," *New York Times* 9 Jan. 1998; and Wilford, "New Measurement Suggests Universe Is Younger Than Believed," *New York Times* 2 June 1999: A19.

[6] Malcolm W. Browne, "Age of Universe Is Now Settled, Astronomer Says," *New York Times* 5 Mar. 1996; and Wilford, "New Data."

[7] Angela Tilby, *Soul: God, Self and the New Cosmology* (New York: Doubleday, 1992): 71, 77. This book was an enormous help to me in dealing with science of the twentieth century. She writes clearly and with insight for those who are not well versed in the subject. I drew upon her work extensively.

[8] The quote is from Banesh Hoffman. Tilby 75.

[9] Tilby, *Soul*, 74.

[10] Tilby 75.

[11] Tilby 74

[12] Tilby 77.

[13] Tilby 103, 115.

[14] Wilford, "Sailing A Wheelchair To the End of Time," *New York Times* 24 Mar. 1998.

[15] Dick Teresi, "Physics Is History," *New York Times* 11 June 1994. See also Browne,"A Millennial Angst for Particle Physics" *New York Times* 19 Jan. 1999: F5.

[16] Teresi, "Physics Is History".

[17] Robin Pogrebin, "Love Letters By Einstein at Auction: Notes Reveal Affair With Possible Spy," *New York Times* 1 June 1998, and Fred Jerome, "Looking at a Genius, Seeing a Spy," *New York Times* 8 June 1998.

[18] Stephen Hawking, *A Brief History of Time: From the Big Bang to Black Holes* (New York: Bantam Books, 1990). 177-8; Pais 11.

[19] Tilby 77, 166.

[20] Tilby 79, 142-143, 158, 164-165.

[21] Hawking 11-12.

[22] Tilby 166-168.

[23] Hawking 156.

[24] This quotation was taken from biographical materials on Jack Kilby issued by the Kilby Awards Foundation.

[25] This problem was further explored in a piece by Louis Uchitelle, "Basic Research Is Losing Out As Companies Stress Results," *New York Times* 8 Oct. 1996.

[26] The paragraphs on Jack Kilby are based on an interview with him in February, 1994, which led to a column in the *National Forum* that same month.

[27] James D. Watson, *The Double Helix: A Personal Account of the Discovery and Structure of DNA* (New York : Atheneum, 1969) front flap of jacket.

[28] Dennis L. Breo, "The double helix—Watson & Crick's 'freak find' of how like begets like," *Journal of the American Medical Association* 269.8 (1993): 1040. This article was a substantial help in assembling the section on Watson and Crick.

[29] Breo 1042.

[30] Watson 7.

[31] Breo 1042.

[32] Breo 1040.

[33] James Watson and John Tooze, *The DNA Story* (San Francisco: W.H. Freeman and Company, 1981) xiv, 2-27.

[34] Lee Cullum, interview with Dr. James Watson for KERA-TV and KDTN-TV, the public television stations in Dallas-Fort Worth, 1994.

[35] Louise Levathes, "A Geneticist Maps Ancient Migrations," *New York Times* 27 July 1993. Stone tools found in Siberia suggest that "primitive humans were there as early as 300,000 years ago," and the "discovery of 400,000-year-old wooden spears in Germany" raises questions about when pre-modern man reached that part of the world. Wilford, "A Discovery Puts Humans In Siberia Ages Ago," *New York Times* 28 Feb. 1997.

[36] Breo 1045.

[37] Stuart Kauffman, *At Home in the Universe: The Search for Laws of Self-Organization and Complexity* (New York: Oxford UP, 1995) 8.

[38] M. Mitchell Waldrop, *Complexity: The Emerging Science at the Edge of Order and Chaos* (New York: Simon & Schuster, 1992) 121-122. See also William J. Broad, "Clues to Fiery Origin of Life Sought in Hothouse Microbes," *New York Times* 9 May 1995.

[39] Waldrop 122-123.

[40] Waldrop 123, 125.

[41] Tilby 224.

[42] Waldrop 103 - 105.

[43] Tilby 166.

[44] Jeffrey Kovac, "Ilya Prigogine," *The History of Modern Chemical Sciences* (Rahway, N.J.: Merck ,1993). The biographical material on Prigogine was drawn from this piece.

[45] Tilby 185, 190.

[46] Tilby 191, 207.

[47] Yevgeny Yevtushenko, *Fatal Half Measures: The Culture of Democracy in the Soviet Union*, trans. and ed. Antonina W. Bouis (Boston: Little Brown, 1991) 46.

[48] Yevtushenko 44-46.

[49] Yevtushenko 44-46.

[50] Yevtushenko 44-46.

[51] Yevtushenko 46.

[52] Yevtushenko 46.

[53] David Remnick, "Can Russia Change?" *Foreign Affairs* January-February 1997: 37-38.

[54] Quoted by David Remnick, "Letter from Jerusalem: The Afterlife," *New Yorker* 11 Aug. 1997: 58.

[55] John Horgan, *The End of Science: Facing the Limits of Knowledge in the Twilight of the Scientific Age* (Reading, Mass.: Helix Books, Addison-Wesley, 1996) 16. This is a fascinating study. Though I don't agree with Horgan's conclusions, I explore extensively his argument and am grateful to him for it.

[56] Horgan 10. Gunther Stent is a biologist. I am using his quote as it appears in Horgan.

[57] Horgan 75. Steven Weinberg is a physicist at the University of Texas at Austin. I am using his quote as it appears in Horgan.

[58] Horgan 27-28. The quote is from Leo Kadenoff, a physicist at the University of Chicago. It is presented as it appears in Horgan.

[59] Horgan 90-91. This quote by Richard Feynman is cited in Horgan.

[60] Hogan 58. This quote by Colin McGinn is cited in Horgan.

[61] Horgan 63. This quote by Sheldon Glashow is cited in Horgan.

[62] Horgan 60. This quote by Einstein is cited by Horgan.

[63] Horgan 87-89. This quote by David Bohm is cited by Horgan.

[64] Christopher Lehmann-Haupt, "The Century Ahead for Science," rev. of *What Remains To Be Discovered: Mapping the Secrets of the Universe, the Origins of Life and the Future of the Human Race* by John Maddox, *New York Times* 16 Nov. 1998: B6.

CHAPTER FIVE

The discussion in this chapter of the lives and careers of modern artists is especially indebted to a few excellent individual studies. Unless otherwise noted, information and quotations concerning an artist will refer to one of the following: Patrick O'Brian, *Picasso: A Biography* (New York: W.W. Norton, 1994); Hayden Herrera, *Matisse: A Portrait* (New York: Harcourt Brace, 1993); Yve-Alain Bois, et al., *Piet Mondrian*, trans. Andrew McCormick and Gregory Sims (Boston: Little, Brown, 1994); Will Grohmann, *Wassily Kandinsky: Life and Work*, trans by Norbert Guterman (New York: Harry N. Abrams, 1958); Charlotte Douglas, *Malevich* (New York: Harry N. Abrams, 1994); Roger Berthoud, *The Life of Henry Moore* (New York: F.P. Dutton, 1987); Radu Varia, *Brancusi*, trans. Mary Vaudoyer (New York: Universe, 1986); James E.B. Breslin, *Mark Rothko: A Biography* (Chicago: University of Chicago Press, 1993).

[1] Gilles Néret, *Matisse*, trans. Josephine Bacon (Cologne: Taschen, 1996) 16-19.

[2] Quoted in O'Brian 153-154, 267. This conversation, with André Malraux in 1937, was reported by that writer 37 years later.

[3] Quoted in O'Brian 153-154.

[4] O'Brian 312, 316, 317, 353, 378. See also Alan Riding, "31 Picassos Are Sold at Paris Auction," *New York Times* 29 Oct. 1998, and Riding, "Dora Maar, 89, Picasso's Muse And a Photographer, Is Dead," *New York Times*, 26 July 1997.

[5] Quoted in O'Brian 383.

[6] Néret, *Matisse* 19, 23; Herrera 3-4.

[7] Bernard Denvir, "The Ferocious Fauve: A look at the prodigious egotism behind the bland benignity of Henry Matisse," *New York Times Book Review* 10 Oct. 1993: 28.

[8] Herrera 20-21, 36, 38, 94-95. See also Denvir 28.

[9] Herrera 23, 70, 110. See also Néret 23.

[10] Néret 8.

[11] Néret 23-24.

[12] He also bought works by Rodin, Gauguin, and van Gogh, financing them with debt (Néret 12, 15).

[13] Stein is cited in Herrera 59-60.

[14] Matisse's son Jean, Herrera reports, also worked in the Resistance. He taught recruits how to use firearms in his cellar.

[15] Néret 60-61; and Herrera 159-161.

[16] Néret 63; and Herrera 101.

[17] Cited in Bois 75.

[18] Mondrian left his estate to Harry Holtzman.

[19] Cited in Grohmann 77.

[20] Susan P. Compton, *The World Backwards: Russian Futurist Books*, 1912-16 (London: The British Library, 1978) 33, 52-59.

[21] Carol Vogel, "The Modern Gets to Keep Malevich Works," *New York Times* 19 June 1999: A17.

[22] Berthoud 211. That assessment came from M.H. Middleton in the *Spectator*.

[23] Berthoud 14, 251, 356. The observation of Moore as a public artist is Hilton Kramer's.

[24] Quoted in Berthoud 104.

[25] The quote in Varia is from Jean Cassou.

[26] Also in WPA were Milton Avery, Willem de Kooning, Arshile Gorky, Philip Guston, Lee Kramer, Louise Nevelson, Jackson Pollock, Ad Reinhardt and David Smith (Breslin 121).

[27] Ann Douglas, "Pollock's Volcanic New York Circle," *New York Times* 27 Nov 1998: B37, B39.

[28] Breslin 489-493, 499. See also Judith H. Dobrzynski, "A Betrayal The Art World Can't Forget: The Battle for Rothko's Estate Altered Lives and Reputations," *New York Times* 2 Nov. 1998.

[29] Roberta Smith, "Frank Lloyd, Prominent Art Dealer Convicted in the 70s Rothko Scandal, Dies at 86," *New York Times* 8 April 1998.

[30] Cited in Breslin 323.

CHAPTER SIX

In this chapter I quote extensively from several works of twentieth-century fiction. The following is a list of the editions to which these quotations refer. They are given here in the order in which I have treated the authors: Marcel Proust, *Remembrance of Things Past, Volume I*, trans. Scott Moncrieff and Terence Kilmartin (New York: Vintage-Random House, 1982); James Joyce, *Ulysses* (New York: Vintage-Random House, 1961); Virginia Woolf, *The Waves*, in *Jacob's Room and The Waves: Two Complete Novels* (New York: Harcourt, Brace & World, 1931); Woolf, *Orlando* (New York: Harcourt & Brace, 1928); Woolf, *To the Lighthouse* (New York: Harcourt, Brace & World, 1927); Woolf, *Mrs. Dalloway* (New York: Harcourt, Brace, & World, 1925); E.M. Forster, *Howards End* (New York: Vintage-Random House, 1921); Edith Wharton, *The Age of Innocence*, in *The Edith Wharton Omnibus* (New York: Charles Scribner's Sons, 1978); Isak Dinesen, *Out of Africa*, in *Out of Africa and Shadows on the Grass* (New York: Vintage-Random House, 1989); Franz Kafka, "The Metamorphosis" and "The Burrow," in *The Complete Stories*, trans. Willa and Edwin Muir (New York: Schocken Books, 1971); Boris Pasternak, *Doctor Zhivago*, trans. by Max Hayward and Marya Harari (New York: Ballantine Books) 1981; Nadine Gordimer, "Safe House," in *Jump and Other Stories* (New York: Penguin Books, 1992); Toni Morrison, *Beloved* (New York: Plume-Penguin, 1988); William Faulkner, *Sanctuary* and *Light in August*, in *Novels, 1930-1935* (New York: Viking, 1985).

[1] Harold Bloom, *The Western Canon* (New York: Harcourt Brace & Company, 1994) 3, 447. He also included in that distinguished list the essays of Freud and the parables and tales of Kafka.

[2] Harold Bloom and David Rosenberg, *The Book of J* (New York: Grove Weidenfeld, 1990) front flap of jacket.

[3] Francesca Premoli-Droulers, *Maisons d'écrivains. English Writers' Houses* (New York: The Vendome Press, 1995) 171-172. Thanks to this lovely survey for information about Virginia Woolf's writing room and the income she made from her books.

[4] Virginia Woolf, *The Letters of Virginia Woolf, Volume Three, 1923-1928*, ed. Nigel Nicolson and Joanne Trautmann (New York: Harcourt Brace Jovanovich, 1977) xx.

[5] Woolf, *Letters, Volume Three* 80.

[6] Bloom 433.

[7] Woolf, *Letters, Volume Three* 80.

[8] Woolf, *A Writer's Diary* (New York, Harcourt Brace Jovanovich, 1954) 349.

[9] Woolf, *Letters, Volume Three* 365.

[10] Quentin Bell, *Virginia Woolf: A Biography* (New York: Harcourt Brace Jovanovich, 1972) 138. This brilliant biography, upon which no one can improve, has been an invaluable source on Virginia Woolf.

[11] Bloom 397-398, 404.

[12] Woolf, *Writer's Diary* 140-141, 138.

[13] Bloom 434, 423.

[14] James Joyce, *Ulysses* (New York: Vintage-Random House, 1961) x.

[15] Woolf, *The Diary of Virginia Woolf, Volume Two*, 1920-1924, ed. Anne Olivier Bell (New York: Harcourt, Brace, Jovanovich, 1978) 322.

[16] Woolf, *Writer's Diary* 136.

[17] Woolf, *Letters, Volume Three* 201.

[18] Woolf, "Joseph Conrad," *The Common Reader* (New York: Harcourt, Brace & World, 1925) 229.

[19] Bloom 439, 436, 446.

[20] James Wood, "Beneath The Waves," *New Republic* 29 Sept. 1997: 37.

[21] Bloom 439.

[22] E.M. Forster, *Virginia Woolf* (London: Cambridge UP, 1942) 23.

[23] Woolf, "Mr. Bennett and Mrs. Brown," *The Captain's Death Bed and Other Essays* (New York: Harcourt Brace Jovanovich, 1950) 96-97, 115-116.

[24] Rosemary Dinnage, "The Whirr of Wings," *New York Review of Books* 29 May 1997: 4.

[25] Woolf, *The Diary of Virginia Woolf, Volume Five, 1936-1941*, ed. Anne Olivier Bell (New York: Harcourt Brace Jovanovich, 1984) 359. Harold Bloom included *Between the Acts* in his list of Woolf's five canonical novels (554).

[26] Dinnage 6.

[27] Woolf, *Letters, Volume Three* 119, 133.

[28] Woolf, *Diary, Volume Two* 135 and unnumbered note.

[29] Woolf, *Letters, Volume Three* 134-135.

[30] Woolf, *The Letters of Virginia Woolf, Volume Six, 1936-1941*, ed. Nigel Nicolson and Joanne Trautmann (New York: Harcourt Brace Jovanovich, 1980) 312.

[31] Woolf, *Diary, Volume Five* 249, 250. Bell adds in a note that Woolf apparently was reading Freud's *The Future of an Illusion* and *Civilization and Its Discontents*.

[32] Woolf, *Diary, Volume Five* 299.

[33] Leonard Woolf, *Downhill All the Way: An Autobiography of the Years 1919 to 1939* (New York: Harcourt, Brace & World, 1967) 168-169.

[34] Bell 8.

[35] Jane Dunn, *A Very Close Conspiracy: Vanessa Bell and Virginia Woolf* (Boston: Little, Brown, 1990) both jacket flaps.

[36] Angelica Garnett, *Deceived with Kindness* (New York, Harcourt Brace Jovanovich, 1985) front flap of jacket, 134-142, 22-23.

[37] Woolf, *Moments of Being: Virginia Woolf, Unpublished Autobiographical Writings*, ed. Jeanne Schulkind (New York: Harcourt Brace Jovanovich, 1978) 28-29.

[38] Woolf, *Night and Day* (New York: Harcourt Brace Jovanovich, 1920) dedication.

[39] Woolf, *Writer's Diary* 118.

[40] Vita Sackville-West, *The Letters of Vita Sackville-West to Virginia Woolf*, ed. Louise DeSalvo and Mitchell A. Leaska (New York, William Morrow, 1985) 403.

[41] Sackville-West 403.

[42] Woolf, "Mr. Bennett and Mrs. Brown" 116-117. She refers to Thomas Babington Macaulay, 1800-1859, British historian, essayist, and politician.

[43] Bloom 436, 434.

[44] Woolf, *A Room of One's Own* (New York, Harcourt, Brace & World, 1957) 18.

[45] Woolf, Virginia, "Evening Over Sussex," in *The Death of the Moth* and *Other Essays* (New York: Harcourt Brace, 1942) 10-11.

[46] Woolf, "The Novels of E.M. Forster," in *The Death of the Moth* 162, 169, 166.

[47] Woolf, "Novels of E.M. Forster" 172, 166.

[48] Forster, *Virginia Woolf* 7-8.

[49] Rose Macaulay, *The Writings of E.M. Forster* (London: The Hogarth Press, 1938) 10.

[50] Macaulay 99-100.

[51] Forster quoted in Macaulay 111-112.

[52] Macaulay 107, 109.

[53] Lionel Trilling, *Howards End* back cover. Reprinted with the permission of the Wylie Agency, Inc.

[54] Woolf, "Novels of E.M. Forster" 167, 164.

[55] Gore Vidal, Introduction to *The Edith Wharton Omnibus* (New York: Charles Scribner's Sons, 1978) viii.

[56] R.W.B. Lewis, Introduction to *The House of Mirth* (New York: New York UP, 1977) vi, xii. Lewis, to my mind, is the authority on Edith Wharton. I am heavily indebted to this introduction and also to his elegant biography of her.

[57] R.W.B. Lewis, *Edith Wharton, A Biography* (New York: Harper & Row, 1975) 83, 74. As mentioned earlier, I have relied gratefully on this superb account of Wharton's life.

[58] Vidal xi.

[59] Lewis, Introduction to *The House of Mirth* vi.

[60] Lewis, *Edith Wharton* xi.

[61] Cynthia Griffin Wolff, *A Feast of Words: The Triumph of Edith Wharton* (New York: Oxford UP, 1977) 318.

[62] Wolff 329 333.

[63] Lewis, Introduction to *The House of Mirth* viii, vii.

[64] Lewis, *Edith Wharton* 276, 275.

[65] Lewis, *Edith Wharton* 277.

[66] Lewis, *Edith Wharton* 544.

[67] Joyce Carol Oates, "Depth-Sightings," rev. of *Sight-Readings: American Fictions* by Elizabeth Hardwick, *New York Review of Books* 24 Sept. 1998: 4-6..

[68] Lewis, *Edith Wharton* 48-50.

[69] Lewis, *Edith Wharton* 285, 478-479.

[70] Lewis, *Edith Wharton* 442. The "Beatrice Palmato" fragment can be found on 544-548. See also 525.

[71] Trilling, "James Joyce in His Letters," in *The Last Decade* 27. Copyright © 1968 by Lionel Trilling. Reprinted with the permission of the Wylie Agency, Inc.

[72] Trilling, "James Joyce in His Letters" 29, 33. Copyright © 1968 by Lionel Trilling. Reprinted with the permission of the Wylie Agency, Inc.

[73] Lewis, *Edith Wharton* 483.

[74] Woolf, *Letters, Volume Five* 305.

[75] Lewis, *Edith Wharton* 483.

[76] Lewis, *Edith Wharton* 402, 403.

[77] Edith Wharton, *A Backward Glance* (New York: Charles Scribner's Sons, 1964) xix.

[78] Vidal xiii.

[79] Trilling, "James Joyce in His Letters" 39.

[80] I am indebted for the material on Isak Dinesen to Judith Thurman, *Isak Dinesen: The Life of a Storyteller* (New York: St. Martin's Press, 1982). This is a masterful work.

[81] Thurman 257, 257n.

[82] Thurman 107.

[83] Isak Dinesen, *Breve fra Afrika. English Letters from Africa, 1914-1931*, ed. Frans Lasson, trans. Anne Born (Chicago: University of Chicago Press, 1981) 33.

[84] Dinesen, *English Letters from Africa* xix.

[85] Dinesen, *English Letters from Africa* 61.

[86] Thurman 5.

[87] Dinesen, *English Letters from Africa* xxv.

[88] Thurman, *Isak Dinesen*, 27-28.

[89] Thurman 429, 467, 487

[90] John Updike, Introduction to *Kafka, The Complete Stories* xvii-xviii.

[91] Yevgeny Yevtushenko, *Fatal Half-Measures* (Boston: Little, Brown, 1991) 341. I have relied heavily on Yevtushenko and his eloquent and insightful work for my section on Pasternak.

[92] Jane Jacobs explores her notion of intellectual dissent in *Systems of Survival* (New York: Random House, 1992). I talked with her about Marxism in an interview for public television in May, 1993.

[93] Yevtushenko 333.

[94] "Olga Ivinskaya, 83, Pasternak muse for 'Zhivago,'" *New York Times* 13 Sept. 1995.

[95] Yevtushenko 341.

[96] "Olga Ivinskaya, inspiration for 'Dr Zhivago,' dies at 83," *Dallas Morning News* 13 Sept. 1995. And "Olga Ivinskaya, 83"

[97] Alessandra Stanley, "Model for Dr. Zhivago's Lara Betrayed Pasternak to K.G.B.," *New York Times* 27 Nov. 1997. See also "Olga Ivinskaya, inspiration."

[98] Olga Ivinskaya, 83; and Stanley, "Model."

[99] Yevtushenko 331, 341; and Stanley, "Model."

[100] Yevtushenko 332.

[101] Yevtushenko 342.

[102] Yevtushenko 333.

[103] Isaiah Berlin, *Personal Impressions* (New York: The Viking Press, 1981) 174, 178-180; Yevtushenko 338.

[104] Michiko Kakutani "A Fatal Triangle in the Long Shadow of Apartheid," *New York Times* 16 Jan. 1998.

[105] Caryl Phillips, "The Beat of History," *The New Republic* 24 Oct. 1994: 34. The piece quotes Gordimer's autobiographical essay, "A Bolter and the Invincible Summer" (1963) from which this material is taken.

[106] Diana Jean Schemo, "A Crusader Adjusts to Life After Apartheid," *New York Times*, 28 Nov. 1994.

[107] Phillips, "The Beat of History," 34-35.

[108] Dinitia Smith, "Mixing Tragedy and Folklore," *New York Times*, 8 Jan. 1998. This is the source of biographical details of Toni Morrison's life.

[109] Faulkner, *Novels 1930-1935*, 1007-1008

[110] Lionel Trilling, "Why We Read Jane Austen," in *The Last Decade: Essays and Revisions, 1965-75* (New York: Harcourt Brace Jovanovich, 1979) 210. Copyright © 1979 by Diana Trilling and James Trilling. Reprinted with the permission of the Wylie Agency, Inc.

[111] Trilling, "Emma and the Legend of Jane Austen," *Beyond Culture* (New York: Harcourt Brace Jovanovich, 1979) 28. Copyright © 1957 by Lionel Trilling. Reprinted with the permission of the Wylie Agency, Inc.

[112] Trilling, "Why We Read Jane Austen" 209. Copyright © 1979 by Diana Trilling and James Trilling. Reprinted with the permission of the Wylie Agency, Inc.

[113] Trilling, "Emma and the Legend of Jane Austen" 34. Copyright © 1957 by Lionel Trilling. Reprinted with the permission of the Wylie Agency, Inc.

[114] Trilling, "Emma and the Legend of Jane Austen." Copyright © 1957 by Lionel Trilling. Reprinted with the permission of the Wylie Agency, Inc.

[115] Trilling, "Emma and the Legend of Jane Austen" 41, 35, 48-49. Copyright © 1957 by Lionel Trilling. Reprinted with the permission of the Wylie Agency, Inc.

[116] Bloom 259-260, 254.

[117] Lionel Trilling, "Mansfield Park," *The Opposing Self* (New York: Harcourt Brace Jovanovich, 1979) 182. Copyright © 1955 by Lionel Trilling. Reprinted with the permission of the Wylie Agency, Inc.

[118] Woolf, *A Room of One's Own* 70-71. Actually, Austen was in London occasionally, and stayed with her brother Henry. But she felt intimidated by the city even when it excited her. (Nigel Nicolson, *The World of Jane Austen* [London: Weidenfeld and Nicolson, 1991] 79-83).

[119] Woolf, "Jane Austen," in *The Common Reader* 148-149.

CHAPTER SEVEN

I am especially indebted in this chapter to a general study of twentieth century music: Phil Hardy and Dave Lang, *The Da Capo Companion to 20th Century Popular Music* (New York: Da Capo Press, 1995). I am also indebted to several biographies of popular musicians. I gratefully acknowledge these sources here; additional sources are cited in endnotes: Charles Schwartz, *Gershwin: His Life and Music* (New York: Da Capo Press, 1973); Charles Schwartz, *Cole Porter* (New York: Da Capo Press, 1992); William G. Hyland, *Richard Rodgers* (New Haven: Yale UP, 1998); Meryle Secrest, *Stephen Sondheim: A Life* (New York: Alfred A. Knopf, 1998); Michael Walsh, *Andrew Lloyd Webber: His Life and Works* (New York: Harry N. Abrams, 1997).

[1] John Rockwell, "Song of the Earth: A biography of Mahler for old and new devotees of his music," *New York Times Book Review* 8 Mar. 1998: 11. See also Richard Bernstein, "Reality Check for the Mythic Mahler," *New York Times* 21 Jan 1998: E9.

[2] Carl E. Schorske, *Fin-de-Siècle Vienna* (New York: Alfred A. Knopf, 1980) 3-4.

[3] James R. Oestreich, "Hearing Bach and Shostakovich in Conversation," *New York Times* 8 May 1998: B4.

[4] David Schiff, "Modernists in the California Sun," *New York Times* 25 Jan. 1998. See also Anthony Tommasini, "Arnold Schoenberg: Pushing Music to Evolve," *International Herald Tribune* (New York Times Service) 2 Feb. 1999.

[5] Oestreich, "How Does Music Turn the Century? Schoenberg Could One Day Sound as Remote as Gregorian Chant," *New York Times* 27 Dec. 1997: A9, A11.

[6] "Tunesmith dies at 74," *Dallas Morning News* (New York Times News Service) 19 Feb. 1998.

[7] Quotations in Schwartz are from Isaac Goldberg's *George Gershwin*, 138-139.

[8] The quotation in Schwartz is from Leonard Bernstein, "A Nice Gershwin Tune," *Atlantic Monthly* (April, 1955) 40-41. This article also appears in Bernstein's book, *The Joy of Music*.

[9] This quotation in Schwartz is from Leonard Bernstein, "A Nice Gershwin Tune" 40-41.

[10] Oscar Levant, "My Life; Or the Story of George Gershwin," *A Smattering of Ignorance* (New York: Doubleday, Doran, 1940) 170.

[11] Schwartz, *Gershwin* 245, 254, 258-267. The Gershwin quote on jazz coming from Africa (254) is from the *New York Herald-Tribune* 5 Jan. 1934. See also Bernard Holland, "Singing the Gershwins: Nice Work if You Can Get It," *New York Times* 17 Mar. 1998: B1, B4.

[12] Brad Leithauser "Let's Face the Music," *New York Review of Books* 22 Apr. 1999: 16-20. I drew heavily upon this excellent piece for my section on Irving Berlin's life.

[13] Alexander Chancellor, "De-lightful, De-licious, De-ceitful: A biography of Cole Porter reveals the unhappy, closeted man behind the facade of urbane insouciance," *New York Times Book Review* 29 Nov. 1998: 9. The quote is from William McBrien, *Cole Porter: A Biography* (New York: Alfred A. Knopf, 1998).

[14] Hardy and Laing 409, 803. See also Ben Brantley, "The Sound of His Music: Richard Rodgers conquered Broadway with remarkable ease," *New York Times Book Review* 17 May 1998: 38.

[15] See Brantley 38.

[16] The quote in Hyland is from the Mary Rodgers introduction to Richard Rodgers' autobiography, *Musical Stages* (New York: Da Capo Press, 1995).

[17] The quote in Secrest is by Susan Blanchard.

CHAPTER EIGHT

In this chapter I have drawn extensively upon general studies of the history of cinema, which have provided the basis of my presentation of individual directors. I gratefully acknowledge these sources here; additional sources are cited in endnotes. David Thomson, *A Biographical Dictionary of Film* (New York: Alfred A Knopf, 1996); and Andrew Sarris, *"You Ain't Heard Nothin' Yet": The American Talking Film, History and Memory, 1927-1949* (New York: Oxford UP, 1998) were indispensable. In addition, I have referred to several individual articles from Geoffrey Nowell-Smith, *The Oxford History of World Cinema* (Oxford: Oxford UP, 1996). These are, in alphabetical order according to the author: John Belton on Howard Hawks; Janet Bergstrom on Friedrich Wilhem Murnan, on Jean Renoir, and on Fritz Lang; David Bordwell on Sergei Eisenstein and on Yasujiro Ozu; Edward Buscombe on John Ford; Phillip Drummond on Jean-Luc Godard; Thomas Elsaesser on Ernst Lubitsch; Douglas Gomery on "The New Hollywood"; Phillip Kemp on Ingmar Bergman; Hiroshi Komatsu on Akira Kurosawa and on Kenji Mizoguchi; Morando Morandini on Vittorio De Sica, on Frederico Fellini, and on Bernardo Bertolucci; Geoffrey Nowell-Smith on Buster Keaton, on Erich von Stroheim, on Max Ophuls, on Luchino Visconti, on Roberto Rossellini, and on Michelangelo Antonioni; Edward R. O'Neill on Alfred Hitchcock, on Martin Scorsese, and on Orson Wells; Roberta Pearson on David Wark Griffith; Eric Rentschler on Leni Riefenstahl; David Robinson on Charles Chaplin; Gaylyn Studler on Josef von Sternberg and on Marlene Dietrich; Paolo Cherchi Usai on Carl Theodor Dreyer and on Victor Sjostrom.

For the treatment of Leni Riefenstahl I am especially indebted to these excellent articles: John Simon, "The Führer's Movie Maker: Leni Riefenstahl paints herself as both the master of her fate and its victim," *New York Times Book Review* 27 Sept. 1993, sec. 7: 1+; Frank Deford, "The Ghost of Berlin," *Sports Illustrated* 65 (4 Aug. 1986): 48; Richard Corliss, "Riefenstahl's Last Triumph," *Time* 142 (18 Oct. 1993): 91; Brian Winston, "Triumph of the Will," *History Today* 47 (Jan. 1997): 24; Richard Grenier, "The Führer's Film Maker," *Commentary* 98.2 (Aug. 1994): 50; and Susan Sontag, "Fascinating Fascism," *Under the Sign of Saturn* (New York: Farrar, Straus, Giroux, 1980).

I am grateful as well for the help of two biographies: Joseph McBride, *Hawks on Hawks* (Berkeley: University of California Press, 1982); and Ronald L. Davis, *John Ford: Hollywood's Old Master* (Norman: University of Oklahoma Press, 1995).

[1] Charles Musser, *The Emergence of Cinema: The American Screen to 1907* (Berkeley: University of California Press, 1994) 417-433.

[2] Ronald L. Davis, *The Glamour Factory* (Dallas: Southern Methodist UP, 1993) 99.

[3] In addition to Bordwell (in Nowell-Smith) and Thompson, see Joshua Rubenstein, "The Dictator's Cut: Stalin made life miserable for Sergei Eisenstein, but the director got his revenge," rev. of *Sergei Eisenstein: A Life in Conflict*, by Ronald Bergan, *New York Times Book Review* 27 June 1999).

[4] Bordwell; and Nancy Ramsey, "Keepers of a Flame That Burned for Russia," *New York Times* 5 July 1998.

[5] Ramsey.

[6] Davis 98. This was the insight of Norman Lloyd.

[7] James Spada, "The Lady and the Tramp: When Oona O'Neill, 18, married Charlie Chaplin, 54, handicappers gave it six months," *New York Times Book Review* 29 Nov. 1998: 11. The quote is from Jane Scovell, *Oona: Living in the Shadows: A Biography of Oona O'Neill Chaplin* (New York: Warner Books, 1998).

[8] Robinson 85; see also David Zinman, *50 Classic Motion Pictures: The Stuff That Dreams Are Made of* (New York: Limelight Editions, 1992) 137.

[9] I am indebted to Charles Silver of the Film Studies Department at the Museum of Modern Art for this insight.

[10] Here again, Charles Silver of MoMA was very helpful in his comments about the work of these two directors.

[11] Pauline Kael, *5001 Nights at the Movies* (New York: Henry Holt, 1985) 175.

[12] This is the observation of Charles Silver of MoMA.

[13] Herbert Mitgang, "An Industrial Stop Before Auschwitz," *New York Times* 26 June 1998: B43.

[14] Simon 28; Deford 48; and Hans Stueck, "Leni Riefenstahl Returns to Olympics," *New York Times* 23 Aug. 1972: 31.

[15] Janet Maslin, "Just What Did Leni Riefenstahl's Lens See?" *New York Times* 13 Mar. 1994, sec. II: 15.

[16] Stueck 31; and Sontag 83

[17] Walter Goodman, "Too brilliant for the World's Good," *New York Times* 5 July 1995, sec. C: 20.

[18] "Torch Reaches Belgrade," *New York Times* 28 July 1936: 12. See also Rentschler, "Leni Riefenstahl" 375.

[19] Tobin Harshaw, "Why Am I Guilty?" box insert in Simon 28.

[20] "Hollywood Ad Hits at Leni Riefenstahl: Anti-Nazi League Bids Industry Close Doors to Hitler Agents," *New York Times* 30 Nov. 1938: 15; Simon 28; and "Protest Olympic Movie: Two Groups Threaten to picket Riefenstahl Film," *New York Times* 4 Nov. 1938: 20.

[21] "Hollywood Ad" 15.

[22] "Leni Riefenstahl Angry," *New York Times* 28 Jan. 1939: 18; and Associated Press, *New York Times* 28 Jan. 1939: 18.

[23] Kai Bird and Max Holland, "Out of the Past," *Nation* 240 (4 May 1985): 520. See also Michael Binyon, "Film women get to grips on Auschwitz gypsies," *London Times* 29 Nov. 1984: 6g.

[24] Bird and Holland 520.

[25] Frank Johnson, "Nazi camp slur stands against top film maker," *London Times* 27 June 1985: 6f.

[26] Associated Press, *New York Times* 18 May 1945: 7.

[27] Simon 28-29. See also *Coral Gardens, Washington Post Book World* 10 Dec. 1978: E6; and Alan Cowell, "Admire Her Art? (Her Camera Adored Swastikas)," *New York Times* 21 Aug. 1997, sec. A: 4.

[28] Harshaw, "Why Am I Guilty?" in Simon 28, 29; Cowell 4; and Rena Andrews, "Hitler's Favorite Filmmaker Honored at Colorado Festival," *New York Times* 15 Sept 1974, sec II: 1.

[29] Maslin 15.

[30] Cowell 4.

[31] Stueck 31.

[32] Amos Vogel, "Can We Now Forget the Evil That She Did?" *New York Times* 3 May 1973, sec. II: 19.

[33] Goodman 20.

[34] Steve Gutow, soon to be a rabbi, observed in a conversation that one's own vision of harmony, imposed upon others as if they were objects, is indeed fascist. But to seek harmony with others in a way that makes a harmony of the whole is a high moral pursuit.

[35] Molly Haskell, "The Ride of a Valkyrie," *Washington Post Book World* 23 (29 Aug. 1993): 1.

[36] Joseph McBride, *Orson Welles* (New York: Da Capo Press, 1996) viii-ix.

[37] McBride 3.

[38] Kael 235.

[39] Bernard Weinraub, "A Life in Hollywood, Yet Never a Niche," New York Times 19 Feb. 1998: B1, B6. See also Walter Murch, "Restoring the Touch of Genius to 'Touch of Evil,'" New York Times 6 Sept. 1998, sec. 2: 16.

[40] Weinraub B1, B6.

[41] Nowell-Smith; and Phillip Lopate, "Master of Motion and Emotion," *New York Times* 20 June 1999, Arts and Leisure: 11-12.

[42] This is from a conversation with Vincent Prothro in Mar. 1998.

[43] Kael 104.

[44] Kael 701; and Sarris 255-256.

[45] Peter Bogdanovich, "Is That Ticking (Pause) a Bomb?" *New York Times* 11 Apr. 1999, Arts and Leisure: 15, 18.

[46] Charles Silver of MoMA was very instructive about Murnau and Eisenstein.

[47] Davis, *John Ford,* p. 63, pp. 98-99.

[48] Davis, *John Ford* 101, 91-93. See also Richard Etulain, Introduction to Davis, *John Ford* x; and Buscombe, 288.

[49] Davis, *John Ford* 264, 106; and Etulain, in Davis, *John Ford* x.

[50] In addition to Sarris and Davis, I am indebted to Charles Silver of MoMA.

[51] Greg Mitchell, "Winning a Battle but Losing The War Over the Blacklist," *New York Times* 25 Jan. 1998.

[52] Kemp; and Van Gelder, "Footlights: Curtain Call," *New York Times* 12 Feb. 1998.

[53] Karen Durbin, "New Film, New Chapter in a Storied Union," *New York Times* 3 Jan. 1999, Arts and Leisure: 9, 14. Thinking back to her first film with Bergman (*Persona,* in 1966), she said. "I knew that I was him."

[54] Rick Lyman, "Akira Kurosawa, Director of Epics, Dies at 88," *New York Times* 7 Sept. 1998: A1, A12.

[55] Lyman A12.

[56] Lyman A12.

[57] Ronald Davis, *Celluloid Mirrors: Hollywood and American Society since 1945* (Fort Worth: Harcourt Brace College Publishers, 1997) 101. See also Richard Brody, "Drowning in the New Wave," rev. of *Truffaut* by Antoine de Baecque and Serge Toubiana, *New Yorker* 24 May 1999: 84-89. This was an excellent source on Truffaut as well as on Jean-Luc Godard.

[58] Thomson. See also Caryn James, "Such a Gorgeous Kid Like Him: François Truffaut wanted the world to see him as a boyishly romantic artist," rev. of *Truffaut* by Antoine de Baecque and Serge Toubiana, *New York Times Book Review,* 18 Apr. 1999: 10. This article too was a useful source on Truffaut.

[59] Kael 100.

[60] Alexander Stille, "Paisans: How Roberto Rossellini and his filmmaker friends made cinematic history," rev. of *The Adventures of Roberto Rossellini* by Tag Gallagher, *New York Times Book Review* 7 Feb. 1999: 20. I drew upon this review for much of the biographical material in this segment.

[61] Kael 551.

[62] Stille.

[63] Jim Shepard, "A Mild Rebellion, Then a Revolution," *New York Times* 27 Dec. 1998.

[64] Kael 862-863.

[65] Rick Lyman, "Scene One: A Fire Escape," *New York Times* 13 Feb. 1998. See also Edward R. O'Neill, "Martin Scorsese," in Nowell-Smith. These were important sources in researching this section on Scorsese. So was Peter Biskind, *Easy Riders, Raging Bulls: How the Sex-Drugs-and-Rock 'n' Roll Generation Saved Hollywood* (New York: Simon & Schuster, 1998: 229, 230), a splendid work. My thanks to all three.

[66] Biskind 250.

[67] Biskind 251.

[68] Biskind 379, 392, 405.

[69] Janet Maslin, "Hollywood Under the Influence," *New York Times* 5 May 1998.

[70] Lyman, "Scene One: A Fire Escape."

[71] Dr. Richard Meyer is insightful on the similarities between Woody Allen and Charlie Chaplin. Also Davis, *Celluloid Mirrors* 125-126.

[72] Gomery. See also Bernard Weinraub, "Deconstructing His Film Crew: Woody Allen's Longtime Staff Is Hit by Cost-Cutting Efforts," *New York Times* 1 June 1998: B1, B4; and Bernard Weinraub, "Switch to a New Agent Is Woody Allen's Latest," *New York Times* 2 July 1998.

[73] Weinraub, "Deconstructing His Film Crew" B4.

[74] Janet Maslin, "Gleefully Skewering His Own Monsters," *New York Times* 12 Dec. 1997: B1.

[75] Maureen Dowd, "Grow Up, Harry," *New York Times* 11 Jan. 1998.

[76] Margo Jefferson, "The New Film Hero: Twisted, Neurotic, Triumphant," *New York Times* 28 Jan. 1998.

CHAPTER NINE

[1] Rebecca West, *Black Lamb and Gray Falcon* (London: Penguin, 1982) 11.

[2] Roger Cohen, "In Sarajevo, Victims of a 'Postmodern' War," *New York Times* 21 May 1995; Thomas Friedman, "New Mexico," *New York Times* 15 Mar. 1995; and Georgia Dullea, "Tarot Goes 'Po Mo,'" *New York Times* 31 Oct. 1993.

[3] For a survey of religious architecture in the United States see Roger G. Kennedy, *American Churches* (New York: Stewart, Tabori & Chang, 1982).

[4] Cited by West 65.

[5] Václav Havel, "The New Measure of Man," *New York Times* 8 July. 1994.

[6] Havel, "The New Measure of Man."

[7] David Cannadine, "Ambition Will Get You Everywhere: A biography of Disraeli as the prototypical post-modern politician, driven and always reinventing himself," rev. of *Disraeli: A Biography* by Stanley Weintraub. *New York Times Book Review* 17 Oct. 1993: 14-15.

[8] Kakutani, Michiko, "Opinion vs. Reality In an Age of Pundits And Spin Doctors," *New York Times* Jan. 28, 1994.

[9] Kakutani, Michiko, "Witness Against the Post-Modern Historians," rev. of *On Looking Into the Abyss: Untimely Thoughts on Culture and Society*, by Gertrude Himmelfarb, *New York Times* 1 Mar. 1994.

[10] Quoted by Richard A. Shweder, "Keep Your Mind Open: And watch it closely, because it's apt to change," *New York Times* 20 Feb. 1994.

[11] This came from a conversation with Barnaby Fitzgerald in 1995.

[12] Peter Berger, *A Far Glory* (New York: Free Press, 1982) 99.

[13] A similar thought was expressed by Eva Hoffman in *Exist Into History* (New York: Viking, 1993) xi-xii.

[14] Timothy Garton Ash, *The Magic Lantern: The Revolution of 1989 Witnessed in Warsaw, Budapest, Berlin and Prague* (New York: Random House, 1990) 79.

[15] Ash 85-86.

[16] Some of these thoughts were included in a commentary by Lee Cullum on KERA-FM in October, 1998.

[17] Paul Berman, "The Philosopher-King Is Mortal," *New York Times Book Review* 11 May 1997: 36-37, 47. Berman notes that Heidegger was a Nazi, with disciples mainly from Marxism and the new-left. But Havel, wedded to literature more than philosophy, found in Heidegger what he needed to express his own view of liberal democracy.

[18] Milan Kundera, "A life like a work of art," *New Republic* 202 (29 Jan. 1990): 16-17.

[19] Hans Wingler, *The Bauhaus: Weimar Dessau Berlin Chicago* (Cambridge, Mass.: MIT Press,

1969) 51. I have relied on this monumental and authoritative work for information about the Bauhaus.

[20] Stephanie Barron and Maurice Tuchman, *The Avant-Garde in Russia, 1910-1930, New Perspectives* (Los Angeles: Los Angeles County Museum of Art, 1980) 184, 279.

[21] Lazar Markovich Lissitzky, "Letter to J.J.P. Oud," 30 June 1924, in *El Lissitzky* (exhibition catalogue) (Cologne: Galerie Gmurzynska, 1976) 73.

[22] Quoted by George Johnson, "The Odds on God: If He understands mathematical physics, He exists," *New York Times Book Review* 9 Oct. 1994: 15.

[23] Gustav Niebuhr, "Scientist Wins Religion Prize Of $1 Million," *New York Times* 9 Mar. 1995.

[24] Peggy Landers, "If science plays God . . . Gene research stirs controversy," *Dallas Morning News* (Knight Ridder News Service) 18 Apr. 1993.

[25] See Barbara Koenig, "Gene Tests: What You Know Can Hurt You," *New York Times* 6 Apr. 1996. To its credit, the State of New Jersey has passed a law prohibiting health insurance companies from using genetic information to deny individuals coverage or charge them higher premiums. Employers also are forbidden to require or use genetic testing. Other states have passed similar laws. Jennifer Preston, "Bill in New Jersey Would Limit Use of Genetic Tests by Insurers," *New York Times* 18 June 1996.

[26] Jessica Mathews, "Genome Project; We'll need guidance on ethical questions," *Dallas Morning News* 18 May 1996.

[27] Laurence H. Tribe, "Second Thoughts on Cloning," *New York Times* 5 Dec. 1997. See also David Bromwich, "Experience Can't Be Cloned," *New York Times* 11 Jan. 1998.

[28] Quoted in Michael Novak, "The Most Religious Century," *New York Times* 24 May 1998.

[29] Gina Kolata, "With Cloning of a Sheep, the Ethical Ground Shifts," *New York Times* 24 Feb. 1997; Lawrence M. Fisher, "Cloned Animals Offer Companies a Faster Path to New Drugs," *New York Times* 24 Feb. 1997; and Kolata, "Scientist Reports First Cloning Ever of Adult Mammal," *New York Times* 23 Feb. 1997. See also "The Philosopher Pope," *New York Times* 21 Oct. 1998: editorial page.

[30] Robert L. Park, "The Danger of Voodoo Science," *New York Times* 9 July 1995.

[31] Carlos Fuentes, *Myself with Others* (New York: Noonday-Farrar, Straus and Giroux, 1990) 186.

[32] Quoted by Molly O'Neill, "As Life Gets More Complex, Magic Casts a Wider Spell," *New York Times* 3 June 1994.

[33] The material from Dr. Wilhelmsen was contained in a letter to the author dated June 24, 1994. He died in 1996. Some of his thoughts also appeared in a commentary by Lee Cullum on KERA-FM, the public radio station in Dallas-Fort Worth, in October, 1998.

[34] Some of the thoughts in this segment were presented in a commentary by Lee Cullum on KERA-FM, the public radio station in Dallas-Fort Worth, in October, 1998.

[35] Peter Drucker, *Managing in Turbulent Times* (London: Heinemann, 1980). For this section I have relied heavily on this admirable work by Peter Drucker, who is always startlingly insightful.

[36] Robert Putnam of Harvard has explored the phenomenon of bowling alone.

[37] Peter Drucker, *Managing for the Future: the 1990s and Beyond* (New York: Truman Talley Books/Dutton, 1992) 1-2.

[38] Drucker, *Managing for the Future* 2-3.

[39] Drucker, *Managing for the Future* 3.

[40] Ray Marshall, "The Global Jobs Crisis," *Foreign Policy* 100 (Fall, 1995) Carnegie Endowment for International Peace, 1995.

[41] Drucker, *Managing for the Future* 5-7.

[42] Drucker, *Managing for the Future* 6-7.

[43] Drucker, *Managing for the Future* 4.

[44] John Holushe, "Lockheed and Marietta Uniting To Survive Lean Arms Budgets," *New York Times* 31 Aug. 1994.

[45] Marshall McLuhan and Quentin Fiore, *The Medium is the Message* (New York: Bantam Books, 1967).

[46] These thoughts on moderation were adapted to a commentary for "All Things Considered" on National Public Radio in 1995.

[47] The quote by Frederick Turner came from a speech he made at the Dallas Institute of Humanities and Culture in February, 1996. Much of the material on the importance of history appeared in a commentary for *All Things Considered* on National Public Radio in February, 1996.

[48] John Russell, *The Meanings of Modern Art* (New York: Harper & Row, 1981) 195.

[49] Some of these observations appeared in a commentary by Lee Cullum on KERA-FM, the public radio station in Dallas-Fort Worth, in October, 1998.

[50] Quentin Bell, *Ruskin* (London: The Hogarth Press, 1978) 50.

[51] For Tammy Wynette I drew upon the following: Jon Parales, "Tammy Wynette, Country Singer Known For 'Stand by Your Man' Is Dead at 55," *New York Times* 8 Apr. 1998; David Gates, "First Lady of Nashville: Country singer Tammy Wynette, 1942-1998," *Newsweek* 20 Apr. 20, 1998: 59; and Tom Gliatto et al., "Heroine of Hardship." *People* 20 Apr. 1998: 54-61.

[52] Some of this material on Jackie Onassis appeared in a column by Lee Cullum published in the *Dallas Morning News* (May 25, 1994) and also in *National Forum*, put out by American Publishing in June, 1994.

[53] Richard Sennett, *The Fall of Public Man* (New York: Alfred A. Knopf, 1997) 38-44, 69-72, 74-77.

[54] Some of the material on Diana appeared in a column by Lee Cullum in the *Dallas Morning News* (September 3, 1997) and in *National Forum*, put out by American Publishing in September, 1997. A few of the insights also were used by Lee Cullum on the *News Hour with Jim Lehrer* September 5, 1997.

[55] Andrew Morton, *Diana: Her True Story* (New York: Simon & Schuster, 1997) 280.

[56] This observation by Lord Owen was contained in a report by Deborah Amos on National Public Radio in 1995.

[57] I am indebted for this insight to Dr. Flo Wiedemann.

[58] This came from a conversation with Dr. Cowan in 1995.

[59] Cited by Thomas Cahill, *How the Irish Saved Civilization* (New York: Doubleday, 1995) 218.

Works Cited

Andrews, Rena. "Hitler's Favorite Filmmaker Honored at Colorado Festival." *New York Times* 15 Sept. 1974, sec. 2: 1.

Armstrong, Karen. *A History of God: The 4000-Year Quest of Judaism, Christianity and Islam.* New York: Alfred A. Knopf, 1993.

Ash, Timothy Garton. *The Magic Lantern: The Revolution of 1989 Witnessed in Warsaw, Budapest, Berlin and Prague.* New York: Random House, 1990.

Barnett, Corelli. *The Collapse of British Power.* Atlantic Highlands, NJ: Humanities Press International, 1972.

Barron, Stephanie, and Maurice Tuchman. *The Avant-Garde in Russia, 1910-1930, New Perspectives.* Los Angeles: Los Angeles County Museum of Art, 1980.

Becker, Ernest. *The Denial of Death.* New York: Free Press, 1973.

Behe, Michael J. "Darwin Under the Microscope." *New York Times* 29 Oct. 1996.

Bell, Quentin. *Ruskin.* London: Hogarth Press, 1978.

—. *Virginia Woolf: A Biography.* New York: Harcourt Brace Jovanovich, 1972.

Berger, Peter. *A Far Glory.* New York: Free Press, 1982.

Berman, Paul. "The Philosopher-King Is Mortal." *New York Times Book Review* 11 May 1997: 36+.

Bernstein, Leonard. "A Nice Gershwin Tune." *Atlantic Monthly* Apr. 1955: 40+.

Bernstein, Richard. "The Inquisition: A Spanish Model for a Final Solution." *New York Times* 23 Aug. 1995.

—. "Reality Check for the Mythic Mahler." *New York Times* 21 Jan. 1998: E9.

—. "What Would Happen if E.T. Did Call?" Rev. of *Are We Alone?* by Paul Davies. *New York Times* 12 July 1995.

Berthoud, Roger. *The Life of Henry Moore.* New York: E. P. Dutton, 1987.

Binyon, Michael. "Film women get to grips on Auschwitz gypsies." *London Times.* 29 Nov. 1984: 6g.

Bird, Kai, and Max Holland. "Out of the Past." *Nation* 240 (4 May 1985): 520.

Biskind, Peter. *Easy Riders, Raging Bulls: How the Sex-Drugs-and-Rock 'n' Roll Generation Saved Hollywood.* New York: Simon & Schuster, 1998.

Bloom, Harold. *The Western Canon.* New York: Harcourt Brace, 1994.

Bloom, Harold, and David Rosenberg. *The Book of J.* New York: Grove Weidenfeld, 1990.

Bogdanovich, Peter. "Is That Ticking (Pause) a Bomb?" *New York Times* 11 Apr. 1999, Arts and Leisure: 15, 18.

Bois, Yve-Alain, Joop Jooster, Angelica Zander Rudenstine, and Hans Jansses.

Trans. Andrew McCormick and Gregory Sims. *Piet Mondrian*. Boston: A Bulfinch Press Book-Little, Brown, 1994.

Brantley, Ben. "The Sound of His Music: Richard Rodgers conquered Broadway with remarkable ease." *New York Times Book Review* 17 May 1998: 38.

Breo, Dennis L. "The double helix—Watson & Crick's 'freak find' of how like begets like." *Journal of the American Medical Association* 269.8 (1993).

Breslin, James E.B. *Mark Rothko: A Biography*. Chicago: University of Chicago Press, 1993.

Broad, William J. "Clues to Fiery Origin of Life Sought in Hothouse Microbes." *New York Times* 9 May 1995.

Brody, Richard. "Drowning in the New Wave." Rev. of *Truffaut*, by Antoine de Baecque and Serge Toubiana. *New Yorker* 24 May 1999.

Bromwich, David. "Experience Can't Be Cloned." *New York Times* 11 Jan. 1998.

Brown, Judith M. *Gandhi: Prisoner of Hope*. New Haven: Yale UP, 1989.

Browne, Malcolm W, "Age of Universe Is Now Settled, Astronomer Says." *New York Times* 5 Mar. 1996.

—. "A Millennial Angst for Particle Physics." *New York Times* 19 Jan. 1999: F5.

Brumberg, Abraham. "Yesterday's Hero." *New York Times Book Review* 7 July 1996.

Burns, James MacGregor. "More Than Merely Power: II." *New York Times* 17 Nov. 1978.

Burns, John F. "With Old Skills and New, India Battles the Plague." *New York Times* 29 Sept. 1994.

Cahill, Thomas. *How the Irish Saved Civilization*. New York: Doubleday, 1995.

Callahan, Daniel. "A Step Too Far." *New York Times* 26 Feb. 1997: Editorial page.

Cannadine, David. "Ambition Will Get You Everywhere: A biography of Disraeli as the prototypical post-modern politician, driven and always reinventing himself." Rev. of *Disraeli: A Biography*, by Stanley Weintraub. *New York Times Book Review* 17 Oct. 1993: 14+.

Cattau, Daniel. "Episcopal diocese's office is exorcised." *Dallas Morning News* 10 Oct 1993.

Chancellor, Alexander. "De-lightful, De-licious, De-ceitful: A biography of Cole Porter reveals the unhappy, closeted man behind the facade of urbane insouciance." *New York Times Book Review* 29 Nov. 1998: 9.

Charmley, John. *Churchill: The End of Glory*. New York: Harcourt Brace, 1993.

Chesterton, G.K. *Saint Thomas Aquinas: "The Dumb Ox."* New York: Doubleday, 1956.

Choiniere, Ray, and David Keirsey. *Presidential Temperament*, Del Mar, CA: Prometheus Nemesis, INTJ Books, 1992.

Churchill, Winston. *History of the English-Speaking Peoples*. New York: Barnes & Noble, 1995.

Clark, Ronald W. *Freud: The Man and the Cause*. New York: Random House, 1980.

Cohen, Roger. "In Sarajevo, Victims of a 'Postmodern' War." *New York Times* 21 May 1995.

Collins, Joseph. "A Fine Madness: May 28, 1922: 'Ulysses' by James Joyce." *New York Times Book Review* 6 Oct. 1996: 23.

Collins, Larry, and Dominique Lapierre. *Freedom at Midnight*. New York: Avon, 1975.

Compton, Susan P. *The World Backwards: Russian Futurist Books, 1912-16.* London: British Library, 1978.

Corliss, Richard. "Riefenstahl's Last Triumph." *Time* 142 (18 Oct. 1993): 91.

"The Counter-attack of God." *Economist* July 1995: 19+.

Cowell, Alan. "Admire Her Art? (Her Camera Adored Swastikas)." *New York Times* 21 Aug. 1997, sec A: 4.

Cullum, Lee. "Jackie O. Made Public Life A Spirited Work of Art." *National Forum* June 1994

—. "Jackie O. understood our dichotomy." *Dallas Morning News* 25 May 1994.

Darnton, John. "50 Years After War, Historians See Era's End." *New York Times* 7 May 1995.

Davis, Ronald L. *Celluloid Mirrors: Hollywood and American Society since 1945.* Fort Worth: Harcourt Brace College Publishers, 1997.

—. *The Glamour Factory*. Dallas: Southern Methodist UP, 1993.

—. *John Ford: Hollywood's Old Master*. Norman: University of Oklahoma Press, 1995.

de Mille, Agnes. "Measuring the Steps of a Giant." *New York Times* 7 Apr. 1991.

Deford, Frank. "The Ghost of Berlin." *Sports Illustrated* 65 (4 Aug. 1986): 48.

Denvir, Bernard. "The Ferocious Fauve: A look at the prodigious egotism behind the bland benignity of Henry Matisse." *New York Times Book Review* 10 Oct. 1993.

Dinesen, Isak Breve fra Afrika. *English Letters from Africa, 1914-1931.* Trans. Anne Born. Ed. Frans Lasson. Chicago: University of Chicago Press, 1981.

—. *Out of Africa* and *Shadows on the Grass*. New York: Vintage International-Random House, 1989.

Dinnage, Rosemary. "The Whirr of Wings." *New York Review of Books* 29 May 1997: 4+.

Dobrzynski, Judith H. "A Betrayal the Art World Can't Forget: The Battle for Rothko's Estate Altered Lives and Reputations." *New York Times* 2 Nov. 1998.

Doder, Dusko, and Louise Branson. *Gorbachev, Heretic in the Kremlin*. New York: Penguin Books, 1991.

Douglas, Ann. "Pollock's Volcanic New York Circle." *New York Times* 27 Nov. 1998: B37+.

Douglas, Charlotte. *Malevich*. New York: Harry N. Abrams, 1994.

Dowd, Maureen. "Grow Up, Harry." *New York Times* 11 Jan. 1998.

Draper, Theodore. "Neoconservative History." *New York Review of Books* 16 Jan. 1986.

Dreifus, Claudia. "Chloe Wofford Talks About Toni Morrison," *New York Times Magazine* 11 Sept. 1994: 73-75.

Drucker, Peter. *Managing for the Future: The 1990s and Beyond.* New York: Truman Talley Books-Dutton, 1992.

—. *Managing in Turbulent Times.* London: Heinemann, 1980.

Dullea, Georgia. "Tarot Goes 'Po Mo.'" *New York Times* 31 Oct. 1993.

Dunn, Jane. *A Very Close Conspiracy: Vanessa Bell and Virginia Woolf.* Boston: Little, Brown, 1990.

Durbin, Karen. "New Film, New Chapter in a Storied Union." *New York Times* 3 Jan. 1999, Arts and Leisure: 9+.

Eberstadt, Nicholas. "The Great Leap Backward: The story behind Mao's policies of the late 1950s, which led to the starvation of tens of millions." *New York Times Book Review* 16 Feb. 1997: 6+.

Egan, Timothy. "Pacific Chiefs to meet where 2 worlds mix." *New York Times* 5 Nov. 1993.

Etulain, Richard. Introduction to *John Ford: Hollywood's Old Master.* By Ronald L. Davis. Norman: University of Oklahoma Press, 1995.

Faulkner, William. *Novels, 1930-1935.* New York: Viking, 1985.

Fisher, Lawrence M. "Cloned Animals Offer Companies a Faster Path to New Drugs." *New York Times* 24 Feb. 1997.

Fitzgerald, Michael. "The Unknown Picasso: A Revolutionary in Clay." *New York Times* 28 Feb. 1999, Arts and Leisure: 46.

Forster, E.M. *Howards End.* New York: Vintage Books-Random House, 1921.

— *Virginia Woolf.* London: Cambridge UP, 1942.

Freud, Sigmund. *Civilization and Its Discontents.* Trans. James Strachey, New York: W. W. Norton, 1961.

Friedman, Thomas. "New Mexico." *New York Times* 15 Mar. 1995.

Fuentes, Carlos. *Myself with Others.* New York: Noonday Press-Farrar, Straus and Giroux, 1990.

Fukuyama, Francis. T*he End of History and the Last Man.* New York: Avon Books, 1992.

Galbraith, John Kenneth. *The Great Crash 1929.* New York: Time, 1962.

Garnett, Angelica. *Deceived with Kindness.* New York: Harcourt Brace Jovanovich, 1985.

Gates, David. "First Lady of Nashville: Country singer Tammy Wynette, 1942-1998." *Newsweek* 20 Apr. 1998: 59.

Gay, Peter. *Freud: A Life for Our Time.* New York: Anchor Books-Doubleday, 1989.

Gelder, Van. "Footlights: Curtain Call." *New York Times* 12 Feb. 1998.

Genovese, Eugene D. "The Squandered Century." Rev. of *The Age of Extremes: A History of the World, 1914-1991,* by Eric Hobsbawn. *New Republic* 17 Apr. 1995: 38.

Gibbs, Nancy. "Angels Among Us." *Time* 27 Dec. 1993: 56+.

Gilliam, Bryan. "For Bruckner, a Vague Nazi Aura Persists." *New York Times* 20 Oct. 1996.

Gliatto, Tom, et. al. "Heroine of Hardship." *People* 20 Apr. 1998: 54+.

Godwin, Malcolm. *Angels: An Endangered Species.* New York: Simon & Schuster, 1990

Goodman, Walter. "Too brilliant for the World's Good." *New York Times* 5 1995, sec. C: 20.

Goodwin, Doris Kearns. *No Ordinary Time: Franklin and Eleanor Roosevelt: The Home Front in World War II.* New York: Simon & Schuster, 1994.

Gordimer, Nadine. *Jump and Other Stories.* New York: Penguin Books, 1992.

Gray, Paul. "The Assault on Freud." *Time* 29 Nov. 1993: 47.

Grenier, Richard., "The Führer's Filmmaker." *Commentary* 98.2 (Aug. 1994): 50.

Grohmann, Will. *Wassily Kandinsky: Life and Work.* Trans by Norbert Guterman. New York, Harry N. Abrams, 1958.

Harbaugh, William Henry. *Power and Responsibility: The Life and Times of Theodore Roosevelt.* New York: Farrar, Strauss and Cudahy, 1961.

Hardy, Phil, and Dave Laing. *The Da Capo Companion to 20th-Century Popular Music.* New York: Da Capo Press, 1995.

Harris, Kenneth. "Wartime Lies: The Churchill-Roosevelt partnership was plagued by deception." *New York Times Book Review* 27 Apr. 1997: 30.

Harshaw, Tobin. "Why Am I Guilty?" *New York Times Book Review* 27 Sept. 1993, sec 7: 28.

Haskell, Molly. "The Ride of a Valkyrie." *Washington Post Book World* 23 (29 Aug. 1993): 1.

Havel, Václav. "The Charms of NATO." *New York Review of Books* 15 Jan. 1998.

—. "The New Measure of Man." *New York Times* 8 July 1994.

Hawking, Stephen. *A Brief History of Time: From the Big Bang to Black Holes.* New York: Bantam Books, 1990.

Henderson, Nicholas. "Their Man in Washington: Anatoly Dobrynin examines the motives and miscalculations of the cold war." *New York Times Book Review* 10 Sept. 1995: 11.

Herrera, Hayden. *Matisse: A Portrait.* New York: Harcourt Brace, 1993.

Himmelfarb, Gertrude. "The Company He Kept: Many of Churchill's countrymen were readier to do him harm than good." *New York Times Book Review* 16 July 1995: 6.

Hoffman, Eva. *Exist Into History: A Journey Through the New Eastern Europe.* New York: Viking, 1993.

Hofstadter, Richard. *The American Political Tradition.* New York: Vintage Books, 1957.

Holland, Bernard. "Singing the Gershwins: Nice Work if You Can Get It." *New York Times* 17 Mar. 1998: B1+.

"Hollywood Ad Hits at Leni Riefenstahl: Anti-Nazi League Bids Industry Close Doors to Hitler Agents." *New York Times* 30 Nov. 1938: 15.

Holroyd, Michael. *Bernard Shaw: The Lure of Fantasy—1951* (Volume 3). London: Chatto & Windus (Random Century Group), 1991.

Holushe, John. "Lockheed and Marietta Uniting To Survive Lean Arms Budgets." *New York Times* 31 Aug. 1994.

Horgan, John. *The End of Science: Facing the Limits of Knowledge in the Twilight of the Scientific Age.* Reading, Mass.: Helix-Addison-Wesley. 1996.

Horne, Alistair. "Tougher Than George C. Scott." *New York Times Book Review* 10 Dec. 1995: 9.

Hyland, William G. *Richard Rodgers.* New Haven: Yale UP, 1998.

Ibrahim, Youssef M. "Mandela Ends Triumphant Visit to Britain." *New York Times* 13 July 1996.

Jacobs, Jane. *Systems of Survival.* New York: Random House, 1992.

James, Caryn. "Such a Gorgeous Kid Like Him: François Truffaut wants the world to see him as a boyishly romantic artist." Rev. of *Truffaut*, by Antoine de Baecque and Serge Toubiana *New York Times Book Review* 18 Apr. 1999: 10.

Jefferson, Margo. "The New Film Hero: Twisted, Neurotic, Triumphant." *New York Times* 28 Jan. 1998.

Jerome, Fred. "Looking at a Genius, Seeing a Spy." *New York Times* 8 June 1998.

Johnson, Frank. "Nazi camp slur stands against top film maker." *London Times* 27 June 1985: 6+.

Johnson, George. "The Odds on God: If He understands mathematical physics, He exists." *New York Times Book Review* 9 Oct. 1994: 15.

Johnson, Haynes. "When the Sleeping Giant Woke: How the War Changed America." *International Herald Tribune* 31 July 1995: 2.

Jones, Timothy. "Rumors of Angels." *Christianity Today* 5 Apr. 1993: 18+.

Joyce, James. *Ulysses.* New York: Vintage-Random House, 1961.

Jung, C.G. "Crazy Times." *New York Times* 19 Nov. 1993.

—. *Modern Man in Search of a Soul.* Trans. W.S. Dell and Cary F. Baynes. San Diego: Harcourt Brace Jovanovich, 1933.

Jung Chang. *Wild Swans.* New York: Doubleday Anchor Books, 1992.

Kael, Pauline. *5001 Nights at the Movies.* New York: Henry Holt, 1985.

Kafka, Franz. *The Complete Stories.* Trans. Willa and Edwin Muir. New York: Schocken Books, 1971.

Kagan, Richard L. "Article of Faith?" *New York Times Book Review* 27 Aug. 1995: 15+.

Kakutani, Michiko. "A Fatal Triangle in the Long Shadow of Apartheid." *New York Times* 16 Jan. 1998.

—. "Magician and Miscreant of Modernism. Continued." *New York Times* 8 Nov. 1996.

—. "Opinion vs. Reality In an Age of Pundits And Spin Doctors." *New York Times*. 28 Jan. 1994.

—. "Witness Against the Post-Modern Historians." Rev. of *On Looking Into the Abyss: Untimely Thoughts on Culture and Society*, by Gertrude Himmelfarb. *New York Times* 1 Mar. 1994.

Kauffman, Stuart. *At Home in the Universe: The Search for Laws of Self-Organization and Complexity.* New York: Oxford UP, 1995.

Keller, Bill. "The Art of the Possible." *New York Times Book Review* 20 Oct. 1996.

Kennan, George. "The Balkan Crises: 1913 and 1993." Introduction to *The Other Balkan Wars.* Washington, D.C.: Carnegie Endowment, 1993.

Kennedy, Roger G. *American Churches.* New York: Stewart, Tabori & Chang, 1982.

Kisselgoff, Anna. "Martha Graham Dies at 96: A Revolution in Dance." *New York Times* 2 Apr. 1991.

Kissinger, Henry. "The Right to be Right." Rev. of *The Downing Street Years,* by Margaret Thatcher. *New York Times Book Review* 14 Nov. 1993.

—. *The White House Years.* Boston: Little, Brown, 1979.

—. "With Faint Praise: A biographer finds traces of clay on the great statesman's feet." Rev. of *The Unruly Giant,* by Norman Rose. *New York Times Book Review* 16 July 1995: 7.

Koenig, Barbara. "Gene Tests: What You Know Can Hurt You." *New York Times* 6 Apr. 1996.

Kolata, Gina. "Scientist Reports First Cloning Ever of Adult Mammal." *New York Times* 23 Feb. 1997.

—. "With Cloning of a Sheep, the Ethical Ground Shifts." *New York Times* 24 Feb. 1997.

Kovac, Jeffrey. "Ilya Prigogine." In *The History of Modern Chemical Sciences.* Rahway, N.J.: Merck, 1993

Kundera, Milan. "A life like a work of art." *New Republic* 202 (29 Jan. 1990): 16+.

Landers, Peggy. "If science plays God . . . Gene research stirs controversy." *Dallas Morning News* (Knight Ridder News Service) 18 Apr. 1993.

Larmer, Brook, Tim Padget, and David Schrieberg. "Politics & Prose." *Newsweek* 6 May 1996: 39+.

Lear, Jonathan. "The Shrink Is In." *New Republic* 25 Dec. 1995: 18.

Lehmann-Haupt, Christopher. "The Century Ahead for Science." Rev. of *What Remains To Be Discovered: Mapping the Secrets of the Universe, the Origins of Life and the Future of the Human Race,* by Jon Maddox. *New York Times* 16 Nov. 1998: B6.

Leithauser, Brad. "Let's Face the Music," *New York Review of Books* 20 Apr. 1999: 16-20.

"Leni Riefenstahl Angry." *New York Times* 28 Jan. 1939: 18.

Levant, Oscar. *A Smattering of Ignorance.* Garden City: Doubleday, 1959.

Levathes, Louise. "A Geneticist Maps Ancient Migrations." *New York Times* 27 July 1993.

Lewis, Anthony. "Mandela the Pol." *New York Times Magazine* 23 Mar. 1997: 43+.

Lewis, R.W.B. *Edith Wharton, A Biography.* New York: Harper Colophon Books-Harper & Row, 1975.

—. "Introduction." *The House of Mirth.* By Edith Wharton. New York: New York UP, 1977.

Lind, Michael. "The Southern Coup." *New Republic* 19 June 1995: 23+.

Lissitzky, Lazar Markovich. "Letter to J.J.P. Oud." 30 June 1924. In *El Lissitzky* (Exhibition catalogue). Cologne: Galerie Gmurzynska, 1976.

Lopate, Phillip. "Master of Motion and Emotion." *New York Times* 20 June 1999, Arts and Leisure: 11-12.

Lutz, Tom. "Macho Men: Exploring Harvard's role in the construction of the late-19th-century manly ideal." *New York Times Book Review* 5 Jan. 1997.

Lyman, Rick. "Akira Kurosawa, Director of Epics, Dies at 88." *New York Times* 7 Sept.1998: A1+.

—. "Scene One: A Fire Escape." *New York Times* 13 Feb. 1998.

Macaulay, Rose. *The Writings of E.M. Forster.* London: Hogarth Press, 1938.

Malcolm, Janet. "The Trial of Aloysha." Rev. of *Letters to Olga: June 1979-September 1982*, by Václav Havel, trans. by Paul Wilson. *New York Review of Books* 14 June 1990: 35.

Mallaby, Sebastian. "Father of His Country: A closer look at the man who brought majority rule to South Africa." *New York Times Book Review* 1 Mar. 1998.

Manchester, William. *The Last Lion, Winston Spencer Churchill, Alone, 1932-1940.* Boston: Little Brown, 1988.

Mandela, Nelson. *Long Walk to Freedom.* Boston: Little, Brown, 1994.

Marshall, Ray. "The Global Jobs Crisis." *Foreign Policy* 100 (Fall 1995).

Maslin, Janet. "Gleefully Skewering His Own Monsters." *New York Times* 12 Dec. 1997: B1.

—. "Hollywood Under the Influence." *New York Times* 5 May 1998.

—. "Just What Did Leni Riefenstahl's Lens See?" *New York Times* 13 Mar. 1994, sec. 2:15.

Mathews, Jessica. "Genome Project; We'll need guidance on ethical questions." *Dallas Morning News* 18 May 1996.

Matlock, Jr., Jack F. "Gorbachev: Lingering Mysteries." *New York Review of Books* 19 Dec. 1996.

McBride, Joseph. *Hawks on Hawks.* Berkeley: University of California Press, 1982.

—. *Orson Welles.* New York: Da Capo Press, 1996.

McLuhan, Marshall, and Quentin Fiore. *The Medium is the Message.* New York: Bantam Books, 1967.

Miller, Arthur. *Timebends, A Life.* New York: Harper & Row, 1987.

Mitchell, Greg. "Winning a Battle but Losing The War Over the Blacklist." *New York Times* 25 Jan. 1998.

Mitgang, Herbert. "An Industrial Stop Before Auschwitz." *New York Times* 26 June 1998: B43.

Molotsky, Irvin. "Freud Show Delayed Amid Criticism." *New York Times* 6 Dec. 1995.

Moore, Thomas. *Care of the Soul.* New York: HarperCollins, 1992.

Morrison, Toni. *Beloved.* New York: Plume-Penguin Group, 1988.

Morton, Andrew. *Diana: Her True Story.* New York: Simon & Schuster, 1997.

Morton, Frederic. *A Nervous Splendor.* Boston: Little, Brown, 1979.

Murch, Walter. "Restoring the Touch of Genius to 'Touch of Evil.'" *New York Times* 6 Sept. 1998, sec. 2:16.

Musser, Charles. *The Emergence of Cinema: The American Screen to 1907.* Berkeley, University of California Press, 1994.

Néret, Gilles. *Matisse.* Trans. by Josephine Bacon. Cologne: Taschen, 1996.

"New Data Hint that Universe May Be Bigger Than Thought." *New York Times* 15 Feb. 1997.

Nicolson, Nigel. *The World of Jane Austen.* London: Weidenfeld and Nicolson, 1991.

Niebuhr, Gustav. "Scientist Wins Religion Prize Of $1 Million." *New York Times* 9 Mar. 1995.

—. "Unitarians Striking Chord of Spirituality: Church's Shift Mirrors a Trend in Society." *New York Times* 8 Dec. 1996.

Nixon, Richard. *In the Arena.* New York: Pocket Books, 1990.

Novak, Michael. "The Most Religious Century." *New York Times* 24 May 1998.

Nowell-Smith, Geoffrey, ed. *The Oxford History of World Cinema.* Oxford: Oxford UP, 1996.

O'Brian, Patrick. *Picasso: A Biography.* New York: W.W. Norton, 1994.

O'Neill, Molly. "As Life Gets More Complex, Magic Casts a Wider Spell." *New York Times* 3 June 1994.

Oates, Joyce Carol. "Depth-Sightings." Rev. of *Sight-Readings: American Fictions* by Elizabeth Hardwick. *New York Review of Books* 24 Sept. 1998: 4+.

Oestreich, James R. "Hearing Bach and Shostakovich in Conversation." *New York Times* 8 May 1998: B4.

—. "How Does Music Turn the Century? Schoenberg Could One Day Sound as Remote as Gregorian Chant." *New York Times* 27 Dec. 1997: A9+.

"Olga Ivinskaya, inspiration for 'Dr Zhivago,' dies at 83." *Dallas Morning News* 13 Sept. 1995.

"Olga Ivinskaya, 83, Pasternak muse for 'Zhivago.'" *New York Times* 13 Sept. 1995.

Pais, Abraham. *'Subtle is the Lord—:' The Science and the Life of Albert Einstein.* Oxford: Oxford UP, 1982.

Parales, Jon. "Tammy Wynette, Country Singer Known For 'Stand by Your Man' Is Dead at 55." *New York Times* 8 Apr. 1998.

Park, Robert L. "The Danger of Voodoo Science." *New York Times* 9 July 1995.

Pasternak, Boris. *Doctor Zhivago.* Trans. by Max Hayward and Marya Harari. New York: Ballantine Books, 1981.

Phillips, Caryl. "The Beat of History." *New Republic* 24 Oct. 1994: 34.

"The Philosopher Pope." *New York Times* 21 Oct. 1998: editorial page.

Pogrebin, Robin. "Love Letters By Einstein at Auction: Notes Reveal Affair With Possible Spy." *New York Times* 1 June 1998.

Premoli-Droulers, Francesca. *Maisons d'écrivains. English Writers' Houses.* New York: Vendome Press, 1995.

Preston, Jennifer. "Bill in New Jersey Would Limit Use of Genetic Tests by Insurers." *New York Times* 18 June 1996.

"Protest Olympic Movie: Two Groups Threaten to picket Riefenstahl Film." *New York Times* 4 Nov. 1938: 20.

Proust, Marcel. *Remembrance of Things Past, Volume I.* Trans. by Scott Moncrieff and Terence Kilmartin. New York: Vintage-Random House, 1982.

Ramsey, Nancy. "Keepers of a Flame That Burned for Russia." *New York Times* 5 July 1998.

Remnick, David. "Can Russia Change?" *Foreign Affairs* Jan.-Feb. 1997: 37+.

—. "The First and the Last: Lenin revealed, and buried by Gorbachev." *New Yorker* 18 Nov. 1996: 122+.

—. "Gorbachev's Last Hurrah." *New Yorker* 11 Mar. 1996: 80.

—. "Letter from Jerusalem: The Afterlife." *New Yorker* 11 Aug. 1997: 58+.

"Return of the Plague." *New York Times* 29 Sept. 1994.

Rev. of *Coral Gardens*, by Leni Riefensthal. *Washington Post Book World* 10 Dec. 1978: E6.

Richardson, John, with the collaboration of Marilyn McCully. *A Life of Picasso, Volume II: 1907-1917.* New York: Random House, 1996.

Riding, Alan. "31 Picassos Are Sold at Paris Auction." *New York Times* 29 Oct. 1998.

—. "Dora Maar, 89, Picasso's Muse And a Photographer, Is Dead." *New York Times* 26 July 1997.

Rockwell, John. "Song of the Earth: A biography of Mahler for old and new devotees of his music." *New York Times Book Review* 8 Mar. 1998: 11.

Rodgers, Richard. *Musical Stages: an Autobiography.* Introduction by Mary Rodgers. New York: Da Capo Press, 1995.

Rohter, Larry. "García Márquez Embraces Old Love (That's News!)." *New York Times* 3 Mar. 1999.

Rubenstein, Joshua. "The Dictator's Cut: Stalin made life miserable for Sergei Eisenstein, but the director got his revenge." Rev. of *Sergei Eisenstein: A Life in Conflict*, by Ronald Bergan. *New York Times Book Review* 27 June 1999.

Russell, John. *The Meanings of Modern Art.* New York: Harper & Row, 1981.

Sackville-West, Vita. *The Letters of Vita Sackville-West to Virginia Woolf.* Ed. Louise DeSalvo and Mitchell A. Leaska. New York: William Morrow, 1985.

Sakharov, Andrei. *Memoirs.* Trans. Richard Lourie. New York: Alfred A. Knopf, 1990.

Salisbury, Harrison. *The New Emperors.* New York: Avon Books, 1992.

Sandel, Michael J. "America's Search for a New Public Philosophy." *Atlantic Monthly* Mar. 1996: 60+.

Sarris, Andrew. *"You Ain't Heard Nothin' Yet": The American Talking Film,*

History and Memory, 1927-1949. New York: Oxford UP, 1998.

Schemo, Diana Jean. "A Crusader Adjusts to Life After Apartheid." *New York Times* 28 Nov. 1994.

Schiff, David. "Modernists in the California Sun." *New York Times* 25 Jan. 1998.

Schorske, Carl E. *Fin-de-Siècle Vienna.* New York: Alfred A. Knopf, 1980.

Schwartz, Charles. *Cole Porter.* New York: Da Capo Press, 1992.

—. *Gershwin: His Life and Music.* New York: Da Capo Press, 1973.

Scovell, Jane. *Oona: Living in the Shadows: A Biography of Oona O'Neill Chaplin.* New York: Warner Books, 1998.

Secrest, Meryle. *Stephen Sondheim: A Life.* New York: Alfred A. Knopf, 1998.

Sennett, Richard. *The Fall of Public Man.* New York: Alfred A. Knopf, 1997.

Shaw, Bernard. *Collected Letters, 1926-1950.* Ed. Dan H. Laurence. New York: Viking, 1988.

Shepard, Jim. "A Mild Rebellion, Then a Revolution." *New York Times* 27 Dec. 1998.

Shweder, Richard A. "Keep Your Mind Open: And watch it closely, because it's apt to change." Rev. of *The Protean Self: Human Resilience in an Age of Fragmentation,* by Robert Jay Lifton. *New York Times* 20 Feb. 1994.

Siegfried, Tom. "Fickle equation now finds universe finite." *Dallas Morning News* 16 June 1991.

Simon, John. "The Führer's Movie Maker: Leni Riefenstahl paints herself as both the master of her fate and its victim." *New York Times Book Review* 27 Sept. 1993, sec 7:1+.

Simons, Marlise. "France Under the Spell of Druids?" *New York Times* 30 Apr. 1996.

Smith, Dinitia. "Freud May Be Dead, But His Critics Still Kick." *New York Times* 10 Dec. 1995.

—. "Mixing Tragedy and Folklore." *New York Times* 8 Jan. 1998.

Smith, Roberta. "Frank Lloyd, Prominent Art Dealer Convicted in the 70s Rothko Scandal, Dies at 86." *New York Times* 8 Apr. 1998.

Sontag, Susan. "Fascinating Fascism." In *Under the Sign of Saturn.* New York: Farrar, Straus, Giroux, 1980. 73-105.

Spada, James. "The Lady and the Tramp: When Oona O'Neill, 18, married Charlie Chaplin, 54, handicappers gave it six months." Rev of *Oona: Living in the Shadows: A Biography of Oona O'Neill Chaplin,* by Jane Scovell. *New York Times Book Review* 29 Nov. 1998: 11.

Stanley, Alessandra. "Communist Struggles for Support as Rivals Back Yeltsin." *New York Times* 20 June 1996.

—. "Model for Dr. Zhivago's Lara Betrayed Pasternak to K.G.B." *New York Times* 27 Nov. 1997.

—. "Neither Ridicule Nor Rancor Halts Gorbachev Election Bid." *New York Times* 17 May 1996.

—. "Stripped of Themes, Yeltsin Wraps Himself in Flag." *New York Times* 19 Apr. 1996.

Steinfels, Peter. "Witch Trial Held in New England." *New York Times* 1 May 1996.

Stevenson, Richard W. "The Pain of British Privatization Has Yielded a String of Successes." *New York Times* 22 Feb. 1994.

Stille, Alexander. "Paisans: How Roberto Rossellini and his filmmaker friends made cinematic history." Rev. of *The Adventures of Roberto Rossellini*, by Tag Gallagher. *New York Times Book Review* 7 Feb. 1999: 20.

Stueck, Hans. "Leni Riefenstahl Returns to Olympics." *New York Times* 23 Aug. 1972: 31.

Suyin, Han. *Eldest Son: Zhou Enlai and the Making of Modern China, 1898 - 1976*. New York: Hill and Wang-Farrar, Strauss and Giroux, 1994.

Teresi, Dick. "The Cosmic Egoist, A life of Edwin Hubble, who had one eye on the universe and the other on himself." *New York Times Book Review* 3 Sept. 1995: 1+.

—. "Physics Is History." *New York Times* 11 June 1994.

"The Thatcher Legacy: the immortal remains of Margaret Thatcher." *Economist* 22 Oct. 1993: 67.

Thatcher, Margaret. *The Downing Street Years*. New York: Harper Collins, 1993.

Thomson, David. *A Biographical Dictionary of Film*. New York: Alfred A. Knopf, 1996.

Thurman, Judith. *Isak Dinesen: The Life of a Storyteller*. New York: St. Martin's Press, 1982.

Tilby, Angela. *Soul: God, Self and the New Cosmology*. New York: Doubleday, 1992.

Tommasini, Anthony. "Arnold Schoenberg: Pushing Music to Evolve," *International Herald Tribune*, (New York Times Service) 2 Feb. 1999.

"Torch Reaches Belgrade." *New York Times* 28 July: 1936: 12.

Trevelyan, Raleigh. "One Nation Under Many Gods." Rev of *In Light of India* and *A Tale of Two Gardens* by Octavio Paz. *New York Times Book Review* 30 Mar. 1997: 25.

Tribe, Laurence H. "Second Thoughts on Cloning." *New York Times* 5 Dec. 1997.

Trilling, Lionel. *Beyond Culture*. New York: Harcourt Brace Jovanovich, 1979.

—. *The Last Decade: Essays and Reviews, 1965-75*. New York: Harcourt Brace Jovanovich, 1979.

—. *The Opposing Self*. New York: Harcourt Brace Jovanovich, 1979.

Tuchman, Barbara. *A Distant Mirror: The Calamitous 14th Century*. New York: Alfred A. Knopf, 1978.

"Tunesmith dies at 74." *Dallas Morning News* (New York Times News Service) 19 Feb. 1998.

Uchitelle, Louis. "Basic Research Is Losing Out As Companies Stress Results." *New York Times* 8 Oct. 1996.

Updike, John. Introduction to *Kafka: The Complete Stories*. Trans. Willa and Edwin Muir. New York: Schocken Books, 1971.

vander Heuvel, William J. "The Holocaust Was No Secret: Churchill knew. We all knew, and couldn't do anything about it—except win the war." *New York Times Magazine* 22 Dec. 1996.

Varia, Radu. *Brancusi*. Trans. by Mary Vaudoyer. New York: Universe, 1986.

Vidal, Gore, "Introduction." *The Edith Wharton Omnibus*. New York: Charles Scribner's Sons, 1978

Vogel, Amos. "Can We Now Forget the Evil That She Did?" *New York Times* 3 May 1973, sec. 2:19.

Vogel, Carol. "The Modern Gets to Keep Malkovich Works." *New York Times* 19 June 1999: A17.

Waldrop, Malcolm. *Complexity: The Emerging Science at the Edge of Order and Chaos*. New York: Simon & Schuster, 1992.

Walsh, Michael. *Andrew Lloyd Webber: His Life and Works*. New York: Harry N. Abrams, 1997.

Ward, Geoffrey C. *A First-Class Temperament: The Emergence of Franklin Roosevelt*. New York: Harper and Row, 1989.

Watson, James D. *The Double Helix: A Personal Account of the Discovery and Structure of DNA*. New York : Atheneum, 1969.

Watson, James, and John Tooze. *The DNA Story*. San Francisco: W. H. Freeman, 1981.

Weinraub, Bernard. "Deconstructing His Film Crew: Woody Allen's Longtime Staff Is Hit by Cost-Cutting Efforts." *New York Times* 1 June 1998: B1+.

—. "A Life in Hollywood, Yet Never a Niche." *New York Times* 19 Feb. 1998: B1+.

—. "Switch to a New Agent Is Woody Allen's Latest." *New York Times* 2 July 1998.

West, Rebecca. *Black Lamb and Gray Falcon*. London: Penguin Books, 1982.

Wharton, Edith. *The Age of Innocence*. In *The Edith Wharton Omnibus*. New York: Charles Scribner's Sons, 1978.

—. *A Backward Glance*. New York: Charles Scribner's Sons, 1964.

"When Children Are Soldiers." *New York Times* 5 July 1998: editorial page.

Wilford, John Noble. "Big Bang's Defenders Weigh Fudge Factor, A Blunder of Einstein's, As Fix for New Crisis." *New York Times* 1 Nov. 1994.

—. "A Discovery Puts Humans In Siberia Ages Ago." *New York Times* 28 Feb. 1997.

—. "Finding on Universe's Age Poses New Cosmic Puzzle." *New York Times* 27 Oct. 1994.

—. "New Data Suggest Universe Will Expand Forever." *New York Times* 9 Jan. 1998.

—. "New Measurement Suggests Universe Is Younger Than Believed." *New York Times*, 2 June 1999: A19.

—. "Sailing A Wheelchair To the End of Time," *New York Times* 24 Mar. 1998.

—. "Scientists, Once Starry-Eyed. Get Clearer View of Universe." *New York Times* 7 Apr. 1997.

Wilson, James Q. "Liberal Ghosts." Rev. of *The End of Reform: New Deal Liberalism in Recession and War*, by Alan Brinkley. *New Republic* 22 May 1995: 31+.

Wingler, Hans. *The Bauhaus: Weimar Dessau Berlin Chicago*. Trans. Wofgang Jabs and Basil Gilbert. Ed. Joseph Stein. Cambridge, Mass.: MIT Press, 1969.

Winston, Brian. "Triumph of the Will." *History Today* 47 (Jan. 1997): 24.

Wolff, Cynthia Griffin. *A Feast of Words: The Triumph of Edith Wharton*. New York: Oxford UP, 1977.

Wood, James. "Beneath The Waves." *New Republic* 29 Sept. 1997: 37.

Woolf, Leonard. *Downhill All the Way: An Autobiography of the Years 1919 to 1939*. New York: Harcourt, Brace & World, 1967.

Woolf, Virginia. *The Captain's Death Bed and Other Essays*. New York: Harcourt, Brace & World, 1950.

—. *The Common Reader*. New York: Harcourt, Brace & World, 1925.

—. *The Death of the Moth and Other Essays*. New York: Harcourt Brace Jovanovich, 1974.

—. *The Diary of Virginia Woolf, Volume Five, 1936-1941*. Ed. Anne Olivier Bell assisted by Andrew McNeillie. New York: Harcourt Brace Jovanovich, 1984.

— *The Diary of Virginia Woolf, Volume Two, 1920 - 1924*. Ed. Anne Olivier Bell assisted by Andrew McNeillie. New York: Harcourt Brace Jovanovich, 1978.

—. *Jacob's Room and The Waves: Two Complete Novels*. New York: Harcourt, Brace & World, 1931.

—. *The Letters of Virginia Woolf, Volume Six, 1936 - 1941*. Ed. Nigel Nicolson and Joanne Trautmann. New York: Harcourt Brace Jovanovich, 1980.

—. *The Letters of Virginia Woolf, Volume Three, 1923 - 1928*. Ed. Nigel Nicolson and Joanne Trautmann. New York: Harcourt Brace Jovanovich, 1977.

—. *Moments of Being: Virginia Woolf, Unpublished Autobiographical Writings*. Ed. Jeanne Schulkind. New York: Harcourt Brace Jovanovich, 1978.

—. *Mrs. Dalloway*. New York: Harcourt, Brace & World, 1925.

—. *Night and Day*. New York: Harcourt, Brace & World, 1920.

—. *Orlando*. New York: Harcourt, Brace & World, 1928.

—. *A Room of One's Own*. New York: Harcourt, Brace & World, 1957.

—. *To the Lighthouse*. New York: Harcourt, Brace & World, 1927.

—. *A Writer's Diary*. New York: Harcourt Brace Jovanovich, 1954.

Yevtushenko, Yevgeny. *Fatal Half Measures: The Culture of Democracy in the Soviet Union*. Trans. and ed. Antonina W. Bouis. Boston: Little Brown, 1991.

Yoffe, Emily. "How the Soul Is Sold." *New York Times Magazine* 23 Apr. 1995: 47.

Young, Hugo. *The Iron Lady*. New York: Noonday-Farrar, Straus and Giroux, 1989.

Zinman, David. *50 Classic Motion Pictures: The Stuff That Dreams Are Made of*. New York: Limelight Editions, 1992.

Photo Credits

Index

About the Author

Lee Cullum, a columnist based at the *Dallas Morning News*, is a regular commentator on *The NewsHour with Jim Lehrer*. She has also done commentaries for *All Things Considered* on National Public Radio. Her interests range from politics and foreign relations to literature and the arts. She has one son, Cullum Clark, who lives in New York with his wife, Nita, and their two daughters, Lili and Annabel.